Tourism in the City

Nicola Bellini • Cecilia Pasquinelli

Editors

Tourism in the City

Towards an Integrative Agenda on Urban Tourism

 Springer

Editors
Nicola Bellini
Groupe Sup de Co La Rochelle
La Rochelle
France

Cecilia Pasquinelli
GSSI Social Sciences
Gran Sasso Science Institute
L'Aquila
Italy

ISBN 978-3-319-26876-7   ISBN 978-3-319-26877-4   (eBook)
DOI 10.1007/978-3-319-26877-4

Library of Congress Control Number: 2016950566

Printed on acid-free paper

This Springer imprint is published by Springer Nature
The registered company is Springer International Publishing AG Switzerland

Contents

Contributors

Göran Andersson is an assistant professor at the Department of Tourism Studies of Södertörn University in Stockholm, Sweden. He founded the discipline Tourism Studies at Södertörn University in 2004 and has been the head of the Department since then. His research focuses on city tourism and the sub-themes of sustainable destinations, heritage attractions, meetings and events, and tourism networks. He was the founder and member of the "Stockholm Centre for Tourism Research" 2002–2007 together with Stockholm University, the Royal Institute of Technology, and the Stockholm Visitors Board, where the focus was the meetings industry. Another network of interest is the Swedish tourism academic network NATU, of which he was the chairman in 2006 and 2013. He has been a strategic partner leader for EU-research projects, publishing articles on community engagements and destination development. As the chairman of the Business Council for Tourism Department since 2002, he has initiated several applied research projects.

Nicola Bellini is a full Professor of Economics and Management at the Institute of Management of the Scuola Superiore Sant'Anna (Pisa, Italy—currently on leave) and Director of the La Rochelle Tourism Management Institute at the Groupe Sup de Co, La Rochelle (France). He is a former Director of IRPET, the Regional Institute for Economic Planning of the Tuscany Region (Florence, Italy), and a former Trustee of the Regional Studies Association. He also works for the European Commission as an expert on smart specialization strategies for European regions. His research interests include local and regional development policies (with a special focus on innovation, internationalization, and tourism), business support services, area marketing, and place branding.

Kamila Borseková is Head of the Research and Innovation Centre at the Faculty of Economics of the Matej Bel University Banska Bystrica, Slovakia. Her research is focused on smart cities, creative cities, spatial and urban development, competitive advantage, and competitiveness. She is currently working on several domestic and international scientific projects and grants, including the national grant "Creative industries as a key source of public sector intangibles in the context of innovations and intelligent growth". She is active in attendance at, as well as the organization of, international scientific events, workshops, and conferences. She is the author or co-author of almost 50 research papers, articles, chapters, and studies.

Nebojša Čamprag is teaching and research associate at the Faculty of Architecture, TU Darmstadt. He has a background in the history and theory of architecture and urbanism, in urban planning and design, and in international cooperation in urban development. His doctoral dissertation "Urban Identity and Change—a Comparison Between Frankfurt and Rotterdam", published in 2014, deals with the problem of identity in contemporary cities and the new means to establish recognizable urban images. His current research interests range from filtration of built heritage and construction of urban identities, through heritage manipulation, to urban identity building by means of contemporary innovative architecture.

Francesco Capone is Assistant Professor in Economics and Management at the Department of Economics and Management, University of Florence. He is member of the Doctorate Programme DELoS of the University of Trento and University of Florence. His research interests focus on networks dynamics and cluster competitiveness in tourism, cultural and creative industries, and Made in Italy. He has published articles on these themes in major journals, including *European Planning Studies*, *Industry and Innovation*, *City, Culture and Society*, *Tourism Geographies*, *European Urban and Regional Research*, and *Annals of Regional Sciences*. He has recently published the book *Tourist Clusters, Destinations and Competitiveness* with Routledge (2016).

Fabio Carnelli is a Ph.D. candidate in Urban European and Local Studies at the Sociology Department of University of Milan Bicocca (Italy) where he is working on disaster risk reduction from a comparative perspective. He has published an edited book and book chapters in volumes concerning sociocultural aspects of the L'Aquila earthquake's aftermath. He recently co-edited an interdisciplinary volume on seismic risk.

Matteo Caroli is full Professor of International Business at the Department of Business and Management of Luiss Guido Carli University, Rome. He heads the Community of Management within the same department and is director of the CERIIS (Centre for Research on Social Innovation). Since 2015, he has been the director of the international master programme in Tourism Management of the Luiss Business School. Territorial marketing and tourism destination marketing are two of his main areas of scientific interest. In these fields, he has also collaborated with many national, regional, and local institutions. Some of his recent books are *Il marketing per la gestione competitiva del territorio (2014)*, *Gestione delle imprese internazionali (2015)*, and *Gestione del patrimonio culturale e competitività del territorio (2016)*.

Patrizia Casadei is a Ph.D. candidate in the "Development Economics and Local Systems" (DELoS) doctorate programme of the University of Florence and the University of Trento. She has worked as a business analyst in the fashion and luxury industry and spent a period of study and research in London in 2014. Her research interests focus on local development, cultural economy, creative and cultural industries, creative cities, economics of fashion and design industries, and the role of fashion in urban economies with a particular focus on the cities of London and Florence. Currently, she is a visiting research student in the Department of Geography at the Royal Holloway University, London.

María Cordente Rodríguez is Assistant Professor of Marketing at the University of Castilla-La Mancha (Cuenca, Spain) with accreditation as Associate since November 2015. She teaches marketing research, commercial management, marketing for social services, and strategic marketing on both B.A. and M.A. programmes. Her research interests include cultural tourism, the image of tourism destinations, consumer behaviour, sustainable marketing and tourism, and e-learning. She is a member of the Spanish Marketing Association. She has presented her research results at national and international conferences and published her work in several national and international journals and books. She has worked in several research projects funded by different national and regional institutions. Currently, she is conducting research on the development of the perception of residents about tourism activity in their cities.

Maria Della Lucia is Associate Professor of Tourism and Business Management at the University of Trento in Italy. Her current research interests include local development, cultural-led regeneration, destination management and governance, sustainable tourism and mobility, and economic impact analyses as investment decision-making tools. Tourism and culture are her main domains of interest, and her field research focuses primarily on fragmented and community-based areas, particularly Alpine and rural destinations and urban areas. She has authored and co-authored journal publications in *Tourism Management, Journal of Sustainable Tourism, Journal of Information Technology and Tourism, International Journal of Management Cases*, and *Journal of Agricultural Studies* and book chapters in volumes published by CABI, Emerald Publishing, ESV Erich Schmidt Verlag, Palgrave Macmillan, and Routledge.

Veronika Dumbrovská is a Ph.D. candidate in Regional and Political Geography at Charles University in Prague. She holds a bachelor's degree in Geography and Cartography (Charles University in Prague, 2009). In 2013, she received a master's degree in Political and Regional Geography from Charles University in Prague with a thesis on "Development of the Status of Prague—Tourist Destination in the Central European Space". During her studies, she completed short research stays at Yale University (2012) and the University of Vienna (2014) and interned at CzechTourism, a state agency for tourism research, in its Prague (2011) and

New York (2012) branches. She participates in the Geography of Leisure Research Center and she is a member of the Czech Geographical Society and the Regional Studies Association. Her research interests encompass issues of tourism geography, urban tourism, heritage, host–visitor relationships, touristification, tourism impacts, and tourism development.

Nadia Fava has a Ph.D. in Architecture from Universitat Politecnica de Catalunya (2004) and was awarded the "Premi extraordinari de la Politecnica" in 2006 for her doctoral thesis titled "Processi in conflitto: la facciata marittima di Barcellona". She is Professor of Urban Planning at the University of Girona. Her research interests include urban history, urban retailing, and urban and rural tourism. She is head of the Architecture and Territory research group (http://daec.udg.edu/arquitectura-i-territori/) at the University of Girona. In 2013–2014, she was coordinator of the European programme titled "New territories for the European maritime coast" and director of the International Seminar "Touristic territories, touristic imagery and the construction of the contemporary landscape". She has published her work in several national and international journals and books.

Luca Ferrucci is full Professor of Corporate Governance and Strategy at the Department of Economics and Business of the University of Perugia. He is also the Chairman of the Bachelor and Master of Science Programmes at the same department. His publications focus on cultural tourism, the economic impact of cultural events, and urban economy for touristic attractiveness. His research interests include small and medium manufacturing competitiveness, Italian industrial districts, and local and regional development policies (with a focus on innovation and internationalization).

Chiara Garau is Assistant Professor of Urban and Regional Planning at the DICAAR (Department of Civil and Environmental Engineering and Architecture) of the University of Cagliari, Italy. She has been a member of the scientific and organizing committee of the YA AESOP (Young Academics—Association of European Schools of Planning, 2011–2013). She has been scientific and technical adviser for the Smart Cities Observatory of Rome (2013–2014), and she has held several postdoctoral fellowships at the DICAAR. In June 2015, she received the Best Paper award at the 15th International Conference on Computational Science and its Applications (ICCSA 2015) with a manuscript entitled *Benchmarking Smart Urban Mobility: A Study on Italian Cities*, co-authored with Francesco Pinna and Francesca Masala. She has recently won a national research competition (the SIR call proposal—*Scientific independence of young researchers*, Domain SH—of the Italian Ministry of Education, University and Research) with the project entitled *Governing the smart city: a governance-centred approach to smart urbanism*. She has also been selected as an international scientist by the Federal Ministry of Education and Research (BMBF) and by the German Academic Exchange Service (DAAD) to be part of the programme "Science Tour 2016: City of the Future—Research for Sustainable Urban Development". Currently, she is a member of the

Resilient Cities RESURBE international programme (coordinated by Hermilo Salas, Nicola Tollin, Jordi Morato, and Ernesto Santibañez). Her research interests focus on urban planning, cultural heritage, ICT, urban governance, smart cities, cultural tourism, and participatory processes. She is author of over 43 scientific publications, including monographs, conference proceedings, and articles in books and national and international journals.

Massimo Giovanardi joined the University of Leicester School of Management as a Lecturer in Marketing in 2014. During his Ph.D. training and postdoc experience, he developed expertise in the study of "place branding"—an umbrella term for research in place marketing, destination image, and place-of-origin effect. More broadly, his research approach takes sociological perspectives to understand the processes whereby places are marketed, communicated, and consumed. His contributions have been published in *Annals of Tourism Research, Marketing Theory, European Planning Studies, Journal of Public Affairs*, and other topical academic journals about territorial development. He is affiliated to the Stockholm Programme of Place Branding and is developing a rich teaching portfolio, including public marketing, tourism and hospitality marketing management, and Ph.D. workshops on methodology and paper development.

Frank M. Go currently holds the Bewetour chair of tourism marketing at the Rotterdam School of Management and serves as senior member of Erasmus@Work, which develops insights into the new ways of working and has received an ERIM Impact Award. Prior to 1996, he served as professor at Hong Kong Polytechnic University, the Haskayne School of Business, University of Calgary, and Ryerson University, Toronto. An editorial board member of eight international journals, he has published independently and as co-author in, amongst others, the Economist Intelligence Unit publications, *Journal of Brand Management*, the *Journal of Place Branding and Public Diplomacy, Journal of Travel Research*, the *Journal of Travel and Tourism Marketing, Annals of Tourism Research, Tourism Management*, and *Information Technology and Tourism*. His present research interests address issues in relation to the dominant service logic, the governance of brand identity/image, event marketing, and partnered sponsorship. He has served as consultant, adviser, and researcher to the private and public sectors, including Microsoft, IATA, and Quality Lodgings and is advisory board member of Media-Tenor. He has served as jury member and invited speaker and conference chairman at events in more than 55 countries. He is co-editor of the *International Place Branding Yearbook* series (2010, 2011, and 2012) and co-author of *Place Branding* (2009) all issued by Palgrave-Macmillan, London. He holds a Ph.D. from the Faculty of Economics and Econometrics, University of Amsterdam; he is visiting professor at the Open University Business School (UK) and Rikkyo University, Tokyo.

Werner Gronau is Professor of Tourism, Travel and Transport at the University of Applied Sciences Stralsund/Germany and is affiliated to the University of

Bergamo/Italy as Adjunct Professor. He holds a German Degree in Human Geography from the Technical University of Munich and a Ph.D. in Mobility Studies ("Leisure mobility and leisure style") from the University of Paderborn. He is member of several research groups in the field of tourism and transport, such as the Transport Geography Research Group of the British Royal Geographical Society, the German Society of Tourism Research (DGT), or the German Transport Geography Research Group (Arbeitskreis Verkehr). He also works as a reviewer for several academic journals, such as *Tourism Management*, *Local Environment*, or *Journal of Transport Geography*. Furthermore, he is chief editor of the transport journal *Studies on Mobility and Transport Research*. His research interests focus on sustainable transport management and tourism-related transport issues. He has worked in several research projects funded by different institutions, for example the German Ministry of Research or the European Commission, and presented the results at international conferences, in various journals and books.

Mihalis Kavaratzis is a Senior Lecturer in Marketing at the University of Leicester School of Management. He holds a Ph.D. on City Marketing from the University of Groningen, Netherlands, and he has taught marketing and tourism-related courses in Hungary, the Netherlands, and the UK. His research centres on marketing and branding places and tourism destinations, with a particular focus on clarifying the processes involved in place brand formation and on refining the ways in which place branding is undertaken in practice. He has published extensively on these topics in marketing, geography, and planning journals, as well as the edited volumes *Towards Effective Place Brand Management* (with Ashworth 2010) and *Rethinking Place Branding* (with Warnaby and Ashworth 2015).

Assya Khiat is Professor at the Université d'Oran 2 Mohamed Ben Ahmed Algérie, coordinator of the Ph.D. in Human Resource Management and Marketing, of the Executive Master programme in Human Resource and Communication, and of the *CNEPRU Audit de la Fonction Ressources Humaines* project. She has worked as a consultant for public and private companies in Algeria. The author of several publications, she is a member of the *Instituts International d'Audit Social* (IAS) and deputy president of the *RESADDERSE International* journal. She is researcher at the LAREEM laboratory (*Laboratoire de Recherche sur les Economies Euro-Méditérranéennes*), currently focusing on the jobs market in the tourism industry.

Barbara Konecka-Szydłowska is a researcher and lecturer at the Department of Regional Analysis, Institute of Socio-Economic Geography and Spatial Management, Adam Mickiewicz University in Poznań, Poland. Her research focuses on structural and functional changes at the local level, especially at the scale of small towns, the role of small towns in regional settlement systems, the significance of endogenous capital for urban development, the operation of new towns in a settlement system, and the use of regionalization methods in geographical studies. She is the author and co-author of more than 70 articles published in national and international journals. She is co-author of two expert reports for the Wielkopolska Marshal Office in Poznań. She has taken part in five research projects, including two international projects carried out in cooperation with the Leibniz-Institut für Landerkunde in Leipzig and one project implemented together with partners from Lithuania and Slovakia (http://www.owsg.pl/). Currently, she is conducting research on the development of small towns located in metropolitan areas and on the endogenous potential of towns belonging to the Polish National Cittaslow Network.

Robert Lanquar is Doctor in "Economy and Law of Tourism"—University Aix-Marseilles III, and has a Ph.D. in "Recreation Resources Organizational Development"—Texas A&M University (USA). A former UNWTO civil servant, he has been an expert of several international organizations like UNWTO, UNEP, UNDP, the World Bank, the European Commission, and the Commonwealth. He has been the tourism coordinator of the Blue Plan for the Mediterranean. He has published more than 350 articles and reports, as well as 17 books, mainly in the Presses Universitaires de France's collection "Que Sais-Je", translated into eight different languages. He has taught in France, Canada, Belgium, Switzerland, Spain, Algeria, and Mexico as well as in various European and African countries.

Luciana Lazzeretti is full Professor of Economics and Management and founding director of the Postgraduate Programme in Economics and Management of Cultural Goods and Museums, University of Florence. She is coordinator of the curriculum in Local Development in the Doctorate Programme "Development Economics and Local Systems" (DELoS) of the University of Trento and Florence. She is Associate Professor at the National Research Institute (CNR) of Applied Physics "Nello Carrara" in Florence. Her current research interests are focused on industrial districts, cultural clusters, and cities of art, creative and cultural industries, innovation, and creativity. She has recently published *Creative Industries and Innovation in Europe*, Routledge (2013), and *Creative Cities, Cultural Clusters and Local Economic Development*, Edward Elgar in 2008 (with Phil Cooke).

Barbara Maćkiewicz is a researcher and lecturer at the Department of Food Management and Rural Areas, Institute of Socio-Economic Geography and Spatial Management, Adam Mickiewicz University in Poznań, Poland. Her research focuses mostly on the real-estate market and changes in the land-use pattern in urban agglomerations. She is the author of several scientific articles and of expert's reports on the real-estate market in the Poznań agglomeration. Her scholarly interests also include rural and urban areas, as well as tourism, especially eco-tourism.

Paola Minoia is Senior Lecturer in Development Geography and Tourism Research at the University of Helsinki. Her research focuses on political ecology, sustainable tourism, environmental justice, and community participation. She is chief editor of *Fennia*, international journal of geography published by the

Geographical Society of Finland. In the past, she has coordinated a EU-LIFE project on eco-tourism in the Venice Lagoon and been involved in participatory planning to address conflicting issues between tourism and residential functions in Venice.

Nathalie Montargot is an Associate Professor of Tourism Management and member of the ESSEC Chair of Change. She teaches and does research in the Sup de Co La Rochelle Group (France). She was Director of International Hospitality Postgraduate Studies at Cergy University (France). She received a Ph.D. in Management at Cergy University, with a thesis titled "The integration of young people with weak educational assets: the case of hospitality and catering sectors". Her current research interests concern organizational socialization, change management, and well-being in the workplace, especially in the hospitality and tourism sectors.

Silvia Mugnano is Assistant Professor of Urban Sociology, and her research interests include housing, urban transformation, and creative industry. She has participated in several international research projects, and she has coordinated the Italian research unit of the EU projects entitled RESTATE (Restructuring Large Housing Estates in European Cities) and ACRE (Accommodating Creative Knowledge—Competitiveness of European Metropolitan Regions within the Enlarged Union). She works on decentralized cooperation programmes in Lebanon and Central America. She is a staff member of *Laboratorio Perimetro* (laboratory on metropolitan peripheries).

Saida Palou Rubio holds a Ph.D. in Social and Cultural Anthropology from the University of Barcelona. She won the Ciutat de Barcelona Agustí Duran i Sanpere d'Història prize (2011) for her doctoral thesis *Barcelona, tourist destination. Public promotion, tourism, images and city (1888–2010)*. She is currently teaching at the Tourism Faculty of the University of Girona. She is a member of the Catalan Institute of Anthropology and coordinator of the *Destination BCN. History of tourism in the city* conference. She has also authored publications in the fields of history of tourism, anthropology, and collective memory. She was a member of the Office of Strategic Tourism Plan of the City of Barcelona (2008–2010).

Cecilia Pasquinelli is a postdoctoral research fellow at the Gran Sasso Science Institute in L'Aquila, Italy. She previously worked in the Department of Social and Economic Geography at Uppsala University, Sweden. She received her Ph.D. in Management, Competitiveness, and Development from the Institute of Management at Scuola Superiore Sant'Anna in 2012. She has experience as a consultant on place marketing and foreign direct investment promotion. She is Associate Editor of the *Journal of Place Management and Development*. Her research interests include place branding, place of origin and the economic geography of brands and branding, cultural economy, local and regional development, and urban tourism. Her work has been published in international journals including *Urban Studies*,

Cities, Local Economy, Environment Planning Studies, Urban Research and Practice, and *Place Branding and Public Diplomacy*.

Marko Perić is Assistant Professor and Head of the Department of Management at the Faculty of Tourism and Hospitality Management, University of Rijeka, Croatia. He is also principal investigator of the research project entitled "Management of Sports Experiences in the Function of Designing Effective Business Models in Less Developed Tourist Destinations" supported by the Croatian Science Foundation. His fields of interest include strategic management, sports management, sports tourism, and project management issues. He is author or co-author of 4 books and over 35 papers on management and tourism issues.

Chiara Rabbiosi was awarded a Ph.D. in Urban and Local European Studies at the University of Milano-Bicocca (Italy) in 2009, and she has been working in the field of tourism since 2012, first as a visiting postdoctoral fellow at the Institut de Recherche et d'Études Supérieures du Tourisme (IREST) at the University Paris I Panthéon Sorbonne (France) and then as a postdoc at the Center for Advanced Studies in Tourism (CAST) at the Rimini Campus of the University of Bologna (Italy), where she is currently working. Her current research and teaching interests deal with the social and spatial dimensions of urban studies and consumer culture, including critical approaches to shopping tourism, the geographies of brand, and place-making debates. Her work has been published in *Cities, The Journal of Tourism and Cultural Change*, and *Gender, Place and Culture*. She is the author of the book *Nuovi itinerari del consumo* (Santarcangelo di Romagna: Maggioli, 2013) and of a number of articles dealing with urban regeneration and participatory research, consumption, and ethnography.

Silvia Sarti is Ph.D. student in Management: Innovation, Sustainability and Healthcare at Scuola Superiore Sant'Anna, Pisa. Her main area of interest is sustainability, and her Ph.D. project is focused on consumer behaviour, paying particular attention to green consumption. Her scholarship is sponsored by Telecom Italia, and she collaborates closely with the JOL White (Wellbeing and Health Innovative Technologies Lab of Telecom Italia), working on a project about healthy nutrition and well-being. She is also conducting research with the Department of Economics of the University of Perugia. In 2014, she received a master's degree with honours in Economics and Management at the University of Perugia, with a thesis on cultural economics. In 2012, she took part in the Erasmus Exchange Programme, spending a semester at Bilkent University in Ankara (Turkey). In 2011, she received a bachelor's degree with honours in Economics and Business Administration at the University of Perugia.

Efe Sevin is a faculty member at the Department of Public Relations and Information of Kadir Has University. His research areas include strategic communication, political communication, place/city branding, and public diplomacy. He is particularly interested in the role of public and non-traditional diplomacy methods in the larger picture of global affairs and the changes brought about in diplomatic practices by online communication methods. His work has been published in several academic journals and books, including *American Behavioral Scientist* and *Cities*. Dr. Sevin received his Ph.D. from American University's School of International Service, Washington, D.C. He completed his graduate studies at Emerson College, Boston, MA, as a Fulbright scholar and his undergraduate studies at Middle East Technical University, Ankara, Turkey.

Simone Splendiani is Assistant Professor of Business Management at the University of Perugia (Italy), where he teaches tourism management and Web marketing. His current main area of research is destination management, with particular regard to communication and branding policies in the tourism planning process. Within this thematic framework, he has conducted several studies on sustainable tourism development initiated by both local agencies and DMOs. In this regard, he has paid particular attention to issues concerning the management of events and measurement of their impact in terms of sustainability. Another area of interest is Internet marketing, with reference to the marketing policies of small and medium-sized enterprises and the opportunities that the Web offers them. This research has been developed with particular regard to social media and new tools related to Web 2.0.

Mariapina Trunfio is Associate Professor of Tourism and Business Management and Director of the Master in Tourism and Hospitality Management at the University of Naples "Parthenope" in Italy. Her current research focuses on governance, destination management, place branding, sustainable tourism, local development, cultural diversity management, culture and creativity, smart destinations, social media, and the MICE industry. She has written several monographs and published authored and co-authored articles in *International Journal of Contemporary Hospitality Management* (Highly Commended Award, 2007), *Journal of Travel and Tourism Research*, *Journal of Agricultural Studies,* and *European J. of Cross-Cultural Competence and Management* and chapters in books published by CABI, ESV Erich Schmidt Verlag, Palgrave Macmillan, and Springer.

Lauren Uğur is a South African born urban development planner and management specialist. She holds a Ph.D. in urban sociology as well as a first-class Master of Business Administration (M.B.A.) degree from the University of South Australia and currently holds a professorship for Tourism and Event Management at the International School of Management in Frankfurt, Germany.

Alfredo Valentino is a postdoctoral fellow at the Department of Business and Management, Luiss Guido Carli University in Rome. He received his Ph.D. in Management at the Luiss Guido Carli University. His research focuses on how marketing tools may be used to improve territorial development and tourism attractiveness. In addition, he is interested in green marketing and the use of eco-industrial parks for sustainable industrial growth. He has worked on

European projects and research projects on place marketing such as Ecomark and MER.

Anna Vaňová is Associate Professor and currently holds the position of Vice Dean for Development at the Department of Public Economy and Regional Development, Faculty of Economics, Matej Bel University in Banska Bystrica, Slovakia. She is a representative of the Slovak Republic at the International Association on Public and Non-profit Marketing (IAPNM). She has wide experience as principal investigator and co-investigator of domestic and international research projects funded by grants from, amongst others, the British KHF, OSF, the European Union, and state institutions. She is the author or co-author of more than 150 publications, several of them on the topics of creative industries, creative economy, creative cities, and their role in territorial development.

Katarína Vitálišová is the Head of the Department of Regional Development and Public Economics at the Institute of Economic Sciences of the Faculty of Economics of the Matej Bel University Banska Bystrica, Slovakia. Her research is focused on the building and maintenance of relationships and networks amongst stakeholders in territories, innovative forms of regional development, creative economy and its importance for regional and local development, and strategic marketing planning. Currently, she is involved in international and national projects dealing with the topic of creative industries. She has published more than 40 papers, studies, and chapters at home and abroad.

Nicholas Wise is an independent researcher in the fields of geography, sport, events, and tourism. His published work has mainly focused on the Dominican Republic, Argentina, Croatia, and Serbia, with work conducted across several disciplines, from human geography and sport sociology to tourism management. His current academic interests deal with interdisciplinary approaches to sports tourism-led regeneration, place image/identity, sense of community, and destination competitiveness. Current work being developed is concerned with the role of communities in urban areas and the immediate regions to assess impacts that go beyond physical and economic change to better understand impacts and social conditions.

Global Context, Policies and Practices in Urban Tourism: An Introduction

Cecilia Pasquinelli and Nicola Bellini

Abstract Tourism is undergoing fundamental changes with regard to market, industry structure and the product itself; changes driven by an even more fundamental transition to 'post-modern' patterns of consumption that makes tourism one of the benchmarks of modes of production and consumption in the knowledge economy. Tourism plays, quantitatively and qualitatively, an unprecedented role in shaping economic development, while consolidated tourism models should rapidly adapt themselves to a new and changing reality. This chapter introduces and provides the background for the discussion developed in this book, which addresses multiple interconnections between tourism and the city from a policy-oriented research standpoint. After an overview of trends characterising city tourism in the global context, the chapter focuses on Europe, where city tourism has been the most dynamic tourism segment. However, besides EU engagement with the development of a tourism policy framework, urban tourism seems to play a secondary role in the European tourism vision, in which tourism is interpreted as a potential economic alternative for lagging areas where other economic drivers have been historically weak. Through discussion of possible explanations, the chapter develops an analysis of the EU Urban Portal to outline tourism representation in connection with the urban agenda of the European Union and concludes by presenting this book's structure.

Keywords Global tourism • Urban • Europe • Tourism policy

C. Pasquinelli (✉)
GSSI Social Sciences, Gran Sasso Science Institute, L'Aquila, Italy
e-mail: cecilia.pasquinelli@gssi.infn.it

N. Bellini
La Rochelle Tourism Management Institute, Groupe Sup de Co La Rochelle, La Rochelle, France
e-mail: bellinin@esc-larochelle.fr

© Springer International Publishing Switzerland 2017
N. Bellini, C. Pasquinelli (eds.), *Tourism in the City*,
DOI 10.1007/978-3-319-26877-4_1

1 Setting the Scene

Tourism is undergoing fundamental changes with regard to market, industry structure and the product itself; changes driven by an even more fundamental transition to 'post-modern' patterns of consumption making tourism one of the benchmarks of the modes of production and consumption in the knowledge economy (Frochot and Batat 2013). Traditional models of tourism management and planning are rapidly adapting themselves to a new reality in which tourism plays, quantitatively and qualitatively, an unprecedented role in shaping economic development.

This book conducts a critical discussion of the interconnections between tourism and the city from a policy-oriented research standpoint. In fact, tourism penetrates and increasingly influences policy decisions in all fields of city development: land-use, site development, building regulations, infrastructures, innovation, environmental quality, social inclusion, entrepreneurship, urban governance, etc. This makes it urgent (and not only for scholars) to include tourism perspectives in the models implemented to face urban issues and challenges. Tourism may support cities in building their reputation, in promoting their relational capital in the global arena, and in proposing and supporting a quality model of urban development.

Furthermore, urban tourism is in itself a multi-faceted phenomenon. A variety of travellers come to a city for very different purposes, and their multiple interactions with the residents and with the city's attractions and infrastructures give rise to a variety of tourisms. Hence a wide range of overlapping tourism models (and business models) must coexist.

Throughout its chapters, this book assumes that tourism is an essential function of contemporary urban contexts. It therefore tests the potential and the limitations of integrating tourism into urban policies. This is done by a multifaceted and multidisciplinary range of contributions. From different perspectives, they discuss how the pursuit of tourism performance may contribute to urban quality and to the well-being of local communities (quality spaces, employment, accessibility, innovation and learning), but may also generate risks, tensions and conflicts, as testified by the rise of anti-tourism movements in reaction to cultural commodification and tourism-induced gentrification. In this regard, as will be further discussed in the conclusions, the integration of tourism into the urban agenda is the condition (both intellectual and political) for critically and positively approaching the asymmetries produced by the city tourism phenomenon. Are these asymmetries leading to a (manageable?) trade-off between the interests of the residents and those of tourists or do they (and under what conditions?) trigger a positive-sum game for the well-being of both permanent and temporary residents?

From this critical perspective, this book provides:

- an updated account and analyses of the urban tourism phenomenon in contemporary cities;
- research-based analyses offering managerial considerations and policy implications;
- a rich array of cases showing practices and policies in diverse urban contexts.

This book is the first result of the joint work of a network of scholars who met for the first time on the occasion of an international workshop held at the Gran Sasso Science Institute (GSSI) in L'Aquila, Italy, in June 2015. The GSSI is a young doctoral school that was established by the Italian government in 2012 in L'Aquila, with the support of the OECD, as part of the strategy for the city's reconstruction following the disastrous earthquake of 2009. The GSSI includes a doctoral programme in urban studies and regional science and a research unit in social sciences that focuses on policy-oriented research concerning the long-term development trajectories of territorial and urban systems and that provides the intellectual and organisational framework for the new network and for that workshop in particular. Testifying to the growing interest in the topic proposed and the need for dedicated research and discussion, the call for papers brought 68 applications from all over Europe, and the selection process allowed wide geographical coverage with case studies and conceptual contributions from both Northern and Southern Europe.

A resurgence of interest in the urban tourism phenomenon has to be connected with a variety of factors of both a contingent and structural nature. Certainly, tourism has been growing and diversifying over the past decade; and in a rapidly changing global context, the travel industry has been transforming. Estimates suggest that the number of international tourist arrivals will increase by 3.3 % yearly on average until 2030 (UNWTO 2012), while, according to the World Economic Forum (2015), the travel and tourism sector is forecast to keep growing by 4 % per year, at a higher speed than other economic sectors such as manufacturing, transport and financial services. Besides the growing trends, the diversification and overall transformation of the tourism phenomenon have started to be observed and questioned. As Hall and Williams (2008) put it, four types of innovation should be brought under scrutiny as summarising the fields in which novelty and emerging trajectories can be sought: *niche* innovation focusing on the opening of new market opportunities through the use of technologies; *regular* innovation following historical patterns of incremental change; *revolutionary* innovation, which derives from intensive use of technologies in specific products or services, yet not involving the entire tourism industry; and finally *architectural* innovation impacting on the tourism industry as a whole. One of current challenges in the tourism research domain consists in the identification of tourism innovations and in the analysis of their social, economic and cultural effects, as well as of their capacity profoundly to change the way in which travellers, on the one hand, and tourism supply players on the other, engage with tourism development.

As this book intends to show, tourism is a 'situated' phenomenon; and throughout its evolution in global society, it has definitely not been a negligible factor in cities' evolving trajectories. And yet urban tourism seems to persist at the margin of the debate on cities. It is rarely studied as part of an urban economy, being mostly confined to treatment as an 'agent' of gentrification and as a direct (and almost taken for granted) result of culture-led regeneration processes. What are the reasons for tourism's marginalisation in urban studies? As we shall see below, this has partly to do with an intellectual history that relegated tourism to playing the role of the 'easy' alternative for lagging peripheral regions that had remained outside industrialisation processes.

Two ideal-types have been proposed: "urbanisation tourism" and "tourism urbanisation" (Hall et al. 2015). Both are meant to signal the embeddedness of tourism in urbanisation processes. The latter (tourism urbanisation) identifies tourism as the main driver of the physical, social and economic shaping of the city: urban tourism and leisure play a predominant role in place production. According to the former (i.e. urbanisation tourism), instead, tourism does not prevail in the urban economy, and it is one of the many dimensions on which to focus in order to explain the evolutionary trajectory of cities. There is growing awareness in the global tourism discourse about the need to converge on a sustainable tourism path that seems to coincide with the 'urbanisation tourism' rationale, where tourism does not take a lead in the local economy but contributes to urban diversity, leisure and culture consumption atmospherics. The sustainable urban tourism conceptualisation is the main response to the negative effects that rapid urban tourism growth has been provoking. However, significant research efforts should address urbanisation tourism, how it takes shape, the policies and practices characterising it, its effects and limits. In investigating the role of tourism in the formation of the social, economic and physical fabric of cities, there is a need to dig deeper into the many *in-between* forms that tourism takes in urban contexts.

Global tourism development, in fact, is closely intertwined with the trajectories of urban transformation and urbanisation. The growth of the urban population will be combined with that of a temporary and oscillating population of visitors, impacting on the urban physical and socio-economic fabric. The disproportionate growth in numbers, increasing revenues, and the expanding presence of tourists in various urban settings beyond central tourism districts, as analysed by neighbourhood studies (Novy 2011), urge treatment of tourism as significant urban fact. Cities, then, are not only the main destinations or major focal points of travellers' itineraries; they are also the origins of most global travellers (Ashworth 1989; Ashworth and Page 2011), since 80 % of tourists are generated from cities (Terzibasoglu 2015).

This is a key reason for reconsideration of tourism as a crucial factor in city development, as stated by the 2012 Istanbul Declaration promoted by the World Tourism Organization (UNWTO), the United Nations agency in charge of responsible, sustainable and universally accessible tourism promotion. Several countries agreed that "tourism is a key resource for cities and local residents" because it may contribute to local income as well as to the maintenance of urban infrastructures and the provision of public services (UNWTO 2012). The Declaration described tourism as the world's biggest industry, creating positive economic benefits and promoting culture and well-being as well as social cohesion and heritage preservation. The UNWTO also stressed the importance of public policies boosting the positive impacts of city tourism, while preventing or mitigating the negative effects. That is, if most tourism policies have to date been conceived as stand-alone marketing and promotion strategies, the time has come to conduct structured reflection on integrated urban policies. The crucial question is, however, how and to what extent academia can help substantiate these statements and guide the debate towards defining theoretically-based and empirically-grounded action for a responsible, sustainable and accessible tourism.

Various international observers have endorsed a positive, often over-optimistic, representation of tourism. A good example of the strongly positive representation of tourism's economic impact is provided by the following statement commenting on the tourism scenario that emerged from the Mastercard 2014 Global Destination Cities Index report:

> The impacts of travel on destination cities that receive visitors are very significant from the business, social, and cultural perspectives. International visitors' spending constitutes an increasingly important source of business revenue in a destination city, encompassing the hospitality, retail, transport, sports, and cultural industries, among many others. In many instances, it is a major economic engine for employment and income generation for the city in question. Along with the flow of visitors comes the flow of new ideas and experiences that benefits both the visitors and the destination cities, which are just as important as the flow of spending. As a result, the more connected a destination city is to other cities, the more vibrant and dynamic it becomes. (Hedrick-Wong and Choong 2014, p. 2).

If, on the one hand, tourism is represented as a Panglossian panacea for many (in some cases even *all*) development problems (as a source of revenue, ideas, employment, connection and dynamism, according to the above quotation), on the other hand, awareness of tourism's many negative effects has nourished increasingly critical interpretations of its impacts and role in urban areas, marking the end of the cities' "honeymoon" with urban tourism (Novy 2014), with the emergence of anti-tourism movements re-claiming the dwellers' right to the city. Various streams in the literature argue the inequitable effects of rent increase and displacement induced by urban dynamics associated with tourism, leisure and consumption, with consequent implications of social, economic, and political exclusion (Novy 2011).

Urban tourism remains an immature field of research, and simplistic descriptions of the city tourism phenomenon are the result. Yet (once again) why do "those studying tourism neglect cities while those studying cities neglect tourism"? (Ashworth and Page 2011, p. 2). Evidently, there has been a kind of implicit consensus on the negligibility of tourism in the process of urban and economic development.

The immaturity of city tourism as analytical domain has historical roots. Until the 1980s the academic literature on urban tourism was very limited (Darcy and Small 2008). Thereafter, urban tourism started to become an integral part of tourism studies, albeit as a quite "distinct phenomenon and area of research" (Edwards et al. 2008). A deep "rural bias" continued to characterise tourism for a long time (Ashworth 1989). Even an "anti-urban bias" (Ashworth and Page 2011) characterised especially the Anglo-American context, where tourism was primarily linked to the idea of outdoor recreation in the countryside where direct contact with nature could be experienced. In contrast, in line with an industrialist vision, cities were conceived as places for hard work, for the "serious tasks of work, trade and government" (Ashworth and Page 2011, p. 3).

Since the 1980s the interest in urban tourism has grown rapidly, in parallel with the increasing attention paid to the need to regulate and counteract the negative externalities of tourism in historic cities (Darcy and Small 2008). As Valls et al. (2014) put it, the "seaside holidays in the sun" model that arose in the 1960s started to diminish, while city tourism has been growing. This trend has been boosted by the emergence and strengthening of low-cost air transport, together with an improvement of European cities' connectivity. The liberalisation of air transportation in the European Union has meant a revolution in tourism, since it impacts strongly on travellers' flows both quantitatively and qualitatively. Low-cost carriers (LCCs) have been moving travellers outside traditional routes, creating new destinations (Iniguez et al. 2014; Ivanovic et al. 2014). 'Emerging' destinations are often small cities and towns, generally not already famous, where low-cost carriers pay lower airport fees and taxes (Olipra 2012). The enthusiasm for a dramatically changing tourism scenario has led to the conception of LCCs as an opportunity not only to expand the geography of tourism but also to reposition well-established destinations. In 2006 the government of Malta, for instance, offered incentives to cheap flight carriers in an attempt to favour short city-breaks and expand cultural/heritage tourism at the expense of the 'sun and beach' model. The result was an increase in the number of arrivals, even though no structural changes in tourism demand occurred (Smith 2009).

At the same time, LCCs have triggered a new wave of discussion on the contribution of tourism to local development. It has been argued that higher tourists flows, like those made possible by LCCs, do not always mean local tourism development, and that, in LCC nodes, tourism destination business models are needed that maximise the benefits while mitigating the negative externalities. The need to reduce or, somehow, balance an overdependence on low-cost carriers has emerged. LCCs, in fact, have the power to decide where, when, and how many visitors will arrive, as well as the power to stop the flows with dramatic consequences on local tourism. This occurred, for instance, in Morocco in 2012 when Ryanair decided to close 34 weekly flights, with the consequent loss of 100,000 visitors annually. This was termed a "Ryanair effect in reverse" (ATW Online 2012).

What are the borders of the urban tourism phenomenon? As this book will show, it is not easy to define detailed and precise contours of the phenomenon because of the multifaceted spatial, cultural, social, economic and political elements that may be argued to be manifestations of city tourism (the following chapters will give an account of this plurality).

A basic definition suggests that city tourism corresponds to those trips to cities (or, more generally, to places of high population density) usually characterised by short stays (UNWTO 2012). Low-cost flights make short city-breaks at affordable prices possible for a growing amount of visitors that choose cities for their weekends or for short vacations. Recent analyses of global travel trends show a rise in city-breaks by 47 % in the period 2009–2013, suggesting that, in numbers, duration is an important aspect for a substantial part of what today is recorded as city tourism (IPK International 2013).

Besides duration, other features distinguish urban tourism (Edwards et al. 2008). Having a wide range of primary and secondary attractions, the urban destination is chosen for a variety of reasons, including leisure, business, shopping, conference attendance, etc. In history, as exemplified by the Grand Tour of Europe from the seventeenth to the nineteenth centuries, cities have always been visited for a "multiplicity of things to see and do"—said Karski in 1990 (Hayllar et al. 2008), suggesting a relationship between variety and length of stay. Thus the traditional criterion of short duration may be too narrow in its focus.

Another aspect qualifying city tourism relates to the fact that, in urban contexts, tourism tends to be only one among economic activities (or one among many economic and social forces), with consequent dynamics of competition for resources between tourism and coexisting urban realities. Tourism is necessarily intertwined to some extent with other socio-economic realities within the urban context because it shares space, skills and, generally, resources with them. There is a "necessary engagement between tourism and the multiplicity of public and commercial organisations with varying levels of involvement with tourism in urban areas" (Edwards et al. 2008, p. 1033). This too, however, is a criterion that is not universally valid, e.g. when we think of resort cities or tourist cities characterised by reducing or simplifying urban functions (this is the case of the tourism urbanisation mentioned above). Urban tourism development must therefore deal with imperative restraints pertaining to the realms of cultural heritage preservation and, on the other hand, to residential needs, which are usually more significant than in other tourist contexts.

In a sense, a keyword with which to explain part of city tourism's essence is the exceptional role of *choice* understood in two senses. First, choice is to be understood as 'opportunity cost', that is, the potential value loss of other alternative land and resource uses when the tourism alternative is chosen in a context that is 'populated' by multiple functions, industries and networks. Secondly, choice concerns the alternative spaces and people that benefit from the value (both symbolic and economic) created by tourism in the city—as this book will amply discuss.

Ashworth and Page, in their literature review based on the identification of paradoxes in the field, remarked that urban tourism has remained a poorly defined and vague concept due to the extraordinarily little attention paid by scholars—in both urban and tourism studies—to tourism "urbanicity" (2011, p. 3) and hence to the distinctive characteristics of those cities that participate in the urban tourism (s) phenomenon. Urban tourism is defined by these authors according to (a) the multi-purpose nature of city visits in a multifunctional context; (b) visitors' use of urban facilities that are not necessarily built for visitors (as Ashworth and Page put it, "if tourists make use of almost all urban features, they make an exclusive use of almost none. Therefore understanding urban tourism is dependent upon a prior understanding of the urban context in which it is embedded", p. 3); (c) the diversity of the urban economy in which tourism takes part. The co-presence of multiple economies in the urban context is fundamental for city tourism, so that cities with the largest and most varied economy will gain the highest benefits from tourism (Ashworth and Page 2011). This sounds like an invitation to reduce the emphasis on the *tourist city* and consider the *tourist function* as embedded in a network of socio-economic realities.

1.1   City Tourism: An Overview of the Global Context

Much emphasis has been put on the magnitude of city tourism as a global phenomenon. For both scholars and policy makers, 'quantity' has often been a source of legitimisation. Numbers have been, in fact, growing very rapidly and are expected to increase steadily at least over the next fifteen years. Global tourism growth is often represented as local opportunity, even though there is increasing awareness of the problems caused by excessive tourism for many 'mature' city destinations (Bremner 2016). The following estimates have been made for global tourism trends by 2030: international arrivals will reach 1.81 billion (Fig. 1), with an annual average growth of 4.4 % (which almost parallels the annual average growth of 4 % in global air passengers according to IATA, Terzibasoglu 2015), world GDP generation of 9.6 % by 2030, and the creation of 300 million direct jobs in a much less concentrated market where new destinations rapidly 'pop up' (UNWTO 2014a).

The World Economic Forum international organisation has started reflecting on the resilience of tourism systems to health, terrorism and economic shocks that might impact on ongoing trends. What has emerged so far is that recovery times are shortening compared to the near past, as a consequence of the implementation of disaster recovery programmes and risk management procedures helping key tourism sectors, e.g. the hotel industry, to be more resilient, but also as a consequence of regional and domestic travellers who, differently from international travellers, are

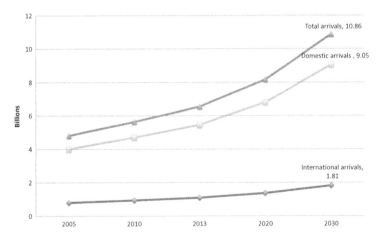

Fig. 1 International and domestic tourist arrivals, 2005–2030. *Source*: Authors' elaboration on Hall et al. (2015)

less sensitive to shocks when planning their journeys (World Economic Forum 2015). There are, however, concerns about possible declining arrivals in some specific cities, even though updated data are necessary to evaluate the actual impact of contemporary global phenomena (Bremner 2016). Further and in-depth analysis of the response of tourism systems to shocks would be welcome, particularly in regard to capital cities in the contemporary global economic and geopolitical context.

Speaking of numbers, it is necessary also to mention that mobile booking and online intermediation have been playing an increasing role. By 2014 they had become a mainstream channel (USD 96 billion) accounting for 12.5 % of global online travel sales (World Travel Market 2015). Intermediary bookings have instead recorded a limited increase (from 1.4 % growth in 2013 to 0.3 % in 2015) mirroring a general tendency of consumers' preferences for direct online purchasing (World Travel Market 2015). This trend is paralleled by the boom in new hospitality providers, with the spread of private rental opportunities brokered through 'sharing economy' platforms like Airbnb. This website has provided travel accommodation to over 30 million guests since its foundation in 2008, impacting negatively on local hotel room revenues and thereby changing consumption patterns, as sustained by Zervas et al. (2016) in the case of the Austin and Texas tourism market.

City tourism recorded significant growth (+58 %) between 2010 and 2014, and it represents 20 % of international tourism (Terzibasoglu 2015). IPK International reports +47 % in the period 2009–2013 (UNWTO 2014a), a much higher percentage than that of other tourism segments such as touring holidays (+27 %), sun and beach holidays (+12 %), and countryside holidays (− 10 %). According to data, city tourism is not only important *per se* but is also a proxy for country/regional tourism because cities are hubs from where visitors start their journeys to surrounding areas. Hence there are two reasons for maintaining that cities are key players in the tourism domain (UNWTO 2014a), since they are both final destinations and 'gateway' ones.

The growth of tourism flows is paralleled by tourism expenditure on international travel. Emerging economies have pushed up growth rates in international tourism expenditure, compensating for traditional source markets—mostly from the European continent and Western countries generally—which are experiencing a slowdown (UNWTO 2014b). According to the Mastercard Global Destination Cities Index report, monitoring 132 destinations around the globe, the top destinations have been London (18.69 million visitors in 2014, +27 % in the period 2010–2014), Bangkok (16.42 millions in 2014, +57 % in 2010–2014) and Paris (15.57 millions in 2014, +17 % in 2010–2014) (Hedrick-Wong and Choong 2014, p. 4). With the exception of first and third positions, which, as said, are occupied by two European capitals, Asian cities and mega-cities such as Singapore, Kuala Lampur, Hong Kong and Seoul lead the ranking. This report also gives information on the total expenditure estimated for the sample analysed. Among the European cities, Barcelona occupies seventh place in the ranking: with 7.3 million visitors, it records growing spend and visitor flows, notwithstanding the many questions raised about the city's tourism model which this book will treat in more detail.

More interestingly, Hedrick-Wong and Choong (2014), on discussing the Mastercard Global Destination Cities Index, drew attention to the pressure that tourism inflows put on the urban system by calculating the ratio of visitors' per resident (Fig. 2). According to their analysis, pressure was evidently growing in the period 2009–2014; yet further insight and in-depth studies would explain how and the extent to which this growth impacted on urban quality and costs. The same report also shows arrivals' expenditure per city residents, spanning from 561 USD in the case of New York City to 3863 USD in the case of Dubai, considering the top ten city destinations. Also in this case, further insight would be necessary to understand who benefits most from tourism expenditure and how these monetary flows trickle down into different parts of local communities. There is also room for exploring who is instead excluded from the 'wealth' created by tourist arrivals—an issue that will also be treated in this book.

The few data presented above direct the attention to the importance of measuring urban tourism, but also to the difficulty of producing data effectively supporting knowledge creation in the field: that is, data able to give a sense of orientation to effective policy-making. The figures outlined above are of a raw nature and certainly suggest that rough measures of tourism 'quantity' are not enough to determine the impact of city tourism and its role in local development and well-being. The need to measure and analyse tourism has been clearly defined in recent times, under the impetus of the UNWTO, which in 2012 initiated the *Cities Project* and then converged on a set of priorities sealed by the Istanbul Declaration. This was signed during the *1st UNWTO Global Conference on City Tourism in 2012*

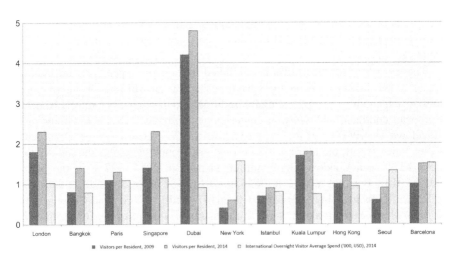

Fig. 2 Destinations by overnight visitor arrivals per city resident, 2009 and 2014 and International Overnight Visitor Average Spend ('000, USD), 2014. *Source*: Authors' elaboration from Hedrick-Wong and Choong (2014)

(UNWTO 2014a), which officially signalled the resurgence of institutions' interest in city tourism. In this context, the importance of going beyond economic performance measurement to encompass the monitoring of impacts on well-being in a broad sense clearly emerged, with advocacy of evidence-based decision-making amongst both public and private stakeholders.

Accordingly, the *Cities Impact Measurement Project* promoted by the World Tourism Organisation, which is a global forum for tourism policy debate and a source of analysis on practices and tourism know-how, drew attention to several fundamental points. First, subnational measurements are required by local stakeholders, given their evident need to rely on these in their everyday activities. Secondly, subnational tourism has to be considered a phenomenon different from regional and national tourism, and it is not possible to 're-use' national data at a subnational scale. From this derives the need to consider city tourism as a distinct field for statistical engagement. Granularity and disaggregation of data responding to city tourism's multifaceted nature are directly connected to the capacity of cities to achieve and maintain their competitiveness over time (UNWTO 2014a).

The World Tourism Organisation also recommended and promoted the standardised production of a set of data and data collection at subnational level so that comparability and benchmarking will be possible across all cities participating in the project. In 2014 a scorecard was proposed to kick off the process of measurement standardisation and harmonisation by providing guidelines for organisations in charge of the monitoring process. The scorecard is composed of three sections: (1) key indicators measuring the economic contribution of tourism in terms of employment and GDP; (2) tourism economic indicators including arrivals, expenditure, jobs per status and seasonality; (3) impact indicators including environmental impacts, tourism pressure counted as number of tourists per day per 100 residents, residents' satisfaction, tourists' use of essential services, congestion and intrusion due to visitors (UNWTO 2014a). The third section emphasises the interconnections between residents' and visitors' terrains in order to highlight complementarities (e.g. use of urban services and the deriving economies of scale), tensions and potential conflicts over spaces, services and resources.

The story of the evolution of monitoring and measuring procedures and tools in city tourism is still in its infancy. Table 1 summarises the initiatives that have made this field progress in recent times.

1.2   The European Context

City tourism has been deemed the most dynamic segment of European tourism. It features the highest growth rates among the various tourism segments, with a dominant role of key source countries such as Germany, United States and United Kingdom, followed by Spain and Italy, which show, however, a slowing trend (European Cities Marketing, ECM 2014). According to the ECM report, which covers 113 cities in Europe including "outstanding cities" (national capitals and

Table 1 City benchmarking initiatives

Initiative	Promoter	Coverage
ETIS—The European Tourism Indicators System	European Commission	'Destination' is not a predefined entity (it can coincide with an administrative unit, a municipality, a region, province, district or country). A range of matters are covered by the indicators, including destination management, environmental, social and cultural sustainability
TourMIS	Department of Tourism and Hospitality Management of MODUL University; financially supported by the Austrian National Tourist Office in collaboration with the European Travel Commission (ETC) and European Cities Marketing (ECM)	TourMIS refers to "city area only" and "greater city area". TourMIS collects information from over 130 cities in Europe. It utilises different and not always harmonised sources
The European Cities Marketing (ECM) Benchmarking Report	ECM is a not-for-profit association dedicated to developing city marketing in Europe	The ECM Report covers tourism statistics from 115 European cities where complete data series are available. It is mostly based on TourMIS
UrbanTUR	UrbanTUR report includes the competitiveness ranking of Spanish city tourism destinations. It is produced by Exceltur (affiliated to UNWTO), which is an association of private tourism companies in Spain	Focus is on Spanish cities, particularly the twenty most visited cities in Spain (Palma de Mallorca is not included)

Source: UNWTO (2014a, pp. 13–18)

power centres) and "core cities" (culturally and economically important destinations), BRIC countries are fast emerging as key source markets. Over the period 2010–2014, while as an aggregate the total number of bednights increased by +20 % in the ECM cities, in the EU28 it did so by +8.9 %. A total of 509 million bednights were estimated in 2014 in the ECM cities; 64 % of them were international bednights (de Delàs 2015). Two different rankings are provided in Table 2, and Fig. 3 gives an overview of the evolution of European cities in terms of international overnight visitors.

The ECM report of 2014 also stressed that smaller European cities may have significant opportunities. Beside the "European Premier League" cities, where city tourism is still growing but may arguably have reached a maturity stage, "Second division" cities (i.e. medium and smaller cities), especially in Eastern Europe, are said to have high potential in the medium-long run and are expected to increase their importance in the urban tourism domain. In terms of city tourism potential to be unlocked, worth mentioning is the World Economic Forum (2015), which, on

Table 2 European Top 10 City Destinations by bednights volume and international overnight visitors

European cities marketing report (Top 10)			MasterCard global destination cities index (Top 10)	
City	Bednights, millions (2013)	%Δ (2012–2013)	City	International overnight visitors, millions (2013)
London	53.7	3.3 %	London	17.3
Paris	36.7	−0.6 %	Paris	15.3
Berlin	26.9	8.2 %	Istanbul	9.9
Rome	24.2	6.2 %	Barcelona	7.2
Barcelona	16.5	3.5 %	Milan	6.8
Madrid	14.9	−4.3 %	Amsterdam	6.7
Prague	14.7	1.5 %	Rome	6.6
Istanbul	14.6	4.8 %	Vienna	5.7
Vienna	13.5	3.2 %	Prague	4.8
Munich	12.9	4.3 %	Munich	4.5

Source: European Cities Marketing (2014) and Hedrick-Wong and Choong (2014)

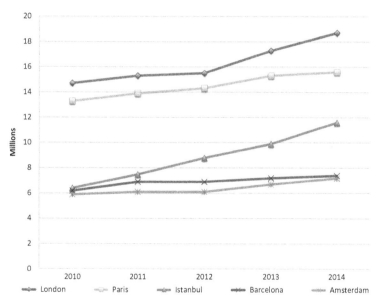

Fig. 3 European Top 5 Destination Cities by International Overnight Visitors, 2010–2014. *Source*: Authors' elaboration on Hedrick-Wong and Choong (2014)

elaborating the Travel & Tourism Competitiveness Report at country level, stressed the outstanding tourism potential of European countries, but it also highlighted differences in terms of realistic tourism development. According to this report, on the one hand, this is due to diverse efforts in tourism promotion, which for some countries is a priority while for others it is a domain for improvisation. On the other hand, it is due to different business environments, which are usually more effective in Northern and Central Europe than in Southern and Eastern Europe.

2 A European Perspective: Tourism Policy in EU

As shown by the previous section, city tourism and tourism more widely are of great importance for Europe, since they directly employ 13.9 million people (3.6 % of total employment; tourism is estimated to indirectly support 32.2 million jobs, 9 % of total employment in Europe)—a number that is growing faster than in other economic sectors according to the European Commission (2010)—and it directly produces 3.4 % and 9.2 % of EU GDP considering connected sectors (World Travel and Tourism Council 2015). Accordingly, the European Commission published in 2010 a communication outlining a new political framework for tourism in Europe, which is celebrated in the running title of the document as "the world's No. 1 tourist destination". Following the Treaty of Lisbon, this document sealed a "new phase" for the European system that, through a process that boosted growing awareness of the importance of tourism in Europe since the 1980s, formally recognised the European tourism policy domain and the EU's competences in this field, which had been the prerogative of Member States (Estol and Font 2016). This communication stated that "European tourism policy needs a new impetus" (p. 14) and recalled that the importance of tourism was defined by the Lisbon Treaty so that the European Union has the capacity to "support, coordinate and complement the action by the Member States" (p. 4) by favouring cooperation and good practice exchange among the States and promoting the integration of tourism into the other EU policies. Action is required because of the new constraints that European tourism has to face. According to this communication, the main challenges are increasing global competition, an ageing population whose travel preferences must be satisfied, since, together with other overlooked segments, e.g. reduced mobility travellers, this represents a significant market potential. Then climate change, scarcity of water, and pressure on biodiversity are presented as key issues. Climate change was likely to boost a restructuring of travel modalities with an impact mostly on a defined set of destinations.

The European Union proposed a "sustainable competitiveness" and stressed the need for a constant updating of the competitiveness variables to be conjugated with the conclusions of the Madrid Declaration for a "socially responsible tourism model". Member States, under the Spanish Presidency of the European Union in April 2010, declared their willingness to participate in the implementation of the EU tourism policy framework, to promote "responsible and ethical tourism and, especially, social, environmental, cultural and economic sustainability of tourism", and agreed on the need to raise awareness of the importance of knowledge, innovation, and new technologies in tourism development and management (Spanish EU Presidency 2010, p. 4).

It seems from the cited documents—which are of key importance for the foundation of a EU tourism policy (for an exhaustive review of the European tourism policy-making process and system, see Estol and Font 2016)—that urban tourism plays a secondary role, while rural and mountain areas, coastal regions, and islands seem to be at the core of the tourism vision in Europe. This has two likely explanations. First, it derived from the process of European tourism policy development that, since the 1980s, was based on an interpretation of tourism as promoting the Internal Market and, through an integration with European cohesion policy, as reducing divergences across regions: rural tourism was, accordingly, identified as a key domain for fostering entrepreneurship and networking in lagging areas (Estol and Font 2016). That is, tourism is supposed to play a specific role in peripheral and backward regions to revitalise their economic development. Secondly, this is also likely to be linked to a historical lack of engagement with, and competence on, the 'urban question' at the European level (something that, as we shall see, has been rapidly changing in recent times).

Besides EU engagement with the development of a policy framework dedicated to tourism, various non-dedicated EU programmes have guaranteed the opportunity to finance tourism-related initiatives in the Member States, such as programmes in the policy domains of cohesion, environment, agriculture, marine and fisheries, culture and education, employment and research, innovation and competitiveness (European Commission 2015c).

For a review of the programmes and types of tourism-related actions that are eligible for funding in the period 2014–2020, it is suggested to read the *Guide on EU Funding For the Tourism Sector*, available at the European Commission web portal. Here some examples are provided that may be of particular relevance to cities and towns and reveal the European rationale for implementing tourism policies. The European Regional Development Fund (ERDF) aims to strengthen economic and social cohesion by removing imbalances amongst regions, and it may support actions improving regional and local competitiveness with an especial focus on industrial and rural declining areas and on urban regeneration. In this frame, tourism-related actions concern innovation, clustering, energy efficiency and entrepreneurship; and, for the period 2014–2020, only small-scale tourism infrastructures can be financed. An example from the previous programming period is the C-Mine project in Genk, Belgium, which was completed in 2011 thanks to 317 million euros from the EU (57 % EU funding on total investment) where a coal-mining site was transformed into a place for creative and cultural economy activities (European Commission 2015c). It will be important to monitor future EU investments in tourism projects to see what projects will be financed for tourism development and if any changes will occur.

Furthermore, Horizon 2020, which is the EU framework programme for research and innovation, is an opportunity to fund tourism-related actions under the *Industrial Leadership* section, including the *Leadership in Enabling and Industrial Technologies* and the *Innovation SMEs* sub-sections. There is a close focus on ICT solutions for cultural and creative sectors with high commercial and innovation potential. One example of a project financed by the Seventh Framework

Programme (then replaced by Horizon 2020) is CHESS (Cultural Heritage Experiences through socio-personal interactions and storytelling) funded by the EU in the period 2011–2014 with 2.8 million euros. It developed devices for delivering personalised interactive stories through the use of various technologies including an augmented reality interface, and it was tested in different cultural venues. The Horizon 2020 Expert Group for Cultural Heritage has recently published a report stressing the economic benefits of cultural heritage as an innovative trigger of employment and growth in a variety of sectors, also beyond tourism and generally in urban contexts; and a heritage-led urban regeneration model was recommended (European Commission 2015b). This was accompanied by the announcement of 100 million euros for research and innovation in the cultural heritage field in 2016–2017 under the Horizon 2020 schemes, to support demonstration projects showcasing the potential of cultural heritage for urban and rural regeneration in Europe.[1]

To conclude, perhaps the most popular EU scheme for towns and cities is the *Creative Europe Programme*, which is designed to support cultural and creative sectors. One of the strands for tourism-related actions is the European Capital of Culture, in the form of an award assigned to one city in two Member States each year. The candidate cities have to develop a cultural programme aimed to emphasise and leverage on the diversity and richness of European cultures. The present chapter and the book will draw further attention to the European Capital of Culture.

2.1   Tourism in the EU Urban Portal

Let us now focus on the urban dimension in the EU's tourism policy. As said above, city tourism does not emerge strongly from the EU framework, which is keener to define a role for tourism as an economic alternative for lagging areas where other economic engines have been historically weak. And, as we shall now see, when dealing with economic development visions for cities, tourism issues do not seem to play a key role despite being mentioned in different documents and in different ways. The lack of a dedicated and focused effort on framing city tourism and its importance in urban settings is certainly connected to the fact that European policy competence does not include urban planning *per se*, although this has rapidly attracted increasing attention due to recognition of a strong urban dimension in economic, social and territorial cohesion. This is instead a core competence of the European policy-making. As a matter of fact, "the European Union does not have a direct policy competence in urban and territorial development, but the last two decades have witnessed an increasing importance of the European level in both urban and territorial development" (European Union 2011, p. 12).

---

[1]http://ec.europa.eu/research/index.cfm?pg = newsalert&year = 2015&na = na-190615. Last accessed 2 March 2016.

If, as stated in the *Cities of Tomorrow* report published in 2011, the "European model of the city" is based on advanced social progress, democracy, cultural dialogue and diversity, green, ecological and environmental regeneration, what is the role that city tourism should play, and at what kind of tourism development should cities aim? As shown above, city tourism has, in fact, a significant and—to a certain extent—growing social, cultural, physical and economic weight in contemporary cities. Hence the topic is no longer avoidable. The *Cities of Tomorrow* report mentions tourism and puts it alongside knowledge-industry business and skilled and creative labour as supposedly attracted by the "European Cities of Tomorrow".

Accordingly, now conducted is a review of the documents archived under the *Urban Portal* of the European Commission.[2] The purpose is to provide a synopsis of a selection of sections called "Urban issues"—*Green Cities, Resilient Cities, Innovative Cities* and *Creative Cities* (see Table 3)—so that the profile(s) of tourism can emerge. As said, a vision for tourism development in the urban domain is at present largely absent, while some sort of "rural bias" (Ashworth 1989) seems to emerge. Attention, in fact, is paid to tourism in that part of the *Urban Portal* referring to urban-rural linkages. It is said that rural-urban partnerships may benefit peripheral areas both in terms of increased accessibility to urban infrastructures and in terms of an upgraded use of cultural assets and landscapes for tourism and recreation through the sharing of a sustainable development vision and marketing strategies (Artmann et al. 2012). Studies categorising the projects arising from urban-rural partnerships have frequently highlighted tourism and cultural heritage as a key field for collaboration. However, the evidence on the effective benefits for

Table 3 Urban issues in the EU Urban Portal: how is tourism represented?

Urban issue	Frameworks	Tourism's representation
Green Cities	EU transport policy and sustainable urban mobility European Green Capital Award	Pressure to be reduced
Resilient Cities	Adaptation Strategies for European Cities EU Strategy on adaptation to climate change	Vulnerable sector that must adapt
Innovative Cities	European Innovation Partnership on Smart Cities and Communities European Capital of Innovation "iCapital"	Field of integration through information, communication, infrastructure and services
Creative Cities	European Capital of Culture (ECoC)	Direct result (not the aim) of ECoC Success factor in ECoC application

Source: The authors, based on http://ec.europa.eu/regional_policy/en/policy/themes/urban-development/portal/

---

[2]http://ec.europa.eu/regional_policy/en/policy/themes/urban-development/portal/. Last accessed 2 March 2016.

rural areas (e.g. in terms of rural employment and housing conditions) is rather uncertain (Artmann et al. 2012).

From the *Green Cities* perspective, the key challenge identified is mobility, whose inefficiencies provoke congestion, pollution, traffic and accidents. This is a major issue considering that yearly 1 % of the EU's GDP (100 billion euros) is lost because of congestion, and that urban traffic produces 40 % of CO2 emissions (European Commission 2007). Tourism is mentioned in this regard because travellers are a key group of transport users with needs, patterns and preferences representing pressure factors on the urban transport system (European Commission 2007). For this reason, CIVITAS, which is an initiative for *Cleaner and Better Transport in Cities*, has supported a variety of sustainable mobility projects in city tourism. One example is the development of new mobility services for tourists in Burgos, Belgium, which provide information, itineraries and guidance on public transport and bicycle access, as well as incentives for collective and cleaner forms of transport, by involving a broad network of hoteliers, taxi drivers and travel agencies.

Not surprisingly, the 'green city' is considered an asset for tourism development in European cities. The European Green Capital Award promoted by the European Commission works as a branding platform yielding advantages in terms of increased tourism, at least according to the dedicated webpage.[3] Although there is no scientific evidence of this positive impact, the green capitals certainly utilise their green profiles to promote tourism, as in the case of Ljubljana, Slovenia, which, as the European Green Capital in 2016, offers 'green' itineraries and a series of dedicated events (http://www.greenljubljana.com). This topic will be further developed in Part III of this book.

From the *Resilient Cities* perspective, the challenge consists in adaptation to climate change, since warmer temperatures and extreme weather events demonstrate the vulnerability of urban systems in coastal zones as well as in other regions. Tourism is a particularly vulnerable sector because climate change is evidently impacting on European regions by increasing summer tourism in Northern Europe while, for example, decreasing summer tourism and probably changing seasonality in Mediterranean coastal cities (this book will deal with this issue). The *Innovative Cities* perspective draws attention to the need for tourism's integration into the wider smart city, and for smart community planning based on a strategic use of information, communication, infrastructure and services (EIP-SCC 2013). The 'innovative' and 'green' city agendas overlap—as proliferating experiences of smart systems for traffic and public transport (e.g. real-time applications) demonstrate—to improve tourism destination competitiveness (World Travel Market 2015).

Finally, the *Creative Cities* perspective intersects with city tourism particularly in the case of the European Capital of Culture (ECoC) scheme based on culture as a trigger of smart, sustainable and inclusive growth. The programme has been recently strengthened by embedding it more firmly in the overall urban cultural

[3]http://ec.europa.eu/environment/europeangreencapital/about-the-award/faqs/. Last accessed 2 March 2016.

strategy, in order to widen and extend the local legacy of the European Capital of Culture (European Commission 2015a). In this framework, sustainable tourism is viewed as the natural result of the ECoC project. On the other hand, tourism supply—including hospitality, transports and soft skills—is considered a success factor of candidate cities (European Commission 2014). However, it is explicitly stated that tourism development is not to be the goal of this framework, which must not be understood and translated into a dedicated programme supporting tourism. It is declared, in fact, that the ECoC is "not a tourism-led project", while the aim is the well-being of citizens and the local population (European Commission 2014). At the same time, however, the guide published for cities preparing to bid in the period 2020–2033 also states that "one of the objectives of the programme is to raise the international profile of a city through culture" (European Commission 2014, p. 7).

2.1.1   What Is 'Urban'?

Section 1 drew attention to the (controversial) definition of urban tourism, whose borders are not easily defined. After describing the European context as regards city tourism numbers and policy framework, it is time to reflect on the notion of 'urban' that, mostly in line with the European definition, will be used in this book, Parts II and III of which will propose a set of case analyses—all of the cases being cities and towns in Europe where multifaceted types of urban tourism are manifest and under scrutiny.

The growth of interest in the 'urban', beyond the lack of formal competence of the European Union mentioned above, has been justified by the figures: over 60 % of the European population lives in urban areas, and approximately 85 % of the EU's GDP is produced in urban areas, so that towns and cities play a driving role in the European economy (European Commission 2007). It was the already-mentioned report *Cities of Tomorrow* that, in attempting to outline a "European model of the city", acknowledged a lack—at first sight paradoxical—of common definitions of 'urban' and 'cities' informing the proposed urban 'model' (European Union 2011). In the same pragmatic fashion as the *Cities of Tomorrow* report, this book defines a city as an "urban agglomeration in general", although it is aware that an urban policy perspective necessarily includes a range of scales extending from the neighbourhood to the administrative city or to the functional urban areas and beyond (European Union 2011). The same report considers an urban agglomeration to be any entity with more than 5000 inhabitants. To be borne in mind is that urban agglomerations in Europe have a total of 350 million inhabitants, which means 70 % of the European population.

The European urban system mostly consists of small and medium-sized cities and towns with between 5000 and 100,000 inhabitants; that is, 56 % of the European urban population, corresponding to about 38 % of the total European population, lives in small and medium cities, while only 7 % of the EU population lives in metropolises of above 5 million dwellers (European Union 2011). This suggests that the European system is polycentric and relatively dispersed, with smaller cities having to play a role in producing wealth and boosting well-being not only for their own inhabitants but also for the surrounding rural areas—as the *Cities of Tomorrow* report stated.

Turning to city tourism, it is evident that "cities of all sizes can be competitive" destinations (UNWTO 2014a, p. 10). In the UK, there has been much debate and effort to redefine the tourist offerings in smaller urban centres. Most of the actions have been based on digitalisation and hi-tech solutions to attract visitors and enhance travellers' experiences, denoting a specific reliance on new technologies to boost smaller cities' competitiveness in the tourism field (World Travel Market 2015). The cases analysed in the book will provide further arguments for a 'loose' definition of 'the urban' where size seems to be of secondary importance when predicting the degree of competitiveness and sophistication of urban tourism models.

3 The Book's Structure

The book provides wide theoretical, empirical and methodological coverage of the urban tourism field of research. It is composed of three parts. While Part I is mostly devoted to reviewing the current debate and to introducing key themes in disentangling the urban tourism phenomenon, Parts II and III analyse a wide range of urban agglomerations and their experiences of tourism development. The geographical scope of this book consists in European and Mediterranean cities, as shown by the rich empirical array of cases analysed.

Part I outlines the research scene and sketches a set of key issues in city tourism. The first chapter by *Pasquinelli* outlines the frontiers of the city tourism debate by making a range of analytical issues explicitly emerge. Four distinct yet closely interrelated domains of analysis are presented: travellers' needs, preferences and tastes; city tourism in the urban fabric; the political economy of urban tourism; and city branding. Throughout the treatment, the core argument states an expanding research agenda in urban tourism both conceptually (because what analysts refer to as tourism in the urban context is expanding) and spatially (encompassing, yet going beyond, conventional tourist hotspots and giving specific meaning to temporary spatialities). The scene is then widened by *Uğur*, who discusses how sustainability goes in parallel with inclusion. In order to disentangle this overused concept, she analytically deploys the notion of integrated access across economic, spatial and institutional spheres. This chapter serves as an introduction to city tourism as sustainable tourism by "recognising the necessity to establish enhanced linkages between urban tourism development and urban planning".

The focus is on the relationship between residents and tourists and a balance between their needs, either explaining a need for equity and equitable access or suggesting a fruitful search for complementarities. These are two different readings of tensions, conflicts and trade-offs which will be examined in more detail in Part III of the book. Research on transport and accessibility is a key field for theoretically and empirically testing growing tensions between local well-being and tourism development which, according to *Gronau*'s contribution to this book, should be further studied without forgetting that tourists' and residents' everyday practices grow increasingly blurred. As also stated above, transport and the related issues are crucial for urban development and as such should be understood as playing a key role in urban tourism development. Amid a general lack of research and, especially, empirical inquiry, this chapter sets the scene for future transport research in city tourism. On the other hand, the technological domain is inevitably part of the smart city frame (or, more broadly, the innovative city as defined by the European discourse mentioned above). In a sense, access to heritage and cultural assets is mediated and even enabled by new technologies that co-produce cultural tourism and cultural consumption. This is the theme addressed by *Garau*, who shows how cultural tourism is today enhanced and re-envisioned in forms of a smart tourism and smart cultural consumption.

The relationship between residents and tourists is then considered through the lens of place branding. In this regard, *Kavaratzis* presents a holistic framework of brand formation interpreted as a negotiation process harmonising residents' internal perspectives with tourism and outward-looking branding actions. The chapter proposes a participatory place-branding process for an interactive destination brand. At issue is whether place brand building works as a platform for tourism destination planning by providing a space for the involvement of local stakeholders and external audiences. *Sevin*'s chapter adds a further perspective on branding by discussing a "new communicative space" in which cities are immersed. In particular, social media enable one-to-one communication amongst residents and visitors whose interactions are boosted in favour of the city's reputation.

Khiat and *Montargot* further investigate the visitor/resident relationship in city tourism by addressing the important theme of human capital and labour market in tourism development. They focus on professionalism in hospitality as playing a significant role in improving visitors' satisfaction. Taking the case of Oran, Algeria, as an example, the authors argue that the volume of students of tourism and hospitality is widely insufficient to meet local needs, while hospitality tends to be left to individuals' welcoming skills. The authors argue that this is a "cultural question" because they find that the culture of service is "delicate and historically sensitive" in Oran, where locals perceive service as form of submission. This contribution to the book opens an important discussion on tourism as a labour market too often overlooked or regarded as unproblematic.

Finally, the theme of measuring and monitoring urban tourism is developed in two chapters that close this first part of the book. Two contributions address this theme from two different perspectives, i.e. the 'macro' dimension and the 'micro' dimension of urban tourism measurement. *Lanquar* puts the case for monitoring the impacts of climate change on urban coastal tourism and introduces the terms of an ongoing discussion for establishing a system of indicators to be used in decision-making by urban planners and local authorities. *Andersson* draws attention to the need to produce knowledge about visitors' segments beyond monolithic market categories by obtaining insight into what visitors really do and where they go. The 'visitor stream' concept is proposed, and it introduces a wider discussion on the use of statistics to measure, monitor, and assess the actual value of urban tourisms.

Parts II and III comprise two different streams of inquiry. In particular, these two sections of the book conduct case analyses in order to expand the discussion through empirical inquiry. **Part II** focuses on the role of culture, creativity, and heritage in the construction of city tourism destinations. It starts with *Čamprag*'s contribution presenting the case of the modernisation of Frankfurt's Altstadt followed by the (re)production of the destroyed medieval city. This draws attention to the 'museumification' of urban centres boosted by tourism-led image making processes. How should this urban trajectory be interpreted? The chapter disentangles a multi-layered context by making a plurality of research perspectives emerge.

Della Lucia, Trunfio and *Go* then reflect on heritage and its pivotal role in urban regeneration and value creation though various forms of "cultural legacy hybridisation". Differences emerge among three Italian cities analysed by the authors where substantially different urban tourism models are apparent; from traditional forms of cultural tourism, through combinations of traditional cultural tourism and creative tourism, to innovative forms of tourism generated by processes of cross-fertilisation and creativity. A further urban tourism model emerges from the case of Košice, Slovakia, presented by *Borseková, Vaňová* and *Vitálišová*. The city was awarded the title of European Capital of Culture in 2013 as part of a transformative process with an impact on the shape and quality of the urban space, on cultural life, attractiveness, and entrepreneurship. An Italian case, the city of Florence, then draws attention to the intertwining of the "city of art", the "creative city" and the "manufacturing and symbolic fashion city", as presented by *Lazzeretti, Capone* and *Casadei*. The authors argue that the re-emergence of Florence as a fashion city is based on thick synergies between the artistic and cultural urban heritage and the local fashion industry. These engender significant tourism niches, ranging among shopping tourism, fashion museum, and fashion itineraries. Interestingly, this happens without any orchestration by local authorities, yet significant potential seems to be untapped.

Moreover, events and their role in the construction of urban destinations are scrutinised by two contributions in this book, one focusing on recurrent events, the other on itinerant ones. *Caroli* and *Valentino* propose six cases of European music festivals where the effects of recurrent events on national and international tourist flows, as well as on demand differentiation, are discussed. *Ferrucci, Sarti, Splendiani* and *Cordente Rodrìguez* instead focus on itinerant events, underlining their innovative use for the promotion of regional tourism and image making.

Finally, *Rabbiosi* and *Giovanardi* conclude this second part of the book by discussing the role of tourism in the urban policy framework of two Italian coastal cities where mass seaside tourism has reached a maturity stage, while the 'cultural city' has started being narrated as an innovative path for change and progress. It seems from the authors' analysis that the urban centre may work as an 'adaptive spatiality' through a culture-led regeneration process. This is because, owing to a variety of physical and symbolic resources, the urban centre is a platform for either tourism diversification or the rejuvenation of the local tourism model through a recombination of old and emerging (i.e. previously not selected nor taken into account) cultural factors.

Part III reconsiders and develops the theme of the relationship between tourists and residents, inclusiveness and access, introduced in the Part I. These chapters scrutinise the tensions, risks and potential trade-offs among tourism, tourism system performance, and urban well-being. *Minoia* presents an iconic case in the tourism debate—the city of Venice—by casting novel light on the role of tourism in changing the historical city through the introduction and sedimentation of forms of cosmopolitan consumption. Not just tourists but also new residents, i.e. super-rich activists of philanthropic associations and intellectuals, participate in the tourism gentrification and simplification of Venice's urban multifunctionality. Rapid and unbalanced tourism growth in the Czech capital city, Prague, is then analysed by *Dumbrovskà*. This chapter discusses the evolution of the historic centre into a 'tourist ghetto', by drawing attention to what can be read as residents' practices of resilience to the pressure of tourism development. Another iconic case in the tourism debate, i.e. Barcelona, is then developed by *Fava* and *Palau Rubio*. The chapter analyses the city's Strategic Tourism Plan launched in 2008. Recent political developments and the newly designed actions to correct the excesses of tourism and boost decongestion confirm this city as a 'hot case' for the urban tourism debate.

Besides the evident tensions and conflicts emerging from urban tourism contexts and which have recently transformed into anti-tourism movements, there is room to reflect upon what (and in what urban contexts) tourism may work as a catalyst for the production of forms of added value benefiting tourists and residents alike. In this regard, and adding further insight into the relation between tourism performance and urban well-being, *Maćkiewicz* and *Konecka-Szydłowska* introduce the theme of urban green tourism as responding to the commonly sustained "need (. . .) to make a city enjoyable to all", tourists and citizens alike. The authors consider ecotourism in urban centres through analysis of the *Cittaslow* movement. In particular, they analyse the green tourism offering developed by diverse towns and cities belonging to the Polish *Cittaslow* Network.

Wise and *Perić*, then propose the case of Medulin, Croatia, to ground a discussion on the social impacts of sport tourism-led regeneration and on the extent to which sport tourism developments provide local communities with benefits. This is a research perspective rarely adopted in the sport tourism development debate. Finally, *Mugnano* and *Carnelli* close the section with their contribution on the interaction between tourism and disasters, casting light on the path of reconfiguration of a "new normality" for residents and tourists in post-disaster contexts. It is argued that a form of disaster tourism may even provide tools for developing "a sense of hereness" that may furnish cultural, social and economic means with which to face a disaster's aftermath.

References

Artmann J, Huttenloher C, Kawka R, Scholze J (2012) Partnership for sustainable rural-urban development: existing evidences. Federal Institute for Research on Building, Urban Affairs and Spatial Development, Deutscher Verband fur Wohnungswesen, Stadtebau und Raumordnung e. V.

Ashworth G (1989) Urban tourism: an imbalance in attention. In: Cooper C (ed) Progress in tourism recreation and hospitality management, vol 1. Belhaven, London, pp 33–54

Ashworth G, Page SJ (2011) Urban tourism research: recent progress and current paradoxes. Tour Manag 32(1):1–15. doi:10.1016/j.tourman.2010.02.002

ATW Online (2012) The Ryanair effect in reverse: flight cuts to Morocco means fewer tourists. ATM Online

Bremner C (2016) Top 100 city destinations ranking. Euromonitor Blog

Darcy S, Small J (2008) Theorizing precincts: disciplinary perspectives. In: Hayllar B, Griffin T, Edwards D (eds) City spaces—tourist places. Elsevier, Oxford, pp 63–92

de Delàs I (2015) Positioning of city tourism in the global marketplace. Quantitative and qualitative approach. Paper presented at the 4th Global Summit on City Tourism UNWTO, Marrakesh

Edwards D, Griffin T, Hayllar B (2008) Urban tourism research. Ann Tour Res 35(4):1032–1052. doi:10.1016/j.annals.2008.09.002

EIP-SCC (2013) European innovation partnership on smart cities and communities—strategic implementation plan. High level group of the European Innovation Partnership for smart cities and communities, Brussels

Estol J, Font X (2016) European tourism policy: its evolution and structure. Tour Manag 52:230–241

European Cities Marketing (2014) ECM presents the results of Tourism in Europe through its Benchmarking report 2014. Available at http://www.europeancitiesmarketing.com/ecm-pre sents-results-tourism-europe-benchmarking-report-2014/. Accessed 18 Mar 2016

European Commission (2007) Green paper. Towards a new culture for urban mobility. vol COM (2007) 551 final. European Commission, Brussels

European Commission (2010) Europe, the world's No 1 tourist destination—a new political framework for tourism in Europe. Vol Communication from the Commission to the European Parliament, the Council, the European Economic and Social Committee of the Regions, Brussels

European Commission (2014) European capitals of culture 2020-2033. Guide for cities preparing to bid. European Commission, Brussels

European Commission (2015a) European capital of culture 30 years. European Union, Brussels

European Commission (2015b) Getting cultural heritage to work for Europe. Report of the Horizon 2020 Expert Group on cultural heritage. Research and innovation. European Commission, Brussels

European Commission (2015c) Guide on EU funding 2014-2020. For the tourism sector. European Commission, Brussels

European Union (2011) Cities of tomorrow. Challenges, visions, ways forward. European Union, Brussels

Frochot I, Batat W (2013) Marketing and designing the tourist experience. Goodfellow Publishers Ltd, Oxford

Hall M, Williams A (2008) Tourism and innovation. Routledge, Oxon

Hall M, Finsterwalder J, Ram Y (2015) Shaping, experiencing and escaping the tourist city. LA. Pleasure Fall 2015:84–90

Hayllar B, Griffin T, Edwards D (2008) Urban tourism precincts: engaging with the field. In: Hayllar B, Griffin T, Edwards D (eds) City spaces—tourist places: urban tourism precincts. Elsevier, Oxford

Hedrick-Wong Y, Choong D (2014) Mastercard 2014 global destination cities index. MasterCard Worldwide Insights, Mastercard
Iniguez T, Plumed M, Latorre Martìnez MP (2014) Ryanair and Spain: air connectivity and tourism from the perspective of complex networks. Tour Manag Stud 10(1):46–52
IPK International (2013) ITB world travel trends report. ITB, Berlin.
Ivanovic S, Vucenovic D, Baresa S (2014) Impact of low-cost air travel on tourism economy in Zadar county. UTMS J Econ 5(1):113–120
Novy J (2011) Marketing marginalized neighborhoods. Tourism and leisure in the 21st Century Inner City. Columbia University, New York
Novy J (2014) Urban tourism—the end of the honeymoon? In: UNWTO (ed) 3rd Global Summit on City Tourism, Barcelona, 9–10 December 2014. UNWTO
Olipra L (2012) The impact of low-cost carriers on tourism development in less famous destinations. In: Cittaslow: il valore della lentenzza per il turismo del futuro. Perugia/Orvieto, pp 41–56
Smith A (2009) Effects of low cost airlines on efforts to develop cultural heritage tourism. Anatolia: Int J Tour Hospital Res 20(2):289–306
Spanish EU Presidency (2010) Declaration of Madrid within the scope of the informal ministerial meeting for tourism under the Spanish Presidency in April 2010 in Madrid under the motto "Towards a socially responsible tourism". Madrid
Terzibasoglu E (2015) Summary and conclusion. Paper presented at the 4th global summit on city tourism, Marrakesh
UNWTO (2012) Global report on city tourism, AM reports: Volume six. UNWTO, Madrid
UNWTO (2014a) Global benchmarking for city tourism measurement, AM reports: Volume ten. UNWTO, Madrid
UNWTO (2014b) Global report on shopping tourism, AM reports: Volume eight. UNWTO, Madrid
Valls J-F, Sureda J, Valls-Tuñon G (2014) Attractiveness analysis of European tourist cities. J Travel Tour Market 31(2):178–194. doi:10.1080/10548408.2014.873310
World Economic Forum (2015) The travel and tourism competitiveness report 2015. Growth through shocks. World Economic Forum, Geneva
World Travel and Tourism Council (2015) Travel and tourism economic impact 2015 Europe. Available at https://www.wttc.org/-/media/files/reports/economic%20impact%20research/regional%202015/europe2015.pdf. Accessed 18 Mar 2016
World Travel Market (2015) World travel market global trends report 2015. WTM, London
Zervas G, Proserpio D, Byers J (2016) The rise of the sharing economy: estimating the impact of Airbnb on the hotel industry. Boston U. School of Management Research Paper, N.2013-16. Available at http://ssrn.com/abstract = 2366898 or http://dx.doi.org/10.2139/ssrn.2366898.

Part I
Urban Tourism: Defining the Research Scene and Dimensions

Tourism Connectivity and Spatial Complexity: A Widening Bi-dimensional Arena of Urban Tourism Research

Cecilia Pasquinelli

Abstract This chapter outlines the frontiers of the city tourism debate and highlights the emerging analytical issues that are widening the urban tourism research agenda. It provides an updated frame for tourism research by attempting to underline the urban character of travelling and, hence, to overcome the view of city tourism as a negligible element in the process of urban and economic development. The chapter is based on a review of academic papers and books, with particular attention paid to recent publications. It advocates a shift of perspective in urban tourism research, which is explained as a change of the unit of analysis for observation in the field and discussed from both a spatial and a conceptual viewpoint. This provides a starting point for future research projects, acknowledging the need for a greater sophistication of the cognitive tools used to analyse the contemporary urban tourism phenomenon.

Keywords City tourism • Travel • Connectivity • Tourism development and planning • Urban system

1 Introduction

There is general and growing agreement that tourism has been considered a negligible element in the process of urban and economic development in the academic debate; and only recently has it been taken into account as an important domain of urban change. Urban tourism is still an immature field of research, which often seems to lag behind the practice of tourism development rather then orienting it. This immaturity has led to biased viewpoints promoting either simplistic descriptions of tourism as a panacea for all development problems, or extremely critical interpretations of the tourism phenomenon. A need for a paradigm shift in city tourism research and practice was affirmed at the *3rd Global Summit on City Tourism* in December 2014, titled "New Paradigms in City Tourism Development". The summit highlighted a need for a paradigm shift and a strong connection

C. Pasquinelli (✉)
GSSI Social Sciences, Gran Sasso Science Institute, viale F. Crispi 7, 67100 L'Aquila, Italy
e-mail: cecilia.pasquinelli@gssi.infn.it

© Springer International Publishing Switzerland 2017
N. Bellini, C. Pasquinelli (eds.), *Tourism in the City*,
DOI 10.1007/978-3-319-26877-4_2

between tourism and the construction of a "smart, sustainable and inclusive city". It invited practitioners and academics to take up the challenge and overcome the weaknesses of current approaches to studying and practising city tourism. A change of path in city tourism development is necessary also in light of the rapid growth of anti-tourism movements in several cities. These movements stress and give voice to problems and asymmetries that urban tourism creates at the expense of local communities, and they reclaim dwellers' right to the city. This draws attention to the necessary construction and management of the relationship between residents and tourists, who play a crucial role in tourism development. Too often this aspect has been overlooked, with the consequence of an explosion of the tourism phenomenon that, in certain contexts, is out of control and reduces the multi-functionality of urban centres (see e.g. chapters "Venice Reshaped? Tourist Gentrification and Sense of Place" and "Urban Tourism Development in Prague: From Tourist Mecca to Tourist Ghetto").

Instead of limiting the analysis of urban tourism to its stigmatisation as the 'big enemy' of the liveable city, there is a need to produce analytical frameworks able to support the planning, managing, and even engineering of city tourism. To this end, academic research may play a role first by identifying the 'character' of urban tourism, distinguishing it from any other kind of tourism by putting the 'urban' at the core of the tourism concept. Secondly, researchers may provide decision-makers with analytical models informing and guiding policies not only through the promotion and marketing of the destination but also through regulation of tourism development and its integration into the broader urban planning and economic development framework.

The purpose of this book is to make a contribution in this direction. The present chapter starts this process by framing the current academic debate on city tourism. It stresses the emergence of analytical domains that, besides more consolidated approaches, are widening the research arena, and it provides evidence of an ongoing shift of perspective in the field. Such domains contribute to restating tourism beyond the post-industrial agenda of the *tourist city*. They draw attention to the complexity of cities where tourism gives shape to the urban space and, conversely, is shaped by that urban space and by the social and economic dynamics occurring within it. The survey of the emerging analytical domains opens and emphasises new research directions and methodological challenges to be addressed in future research.

This chapter is based on a review of academic sources focused on urban tourism, with particular regard to recent publications. These were collected through the ISI Web of Science, complemented with other channels including Google Scholar (especially for book searches). The lists of references were compiled by inserting "urban tourism" and "city tourism" as keywords. By means of the ISI Web of Science, a range of research areas was selected to filter the search, such as business economics, urban studies, geography, sociology, public administration and cultural studies. The review of the listed references was selective, and special attention was paid, as said, to recent contributions (2013–2014) and literature reviews in an attempt to track recent changes in scholarship. The review process was incremental, and the focus was gradually narrowed until, in the last stages, only those contributions matching the chosen urban tourism domains were considered. This procedure led to the identification of four distinct—yet closely interrelated—analytical domains discussed in this chapter: (1) travellers' needs, preferences and tastes, (2) spatialities of urban tourism, (3) the political economy of urban tourism, and (4) city branding. It is evident that some salient domains remained excluded. For instance, the technological dimension of urban tourism is certainly relevant to description of the emerging urban tourism research agenda: the chapter "Emerging Technologies and Cultural Tourism: Opportunities for a Cultural Urban Tourism Research Agenda" will outline the debate and suggest research streams for further engagement. This domain is connected to cultural heritage management, enhancement and dissemination and, more broadly, to the Internet and the role of social media in the construction of the destination brand (in this regard see also chapter "Globetrotters and Brands: Cities in an Emerging Communicative Space"). Furthermore, entrepreneurship, innovation and human capital are important domains in the city tourism research arena, but they are not covered in this chapter. Instead, the contribution by Khiat and Montargot, "The Construction of an Emerging Tourist Destination and Its Related Human Capital Challenges" will advance this crucial theme to tourism development.

As we shall see, the discussion of research findings will support the argument of a shift of perspective consisting in a necessary change of the unit of analysis employed in the study of city tourism, from both the spatial and conceptual viewpoints. This is a potential starting point for urban tourism scholars who have to choose their lens of observation for undertaking theoretical and empirical inquiry. The chapter is structured as follows. Section 2 reports key elements of the debate on urban tourism framed by the four analytical domains mentioned above. Section 3 will discuss the findings and will argue for a 'bi-dimensional arena' representing the urban tourism research agenda that emerges from recent evolutions. Accordingly, tourism connectivity and spatial complexity are the two axes that frame the evolutionary trajectory in the field.

2 Urban Tourism: A Widening Research Agenda?

The urban tourism research agenda testifies to an evident attempt by scholars to catch up with changes in tourism practices and with constant urban transformations. An emerging *shift of perspective* is described below. It is discussed as a process of expansion of a research agenda that acknowledges a changing object of observation, i.e. the city tourism phenomenon. The set of spaces, activities and actors that should be observed when studying city tourism seems to be expanding. While consolidated analytical approaches are not forgotten—since they are still meaningful to city tourism analyses—emerging issues take part in a renewed framework for urban tourism, thus enriching, complementing, or instead in some cases challenging, the traditional analytical perspectives. There follow four distinct, yet closely interrelated, analytical domains for urban tourism research.

2.1 Travellers' Needs, Preferences and Tastes

Awareness of the proliferation of tourist niches has increased (Novelli 2005). And as micro-niches become global in a fast-expanding outbound tourism market, they play a key role in the development of a variety of tourism 'products'. In other words, it is evident that the tourism industry has become much more fragmented in response to a growth of tourists' special interests (Lisle 2007). A few examples are useful. Consider the proliferation of youth travel niches, which include expanding student travel segments seeking a variety of study opportunities, volunteering and work, and diverse cultural experiences. These niches are growing in importance and, according to some global players in the field, will record 300 million global arrivals by 2020 for a market value of 320 billion USD (Student Universe and Skift 2014). Targeting student travellers requires responding to their preferences: for instance, they seem to prefer alternative accommodations to traditional hotels, and spend longer average stays than any other segments (Student Universe and Skift 2014; Richards and Wilson 2004, 2005).

Another example of a niche is provided by film-induced tourism involving visits to film-related theme parks (see Croy and Heitmann 2011) and pilgrimages to places that are (even loosely) related to films. The example of the town of Volterra, Italy helps clarify the point. Volterra, a small town in Tuscany with significant cultural heritage mostly deriving from the Etruscan and Roman ages, saw flows of "vampire-loving, mostly teenage-girl tourists from around the world" (Ehlers 2010) simply because the town was named in the popular *Twilight* series and identified as the place of provenance of the *Volturi* vampire family. Even though the film's shooting set was not in Volterra, tourists arrived to experience the 'vampire land', so that local agencies started organising "New Moon Walks on Edward's and Bella's path" (Lazzeroni et al. 2013).

Another example is slum tourism. The key global destinations are, for instance, in South Africa, where township tourism emerged as form of education for white local policymakers fighting against apartheid and then grew in size, and in Brazil— especially in Rio de Janeiro favelas (Frenzel and Koens 2012). Here tourist agencies organised 'favela tours' for delegates during the Rio 1992 Earth Summit, and afterwards certain favelas became popular among tourists wanting to experience 'authentic' local culture (Frenzel and Koens 2012). A discussion on the ethics of poverty tourism, of the "commodification of poverty", or of the actual impact in terms of economic revenue for the communities involved is certainly worthwhile, but it falls outside the scope of this chapter (see e.g. the Special Issue *Global Perspective on Slum Tourism* published by Tourism Geographies in 2012). Another example of a tourism niche is LGBT tourism. According to Southall and Fallon (2011), it is growing fast so that many more destinations have been targeting this segment, both recognising the economic potential of a potentially high income, high travel spend and high travel propensity niche, and following political and social change. The city of Zurich, Switzerland, for example, has invested in this niche in order to affirm that: "over the last decades, the tolerant, liberal-minded city of Zurich has become home to a lively gay and lesbian scene" (see Zurich Tourism website, https://www.zuerich.com/en/visit/lgbt-zurich#).

These examples are part of what is termed 'niche tourism', which covers various markets fuelled by diverse travel motivations. According to some, the common feature across such diversity is visitors' attitude to the destination, which is the opposite of the one characterising "the villain of the piece, consuming without care or understanding"; this, instead, is at the core of how contemporary modern mass tourism ended up being represented (Marson 2011, p. 8). This sharp difference between niche and mass tourism, however, should be taken with a pinch of salt. Doubts may be raised about the degree of care and attention that, to refer to previous examples, is really paid to local communities and their complexities by film-induced tourists in Volterra (who, after all, arrive in town primarily to be physically immersed in fictional imagery) or by slum tourists in Rio de Janeiro. These, instead, are likely to search for evidence of that specific aspect of reality that interests them, and to be satisfied by a "staged authenticity" (MacCannell 1973). This has a great deal to do with a choice between the matching of tourists' expectations and predefined preferences and, instead, the construction of the destination that, given the window of opportunity opened by niche tourism, makes travellers find what destination planners have strategically decided to provide.

However, there is no doubt that, on reaching maturity, mass tourism products have shown increasingly weak competitiveness; and their negative impacts, which are mostly related to the large size of reference markets, have clearly emerged. Tourism niches have created new market spaces and, in some cases, have rejuvenated 'old' tourism products by means of the progressive specialisation and fragmentation of demand. But, as Marson (2011) asked, are we actually witnessing "a movement towards mass tourism"? This question stresses that niche tourism is in fact growing fast and is reaching—as an aggregate—a large size. It may eventually become a mass product (with an evolution similar to that of what is properly called mass tourism), while other 'new' micro-niches might spill over (and, then, similarly enter global tourism's lifecycle towards a 'massification'). This means that what we are currently interpreting as niche tourism may prove to cause problems and weaknesses just like those caused by what we currently name 'mass tourism'. It seems that tourism destinations must be flexible and able to intercept the emerging micro-niches, and promptly adapt to change. One possibility for tourism destinations is to break the global tourism lifecycle and proactively create micro-niche markets by pursuing a regime of monopolistic competition (Part II will also tackle this issue).

Focusing on niches and micro-niches proliferation, the literature has suggested the emergence of a visitor profile characterised by sophisticated and specialised motivations. Here this is called the *urban traveller*, who is to be understood as flanking (and not replacing) the traditionally studied *urban tourist*. The urban traveller notion connects to the blurred boundaries between tourism and other forms of mobility including temporary migration (e.g. exchange students, second homeowners, mobile workers and "migratory elites", see chapter "Venice Reshaped? Tourist Gentrification and Sense of Place"), as well as to the blurred boundaries between tourism and other forms of leisure and place consumption. There seems to be a growing belief that, while city visitors behave as temporary residents, residents—at least to some extent—behave "as if tourists" (Clark 2001 cited in Novy 2014) so that the process of de-differentiation of tourism activity envisaged by Urry (2002) can no longer be taken as a purely theoretical notion.

The notions of *urban traveller* and *urban tourist* summarise a variety of travel propensities, needs, and tastes in relation to the urban experience (Table 1). The urban tourist can be described as a traditional type of cultural tourist. This mainly refers to standardised visits to cultural hotspots, e.g. museums and monuments (Richards 2003), with the aim of *seeing* an "aesthetic or historic perfection" (Ashworth and Page 2011). Once such aesthetic or historic perfection has been *seen*, according to Ashworth and Page (2011), the urban tourist has no reason to visit the city a second time. The urban tourist wants to create memories of the city and, accordingly, he/she *buys* cultural products or artefacts with high local (standardised) symbolic content. This is termed "a passive reception of culture", and the relation between culture and tourism is exclusively mediated by a commercial exchange (Richards 2014c).

The urban traveller, instead, is said to actively engage with construction of the urban experience. This active engagement is summarised by the expression 'experiential learning'; a learning process enabled by direct experience of the urban ordinary; and a learning process based on the opportunity to trace a link between the city's history and the urban path of progress. A review of creative tourism (see chapters "Heritage and Urban Regeneration. Towards Creative Tourism" and "Building Košice European Capital of Culture. Towards a Creative City?") has recently been carried out by Richards (2014a). This form of tourism is defined as an opportunity to develop individuals' creative potential through participation in *learning* experiences situated in the city. This means *direct involvement* in local culture and proactive co-creation of it, rather than mere admiration of others'

Table 1 Urban tourist *versus* urban traveller

The urban tourist	The urban traveller
Tourism is a non-essential good	Travelling is a 'right'
Buys a tourist package	Co-creates the travel experience
Visits cultural heritage	Active engagement, exercises creativity
Buys cultural products	Experiential learning (e.g. DIY)
Is satisfied with staged authenticity	Lives like a local
Looks for aesthetic/historic perfection	Looks for daily life, risks and futures, progress and ways to cope with contemporary challenges

Source: the author

creativity. Iconic examples are *tango* dance tourism in Buenos Aires, or the workshop tourism in visual and performing arts, crafts, music, photography and cinema offered by *Creative Paris* (http://creativeparis.info/en/). The latter is an online platform dedicated to the promotion of creative workshops and courses with the support of the Municipality of Paris. It was then extended to the national level as a creative tourism platform with the name of *Creative France* (http://www. creativefrance.fr/), following the success achieved in the Parisian context. Through interactions with the urban environment and local instructors, the urban traveller gains first-hand genuine experience of the city, which gives a sense of achievement and unique learning (Hung et al. 2014). The idea of learning through travelling is certainly not new, and in fact is well rooted in history; the novelty is its rapid growth and multifaceted form.

Learning 'the urban ordinary' is imperative for the urban traveller. This corresponds to the "live like a local" rule (Richards 2014a) and implies the establishment of relationships and connections with locals who are brokers of local culture. The urban ordinary is 'learnt', for instance, through the use of public transport by visitors who increasingly impact on urban mobility (see chapter "On the Move: Emerging Fields of Transport Research in Urban Tourism"). Whilst public transport has traditionally been considered to be for lower-income visitors, recent evidence shows the opposite: high-income, educated, young visitors are keener on low-carbon tourism and a sustainable urban lifestyle that contributes to an appealing urban self-identity (Le-Klähn and Hall 2014).

Learning about the links between the city's history and the path of progress is imperative for the urban traveller. It is not a novelty that travellers are in search of infiltration points into the 'reality' of the place (consider for instance MacCannell's study of 1973); however, to show how radical this motivation to travel has been, the case of tourism fuelled by a search for the 'dark' side of local history has been selected from the tourism literature and is presented here. 'Dark tourism' consists in visits to sites of "death, disaster and atrocity" where an unmediated encounter with 'the real' may occur. Cities hit by natural disasters, like tsunamis or earthquakes, places of conflict, war, or terrorism attacks, become tourism destinations. A recent study (Isaac and Çakmak 2014) analysing the reasons for visiting 'dark sites' has shown that dark tourists well embody the profile of the urban traveller interested in learning about the 'urban ordinary' in the phase of recovery, as a visible manifestation of the local path of progress. This is an aspect that is often interpreted as secondary to voyeurism and curiosity about human sorrow and drama. Instead, forms of disaster tourism may contribute to the building of a "sense of *hereness*" and a "new normality" providing cultural, social and economic means to cope with a disaster's aftermath, as Mugnano and Carnelli will discuss in chapter "A 'New Normality' for Residents and Tourists: How Can a Disaster Become a Tourist Resource?".

The city is an 'open-air laboratory' in which to observe lifestyle and human progress in terms of knowledge and technology, for instance. An 'urban model' may be performed through both the urban ordinary and the design of venues or itineraries staging stories about the relation between history and future. An example is the Barcelona Guide Bureau (http://www.barcelonaguidebureau.com/), a travel agency offering a variety of city tours in this renowned Mediterranean destination. The agency proposes the *Smart and Sustainable Barcelona tour*, allowing visitors to "discover one of the most spectacular urban transformations in Barcelona, from old industrial to a model of compact city. Includes Olympic Village, Forum and 22@Barcelona district.".[1] As said, this tour includes a regenerated area of the city dedicated to the innovation district named 22@Barcelona, which is a space for innovative start-up companies and business incubators. Through the tour, this area becomes a target for those travellers wanting to see where the city is currently going as regards innovation, technology, and seeking to understand the city's capacity to engage with crucial global challenges, such as sustainability and smartness. In a city like Barcelona, which hosted over eight million tourists in 2014 and 18 million overnights (Barcelona Turisme 2014), the issue does not concern the quantity of visitors drawn to this 'extraordinary' attraction; instead, the meaning and role of this niche tour should be analysed in relation to the narration of the city emerging from an integration of tourism with other local industries (this point will be further discussed in the *Political economy of urban tourism* section below), as well as in relation to the processes of city image building (as further discussed in the *City branding* section of this chapter).

2.2   Spatialities of Urban Tourism

In this domain pertaining to the physical space of the tourism phenomenon, the shift of perspective coincides with a redefinition of the spatialities of interest for the study of city tourism. Urban tourism has been mainly studied as concentrated either in circumscribed and well-defined spots (tourism precincts), or in itineraries composed of connected urban locations, e.g. iconic sites, flagship shopping districts, cultural institutions, and sites providing tourism-related services (Hayllar et al. 2008).

Self-contained tourist precincts are proven to be at risk of congestion. Congestion reduces the chance for locals to spend time in tourist areas that mostly coincide with cultural institutions and venues, until they are displaced and excluded from cultural life; it impacts on the quality of the environment and challenges preservation of the cultural heritage. Congestion means not only a high concentration of visitors but also a high concentration of advertising in the most visited public spaces in the city that potentially causes a 'brand saturation' of the urban ecosystem (Bellini and Pasquinelli 2016) and, consequently, a 'symbolic congestion'. The municipality of Barcelona has recently imposed a 20% reduction on street

---

[1]http://www.barcelonaguidebureau.com/private-tours-and-transfers/smart-sustainable-bcn-tour/
Last accessed 21 March 2016.

advertising, considering it to be a form of pollution detrimental to the cultural and aesthetic value of the urban public space (O'Sullivan 2016).

Tourism precincts are characterised by a 'spatial thematisation', which, as a model, may also extend to the entire urban context. This is the case of the 'tourist city', where tourism becomes the main economic and social driver affecting the shape and functioning of the city as a whole. Examples are resort cities like Las Vegas, tourist-historic cities like Venice (see chapter "Venice Reshaped? Tourist Gentrification and Sense of Place"), or traditional mass tourism destinations like Rimini, where a tourism mono-culture has imposed a well-defined and static discourse on tourism (Conti and Perrelli 2007) which has been slightly changing in recent times, as Rabbiosi and Giovanrdi will discuss further in chapter "Rediscovering the 'Urban' in Two Italian Tourist Coastal Cities".

Based on these premises, the recently argued 'new urban tourism' emphasises a growing "preference for off the beaten track areas" (Füller and Michel 2014, p. 1304), with a consequent need for analysts to look beyond the narrow notion of the tourist city as a tourist enclave disconnected from ordinary urban life. Experienced travellers in an increasingly mobile world may be no longer relying on the gateway function usually performed by tourist precincts (Hall and Page 2009), which were traditionally conceived as 'free zones' of simplified accessibility targeting standard tourists' needs. This is certainly caused by mobile technologies that reduce the cognitive, cultural and emotional distance from the destination. To some extent this is connected to the discussion in Sect. 2.1, which argued for a fragmentation of demand and hence the diminishing importance of standard tourists' needs. However, the urban tourism precinct has not completely lost its role. Contrary to an overemphasis on the role of technologies in shaping the destination and the urban experience, in some cities, empirical research has proved that travellers' paths remain fairly concentrated in specific areas rather than being dispersed (Valls et al. 2014). Indeed, further research should investigate the factors that, given a certain endowment of technology, influence the spatiality of travellers' urban experiences.

Though acknowledging that the tourist precinct still plays a role (i.e. a functional, social and psychological one), analysis of the complex urban forms assumed by city tourism is necessary. There is a need to test whether, and evaluate the extent to which, the tourist city is being diluted into the notion of 'third generation metropolis', according to which a 'third population', which impacts on the urban fabric, is composed of 'city users' who spend time in urban contexts using collective goods (e.g. streets, airports, museums, parks), as well as private services and spaces, e.g. shops, cinemas and other facilities (Martinotti 1994). It has been argued that cities are becoming places for visitors and guests rather than places for inhabitants, so that they increasingly resemble the 'hospitable city'. This highlights a style of cultural consumption showing common features across a variety of city users, thereby closing the gap between hosts and guests (meaning between tourists and residents). That is, the hospitable city may overcome tensions and conflicts over the use, appropriation, and control of the urban space. This does not seem to happen, however, and quite the opposite emerges in many capital cities where an anti-tourism sentiment is apparent. Further analytical effort is necessary to orient urban (tourism) planners, and Part III will deal with this key theme in urban tourism's evolution.

Temporary spaces of urban tourism warrant attention. Temporary urbanism has been widely discussed from a range of perspectives. They include awareness of social practices and a capacity to stimulate flexibility, innovation and imagination in urban development; and, in contrast, arguments for its instrumental use in place marketing, opening the way to profit-oriented urban redevelopment processes (Tardiveau and Mallo 2014). Even though temporary spaces do not concern direct modifications of the built and physical environment, they host new activities and practices that may have enduring effects in the urban context. Festivals and events—which in some cases become a prominent economic and development planning strategy in the "eventification" turn (Jacob 2012)—represent the time frame in which spatialities of city tourism 'pop up' and may impact on medium/ long term space representation and use. This has been described by Rota and Salone (2014), who analysed the contemporary art festival, *Paratissima*, in Turin, Italy. The event, organised by local associations and art movements in the San Salvario neighbourhood, aims to create a meeting point for art, artists and art consumers, while becoming a place-making process which refreshes and improves the area's image, as well as being a temporary attractor for visitors with a lasting impact on the area.

The temporary use of buildings, streets and squares creates "pop-up cultural spaces" (Richards 2014b) visited by both travellers and residents, constantly transforming the urban geography of cultural consumption. An example is the establishment of temporary art scenes by visual artists, in pubs or in their own studios, creating new spaces to exhibit, sell their work, build their own brands and thus build their strategies of resilience to pursue an artistic career (Sjöholm and Pasquinelli 2014; Pasquinelli and Sjöholm 2015).

Pop-up attractions heighten the dispersed nature of urban tourism. Such dispersion is further sustained by recent trends in hospitality with an expansion of holiday flats in neighbourhoods outside tourist precincts. This is the case of Kreuzberg in Berlin (Füller and Michel 2014), where a number of rental flats are being converted into holiday apartments in an 'ordinary' area which, lacking tourist attractions, is rich in Berlin's bohemian spirit. Here the traveller can "stop being a tourist", as the marketing slogan of a short-term accommodation provider puts it, and break into the spatialities of the ordinary urban life, as reported by Füller and Michel (2014). Travellers' urban dispersion may boost processes of gentrification because of a likely increase in rental and living costs in ordinary neighbourhoods. Such processes have caused the proliferation of anti-tourism movements, which identify tourists—and particularly independent tourists, i.e. those searching for information and organising their travel on their own—as contemporary gentrifiers. So far, in some cases, the conflict between residents and visitors over the urban space may have been based on disproportionate fears and on an identification of tourism as the cause of much broader housing market dynamics that urban tourism is, instead, simply contributing to (Füller and Michel 2014). A discursive mechanism in public debate singles out city tourism trajectories from much more complex urban transformation processes; particularly, the contemporary representation of tourism in political discourse certainly deserves dedicated research efforts as being connected with the production of regulation frameworks and decision-making.

As mentioned in the introduction of this book, global online travel sales and mobile booking have recently become mainstream channels, and platforms like Airbnb are booming, with individuals choosing rental accommodations in private apartments as alternatives to traditional hospitality circuits. Is this an invasion of tourists breaking into and distorting urban everyday life, or is it a process that—if regulated—may spatially spread social and economic benefits and costs across the urban system? On the one hand, as Zervas et al. (2016) assessed, an 'Airbnb effect' consists in reducing local hotel room revenues, evidently creating alternative fragmented and dispersed micro-economies; on the other hand, a major issue concerns the "Airbnb occupancy model", and importantly there is a need to clarify whether residential properties are rented permanently as if they are hotels or, instead, they are shared occasionally (see *Inside Airbnb*, "an independent, non-commercial set of tools and data" exploring how Airbnb is used in cities worldwide, http://insideairbnb.com/about.html). This is important in order to evaluate if and to what extent tourism hospitality may be expanding at the expense of the residential function. As the *Inside Airbnb* website shows, for instance, there were 14,855 listings for Barcelona in Airbnb (on 3 January 2016), 53 % entire apartments, 46 % private rooms, and 1.1 % shared rooms. According to this source, 78 % of the advertised listings did not display the licence number, contrary to the Catalan Tourist Act imposing the registration of homes rented for tourism for a duration of under 30 days; as the website reports, these might correspond to unlicensed rentals. This dynamic challenges regulation and monitoring, while there is a growing and evident need to explain the impacts and effects of this mostly urban phenomenon, in order to support evidence-based regulation.

To conclude this section on the spatiality of urban tourism, a link to the profiling of the urban traveller stated in the previous section is proposed. The growing demand for diversity in the tourism market may be summarised as an explosion of cultural tourism niches featuring multifaceted spatial patterns in the city. If traditional cultural tourism mainly involves city-break visits targeting hard-branded urban attractors, e.g. cultural institutions, it must be borne in mind that "cultural tourism is not just about visiting sites and monuments, which has tended to be the 'traditional' view of cultural tourism, but it also involves consuming the way of life of the visited areas" (Richards 2003, p. 5). As also the World Travel Organization states, cultural tourism includes "all movements of persons (...) because they satisfy the human need for diversity, tending to raise the cultural level of the individual and giving rise to new knowledge, experience and encounters" (Richards 2003, p. 5). This is a very broad definition of cultural tourism which puts the idea of 'learning by travelling' at the core of the concept. In the urban context, 'learning by travelling' explains the variety of travel logics and mirrors the complex spatiality of cultural niches. Table 2 summarises the differences between what is here called *cultural urban tourism*, understood as a form of mass tourism flowing to cities for

Table 2 Cultural urban tourism and cultural urban travelling

Cultural urban tourism	Cultural urban travelling
Visit target: mainly proper cultural institutions such as monuments, museums, art galleries, etc.	**Visit target**: cultural institutions *in a broad sense* including schools, scientific laboratories, construction sites, research centres, temporary cultural spaces
Cultural content: mostly looking for the past and generally the achievements of humankind by means of a well-defined and packaged narration of facts in a polished environment designed to tell a certain story to be consumed	**Cultural content**: mostly looking for current developments explaining the contemporary city and the links to past and future, by means of a narration which is made of the urban ordinary that is experienced "in the street" as well as in venues staging stories about the past/present/future relations
How: purchasing a ticket, buying memories/products with high local symbolic value	**How**: study visits, learning periods, workshops, festivals and events (some examples)

Source: the author

fairly passive cultural consumption, and *cultural urban travelling* referring to diverse forms of closer engagement with the city, local community and its living heritage. These represent extremes of a wide range of urban tourism forms that depend upon travellers' diverse attitudes to the city and different travel motivations, and that are mirrored in a variety of spatial paths and urban experiences.

2.3   The Political Economy of Urban Tourism

The urban tourism literature has been characterised by a bias towards an interpretation of tourism as a mere manifestation of global consumerism. No doubt this is part of the phenomenon, yet this interpretation has displaced or made marginal any other possible angles of observation. The rise of interest in city tourism during the 1980s followed the emergence of the post-industrial city model redesigning the urban physical and economic fabric. In this frame, the construction of the tourist city and its urban precincts has worked as a 'spatial fix' to correct an over-accumulation of capital (i.e. buildings, infrastructures), by means of an expansion of consumption, the purpose being to prevent capital depreciation and overcome crises. The growing importance of leisure, quality of life, cultural amenities, and entertainment for residents (rhetorically represented as willing to move and choose a good place to live and work—Florida's creative class theory has contributed greatly to this representation) can be further interpreted as deriving from a need to extend urban consumption practices to a widening pool of dwellers, in order to strengthen the spatial fix in favour of contemporary capitalism.

Tourism has been narrated by scholars, policy-makers and, generally, by tourism practitioners as way to pursue a resilient path for many cities facing radical and often traumatic transformation into a post-industrial economy. Several cities have entered the tourism market, in many cases by creating the destination mostly from scratch. This path has been undertaken by several European cities envisioning a transition towards a consumption-based economy. The undisputed centrality of consumption in urban tourism is well explained in these critical lines:

> the idea that 'consumption' is taking precedence over 'production', one of the most widely debated facets in urban studies and tourism analyses, maintains that the expansion and deepening of commodity markets has transferred the logic and rationality of 'production' to the sphere of 'consumption' (…) Stressing the emergence and centrality of new forms of consumption, thinkers draw attention to the role that tourism plays as a form of commodified pleasure, tourism-as-spectacle that defines individual travellers and tourists as consumers (Gotham 2002, p. 1737).

As Gotham put it, cities have been transforming from spaces of production to spaces for consumption due to the action of power networks that have produced cultural signifiers for the sake of their own economic interest, not without social consequences (2002). Many cities converged upon cultural tourism development in the frame of culture-led regeneration processes (Beiley et al. 2004; O'Brian and Miles 2010), which turned an 'industrialised' consumption ('industrialised' for the systematisation of consumption practices and processes that are engineered to be scaled up) into a paradigm for urban planning and city management. This has globally led to a serial reproduction of clone tourism destinations. Beyond differences intrinsic to cultural expressions and geographical contents, the mode of representation of the cultural destination has often been the result of a mimetic process (Czarniawska 2002) involving hard investments in iconic buildings whose global commercial brands may provoke their 'placelessness' (Evans 2003), and an entertainment-led regeneration bringing the risks of an empty "eventification" (Jacob 2012).

De facto, a consumption-based view of tourism has inspired research methodologies and measurement of tourism economic impacts mostly based on the monetary payments entering the urban economy and moving through it from one sector to another (Tyrrell and Johnston 2006). The tourism-led growth hypothesis is based on the definition of international tourism as a non-standard type of export, since it implies forms of on-site foreign consumption (Brida et al. 2014), and limits the conceptualisation of tourist flows and their impact to an account of visitors' expenditure and, hence, to an account of consumption.

In contrast to the dominant *consumption-based view*, some scholars, who have stressed the limitations of this approach to explaining and studying tourism, have maintained that a development of *production-based views* is necessary. Urban tourism is, in fact, part of "the production process of a city" in the frame of a flexible accumulation which has been obfuscated in the representation of the urban post-industrial economy (Spirou 2008). The flexible accumulation regime plays a role in explanation of the nature and role of tourism in urban economies, as recent literature seems to suggest. 'Flexible accumulation' refers to the role of diversity and differentiation in post-Fordist economies, and it is based on the capacity of firms and industries to anticipate and adapt to changes in consumer tastes. This is viable through the definition of business models seeking economies of scope, which have brought cities and regions back to the core of industrial studies (Gregory et al. 2009). Acknowledging a production-based view means reflecting on how and to what extent urban tourism supports city's networks and industries in their participation in global circuits of flexible accumulation. Scholarship should further develop this perspective, which remains largely overlooked in the academic debate. In contrast, emerging practices and policies of tourism development seem to have started to consider tourism as a driver of value production and a source of innovation for a variety of industries.

Intersections and crossovers between tourism and creative industries (see also chapter "Heritage and Urban Regeneration. Towards Creative Tourism") seem promising, and international institutions, such as the UNESCO Creative Cities network, the OECD and to some extent the European Commission, have recently promoted frameworks in support of this rationale (Richards 2014a). The OECD has released a report, titled *Tourism and the Creative Economy* (2014), arguing that an integration of creative content with tourism experiences produces value, may reach new targets, and enhance place image and competitiveness, while sustaining the growth of creative industries. The report posits an almost 'natural' integration between these fields, because creative industries (including advertising, animation, architecture, design, film, gaming, gastronomy, music, performing arts, software and interactive games, television and radio) are defined as "knowledge-based creative activities that link producers, consumers and places by utilising technology, talent or skill to generate meaningful intangible cultural products, creative content and experiences" (OECD 2014, p. 7). The same report, however, stresses the lack of attention by policies to such integration; instead, governments should play an "enabling role" by steering cross-sectoral collaboration and by boosting "convergence and innovation" (OECD 2014, p. 8), while destination management organisations (DMOs) should proactively foster creative content production and circulation.

Even though there is no doubt that much has to be done in this direction, national and local governments are increasingly paying attention to the connections between tourism and creative industries. For instance, Rogerson (2006) stresses that in Johannesburg, South Africa, tourism planning has sought to reposition the city not only in shopping and business tourism segments (in line with a consumption-based view) but has also introduced investments in building links between craft and tourism to strengthen local cultural production. It is then evident that ICTs and digital media sectors intersect with the construction of the urban experience. Cultural heritage, its diffusion, promotion and protection become 'raw materials' for nurturing start-ups and embedding firms in the smart city business market (Pasquinelli 2015a). There is a connection between fashion industries and city tourism. This, in fact, may become a geographically situated platform for improving the experiential value of global fashion brands. To exploit this opportunity, firms seemingly devise their own urban destination strategies, as argued in the case of Florence, Italy (Bellini and Pasquinelli 2016), where fashion companies have opened fashion museums, have organised art exhibitions in stores and firm headquarters, and have collaborated with cultural institutions. In so doing, fashion companies are not only boosting local consumption but are also producing global brand value (on fashion and tourism in the case of Florence, see also chapter "The Role of Fashion for Tourism: An Analysis of Florence as a Manufacturing Fashion City and Beyond").

Another case deserves attention. The city of Milan, with an international positioning as a design capital, demonstrates the support that design and tourism have given to each other over time (OECD 2014). Particularly furniture and home accessories design has entered a looping mechanism of tourism-creative industry growth, thus supporting the validity of integration policies. Design "is an element that is now able to 'sweeten' the business component of Milanese tourism by offering new ways of experiencing the city through events, places and services, thus contributing to the innovation of the city's tourism supply" (OECD 2014, p. 117). The *International Furnishing Accessories Exhibition*, a major trade show, was accompanied by complementary smaller events (*Fuorisalone*) that, spread around in the city (over 700 in 2013), became targets of leisure tourists and showcases for emerging creative designers and architects. This not only strengthened the design capital brand but also boosted the activity of the design district, whose production then entered the tourism market by becoming involved in innovation of the hotel industry (in both the luxury and low-budget accommodation segments). Design hotels innovated local hospitality and attracted investments (OECD 2014). Figure 1 represents the dynamic integration of design and the tourism industry in the case of Milan, as described by the OECD report.

To conclude, this section has underlined the importance of two main alternative views on urban tourism which promote the study of cities not only as *places of consumption* but also as *places of production*. That is, if on the one hand the

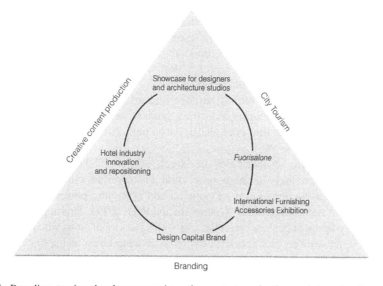

Fig. 1 Branding, tourism development and creative content production: an integration framework for Milan Design Capital. *Source*: author's elaboration on OECD (2014)

organisation of the contemporary city has been mostly read as centred more on "consumption and spectacle" than on production (Urry 1988, p. 52), on the other hand there is increasing room to reflect on the extent to which an "immense accumulation of spectacles" (Harvey 1987 cited in Urry 1988) has become functional to a city's production capacity.

2.4   City Branding

A shift of perspective in analysing and framing the symbolic and discursive representation of cities has been recorded by the city branding debate (see also chapters "The Participatory Place Branding Process for Tourism: Linking Visitors and Residents Through the City Brand" and "Globetrotters and Brands: Cities in an Emerging Communicative Space"). In particular, an "integrated place branding" approach has emerged (Ashworth and Kavaratzis 2009) in contrast with traditional distinctions among city brands targeting different single audiences, e.g. tourists, investors and residents. Integrated branding implies understanding the place brand as an umbrella under which multiple aspects of local development are pursued. That is, the city brand resides in a "melting pot" or a "concentration, variety, and quality of activities and attributes" (Karski 1990 in Hayllar et al. 2008), although this raises not a few issues in terms of implementation.

Integrated branding is in contrast with conventional tourism destination marketing and branding, which focused on single destination products, often projecting monolithic images of tourist precincts or of the tourist city. It would be wrong, though, to say that integrated city branding makes the tourism precinct brand disappear. In many cases, the latter simply becomes part of a more complex "brand architecture" (Dooley and Bowie 2005) within which multiple brands are framed and interact. Brand architectures are not easy to manage, however. The literature has reported the capacity of a destination image (or of the 'narrow' tourism precinct image) to displace any other city image. Particularly difficult is the co-existence of strong cultural heritage and art destination images with the narrations of local manufacturing industries, productive and technological realities characterising a place (Bellini et al. 2010; Pasquinelli 2010; Pasquinelli and Teräs 2013).

It is worth mentioning that cities are targets of visitors' flows for a variety of reasons. Not surprisingly, a high proportion of travel to cities is due to the concentration and agglomeration of political and economic power, rather than to culture, leisure and entertainment (Ashworth and Page 2011). This applies to world cities hosting flows of business travellers, as well as to global cities whose degree of connection, networking and accessibility *per se* (enabled by a technological, political and economic capacity) generates appealing destination images. Those travellers interested in learning about contemporary society have a high propensity to consume these images. City tourism is hence sustained by the brand images of a 'multifunctional' cityscape and, at the same time, it contributes to the development of the world city's image as a place in which to live, do business, study and work. "From a tourism standpoint it is the use of visitor attractions and the infrastructure of cities [to] repackage and represent the accessibility of world cities", say Ashworth and Page (2011, p. 6). This process is, however, not free from pitfalls. As argued in the case of Rio de Janeiro, Brazil, recent sport mega-events that theoretically represented a unique ground for branding the city and the nation, have turned out to be platforms for counter branding, making "counter-imaginaries explicit in the context of urban transformation" (Maiello and Pasquinelli 2015, p. 118; Pasquinelli 2015b). This warns against the temptation of considering the place brand as "controllable and fully manageable" and instead supports an understanding of city branding as a process encompassing, yet going beyond, "coordination, alignment and strategic consistency" (Medway et al. 2015, p. 66).

The city branding literature (and, even more so, branding practice) features increasing awareness of the relations between tourism and other socio-economic domains; that is, as the destination brand speaks to tourists, it is 'heard' also by other potential stakeholders. In this regard, urban tourism was said to give business investors an opportunity to gain first-hand experience of the city as visitors (Fereidouni and Al-mulali 2014), so that there is a link between destination branding and investment promotion, even though this has been rarely taken into account. This link is based on the observation that cities are marketed to potential investors not only by means of cognitive techniques (typical of industrial marketing), but also by means of affective techniques that pertain to consumer marketing and so to the tourism domain (Pasquinelli 2014). In this sense, tourism may be conceived as a mode of city representation or a channel through which to 'broadcast' the city and make it familiar to a wide range of potential stakeholders extending well beyond the relatively narrow audience of actual and potential leisure tourists and which includes all those actors that may have an interest in establishing a relationship (even a long-term one) with the city (e.g. investors, students and workers).

3 Drawing a Bi-dimensional Arena for Research

It has been argued that a shift of perspective in the academic debate on urban tourism is taking place, broadening the research agenda in the field and suggesting a change of the *unit of analysis* adopted when dealing with city tourism. This means a change of the object of observation that acknowledges the complexity and the multifaceted form of urban tourism, i.e. its 'urban character'. This goes in the direction of operationalising the idea that city tourism should be no longer isolated from the study of broader dynamics of urban change; instead, academic research should devise theoretical approaches and methodologies with which to analyse urban tourism as a "supporting infrastructure" (Hall and Page 2009) for the urban system, while outlining frameworks that, starting from this rationale, can orient urban (tourism) policies.

While not leaving consolidated approaches behind, the borders of the debate seem to have moved forward. The concept of city tourism itself has been expanding from both the spatial and conceptual perspectives. That is, the evolutionary trajectory of the literature in the field seems to suggest an expansion of 'what' we look at when analysing city tourism and 'where' city tourism takes shape in the urban context.

The shift of perspective to be observed can be explained as follows (Fig. 2). On the one hand, the spatial unit of analysis has been changing, shifting from self-contained tourism precincts to complex urban forms characterising a dispersed urban geography of tourism. The deriving spatial complexity is due to visitors pushing themselves out of traditionally tourist areas of the tourist city, as, for instance, described in the case of Kreuzberg, Berlin (Füller and Michel 2014). This does not mean that the study of tourism precincts is or should be abandoned; instead, their analysis is complemented by multiple spatial standpoints that expand the borders of the research arena. As stated above, the urban traveller is interested in engaging with the city and in experiential learning; he or she wants to learn the urban ordinary and the urban path of progress. For this purpose the urban traveller looks for infiltration points, thus breaking away from well-established paths and redefining—we can also say co-producing—the set of cultural attractions in the city (with a consequent need to adopt appropriate methodologies for tracking and monitoring urban tourists; see chapter "Visitor Streams in City Destinations: Towards New Tools for Measuring Urban Tourism"). As seen above, an innovation district, i.e. 22@Barcelona, becomes a cultural hotspot. Similarly, business incubators and urban labs potentially become targets of niche urban travellers interested

Fig. 2 Recasting the urban tourism research agenda: A shift of perspective in the field

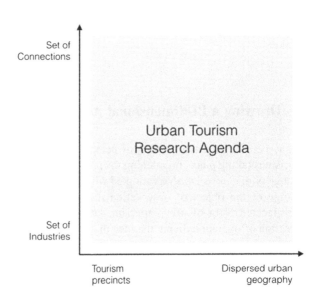

in understanding technological advancements, economic progress, and ways for the city to face global challenges, such as that of sustainability in the smart city. The emerging spatialities of urban tourism—their physical shape, the hosted cultural consumption, and their mode of representation—are necessarily impacted by niche visitors' preferences and behaviours that—to some extent—mix the outsider's expectations with the insider's lifestyle. In this regard, the media have proclaimed the 'advent' of post-tourism (Rogers 2015). The expression 'post-tourism' is not a novelty, however. In 1988 Urry discussed contemporary tourism transformations referring to post-tourism as a development parallel to postmodern culture. Post-tourism remains a sensational journalistic expression (as also pointed out by Urry in the 1980s) drawing attention to 'tourists becoming temporary residents'. Beyond sensationalism, however, there is a need to gauge the phenomenon and understand its meaning and implications in order to translate analytical insight into policy-making and actions.

A second dimension is used to describe the shift of perspective in the city tourism debate. It concerns the conceptual unit of analysis adopted to study urban tourism (Fig. 2). This is here explained as connectivity, suggesting a shift from analysis only of tourism industries—mainly hospitality in the broad sense—to analysis of a set of connections established among tourism industries and between these and non-tourism ones. Instead of focusing only on tourism as an industry *per se*, and thus measuring solely its industrial performance and profit-making capacity (how many visitors arrive in the destination, how much money they spend, and what money leakages take place in the local or regional system), efforts have begun to determine and measure urban tourism connectivity, i.e. the capacity or intrinsic characteristic of city tourism to connect with multiple components of local economic systems.

Tourism is only one among diverse urban economies. This feature is central to the 'urbanicity' of tourism, which is defined according to the multipurpose nature of city visits within a multifunctional context (Ashworth and Page 2011). Cities with the largest and most varied economies will gain the highest benefits from tourism (Ashworth and Page 2011). These are the foundations of the urban character of tourism, and connectivity is meant to be an analytic perspective enabling the detection and evaluation of that character. Especially, connectivity is based on the interpretation of city tourism as *functional* to the competitiveness of the urban system as a whole and, hence, to the competitiveness of local economies. These—producing goods and services typically not for tourists or not exclusively consumed by them—may draw material and/or symbolic value from tourism. Consider the examples cited in Sect. 2.3; accordingly, there is room for inquiry into the ways in which city tourism can support the urban system's participation in global circuits of flexible accumulation. A sort of *soft connectivity* of urban tourism comes to the fore. This comes about at a symbolic and intangible level of image creation, as Sect. 2.4 suggested. Image creation may be considered as purely ephemeral, but the role of city tourism in supporting a "singularisation" (Callon et al. 2012) and differentiation of local products and services should not be overlooked in the frame of a flexible accumulation regime. Connections between city tourism and creative industries have suggested that tourism is a "means of creating and capturing value" (Richards 2014a), and that it may catalyse the formation of an urban value ecosystem. Conversely, however, it may bring forms of brand saturation, hard thematisation, and cultural commodification impoverishing the urban capacity to create symbolic value (Bellini and Pasquinelli 2016).

Finally, there is room for further exploration of an *external* tourism connectivity that may regard tourism's contribution to the establishment of a city's relationships with the outside world. Tourism, in fact, plays a role in the production and circulation of those city images that are consumed not only by tourists but also by other potential stakeholders, e.g. investors, workers and students (see Sect. 2.4). To what extent and how can a city's cultural, scientific, entrepreneurial, educational and productive characteristics be narrated by means of tourism? This suggests a research stream devoted to the study of tourism as 'gateway to the city' by analysing the ways in which cities build their external connections and positioning in global networks.

Acknowledgements The author thanks Adam Radzimski and Nicola Bellini for their comments on an early draft of the manuscript, titled "Urban Tourism(s): Is There a Case for a Paradigm Shift?" included in the *GSSI Social Sciences Working Paper Series*.

References

Ashworth G, Kavaratzis M (2009) Beyond the logo: brand management for cities. J Brand Manage 16:520–531
Ashworth G, Page SJ (2011) Urban tourism research: recent progress and current paradoxes. Tour Manag 32(1):1–15. doi:10.1016/j.tourman.2010.02.002
Barcelona Turisme (2014) 2014 Barcelona tourism annual report. Barcelona Turisme, Barcelona
Beiley C, Miles S, Stark P (2004) Culture-led urban regeneration and the revitalisation of identities in Newcastle, Gateshead and the North East of England. Int J Cult Policy 10(1):46–65
Bellini N, Loffredo A, Pasquinelli C (2010) Managing otherness: the political economy of place images in the case of Tuscany. In: Ashworth G, Kavaratzis M (eds) Towards effective place brand management. Branding European cities and regions. Edward Elgar, Cheltenham, pp 89–116
Bellini N, Pasquinelli C (2016) Urban brandscape as value ecosystem: the cultural destination strategy of fashion brands. Place Brand Public Dipl 12:5–16. doi:10.1057/pb.2015.21
Brida JG, Cortes-Jimenez I, Pulina M (2014) Has the tourism-led growth hypothesis been validated? A literature review. Curr Issues Tourism 1–37. doi:10.1080/13683500.2013.868414
Callon M, Méadel C, Raberharisoa V (2012) The economy of qualities. Econ Soc 31(2):194–217
Conti G, Perrelli C (2007) Governing tourism monoculture: Mediterranean mass tourism destinations and governance networks. In: Burns PM, Novelli M (eds) Tourism and politics. Global frameworks and local realities. Elsevier, Oxford
Croy G, Heitmann S (2011) Tourism and Film. In: Robinson P, Heitmann S, Dieke P (eds) Research themes for tourism. CAB International, Cambridge, MA, pp 188–204
Czarniawska B (2002) A tale of three cities: or the globalization of city management. Oxford University Press, Oxford
Dooley G, Bowie D (2005) Place brand architecture: strategic management of the brand portfolio. Place Brand Public Dipl 1(4):402–419

Ehlers F (2010) Teen twilight vampire tourism: Volterra's battle for authenticity. Spiegel Online International. http://www.spiegel.de/international/europe/teen-twilight-vampire-tourism-volterra-s-battle-for-authenticity-a-690073.html. Accessed 21 Mar 2016

Evans G (2003) Hard-branding the cultural city—from Prado to Prada. Int J Urban Reg Res 27 (2):417–440

Fereidouni HG, Al-mulali U (2014) The interaction between tourism and FDI in real estate in OECD countries. Curr Issue Tour 17(2):105–113. doi:10.1080/13683500.2012.733359

Frenzel F, Koens K (2012) Slum tourism: developments in a young filed of interdisciplinary tourism research. Tour Geogr 14(2):195–201

Füller H, Michel B (2014) 'Stop being a tourist!' New dynamics of urban tourism in Berlin-Kreuzberg. Int J Urban Reg Res 38(4):1304–1318. doi:10.1111/1468-2427.12124

Gotham KF (2002) Marketing Mardi Gras: Commodification, spectacle and the political economy of tourism in New Orleans. Urban Stud 39(10):1735–1756

Gregory D, Johnston R, Pratt G, Watts M, Whatmore S (2009) Flexible accumulation. The dictionary of human geography, 5th edn. Blackwell, Singapore

Hall CM, Page SJ (2009) Progress in tourism management: from the geography of tourism to geographies of tourism—a review. Tour Manage 30(1):3–16. doi:10.1016/j.tourman.2008.05.014

Hayllar B, Griffin T, Edwards D (2008) Urban tourism precincts: engaging with the field. In: Hayllar B, Griffin T, Edwards D (eds) City spaces—tourist places: urban tourism precincts. Elsevier, Oxford

Hung W-L, Lee Y-J, Huang P-H (2014) Creative experiences, memorability and revisit intention in creative tourism. Curr Issues Tour 1–8. doi:10.1080/13683500.2013.877422

Isaac RK, Çakmak E (2014) Understanding visitor's motivation at sites of death and disaster: the case of former transit camp Westerbork, The Netherlands. Curr Issue Tour 17(2):164–179. doi:10.1080/13683500.2013.776021

Jacob D (2012) The eventification of place: urban development and experience consumption in Berlin and New York City. Eur Urban Reg Stud 20(4):447–459

Lazzeroni M, Bellini N, Cortesi G, Loffredo A (2013) The territorial approach to cultural economy: new opportunities for the development of small towns. Eur Plan Stud 21(4):452–472

Le-Klähn D-T, Hall CM (2014) Tourist use of public transport at destinations—a review. Curr Issue Tour 1–19. doi:10.1080/13683500.2014.948812

Lisle D (2007) Defending Voyeurism: dark tourism and the problem of global security. In: Burns PM, Novelli M (eds) Tourism and politics. Global frameworks and local realities. Elsevier, Oxford, pp 333–346

MacCannell D (1973) Staged authenticity: arrangements of social space in tourist settings. Am J Soc 79(3):589–603

Maiello A, Pasquinelli C (2015) Destruction or construction? A (counter) branding analysis of sport mega-events in Rio de Janeiro. Cities 48:116–124

Marson D (2011) From mass tourism to niche tourism. In: Robinson P, Heitmann S, Dieke P (eds) Research themes in tourism. CABI, Cambridge, MA, pp 1–15

Martinotti G (1994) The new social morphology of cities. In: Paper presented at the UNESCO/MOST, Wien, 10–12 Feb 1004

Medway D, Delpy Neirotti L, Pasquinelli C, Zenker S (2015) Place branding: are we wasting our time? Report of an AMA special session. J Place Manag Dev 8(1):63–68

Novelli M (ed) (2005) Niche tourism. Contemporary issues, trends and cases. Elsevier, Oxford

Novy J (2014) Urban tourism—the end of the honeymoon? UNWTO, 3rd Global Summit on City Tourism, Barcelona, 9–10 Dec 2014. UNWTO

O'Brian D, Miles S (2010) Cultural policy as rhetoric and reality: a comparative analysis of policy making in the peripheral North of England. Cult Trends 19(1/2):3–13

O'Sullivan F (2016) Barcelona is targeting billboards it sees as 'pollution'. CityLab, http://www.citylab.com/cityfixer/2016/02/barcelona-reduce-advertising-billboard-public-space/463359/. Accessed 21 Mar 2016

OECD (2014) Tourism and the creative economy. OECD Studies on Tourism, Paris

Pasquinelli C (2010) The limits of place branding for local development. The case of Tuscany and the Arnovalley brand. Local Econ 25(7):558–572

Pasquinelli C (2014) Innovation branding for FDI promotion: building the distinctive brand. In: Berg PO, Björner E (eds) Branding Chinese mega-cities. Policies, practices and positioning. Edward Elgar, Cheltenham, pp 207–219

Pasquinelli C (2015a) City branding and local SMEs: a smart specialisation perspective. Symphonya Emerg Issues Manage 1:63–76

Pasquinelli C (2015b) The Olympic bidding process: a matter of branding? CritCom—A Forum for Research & Commentary in Europe. http://councilforeuropeanstudies.org/critcom/the-olympics-bidding-process-a-matter-of-branding/. Accessed 21 Mar 2016

Pasquinelli C, Sjöholm J (2015) Art and resilience: the spatial practices of making a resilient artistic career in London. City Cult Soc 6(3):75–81

Pasquinelli C, Teräs J (2013) Branding knowledge-intensive regions: a comparative study of Pisa and Oulu high-tech brands. Eur Plan Stud 21(10):1611–1629

Richards G (2003) What is cultural tourism? In: van Maaren A (ed) Erfogoed voor Toerisme. Nationaal Contact Manumenten. https://www.academia.edu/1869136/What_is_Cultural_Tourism. Accessed 21 Mar 2016

Richards G (2014a) Creativity and tourism in the city. Curr Issue Tour 17(2):119–144. doi:10.1080/13683500.2013.783794. Accessed 21 Mar 2016

Richards G (2014b) Tourism trends: the convergence of culture and tourism. https://www.academia.edu/9491857/Tourism_trends_The_convergence_of_culture_and_tourism

Richards G (2014c) Guimaraes and Maribor European Capitals of Culture 2012. ATLAS, Arnhem

Richards G, Wilson J (2004) The international student travel market: travel style, motivations, and activities. Tour Rev Int 8(2):57–67

Richards G, Wilson J (2005) Youth tourism—finally coming of age? In: Novelli M (ed) Niche tourism. Contemporary issues, trends and cases. Elsevier, Oxford, pp 39–46

Rogers T (2015) Berlin is the 'post-tourist' capital of Europe. NYMag, http://nymag.com/next/2015/03/berlin-is-the-post-tourist-capital-of-europe.html. Accessed 21 Mar 2016

Rogerson CM (2006) Creative industries and urban tourism: South African perspectives. Urban Forum 17(2):149

Rota FS, Salone C (2014) Place-making processes in unconventional cultural practices. The case of Turin's contemporary art festival Paratissima. Cities 40:90–98. doi:10.1016/j.cities.2014.03.008

Sjöholm J, Pasquinelli C (2014) Artist brand building: towards a spatial perspective. Arts Mark Int J 4(1/2). doi:10.1108/AM-10-2013-0018

Southall C, Fallon P (2011) LGBT tourism. In: Robinson P, Heitmann S, Dieke P (eds) Research themes for tourism. CABI, Cambridge, MA, pp 218–231

Spirou C (2008) The evolution of the tourism precinct. In: Hayllar B, Griffin T, Edwards D (eds) City spaces—tourist places: urban tourism precincts. Elsevier, Oxford, pp 19–38

StudentUniverse, Skift (2014) The State of student travel. Skift report

Tardiveau A, Mallo D (2014) Unpacking and challenging habitus: an approach to temporary urbanism as a socially engaged practice. J Urban Des 19(4):456–472

Tyrrell TJ, Johnston RJ (2006) The economic impacts of tourism: a special issue. J Travel Res 45(3):3–7. doi:10.1177/0047287506288876

Urry J (1988) Cultural change and contemporary holiday-making. Theor Cult Soc 5(1):35–55

Urry J (2002) The tourist Gaze, 2nd edn. Sage, London

Valls J-F, Sureda J, Valls-Tuñon G (2014) Attractiveness analysis of European tourist cities. J Travel Tour Mark 31(2):178–194. doi:10.1080/10548408.2014.873310

Zervas G, Proserpio D, Byers J (2016) The rise of the sharing economy: estimating the impact of Airbnb on the hotel industry, Boston University, School of Management Research Paper, N.2013-16. doi:10.2139/ssrn.2366898

Mind the Gap: Reconceptualising Inclusive Development in Support of Integrated Urban Planning and Tourism Development

Lauren Uğur

Abstract This chapter proposes a model of integrated access in the promotion of an integrated agenda for urban planning and urban tourism development. The underlying assertion of the conceptual framework presented is that sustainable urban tourism development is reliant on inclusive development that works to balance the needs of both visitors and locals in the production of urban tourisms. The core challenge in achieving an integrated approach lies in the identified disconnect between existing tourism development and urban planning practices. In addressing this challenge, a reconceptualisation of inclusive tourism development is offered, which focuses on the promotion of integrated access across economic, spatial and institutional spheres.

Keywords Integrated urban planning • Tourism development • Inclusive tourism • Accessible tourism

1 Introduction

Undoubtedly the most prominent statistic circulating in urban studies literature concerns the fact that already over half the world's population call cities home (United Nations 2012). Coupled with forces of globalisation and highly networked increases in global exchange urban areas continue to face processes of dynamic change, as a host of professionals, including planners, seek to determine development trajectories for our cities that (re)position urban centres as economically and socially viable spaces of production and consumption for residents and visitors alike. The emergent competition for global positioning has resulted in urban development strategies focused primarily on solidifying economic prosperity, reliant on the attraction of foreign investment, trade and importantly, tourism; the latter being viewed as a source of much opportunity. Accordingly, urban tourism constitutes a key factor in contemporary urban development (UNWTO 2012) with increasing focus being placed on the creation of the urban tourism "product".

L. Uğur (✉)
International School of Management, Frankfurt, Germany
e-mail: lauren.ugur@ism.de

© Springer International Publishing Switzerland 2017
N. Bellini, C. Pasquinelli (eds.), *Tourism in the City*,
DOI 10.1007/978-3-319-26877-4_3

In light of this global "urban revolution" (Lefebvre 2003 [1970]), cities nowadays not only constitute a foundational element on the tourist route, they also constitute the places of origin and thus home for our global populations' majority (Ashworth and Page 2011), thereby rendering cities as spaces of simultaneous consumption by local residents and visitors as the norm. A core challenge to this simultaneous consumption is the ability to realise a balance between the various needs placed on the urban environment by locals and visitors, especially if the liveable functionality of cities as well as the social and economic potential of urban tourism is to be optimised.

The growing importance of urban tourism and the impact that existing forms of consumption have on achieving the development of cities that are socially and economically successful forms the focus of this chapter. The premise on which this input is based extends from the fact that along with the ever-increasing number of people living, working in and visiting cities, we cannot engage in debates concerning sustainable urban development without considering tourism; without considering the impact of visitors on local populations, or the unrelenting need for cities to compete on a global scale in attracting both leisure and business tourists and, primarily, without considering the unrealised potential of urban tourisms.

This chapter thus reflects on the relationship between urban planning and tourism development, guided by the central question "*How can we understand urban development and urban tourism dynamics in pursuing the development of more sustainable, more inclusive cities?*" Drawing on a variety of illustrative examples, including some from within this volume, this contribution argues for the need to reconsider sustainable urban tourism development as it relates to ideologies of inclusion in attempting to better integrate tourism with broader urban planning and development practices. Furthermore, the foundation of inclusion is used as a platform from which to reconceptualise the more pragmatic means by which urban [tourism] planning can react to the challenge of creating tourism products that extend economic and, importantly, social benefits to a far larger proportion of urban societies on the basis of spatial, institutional, and economic access.

2   Mind the Gap: The Urban Planning-Tourism Disconnect

A core severity in the challenge to successfully harnessing any form of tourism-centred urban development in the pursuit of sustainability concerns the persistent disconnect between overwhelmingly economics-oriented tourism development agendas and urban planning. Illustratively, tourism research has thus far failed to engage with the broader field of urban studies, remaining plagued by a persistently "inward looking approach" (Ashworth and Page 2011, p. 1). Additionally, in relation to the construction of tourist attractions and their consumption, it is city *marketing* that has in many ways substituted urban planning in the development process (Deffner and Liouris 2005; Deffner and Metaxas 2006). What must be acknowledged, however, is that due to on-going urbanisation coupled with the continuing growth in urban tourism, any questions concerning the sustainable development of urban areas are rendered inseparable from questions concerning the way in which urban tourism development takes, or should, take place. In other words, the development and continuing consumption of cities as tourism destinations is inextricably linked to the potential for cities to pursue trajectories aimed at achieving sustainable development. For this reason, it is the concept of sustainability, from which initial correlations between tourism and urban studies literatures may be drawn, that provides the starting point in establishing common ground on the basis of which the urban planning-tourism disconnect may be tackled.

2.1 Sustainability and the Economic Bias of Tourism Development

As a cross-cutting thematic present in discourses across an extensive range of contemporary fields and disciplines the notion of sustainability encompasses a diversity of definitions, theoretical positions and underlying ideologies, which underpins how the practice of sustainable development has been approached; the domains of urban planning and tourism being no exception. One of the primary tribulations of attaining any form of sustainability lies in the absence of agreement and clarity over the concept itself (Day 2012; Berno and Bricker 2015). The nature and prime objectives of this chapter precludes any attempt to provide a conclusive definition of sustainability for the diverse industry that is tourism but what it does attempt to do is to re-consider how the common objective of sustainability can be used as the basis from which to further the aim of drawing urban studies, development and tourism discourses closer together.

Pursued as the ultimate goal of [urban] development, sustainability has developed significantly in terms of the extension of the concept from a purely environmental focus to an understanding of sustainability as a more diverse, dynamic issue, strongly reliant on the promotion of social well-being. Within tourism, it is as recently as the turn of the century that reviews on sustainable tourism critiqued the dominant, narrow environmental focus of sustainability (e.g. Butler 1999; Hardy et al. 2002) and argued more strongly for the necessity to extend definitions to include the human environment, specifically calling attention to the requisite for community involvement as a key factor in developing more sustainable tourism destinations and products.

Respectively, the World Tourism Organisation (2005) defines sustainable tourism as "tourism that takes full account of its current and future economic, social and environmental impacts, addressing the needs of visitors, the industry, the environment and host communities" and has over the past decade lobbied for the involvement of local communities in tourism development, highlighting the necessity to consider the social, economic and environmental needs of both visitors and host communities in the production and consumption of tourism. In light of this shift towards a more integrated understanding of sustainability and its influencing factors, the involvement of communities in tourism development has emerged as an essential "cornerstone of sustainable tourism" (Nkemngu 2012).

Within urban studies the discourse is akin, similarly recognising the importance of placing inhabitants' needs at the centre of development practice in the attempt to create more sustainable cities, supported by the emergence of communicative theories of planning (Forester 1989; Innes 1995; Healey 1996) that have replaced systematic planning models and which have progressed to foster collaborative planning processes (Innes and Booher 2003; Innes and Booher 2010; Healey 2003) where stakeholder dialogue is extended in support of active citizenship and co-production (Watson 2014). Here, co-production refers to collaboration between those who supply a service and those who benefit from the use of a service (Ostrom and Ostrom 1999). In tourism, co-production would thus refer, for example, to collaboration between public and/or private entities and civil society in the development of urban tourisms or between civil society and visitors, as primary consumers of the tourist product. Most importantly, co-production requires a balanced interplay between strategies of production and strategies of consumption (ibid.) and is thus viewed as a key component in working towards the development of urban tourism strategies and products that are able to achieve a more equitable balance in addressing the needs of visitors and local residents. In the broadest sense, the development of the sustainable city has therefore become synonymous with the challenge of working collaboratively with multiple stakeholders in balancing social and economic development with environmental management and urban governance.

The focus on social issues as a core element of long-term sustainability has meant that significant bodies of literature have amassed, drawing out definitions and approaches towards community-oriented, collaborative planning, participation and co-production. Within tourism, many of these discourses fall under the larger umbrella of community-based tourism (Jamal and Getz 1995; Blackstock 2005; Okazaki 2008), which advocates for the establishment of tourism products and development processes that extend benefits to local communities. Accordingly, the notion of community involvement, along with the identified potential for tourism to aid in poverty alleviation through leveraging the diversity of the tourism sector, has seen pro-poor tourism (PPT) initiatives levy focus on the generation of direct and indirect benefits for the poor (Ashley et al. 2000). PPT, as an overall approach to tourism development, whether it be through community-based tourism or otherwise, is fundamentally justified on the basis of improved incorporation of the poor into capitalist markets, based on the promise of extensive economic opportunity and the development of the various infrastructures required to facilitate the provision of tourism-related goods and services. Fundamentally, as one of the world's largest industries, realising contributions of over $7.5 billion in GDP and approximately 277 million jobs (World Travel and Tourism Council 2015), tourism is touted as the basis of local economic development. Strategic tourism plans the world over thus highlight the potential for tourism to contribute to growth and prosperity for all levels of society and thus, supported by the notion of the tourism sector as a vehicle for urban economic improvement, remains one of the most common local development strategies in cities (Rogerson and Rogerson 2014).

The overarching "success" of PPT has however been drawn into question, underpinned by the assertion that tourism benefits remain unevenly distributed, in that "rather than attending to the need for structural change, redistribution of wealth and resources, and addressing international and national power structures, they tacitly accept a neoliberal approach to development and tinker with the capitalistic international tourism system at the edges, eking out a few resources for small, selected groups of the poor (or relatively poor) in destination areas" (Harrison 2008, p. 858). Similarly, studies into resident attitudes towards local tourism development demonstrate community concern over being left out of the economic benefits, despite paying a disproportionate cost for tourism development (Harrill 2004). The critique thus remains that tourism development remains so overwhelmingly economics-oriented that the processes supporting tourism development fail to consider the multi-level, interrelated elements required to achieve development that contributes effectively to propagating benefits for local residents.

It is not to say that an economic growth focus for tourism development is negative in its entirety, however arguably one of the strongest criticisms against the economic bias, with which tourism development is approached in so many cities across the world, is that overall benefit is so often peddled on the basis of diffusion economics (Hardy et al. 2002) whereby positive economic and social impact is reliant on the dispersion of economic benefit associated with multiplier effects and the largely unsubstantiated trickle-down effect (Goodwin 2008). For example, in discussing the issues of tourism multipliers and the interplay between industry linkages and leakages across more than 150 countries Lejárraga and Walkenhorst demonstrate the limitations of diffusion principles in that, "with the exception of wages, most of the income generated through direct effects within the tourism economy goes to hotel owners, which are often local or international elites" (2010, p. 420). In contrast to direct effects, the authors further maintain that trickle-down effects, through which lower-income strata of society are supposed to benefit, are linked primarily only to income generated through indirect effects whereby income derives from tourist expenditures in the general economy, for example through the purchase of non-tourism related goods and services (ibid.). In this light, the benefit of the creation of more intensive linkages between the tourism sector and general economies becomes obvious, as such linkages would increase the supply of goods and services to the tourism sector and in turn generate resource shifts, expanding productive activities within the wider economy. After all, it is those cities that are characterised by a large and varied economy that are able to gain most from tourism whereas cities that are over-proportionally dependent on tourism industries tend to benefit least (Ashworth and Page 2011).

The economic bias described, coupled with a lack of agreeable evidence that current urban tourism development trends in fact contribute to creating more liveable cities, reinforces the argument that the disconnect in urban planning and urban tourism development poses an on-going threat to the realisation of sustainable cities. Moreover, the establishment of more varied urban economies, better able to exploit the benefits of urban tourism, is therefore argued as being dependent on a more integrated, coordinated approach to urban tourism planning and underscores the sense of urgency for exploring new means by which to consider how sustainability objectives may be reconciled. Academics and practitioners therefore need to place a more concerted effort on delineating sustainability on a contextual basis so as to develop approaches that better foster the inclusion that community-based approaches have been calling for. This in itself demands an integrated consideration of what inclusion means, how this correlates with contextually-specific availability of "assets" in light of local inhabitants' needs and calls for alignment in identifying the most appropriate forms of urban tourism to be promoted.

2.2   Establishing Common Ground: Delineating Sustainable Development Through Inclusion

The persistent commodification of urban "assets", natural, cultural or otherwise and the variant patterns of consumption that emerge unarguably shape the spatial development of cities and determine the movement of visitors and ordinary citizens in one way or another. It is this determination of movement, at times encouraging and at times restrictive, that is at the heart of the attempt to reconsider the concept of inclusive urban tourism as a more integrated part of the urban development process.

Equality of opportunity and the equitable allocation of resources lie at the heart of promoting inclusion. The practice of inclusive development thus requires a dual-focused approach in targeting barriers that foster forms of exclusion while concurrently engaging those groups that remain excluded. Inclusion thus infers a reduction of present inequalities, working in opposition to patterns of "perverse growth" that limit participation in consumer markets and concentrate income and wealth to the benefit of a privileged few (Sachs 2004). Just as with the critique on the failure of much tourism-related development to achieve even economic inclusion, the neo-liberal capitalist structure that has driven contemporary urbanisation processes is likewise criticised for its failure to promote broad-based inclusive development, having favoured the generation of private profit (van Vliet 2002).

Contemporary neoliberal development policy disseminated and adopted at a global scale, sought to leverage rapid urbanisation and promoting economic prosperity through deregulation, privatisation and austerity. Within urban development discourses, the strong neoliberal approach to urban development has similarly been denounced as having facilitated the entrenchment of unequal development (e.g. Miraftab 2007; Parnell and Pieterse 2010), restricting access on the basis of non-distributive resource allocation and a catered bias to visitor demand. This has so too been blamed on the "syndrome" of assuring global competitiveness and the attainment of world city status pursued by so many urban destinations (McDonald

2008). Others even brand contemporary neoliberal development practices as a form of structural violence, labelling it "an ideology that has little to say about the social and economic inequalities that distort real economies and instead, reveals yet another means by which these economies can be further exploited" (Farmer 2004, p. 313). It is on the back of these criticisms that the call for cities to act not only as engines of growth but as agents of change has resonated, strengthening arguments that development processes will have to re-focus the current utilisation of public resources and revert planning to its former intentions of "…protecting the needs of ordinary people rather than privileged minorities, the public rather than private interest, the future rather than the present" (Lovering 2009, cited by Watson 2009, p. 153). Therefore, redress comes in the form of enabling local populations to enact their "right to the city" (Lefebvre 1991; Harvey 2003; Purcell 2014) under the auspices of which ownership supersedes individual control over assets. Rather, ownership is understood in a collective sense and thus defined on the basis of a group's ability to access these assets (Fainstein 2005). Harvey argues that "the right to the city is not merely a right of access to what already exists" (2003, p. 939) but also constitutes a right to participate in what may come to exist in the future—that is in utilising potential for future gain. Inclusion therefore extends beyond economic access to include access to culture, the right to live in a decent home within a sustainable living environment, the right to access education and employment, to maintain personal security, and to participate in urban governance (Fainstein 2005).

3 Narrowing the Gap: Inclusion Through Integrated Access

Abundant in planning literature is the ideology of [inclusive] urban development as a task dealing in social complexity (Byrne 2003; de Roo and Silva 2010; de Roo et al. 2012). The growing realisation of complexity within the social sciences (Urry 2005) and the recognition that within complex social systems experts are limited in their ability to prescribe ready-made solutions has led the movement from comprehensive master planning and technical rational approaches to development towards the collaborative processes described earlier on in this chapter. Beyond the necessity for collaborative approaches to planning, the acknowledgement of the non-linear interrelatedness of the multitudinous factors that impact how urban communities function has led to the prerequisite to tackle questions of sustainability and inclusion from a variety of perspectives. Essentially, the planning response to systemic complexity has come in the propagation of integrated approaches that work to simultaneously address the multiple factors that contribute to determining the (dys)functionality of urban communities.

The recognition of the complexity of social systems remains limited in tourism discourses and linked to the fact that a strong, linear economic bias prevails, it can be argued that tourism planning remains somewhat stuck in the pursuit of technical rational approaches (Lew 2007), whereby linear causality of tourism development interventions is assumed. Consequently, tourism planning remains characterised by a lack of integrated approaches that work towards recognising linkages and connecting broader community interests to the planning of tourism attractions.

For this reason, using the common objective of inclusive development, a conceptual framework has been developed through which the meaning of integrated urban tourism development may be focused. Here, inclusive development is extended through a conceptualisation of *integrated access*.

3.1 Inclusive Tourism: A Matter of Integrated Access

In having elaborated inclusion as being fundamentally about access we can thus consider how access is to be defined in terms of better integrating urban planning and tourism development. This approach seeks to support the development of a more integrative approach to urban tourism planning so as to more effectively cater to the variety of needs of both locals and visitors, thereby creating more diverse, liveable cities where tourism, as one source of economic potential and extended social well-being, is embedded within the urban fabric. The prime objective is to seamlessly integrate tourism within the city rather than super-impose tourism on parts of the city, which fosters non-inclusive patterns of consumption. The value-add of this approach rests in the potential that the notion of access provides as a pragmatic framework for establishing common ground through which to bridge the gap between tourism development and the practical realities and necessities of inclusive urban planning.

Evolved from the recognition of social complexity in planning, requiring integrated, collaborative approaches to development, access is defined here across a spectrum of the following distinguishable yet highly interdependent spheres; (i) access to leveraged economic opportunity, (ii) physical access to urban space and (iii) institutional access through which social progression may be achieved (Fig. 1).

Within this framework, each of the identified forms of access are highly interdependant on one another and it must also be recognised that any outcome of such an integrated approach will be reliant on local contextual specificities.

Economic Access
The potential of tourism to contribute to the broader economic prosperity of cities is widely recognised and is not called into question here. What is being called into question is the way in which the focus on ensuring extended access to the economic benefits generated through urban tourism has thus far been approached. Here, economic access simply refers to the necessity to enable a larger portion of urban populations to engage with and benefit from the diversity of economic potential that the tourism industry offers.

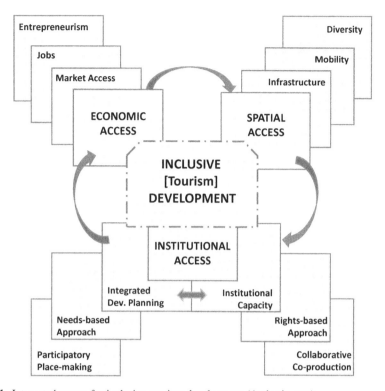

Fig. 1 Integrated access for inclusive tourism development (Author's own)

Integrated economic access therefore requires aligning the development of tourist attractions within cities so as to ensure local access to tourism markets. This may be achieved through the provision of a diversity of employment opportunities, the ability to engage in entrepreneurial activity and in the targeted creation of extended economic linkages that work towards embedding tourism within a more diversified economic base. The assertion is that the challenge of high levels of economic leakage associated with many forms of urban tourism can be combatted through more integrated economic practices that promote locally-oriented economic linkages. For example, enabling access for local suppliers to the tourism value chain by establishing supply chain linkages is one method that has shown promise in achieving more inclusive development (Scheyvens 2011). Furthermore, economic leakage may likewise be reduced through encouraging local entrepreneurship and ensuring the use of local labour forces in tourism development (Ritchie 2008).

Therefore, ensuring economic access itself refers to an integrated process for inclusive development and goes beyond the traditional rhetoric of dispersion benefits. Although job creation remains an important contributor of tourism to local economies, the proposition is that a more diversified urban economy to which tourism can more effectively contribute is reliant on the development of tourist attractions that provide a diversity of opportunities that support local livelihoods through revitalising local cultures and making them accessible to tourists in a way that reduces isolation. Unfortunately, all too often, economic access is restricted in how urban tourism products are produced for the consumption of an intended (read privileged) few, particularly where the city has been "staged" for such consumption (Greene 2003; Čamprag 2016). For example, despite its various limitations and critiques, the rise of township (slum) tourism in many parts of the developing world has been praised as a catalyst for locals to access tourist markets. However, where private capital takes precedence over inclusion, engagement with the complexities of establishing more inclusive economic development gives way to the (re)creation of slum tourism in a less accessible setting. Emoya Shanty Town, located just outside the City of Bloemfontein in South Africa as an illustrative example, offers the "ideal venue for your family and friends to experience a township in a safe and relaxing environment".[1] In such a case, entrepreneurial economic activity for local residents is not promoted and economic access is thus limited to the provision of jobs and perhaps a certain level of extended economic benefit through the private company's corporate social responsibility programme, which, to varying degrees, invests in local community development projects. Importantly, this kind of phenomenon is not only limited to developing contexts and anti-tourism movements have gained momentum in cities such as Berlin where residents demonstrate frustration, attempting to reclaim their right to the city (Novy 2014, cited by Pasquinelli 2015). Moreover, in Barcelona, existing conflict is being tackled head-on as new tourism strategies and public administration approaches seek to redress the negative impacts of the unbalanced consumption of urban space by tourists in the city (see Fava and Palou Rubio 2016).

Integrated economic access cannot however be achieved in isolation and, due to the complex nature of the system, is dependent on a conducive environment, contingent on the promotion of spatial and institutional access.

Situational or Physical Access

In cities across the world economic inequality is often recognisable through spatial forms of exclusion, whereby access to particular urban areas is restricted for certain—usually lower-income—populations. This exclusion is often embedded in socio-economic constructs but is also entrenched through factors such as infrastructure deficits that restrict mobility, as well as urban policy and its enforcement, such as regulations on street vending. Looking at the dynamics of urban-tourism, spatial exclusion, whether involuntary or voluntary, represents an often-cited challenge, particularly in relation to the development of tourist enclaves. In relation to spatial exclusion and urban tourism, it is most important to distinguish forms of exclusion on the basis of restriction and avoidance; differentiated here as *active* and *passive restriction* and *voluntary avoidance*.

---

[1] See Emoya Shanty Town's website, http://www.emoya.co.za/p23/accommodation/shanty-town-for-a-unique-accommodation-experience-in-bloemfontein.html. Accessed 23 October 2015.

Exclusion on the basis of active or passive restriction takes many forms, determined by a number of contextual factors and concerns the creation of the tourist enclave juxtaposed with the provision and extension of the public good through tourism. Physical, economic and institutional factors all play a role in determining the level and effect of spatial restriction and relate directly to stakeholder dynamics and power over the investment process. For example, a scenario of power dominance of private interests in the neoliberal city, coupled with rising socio-economic inequalities and issues of security have rendered many a carefully constructed tourist city far from accessible, both physically and economically, to large portions of society. Furthermore, in cases of weak governance, failure to deliver urban infrastructure and services in an integrated manner entrenches this exclusion, albeit more passively. Passive restriction thus facilitates the ingraining of exclusion where, due to tourism development, particular areas of the city become unaffordable to local populations as residents are unable to maintain pace with rising prices in highly patronised tourism spaces, thus changing consumption habits within the city. Such forms of passive restriction are most often pronounced in urban areas where focus is placed on the attraction of foreign visitors, as expectations and needs vary most dramatically from those of local residents, making access more difficult to reconcile.

Similarly, exclusion may also occur on the basis of choice. In highly tourism-oriented urban areas, voluntary avoidance results as local residents respond to perceived tourist saturation, seeking solace from those areas where tourism intensity is highest. Whether through exclusion on the basis of gentrification and unaffordability or through the choice of residents to avoid tourist crowds, as with restriction, so too does this retreat impact consumption patterns, creating barriers between tourism and other local economies. Furthermore, the tourist product itself comes into question regarding authenticity, as the primary draw to cities that exhibit dense cultural heritage, such as Venice, become increasingly overshadowed by cosmopolitan consumption and the tourist monoculture (see Minoia 2016).

Therefore, inclusive spatial development is reliant on the physical accessibility of urban spaces for local populations as well as for visitors. Inclusive tourism development thus requires a focus on ensuring connectivity and mobility that not only maintain access to public spaces for local residents but that also facilitates the dispersion of tourists within cities, diluting traditional tourist precincts. The concept of tourism "off-the-beaten-track" that seeks to extend tourism beyond traditional tourist precincts (Maitland and Newman 2009), most often supported by a need for authenticity (Füller and Michel 2014), further supports the position being taken that if tourism potential is to be more fully realised, tourist experiences must extend beyond the bounds of traditionally isolated tourist precincts. This extension is, however, inherently reliant on an integrated approach to urban development and tourism planning, which in itself is dependant on ensuring access to local governance and the strengthening of institutional capacities.

Institutional Access

Ultimately, exclusion occurs where access (in all its forms) is denied on the basis of a failure to represent the needs of residents in the development process and where, rather than promoting access, development trajectories place restrictions on residents in favour of tourist needs. The achievement of integrated tourism cannot be realised without the establishment of an accessible institutional environment, as inclusive growth linked to tourism requires greater policy intervention (Rogerson 2013). Institutional access as it is being referred to here, is thus not simply about advocating a bottom-up approach to tourism development. Rather, it is about facilitating a balance between bottom-up and top-down mechanisms of governance in the planning of urban tourism, which recognises the evolving role of government and the need for certain "command and control" approaches to ensuring sustainability mechanisms (Bramwell and Lane 2010), as obligation rests with the institution of the state in guaranteeing the right to the city (Purcell 2014). In other words, integrated institutional access is about the pursuit of urban governance on the basis of a rights-based approach (Parnell and Pieterse 2010). In this sense, institutional access involves two key streams; inclusion through integrated planning that enables the participation of locals in decision-making and the assurance of access to tourism markets via well-capacitated institutional support.

The enablement of the right to the city requires the right to participate in urban governance (Fainstein 2005); that is the right to partake in decision-making that determines local development, including the use of local assets for touristic purposes. Therefore, an integrated approach to inclusion cannot ignore the need for participation and the collaborative involvement of local communities in the tourism development process whereby residents are afforded the ability to proactively contribute to determining development trajectories. This does not only refer to spatial planning, but also to inclusive place-making that establishes local identity and meaning through the involvement of locals in city-branding (Kavaratzis 2016).

The assurance of institutional access and collaborative tourism development that goes beyond consultative participation may also better support the identification of more appropriate forms of tourism and the creation of visitor attractions that are better situated to ensure a variety of economic opportunities and more equitable access to space. For example, this may mean the development of additional tourism offerings to attract middle income tourists where concentration has previously been on upper-class visitors or in the increased promotion of regional tourism, particularly in the visiting friends and family (VFF) segment. What is required is a coordinated, horizontal and vertical alignment of governance that links local-level tourism and urban planning, supported by national and regional tourism strategies, facilitated through common objectives and appropriate funding mechanisms. Although some cases highlight significant progress in structuring local integrated development plans that include tourism and which are embedded in (at the very least legislated) participatory planning processes (van Niekerk 2014), the fact remains that the process of integrated development requires inclusive practices that address the multitudinous implementation challenges associated with managing community-based tourism offerings such as limited, divergent demand, functional deficits in the training of local residents and communities to enable the tourism experience and in the provision of appropriate forms of support for small, medium and micro enterprises (SMMEs) (Rogerson 2004, 2005; Rogerson and Rogerson 2014).

All in all, the diversification of tourism markets on the basis of identified local dynamics and needs is not a one-way street, as the embedding of tourism within a more diversified urban context brings with it the benefit of increased authenticity in the urban tourism experience where tourism forms a more closely related part of everyday urban life.

4 Moving Forward: So Where to Next?

This chapter has argued that the road to sustainable urbanism requires inclusive development practices that take account of the multiple influencing factors that contribute to establishing broad-based economies that are well-positioned to take advantage of the potential of urban tourisms. This argument is reinforced through recognising the necessity to establish enhanced linkages between urban tourism development and urban planning and advocates for focus to be placed on attaining a more equitable balance between the economic and social well-being of locals and the satisfaction of tourist needs.

There is little doubt that the management of urban tourism is a complex task requiring integrated approaches that aim to achieve the balancing of a large number of competing interests and needs of local residents, private businesses and tourists themselves. Cities and city regions continue to expand rapidly and change is dynamic for both the public and private sector, a situation which offers many challenges but also a significant number of opportunities if recognised and responded to accordingly. It is on these opportunities and the means of harnessing latent potential that focus should be oriented.

Far beyond the scope of this short contribution to fully engage with the concept of access and how it relates to urban tourism and development in practice, much work remains to be done in refining the conceptual standpoint being taken. Simply, the notions of access and inclusive development in relation to the creation of the urban tourism product and the leveraging of existent potential need to be better defined and elaborated on the basis of continuing empirical work. The chapters that follow are the starting point, as the contributions to this volume explore the potential and existing tensions associated with the production and consumption of urban tourisms.

References

Ashley C, Boyd C, Goodwin H (2000) Pro-poor tourism: putting poverty at the heart of the tourism agenda. Nat Res Perspect 15:1–6
Ashworth G, Page SJ (2011) Urban tourism research: recent progress and current paradoxes. Tour Manag 32:1–15
Berno T, Bricker K (2015) Sustainable tourism development: the long road from theory to practice. Int J Econ Dev 3:1–18
Blackstock K (2005) A critical look at community based tourism. Community Dev J 40:39–49. doi:10.1093/cdj/bsi005
Bramwell B, Lane B (2010) Sustainable tourism and the evolving roles of government planning. J Sustain Tour 18:1–5. doi:10.1080/09669580903338790
Butler RW (1999) Sustainable tourism: a state of the art review. Tour Geogr 1:7–25. doi:10.1080/14616689908721291
Byrne D (2003) Complexity theory and planning theory: a necessary encounter. Plan Theory 2:171–178
Čamprag N (2016) Museumification of historical centres: the case of Frankfurt Altstadt reconstruction. In: Bellini N, Pasquinelli C (eds) Tourism in the city—towards an integrative agenda on urban tourism. Springer, Heidelberg
Day J (2012) The challenges of sustainable tourism. J Tour Res Hosp 1:1–2
de Roo G, Silva E (2010) A planner's encounter with complexity. Ashgate, Surrey, England
de Roo G, Hillier J, Van Wezemael J (2012) Complexity and planning: assemblages and simulations. Ashgate, Surrey, England
Deffner A, Liouris C (2005) City marketing: a significant planning tool for urban development in a globalised economy. In: 45th congress proceedings of the European Regional Science Association, Amsterdam
Deffner A, Metaxas T (2006) Is city marketing opposed to urban planning? The elaboration of a pilot city marketing plan for the case of Nea Ionia, Magnesia, Greece. In: 46th congress of the European Regional Science Association (ERSA). Volos, pp 1–31
Fainstein SS (2005) Planning theory and the city. J Plan Educ Res 25:121–130. doi:10.1177/0739456X05279275
Farmer P (2004) An anthropology of structural violence. Curr Anthropol 45:305–325
Fava N, Palou Rubio S (2016) From Barcelona: The Pearl of the Mediterranean to Bye Bye Barcelona. Urban movement and tourism management in a Mediterranean city. In: Bellini N, Pasquinelli C (eds) Tourism in the city—towards an integrative agenda on urban tourism. Springer, Heidelberg
Forester J (1989) Planning in the face of power. University of California Press, Berkley
Füller H, Michel B (2014) "Stop Being a Tourist!" new dynamics of urban tourism in Berlin-Kreuzberg. Int J Urban Reg Res 38:1304–1318. doi:10.1111/1468-2427.12124
Goodwin H (2008) Pro-poor tourism: a response. Third World Q 29:869–871. doi:10.1080/01436590802215287
Greene SJ (2003) Staged cities: mega-events, slum clearance, and global capital. Yale Hum Rights Dev LJ 6:161–187
Hardy A, Beeton RJS, Pearson L (2002) Sustainable tourism: an overview of the concept and its position in relation to conceptualisations of tourism. J Sustain Tour 10:475–496. doi:10.1080/09669580208667183
Harrill R (2004) Residents' attitudes toward tourism development: a literature review with implications for tourism planning. J Plan Lit 18:1–16
Harrison D (2008) Pro-poor tourism: a critique. Third World Q 29:851–868. doi:10.1080/01436590802105983
Harvey D (2003) The right to the city. Int J Urban Reg Res 27:939–941
Healey P (1996) The communicative turn in planning theory and its implications for spatial strategy formation. Environ Plan 23:217–234

Healey P (2003) Collaborative planning in perspective. Plan Theor 2:101–123

Innes J (1995) Planning theory's emerging paradigm: communicative action and interactive practice. J Plan Educ Res 14:183–189

Innes JE, Booher DE (2003) Collaborative policymaking: governance through dialogue. In: Hajer M, Wagenaar H (eds) Deliberative policy analysis: understanding governance in the network society. Cambridge University Press, Cambridge, MA, pp 33–59

Innes JE, Booher DE (2010) Planning with complexity: an introduction to collaborative rationality for public policy. Routledge, Oxon

Jamal TB, Getz D (1995) Collaboration theory and community tourism planning. Ann Tour Res 22:186–204. doi:10.1016/0160-7383(94)00067-3

Kavaratzis M (2016) The participatory place branding process for tourism: linking visitors and residents through the city brand. In: Bellini N, Pasquinelli C (eds) Tourism in the city—towards an integrative agenda on urban tourism. Springer, Heidelberg

Lefebvre H (1991) The production of space. Wiley-Blackwell, Oxford

Lefebvre H (2003) The urban revolution. Universit of Minnesota Press, Minneapolis, MN

Lejárraga I, Walkenhorst P (2010) On linkages and leakages: measuring the secondary effects of tourism. Appl Econ Lett 17:417–421. doi:10.1080/13504850701765127

Lew A (2007) Invited commentary: tourism planning and traditional urban planning theory: planners as agents of social change. Leis J Can Assoc Leis Stud High Educ 31:383–392

Maitland R, Newman P (eds) (2009) World tourism cities: developing tourism off the beaten track. Routledge, London

McDonald D (2008) World city syndrome: neoliberalism and inequality in Cape Town. Routledge, New York

Minoia P (2016) Venice reshaped? Tourist gentrification and sense of place. In: Bellini N, Pasquinelli C (eds) Tourism in the city—towards an integrative agenda on urban tourism. Springer, Heidelberg

Miraftab F (2007) Governing post apartheid spatiality: implementing city improvement districts in Cape Town. Antipode 39:602–626. doi:10.1111/j.1467-8330.2007.00543.x

Nkemngu AP (2012) Tourism and hospitality community benefit from tourism : myth or reality a case study of the Soshanguve Township. Tour Hosp 1:1–6. doi:10.4172/2167-0269.1000105

Okazaki E (2008) A community-based tourism model: its conception and use. J Sustain Tour 16:511. doi:10.2167/jost782.0

Ostrom V, Ostrom E (1999) Public goods and public choices. In: McGinnis M (ed) Polycentricity and local public economies. Readings from the workshop in political theory and policy analysis. University of Michigan Press, Ann Arbor, pp 75–105

Parnell S, Pieterse E (2010) The "Right to the City": institutional imperatives of a developmental state. Int J Urban Reg Res 34:146–162

Pasquinelli C (2015) Urban tourism(s): is there a case for a paradigm shift? L'Aquila

Purcell M (2014) Possible worlds: Henri Lefebvre and the right to the city. J Urban Aff 36:141–154. doi:10.1111/juaf.12034

Ritchie B (2008) Contributiong of urban precincts to the urban economy. In: Hayllar B, Griffin T, Edwards D (eds) City spaces tourist places. Elsevier, Oxford, pp 151–177

Rogerson CM (2004) Urban tourism and small tourism enterprise development in Johannesburg: the case of township tourism. GeoJournal 60:249–257

Rogerson CM (2005) Unpacking tourism SMMEs in South Africa: structure, support needs and policy response. Dev South Afr 22:623–642. doi:10.1080/03768350500364224

Rogerson CM (2013) Urban tourism, economic regeneration and inclusion: evidence from South Africa. Local Econ 28:188–202. doi:10.1177/0269094212463789

Rogerson CM, Rogerson JM (2014) Urban tourism destinations in South Africa: divergent trajectories 2001–2012. Urbani izziv 25:S189–S203. doi:10.5379/urbani-izziv-en-2014-25-supplement-014

Sachs I (2004) Inclusive development strategy in an era of globalization. International Labour Office, Geneva

Scheyvens R (2011) Tourism and poverty. Routledge, London

UNEP & WTO (2005) Making tourism more sustainable: a guide for policy makers. UNEP & WTO, Paris

United Nations (2012) World urbanization prospects, The 2011 revision. United Nations, New York

UNWTO (2012) Global report on city tourism. UNWTO, Madrid

Urry J (2005) The complexity turn. Theor Cult Soc 22:1–14

van Niekerk M (2014) Advocating community participation and integrated tourism development planning in local destinations: the case of South Africa. J Destin Mark Manag 3:82–84. doi:10.1016/j.jdmm.2014.02.002

van Vliet W (2002) Cities in a globalizing world: from engines of growth to agents of change. Environ Urban 14:31–40

Watson V (2009) The planned city sweeps the poor away…: Urban planning and 21st century urbanisation. Prog Plann 72:151–193

Watson V (2014) Co-production and collaboration in planning—the difference. Plan Theor Pract 15:62–76

World Travel and Tourism Council (2015) Travel and Tourism in 2015 will grow faster than the global economy. http://www.wttc.org/press-room/press-releases/2015/travel-tourism-in-2015-will-grow-faster-than-the-global-economy/. Accessed 23 Nov 2015

Emerging Technologies and Cultural Tourism: Opportunities for a Cultural Urban Tourism Research Agenda

Chiara Garau

Abstract The aim of this work is to highlight how the 'traditional' approach to cultural tourism should be rethought as part of a broader vision, in which the latest technological devices (smartphones, tablet PCs) and new developments in the 'smart city' paradigm can help in the planning and programming of cultural tourism. To this end, this chapter is organized into three main sections: the first shows how cultural tourism is enhanced today because of new technologies, the second offers a brief overview of how the tourism of cultural heritage has been inserted into the domain of smart tourism and how it is being enhanced today, and the third focuses on opportunities for taking a strategic approach to cultural tourism, in order to go beyond local fragmentary promotions, allowing tourists to perceive all cultural offers for a single destination as unique. Finally, conclusions are drawn, with particular attention given to the construction of specific recommendations for the strategic planning and programming of cultural tourism.

Keywords Cultural tourism • Smart tourism • Smart cities

1 Introduction

Tourism represents a strategic pillar of urban development for its ability to produce income and employment, thereby enhancing the local resources. The role of tourism has increased quickly, not only in cities with their own specific vocation for tourism, but also in cities with less well known resources yet characterized by new and attractive factors, such as the authenticity of the experiences offered (Ferrari and Adamo 2012). However, nowadays the 'authenticity' concept seems controversial and problematic, not so much for the integrity with which the context is maintained, but rather for the attribution of meaning that makes it authentic and unique to the tourists' eyes (Williams and Lew 2014). In a cultural context therefore, how the tourist destination is valued in the tourists' eyes for its ability

C. Garau (✉)
Department of Civil and Environmental Engineering and Architecture (DICAAR), University of Cagliari, via Marengo 2, 09123 Cagliari, Italy
e-mail: cgarau@unica.it

© Springer International Publishing Switzerland 2017   67
N. Bellini, C. Pasquinelli (eds.), *Tourism in the City*,
DOI 10.1007/978-3-319-26877-4_4

to appear authentic and unique becomes important, on the one hand protecting the cultural and architectural heritage, on the other hand, expanding the traditional concept of a museum without isolating the individual buildings from their environment. This is accomplished only through the appropriate integration of the museum buildings, monuments, cultural and social identities, traditions, memories, intangible connections, local peculiarities, and landscapes. These aspects interconnect new and traditional trends, the permanent with the transitory culture, through the reconstruction in the present of social relationships, and of these social relationships in connection to place-based spaces. For this reason, they concern the cultural heritage and identity of a place; not only do they consider places where physical monuments and artworks (buildings) are concentrated, but also the evolution and testimony of the history of the local community (the immaterial aspects of society). From this perspective, cultural heritage appears to be a resource for preserving and enhancing the local context, and also a strategic element that can meet the growing needs of innovation and entrepreneurship (Lazzeretti 2012; Lehman and Wickham 2014).

Global organizations—the International Council on Monuments and Sites (ICOMOS), the United Nations Educational, Scientific and Cultural Organization (UNESCO), and the World Tourism Organization (WTO)—have always shown great interest in the tourism development of cultural heritage, and, over time, have been able to adapt to globalization and to the evolution of new technologies, by responding to new tourist demands, through the innovative techniques of digitization or reconstruction, and through more active and engaging communication strategies to disseminate and better understand cultural heritage.

From this perspective, it is also important not to underestimate the growing convergence of culture and economy in the process of city branding (Zenker and Erfgen 2014). Cities have long understood the importance of promoting themselves through branding, and, over time, practices and different methods of city branding have been improved and refined (see chapter "The Participatory Place Branding Process for Tourism: Linking Visitors and Residents Through the City Brand"). In fact, city branding can increase the value and attractiveness potential of urban images, involves social and political practices, and can rebuild representations/ narrations of urban spaces, particularly in an urban setting with an immaterial and material cultural heritage (Graziano 2014). The 'cultural' objects are interpreted in relation to the personal cognitive space of the tourist; urban spaces acquire and lose their meaning according to 'how' they are perceived, from 'where' they are narrated (official and unofficial channels, i.e. promotion campaigns, news articles, reviews by visitors), and 'how' the city decides to promote itself (see also chapter "Globetrotters and Brands: Cities in an Emerging Communicative Space"). However, according to Vanolo (2015), city representations may appear as selective storytelling, because, at least in the beginning, they collected stories of a small optimistic audience that did not represent the totality of the context of the users involved (Vanolo 2015).

The process of population involvement in cultural heritage has grown gradually over time, causing an evolution of everyday life and the continuous development of the same concept with regard to its cultural heritage; today's entire cultural system is the result of a radical change, in which museum offerings are no longer composed of a single building (the museum), but are a coordinated system of widespread and useable buildings throughout the urban context, on the basis of the user's choices (Garau and Ilardi 2014). Individual buildings appear to be strongly rooted in the urban context, and together propose a tourism cultural offering in which the city as a whole becomes the cultural 'product', which assumes the expositive function.

From this perspective, the main innovations in the field of cultural tourism have included synergies with new communication technology products, through the creation of specific Internet portals, smart cards, fostering cultural heritage, and, the diffusion of mobile tourism applications. The growing invasiveness of the mobile web has been re-drawing virtual aggregation clusters, as well as patterns of interaction between real and virtual domains, allowing the user to be at the core of the cultural tourist offer. The user shares feedback to improve the visitor experience, and sometimes entrusts him/herself to narratives, coming from mobile applications that create more dynamic and 'immersive' relationships between tourists, monuments (cultural products), and urban spaces (Garau and Ilardi 2014).

Therefore, the development of cultural tourism largely depends on (i) the growing awareness of tourists and operators about the cultural, social, and economic relevance of enhancing cultural goods (Silvestrelli 2012), and (ii) the ability to plan and program appropriate strategic policies for training, organizing, and promoting the local cultural heritage, without overshadowing the need to protect it. The first also concerns the expansion of the ubiquitous technologies (namely, emerging technologies able to offer stunning new technical capabilities)—such as Social Media, Quick Response (QR) codes, near-field communications (NFCs), Augmented Reality, Ubiquitous Computing, Cloud Computing, and the Internet of Things (IoT) (Garau 2014; Wang et al. 2016)—and their effects on cultural tourism in the urban context. The processes of city branding that often support pictures circulating globally are also linked to this. For example, over the last few decades, European urban users have represented their city as a 'creative', 'cultural', and 'smart' city, in order to make it a more attractive destination (Vanolo 2015; Lamsfus et al. 2015). The second factor related to the development of cultural tourism refers to the ability to define strategic planning and programming processes, in order to create long-term policies in the tourism industry, taking into account culturally-led targets and creating market opportunities. This also aids the government's ability to recognize the strengths, weaknesses, opportunities, and threats that need to be addressed when improving and enhancing the benefits of the tourism industry.

Thus, the development of cultural tourism must contemplate the integration of a 'strategic set' of factors and initiatives, which, through new technologies and digital services, fosters not only improved performance and the economic attractiveness of the cultural heritage, but also its significant contribution in terms of cohesive policy, identity, and local development. Cultural endowment, understood as a strategic tourist attraction, can therefore provide synergistic opportunities between culture, tourism, and other local resources and services distributed in the urban context, although with an increasing intensity it depends on the ability to create a unique and innovative tourism supply system, regarding different cultural tourism targets. Therefore, a cohesive strategy of local public-private partnerships is fundamental, and, necessarily, has to deal with a 'cultural product' that is increasingly competitive, setting a goal to stimulate the local identity and specificity, as, for example, in emphasizing local identities and specificities, with a tourist and cultural vocation set in the urban context.

Based on these assumptions, this article presents a research agenda that aims to develop the transition from insights and theoretical potentialities to concrete practices and operational applications, a step that has not yet been accomplished in the current literature.

2 Cultural Tourism of Today and New Technologies

From a tourist's perspective, cultural productions become complementary to the tourism experience when the destinations respond to their demands. This complementarity implies the need to develop and maintain a strong network of partnerships among tourism operators, cultural organizations, and institutions at various levels. In this sense, through their rapid evolution, new information technologies and the increasing digitization of cultural resources have made a significant contribution, and innovative models of the management of cultural heritage have been tested. An example is 'Six itineraries to discover Giotto's places in Italy' (http://www. luoghigiottoitalia.it/en/). It provides tourists with the opportunity to choose and build a customized path between six tours scattered across Italy (Padova, Milan, Bologna, Florence, Assisi, and Naples), to discover Giotto. Another example is the mobile application called Tuscany+, in which histories of monuments are narrated, by simply watching and pressing a finger on the screen of a smartphone. In this way, the tourist receives information on monuments, on services offered near a monument (such as restaurants, museums, hotels), and can provide and receive reviews on a monument. This latter is based on bottom-up and community-driven development processes, in which users are able to contribute to the co-creation of the offer, and administrators have access to the tools that can help them in their understanding and interpretation of the demand, in order to differentiate and increase the competitiveness of their territory.

Cultural tourism has therefore had to deal with a new, more dynamic vision of the concept of culture. It is simultaneously the history, the material and immaterial culture, the identity, the *genius loci*, and the peoples' lives. The focus has moved from the informative enrichment of cultural products to the experience of cultural heritage; from physical objects to the visitors; from exceptionality to representativeness—the same community recognizes what for it is more representative (Cerquetti 2015). The centrality of the experience within tourism planning changes significantly: if on one occasion the experience has been the natural result of a trip, now the experience becomes a central issue on which to focus, and in which to invest for place-based redevelopment.

To better understand what results have been achieved in the field of technologies applied to culture, it is necessary to make a small digression to how the technology is placed at the service of cultural tourism. *Informative platforms* can be considered as the first and the simplest tools. They are used to make data (or databases) for the area of interest (information, images, and lists of services present at the destination) accessible. *Connection platforms* offer the possibility of booking or buying some services. However, they are tools for mediation, because the actual transaction then takes place on sites chosen by the user. *Integrated platforms* have allowed further evolution of online platforms. They are, in fact, more complex than the previous ones, in that they use a single integrated platform, common to several companies, for the management of information, booking activities, and direct purchases.

The involvement of local actors is, in this case, intense. They constantly update the information, and manage reservations and purchases generated with it. As a result, tourists are able to view different types of tourist information (such as hotels, modes of transport, and events). A tourist can perform a detailed search by type of service and/or area of interest: he/she can find useful updated information (such as climate information) in real time; he/she can download pictures and audio-video material; and he/she can plan his/her travel route based on the coincidence of different means of transport, and simultaneously provide useful information on how to use public transport to arrive at the tourist destination (as Gronau suggests in chapter "On the Move: Emerging Fields of Transport Research in Urban Tourism", there is a lack of awareness on this issue in today's scientific debate, and among local administrators).

Alongside the birth of more complete and interactive platforms, technology in the tourism sector has led to the testing of smart cards for making payments, and integrating the elements of the offer. Smart cards—real and rechargeable prepaid cards—not only put cultural goods and services online, but collect information on the movements and preferences of tourists, as shown in the project Radio Frequency Identification (*RFID*) *for Festival* realized in Trento. For this project, the municipality of Trento, using RFID technology, has been able to evaluate and analyse the economic impact of this important cultural event, noting the actual consumption behaviour of the participants, and not merely the intentions declared by visitors in the commonly used survey questionnaires (Zeni et al. 2009).

The latest technological developments have created a more dynamic relationship between the visitor and the site's cultural heritage, especially with the museum, and it now seems increasingly less isolated from the reference territory (Garau and Ilardi 2014). The technology is, in fact, more and more detached from the dimensions of the hardware, the physicality of the house, of the museum, or of the building, in general. Solutions for the cultural fruition of both the indoors and outdoors are offered, thanks to (1) 'virtual reconstruction' (that, in a clear manner, allowed the emergence of the links between the single building and its place-based, historical and cultural context); (2) the geolocation of the user; and, (3) the presence of tags, cameras, and sensors for guidance (Garau 2014).

Table 1 Some experimental projects with augmented reality

Project names	Countries	Descriptions
i-MIBAC Voyager	Italy	This app virtually reconstructs the Roman Forum in the age of Constantine, in 3D and in real time, in the display of your smartphone, as you walk inside the archaeological area
Tuscany+	Italy	This app identifies information on museums, accommodation, restaurants, monuments, and reviews, in proximity of the framed and selected point of interest (POI) on the smartphone screen. The POIs offer a map that allows getting directions on how reach them. POIs also have different colours, depending on the category to which they belong
ARCHEOGuide (Augmented Reality-Based Cultural Heritage On-Site Guide)	Greece	This project provides information on the cultural heritage sites of Olympia, using a system based on advanced IT techniques including augmented reality, 3D-visualisation, mobile computing, and multi-modal interaction. Visitors are provided with a see-through Head-Mounted Display (HMD), earphone, and mobile computing equipment
Streetmuseum (Museum of London)	UK	This app is able to recognise the position of a user in London, and overlay historical images of that same place (from 1930 or 1950) on present-day images captured by the user's camera. Each image can be expanded and explored, and it also provides historical commentary
Digital Pen (Cooper Hewitt, Smithsonian Design Museum)	New York	The Digital Pen is a multifunctional pen. Touching its upper end to a symbol on the corresponding panels, you can: (1) 'save' certain works to remember or to share at the end of the visit; (2) draw freehand on any screen available in the museum, in order to have as images the pieces of the collection that have a similar shape at the end of the visit; (3) design patterns, and view them on the walls of the room in which you are modifying the design on the interactive display. At the end of this creative process you can print your project or use it as a background on your smartphone
Smart Glasses (Young Museum)	San Francisco	Smart glasses support augmented reality, and, through a micro projector, allow users to view images and information on the lenses. In addition, these glasses allow sending, receiving, and viewing

(continued)

Table 1 (continued)

Project names	Countries	Descriptions
		information, and they can transmit to the wearer messages via bone conduction. The Young Museum has adopted these glasses as tour guides for the exhibition dedicated to Keith Haring
Smart Glasses for the Exposition of Experience Velazquez (Grand Palais of Paris)	France	With these glasses, tourists can approach a Velazquez painting by viewing projected images on the same theme in their lenses, and hearing in a contextual way an explanatory audio

Such applications are therefore strongly linked with the act of first visiting the place, and then the chosen tourist path and its stops. The transition from personal computers to various mobile communication devices has allowed the development of specific applications for mobility and tourism consultations in the territory, available for everyone. At this turning point, the self-service cutting-edge technologies of augmented reality (AR) play a key role (Chung et al. 2015). Their developments have amply demonstrated how simple cultural fruition is transformed into a dynamic and engaging experience (Table 1).

The user is helped to understand 'how it was' in relation to 'what is there', and he/she can also use its creativity not only to better understand culture and art, but also to improve the experience of visiting and being involved. Today, technologies are focusing on providing adequate cultural offers, modulated on different users' targets. They have improved, trying to concentrate on the philosophy of 'edutainment' and of 'learning by consuming', without losing their historical and scientific references. In other words, technologies have made possible a major cultural shift, one that has led from simple information on the cultural good to the acquisition of culture, in which learning is strongly influenced by direct experience with the cultural good.

3   Smart Tourism in the Cultural Heritage Field

Before discussing the relationship between smart tourism and cultural heritage, it is important to define the 'smart city' concept, and how it has been contemplated in the field of tourism. The literature seems rather discordant in framing the smart city concept. Some authors define it as a paradigm (Kunzmann 2014); others as a fashionable trend of the moment (Lu et al. 2015); others simply as a label (Caragliu et al. 2011). In contemporary communities, mobility, economy, governance, environment, living, and people are the six pillars identified by Giffinger et al. (2007) as being crucial for a smart city. The essence of ICT is to support different activities aimed at (1) improving the citizens' quality of life, (2) supporting new forms of collaboration and value creation, and (3) simultaneously enhancing the innovation, entrepreneurship, and competitiveness of the city (Ferrara 2015).

According to Boes et al. (2015) "the smart city concept can be seen as an 'organic whole' and as a linked system where the people, visitors and citizens alike, are the most important aspect. Still, the Smart City concept does not stand on its own, and covers a variety of industries, including the tourism industry" (Boes et al. 2015, p. 393).

Especially in Europe, the technologizing of the tourism sector and the spread in recent years of the smart city model appear to be two interrelated processes, which work together in shaping the profile of what we call smart tourism. In particular, the different forms of technologies are the main drivers of change in the tourism industry, and their focus is on supporting enriched tourism experiences, using already existing data combined and processed in new ways (Gretzel et al. 2015). The term smart tourism can identify, therefore, both forms of technological evolution in tourism, and new projects within the smart destinations. These latter explicitly apply smart cities' principles to urban contexts, considering "residents and also tourists in their efforts to support mobility, resource availability and allocation, sustainability and quality of life/visits" (Gretzel et al. 2015, p. 180). In other words, the destinations become smart when they integrate smart cities' principles in developing urban tourism, without making some urban areas where the intensity of tourism is highest inaccessible to residents (about access see chapter "Mind the Gap: Reconceptualising Inclusive Development in Support of Integrated Urban Planning and Tourism Development"), or where the technological equipment is not consistent with the social context.

From this perspective, cultural heritage appears to be a strategic factor for operators and urban planners, as they can leverage the enhancement of cultural DNA that has shaped the look of the city, making it visible and easily accessible to a wider audience.

Therefore, the smart concept associated with urban cultural tourism attracts at least two interconnected meanings. On the one hand, the first meaning calls attention to the close link between this form of tourism and the broader competitive configuration that European cities are required to take, in relation not only to the European directives, but also in relation to the evolution of the competitive stresses due to globalization. On the other hand, the second meaning leads the city to innovate its dynamics in a smart and flexible way. This smartness implies a strategic planning and a synergistic programming of the same cultural tourism, between culture, heritage, tourism, marketing, transport, accommodation, policy-making, human capital, and ICTs. Flexibility considers "forming innovative governance styles as a common European opportunity: each city has scope in adopting its own governance approach according to the local context, opportunities, cultural tourism development's specifics, and interrelations with other actors and levels of decision-making" (Paskaleva-Shapira and Besson 2006, p. 64).

The importance of the role that urban cultural tourism assumes inside and outside cities, and the global scenario in which urban cultural tourism is situated, requires a renewed focus on the research and adoption of models and tools of intervention, that, following the paradigm of smart cities, takes into account, on the one hand, the systemic nature of the phenomenon and its complexity, and, on the other hand, the global dimension of the phenomenon correlated with its local consequences in terms of economic, environmental, and social sustainability. The interactions of all the above factors lead then to seeking a strategic coordination between the bottom-up and top-down mechanisms of governance in the planning of urban cultural tourism. In addition, its governance is reflected both at the local level, and at the international level, despite the fact that policies of cultural tourism traditionally are influenced by the high number of stakeholders and by their small size. For these reasons, the next section analyses European initiatives that are intended to boost a cultural tourism research agenda.

4 Opportunities for a Strategic Cultural Tourism Research Agenda from a Smart City Perspective

The system of cultural tourism involves a number of issues widely discussed by experts in the field, including the interference of (local and national) governments in culture, the vision of residents not always being in line with that of the tourists, and differences objectively existing in European countries that make it difficult to implement common and shared cultural planning in the European framework. Despite these factors, the potentialities that technology has to offer the cultural tourism industry remain undisputed.

As mentioned in the previous paragraphs, technologies allow the intertwining of cultural content among various tangible and intangible goods, through continuous hypertext and multimedia links. This allows the user to freely determine his/her cultural path. When planning and designing a multimedia cultural circuit, it is essential to try to catalyse the most positive consequences while attempting to counterbalance the negative effects. That is to say, the definition of a cultural circuit works on spatial relationships, even in terms of the inclusion or exclusion of spaces, places, and people. This triggers a necessary spatial reorganization of access to the territories, cultural heritage, and the city, also in relation to tourism. One of the main risks may be, for example, a spread of 'cultural polarity' that remains so— such as 'leopard spots' in the territory—if they are not planned and interconnected within the logic of a wider and place-based project.

On 26 April 2010, the European Commission adopted a recommendation asking the Member States to define a common strategic research agenda that could identify research needs and objectives for the medium and long-term, regarding the conservation and use of cultural heritage in the context of global changes. To this end, Italy began to coordinate the Joint Programming Initiative (JPI) called 'Cultural Heritage and Global Change: A New Challenge for Europe' in 2011 (http://www.jpi-culturalheritage.eu/). A report entitled *Strategic Research Agenda* was published in June 2014. In this report, Member States that are part of this Joint

Programming Initiative[1] try to define strategic visions, goals, and shared operational measures for research on cultural heritage. This is intended to introduce the necessary innovations in both products and processes that will make the sustainable preservation of Europe's immense cultural heritage possible. The priorities that have been identified are "(1) developing a reflective society; (2) connecting people to heritage; (3) creating knowledge; [and] (4) safeguarding the cultural heritage resource" (Van Balen 2014, p. 8).

The strategic agenda is an excellent opportunity, on the one hand, to give new inputs to European programs, and, on the other hand, to strengthen the system of research and management of cultural heritage. At the same time, the focus is also on strengthening the local business systems and the production chain associated with the technical and scientific cultural world, for the realization of prototypes and operational and experimental solutions generated by research.

Obviously, better management of the entire cultural sector at the European level would have a significant impact on tourism, and could change different national targets of knowledge, protection, enhancement, and the enjoyment of cultural heritage[2] is well known for its quality, quantity, and distribution (Iaffaldano 2013).

The next step in the creation of this research agenda could be a greater strategic focus on cultural tourism, which could be achieved, for example, by providing answers to the following questions: (1) How can we move from theoretical concepts to practical and operational choices, after having identified appropriate tourism governance models? (2) How can we promote an often-fragmented cultural heritage? (3) How can we identify and increase the number of enterprises active in the cultural tourism sector? (4) What other sectors could help to promote the activation of good policies in the cultural tourism sector? (5) Finally, how can we 'create a smart system' that will foster the conditions needed to encourage dialogue between public and private interests, following the smart city model?

A place does not necessarily appear attractive just because it is endowed with cultural resources of a very high quality. The attractiveness of a location is determined by how its cultural patrimony is inserted into an active process that moves from knowledge to valorisation—through preservation and restoration—thereby having a positive and large-scale effect on its cultural and economic development.

If every cultural experience is unique, then a landscape, city, monument, or museum is not replaceable by any other; on the other hand, from the perspective of

---

[1]Eighteen Member States and seven other States are included in the initiative as Observers.

[2]Italy has the broadest cultural heritage worldwide. It occupies first place on the World Heritage List with its fifty recognized sites (one more than last year, see www.unesco.org). It owns nearly half of the national territory, subject to protections imposed by the Code of Cultural Heritage and Landscape (Legislative Decree No. 42 on 22 January 2004), and cultural goods (archaeological, architectural and museum) surveyed by the Ministry of Cultural Heritage and Activities (MIBAC) exceed 100,000 units (Rapporto Bes 2013 pp. 186–187).

a scale of priorities in a globalized world—where a steady growth of tourism and leisure is expected—a close connection between the cultural and economic sector is necessary, in order to be competitive, inclusive, and to substantiate a sustainable development.

5 Conclusions

This chapter focused on how important European-level joint action is for the management of cultural heritage, whose impacts are inevitably also reflected in the tourism sector. Not only public institutions, but also the dense network of private institutions and cultural institutions may have, for various reasons, a strategic vision better adapted to the local and socio-cultural context. From this perspective, the interaction between smart tourism and cultural heritage is important for an effective strategic agenda. In fact, the relationship between innovation and cultural heritage appears inevitably destined to become even more successful, especially if that relationship will lead to solutions that meet, in a simple and accessible way, the emerging needs of knowledge, in-depth 'guidance' for understanding the history and stories of the places, and also a potential factor of place-based development (Migliori et al. 2015).

However, the innovation to which the author refers is considered both from a technological and social point of view, overcoming the purely technicist vision that characterises the smartness. In other words, an effective cultural urban tourism research agenda, seen under the smart cities' model, cannot innovate exclusively through technology. The technology is in fact a tool, and its evolution and spread can have not only positive but also negative consequences, when, for instance, technology is not calibrated with the local social context in which it is applied, or when information of the technological medium is not calibrated with the user (i.e. there is too much information and this confuses him/her, or it is too limited and does not give him/her enough information). One of the main roles of the strategic agenda is precisely to plan for, and at least anticipate possible problems in its use and in its management.

There is awareness that the strategic agenda cannot achieve great results in a short time, with regard to a number of the structural problems inherent in every state. This is so, because their resolution depends on the dynamics articulated, and joint responsibility at different levels of decision making.

However, the strategic agenda for cultural tourism can make a significant contribution to an organization in pursuit of sustainable operating strategies, while simultaneously promoting the territory, culture, and tourism.

Based on these assumptions, specific policy-making recommendations such as the following deserve consideration:

- Improve communication and the promotion of cultural heritage and culture in general, to encourage tourism. The key is to bring the cultural heritage close to users, and to involve the tourists and local community in the promotion.
- Link the cultural heritage with local daily life. The problem is less one of 'introducing' the tourist destination than it is the transmission of the complete contents of the tourist destination to the user (through immersive and interactive technologies), and including the cultural goods in a virtual and actual context.
- Support the capacity of European cultural sectors to operate transnationally, through the promotion of networks, and the circulation of artworks and operators in the cultural sector.
- Develop models of public-private cooperation.
- Strengthen the financial capacity of the cultural sectors.

These recommendations certainly seem very difficult to achieve, if one goes directly to the conclusive outcomes of the specific goals outlined above. Some important steps can lead to change, starting from a local level. For instance, thinking in a multifaceted and organic way and including the various stakeholders will create advantages for both cultural heritage policy, and for tourism development.

Moreover, the arguments discussed in this article have reinforced the idea that a territory can have a vast potential of resources. Because it is recognized as a 'cultural product', it has to have a sufficient tourism infrastructure, supported by its citizens, governments, enterprises, research centres, universities, and institutions. It is also important that cultural operators adapt and create a system with the existing cultural offer, without engendering a conflict of interest (between existing economic resources and the demands of citizens and tourists).

These recommendations are nevertheless strategies that primarily allow planners to ask research questions regarding the responsibilities of the local authorities. In fact, they are closest to the territory, to the cultural heritage, and to the citizens and their expectations. For this reason, they are best positioned to identify needs, and to cooperate in implementing strategies that support economic and cultural revitalization.

Acknowledgments This study is supported by the MIUR (Ministry of Education, Universities and Research, Italy) through a project entitled *Governing tHe smart city: a gOvernance-centred approach to SmarT urbanism—GHOST* (Project code:RBSI14FDPF; CUP Code: F22I15000070008) financed with the SIR (Scientific Independence of young Researchers) programme. Any opinions, findings and conclusions or recommendations expressed in this material are those of the authors and do not necessarily reflect the views of the MIUR.

References

Boes K, Buhalis D, Inversini A (2015) Conceptualising smart tourism destination dimensions. In: Tussyadiah I, Inversini A (eds) Information and communication technologies in tourism 2015. Springer, New York, pp 391–403

Caragliu A, Del Bo C, Nijkamp P (2011) Smart cities in Europe. J Urban Technol 18(2):65–82

Cerquetti M (2015) Dal materiale e all'immateriale Verso un approccio sostenibile alla gestione nel contesto glocale. Il Capitale Cult Stud Value CultHeritage 2:247–269

Chung N, Han H, Joun Y (2015) Tourists' intention to visit destination: role of augmented reality applications for heritage site. Comput Hum Behav 50:588–599. doi:10.1016/j.chb.2015.02.068

Ferrara R (2015) The smart city and the green economy in Europe: a critical approach. Energies 8 (6):4724–4734

Ferrari C, Adamo GE (2012) Autenticità e risorse locali come attrattive turistiche: il caso della Calabria. Sinergie 66(05):79–113

Garau C (2014) Smart paths for advanced management of cultural heritage. Reg Stud Reg Sci 1 (1):286–293

Garau C, Ilardi E (2014) The 'non-places' meet the 'places': virtual tours on smartphones for the enhancement of cultural heritage. J Urban Technol 21(1):79–91

Giffinger R et al (2007) Smart cities: ranking of European medium-sized cities. Vienna University of Technology, Vienna

Graziano T (2014) Boosting innovation and development? The Italian smart tourism, a critical perspective. Eur Assoc Geogr 5(4):6–18

Gretzel U, Sigala M, Xiang Z, Koo C (2015) Smart tourism: foundations and developments. Electron Mark 25(3):179–188

Iaffaldano N (2013) Il' museo diffuso' e le risorse immateriali quali determinanti della competitività di una destinazione turistica culturale. Esperienze d'impresa 2:43–67

Kunzmann KR (2014) Smart cities: a new paradigm of urban development. Crios 4(1):9–20

Lamsfus C, Martín D, Alzua-Sorzabal A, Torres-Manzanera E (2015) Smart tourism destinations: an extended conception of smart cities focusing on human mobility. In: Tussyadiah I, Inversini A (eds) Information and communication technologies in tourism 2015. Springer, New York, pp 363–375

Lazzeretti L (2012) Cluster creativi per i beni culturali. Aestimum 19:90

Lehman K, Wickham MD (2014) Marketing orientation and activities in the arts-marketing context: introducing a visual artists' marketing trajectory model. J Mark Manage 30 (7/8):664–696

Lu D, Tian Y, Liu VY, Zhang Y (2015) The performance of the smart cities in China—a comparative study by means of self-organizing maps and social networks analysis. Sustainability 7(6):7604–7621

Migliori S et al (2015) ICT per il cultural heritage: possibili interazioni con SITAR. Archeol Calcolatori 7:83–88

Paskaleva-Shapira K, Besson E (2006) Integrated management of urban cultural tourism in European small and mid-sized cities: a governance approach. In: Brebbia CA, Pineda FD (eds) Sustainable tourism II. WIT Press, Wessex, pp 59–69

Rapporto Bes 2013 Il benessere equo e sostenibile in Italia. Cnel e Istat (2013) http://www.istat.it/it/files/2013/03/bes_2013.pdf. Accessed 17 Jun 2016

Silvestrelli P (2012) Entrepreneurial innovation for cultural tourism development. Impresa Progetto-Electron J Manage 2:1–18

Van Balen K (2014) Creating the strategic research agenda. In: JPI cultural heritage coordination unit, strategic research agenda. http://www.jpi-culturalheritage.eu/wpcontent/uploads/SRA-2014-06.pdf. Accessed 17 Jun 2016

Vanolo A (2015) The image of the creative city, eight years later: Turin, urban branding and the economic crisis taboo. Cities 46:1–7

Wang X, Li XR, Zhen F, Zhang J (2016) How smart is your tourist attraction? Measuring tourist preferences of smart tourism attractions via a FCEM-AHP and IPA approach. Tour Manag 54:309–320

Williams S, Lew AA (2014) Tourism geography: critical understandings of place, space and experience, 3rd edn. Routledge, New York

Zeni N, Kiyavitskaya N, Barbera S, Oztaysi B, Mich L (2009) RFID-based action tracking for measuring the impact of cultural events on tourism. In: Höpken W, Gretzel U, Law R (eds) Information and communication technologies in tourism 2009. Springer, New York, pp 223–235

Zenker S, Erfgen SZC (2014) Let them do the work: a participatory place branding approach. J Place Manage Dev 7(3):225–234

On The Move: Emerging Fields of Transport Research in Urban Tourism

Werner Gronau

Abstract Urban centres and metropolitan regions have become increasingly prominent amongst tourist destination choice, at the same time they are in many cases characterised by huge transport and accessibility problems in the form of traffic congestions, packed public transport systems and overcrowded pedestrian zones. Therefore the contribution aims at a broader understanding of the interrelation of tourism and transport studies, when it comes to dealing with urban tourism development. The article will address sociological aspects such as the blurring nature of tourists and residents, as well as psychological issues in relation to the role of identity and motivations when it comes to transport behaviour, and last but not least technical changes and innovations such as intermodality and the growing role of e-ticketing systems. Resulting in a brief research agenda on transport related topics in the context of urban tourism studies.

Keywords Public transport • Urban tourism • Integrated ticketing • Tourism behaviour

1 Introduction

The chapter is looking at a basic understanding of the role of transportation in the context of a constantly growing urban tourism. Therefore it provides a brief overview on existing but also arising research fields related to the field of transport and urban tourism. The contribution builds upon a brief review of the existing research agenda while aiming at identifying future research fields, based upon existing practices in the field.

Tourism is on the rise for several decades now and continues to grow, as outlined by the UNWTO World Tourism Barometer, reporting that international tourist arrivals are expected to increase from 898 million arrivals to almost 1.6 billion by the year 2020. While growing, tourism also becomes more and more heterogeneous, displayed for example by a constant increase of geographical diversity, but

W. Gronau (✉)
University of Applied Sciences Stralsund, Stralsund, Germany
e-mail: werner.gronau@fh-stralsund.de

© Springer International Publishing Switzerland 2017
N. Bellini, C. Pasquinelli (eds.), *Tourism in the City*,
DOI 10.1007/978-3-319-26877-4_5

also by new types of destinations. In fact, "many cities in Europe have actively promoted the tourist industry in recent decades. Some examples are Barcelona (Spain), Berlin (Germany) and Amsterdam (The Netherlands), where the number of tourist visits has increased spectacularly over this period." (Albalate et al. 2008, p. 1).

Due to the fact that cities and especially European cities have become hotspots of national as well as international tourism arrivals, they have shifted into the focus of public as well as academic debate. While local governments are increasingly engaged in the creation and maintenance of attractions and accommodation infrastructure or in marketing and promotion of local tourism products, issues related to mobility and accessibility management for tourists have not been focused on.

Despite the disregard of officials, scholars such as Halsall (1992) have outlined the essential role of transport for tourism. According to the author, transport is an essential part of tourist recreational behaviour and, additionally, it advances the achievement of recreation objectives while representing a recreational activity itself. The dramatic changes in transport framework conditions for tourism exemplified by continuous decrease in relative travel costs and distances, resulted in a clear increase in recreational travel (Schiefelbusch et al. 2007; Chapmann 2007; Gronau 2010). The increasing use of cars for tourism has especially increased real travel distances (Duval 2007; Page 2005). Furthermore, the importance of transport networks and infrastructure in tourism development has been elaborated already in past (Prideaux 2000). However, Lumsdon and Page (2004) warn that academic specialists in the areas of transport and tourism have largely remained compartmentalised. Specifically, little attention has been given to competition between tourists and 'hosts' for public transport (Hall 1999), although today's congested cities with often inadequate public transport networks have to accommodate additional demand through tourists. In fact, tourists may end up competing with residents for limited urban resources, a situation that, on the one hand may cause significant negative local externalities, but also on the other hand might negatively influence the urban tourism experience. Therefore attention has to be given, to the internal as well as external accessibility of destinations, in order to assure a long-term sustainable development of urban tourism. Until today, the majority of cities does not seem to address the issue of a rising transport demand through increasing tourism arrivals in the least. Neither transport infrastructure nor transport supply e.g. public transport clearly considers tourist needs. Beside the lacking awareness amongst public stakeholders, there is also a clear lack of research on how tourists use and perceive existing urban transport systems or how existing public transport systems could meet expectations of tourists in a better way. While public transport use in tourism has been extensively studied since 2000 (Gronau and Kagermeier 2007; Guiver et al. 2008; Dickinson et al. 2013; Le-Klähn and Hall 2014) and several case studies from different geographical and cultural contexts exist, there is still a research gap in the field of transport use within destinations, and more specifically in urban destinations, since the majority of studies concentrated on transport to and from destinations (Scott et al. 2012). Therefore there is a strong need for studying destination internal transportation requirements in general and public transport use more specifically, in order to provide an insight on how public transport is used at a destination level, and it what way it should be developed in order to become an even more popular transportation mode for tourists.

2   Towards an Agenda of Transport Studies in Urban Tourism

2.1   Transport Behaviour in Urban Tourism: Impacts of Tourism Identity

As Larsen put it, "tourism is traditionally treated as an escape from everyday life and tourism theory is concerned with extraordinary places. Tourism and everyday life are conceptualized as belonging to different ontological worlds" (2008, p. 21). Referring to Hall (2014), this approach to understand tourism as something outside the ordinary life of both tourists and destination residents has meant that tourism researchers have paid insufficient attention to the "new mobilities paradigm" (NMP) described by Sheller and Urry (2006). Urry's approach stressing the increasing blurring of traditional segmentation such as locals and tourists or hosts and visitors and also other theoretic concepts of related disciplines, have only to a minor degree been integrated in the research agenda on tourism and transportation. Research in the field is still to a large extent concentrating on one or the other group, instead of accepting the decreasing relevance of such categories. Beside the blurring of classical categories of customers, also the ongoing diversification of societies and the related individualisation of consumption seems kind of neglected in transport studies, which is, especially in the case of urban tourism, a real challenge, as urban tourism is strongly affiliated with individual life-styles and ways of consumption. Therefore questions, i.e. to as what role individual life-styles play in transportation needs and the transport behaviour of tourists within urban destinations, have to be put forward. Hibbert for example outlines the fact, "that for many people, holidays play an important part in who they are. Memories are not always just stored away, they can shape the future self of the traveller" (2013, p. 18). Desforges (2000) suggests that understanding identity can give insight into tourism consumption because, by understanding the person and their needs and desires, it could be possible to predict their future travel patterns. If the tourism identity process of an individual could be understood, it might be possible to influence desired identities and consequently travel behaviour, as well as transport choice. Beside such psychological reflections, sociological influences have also been introduced into the debate of the interrelation of tourism and transport. Bourdieu's concept of life-styles has been taken up and paired with specific attitudes towards transportation. This integration of sociological aspects within in the field of—traditionally rather engineering and natural science orientated—transport research has opened up new perspectives. In the way Bourdieu emphasises the connection between lifestyle and what he calls the 'field' and the 'habitus', he questions the traditionally rational choice driven approaches within transport studies and yet creates an interesting link to the state-of-the-art discussion on cultural capital and individualisation of consumption in the field of urban tourism. Transport choice of tourists in an urban context might therefore more likely be interpreted as part of tourism lifestyles rather than a rational choice driven activity, consequently research focused on identifying motivations for using public transport in the leisure and tourism context and identifying possible target groups for such supply. "The modern traveller is described as a hybrid, multi-optional and multi-mobile human being, whose behaviour oscillates between rational aspects such as cost-awareness and emotional aspects like pleasure", as Barr et al. stated (2009, p. 104). Elaborating on the work of Lanzendorf (2001), Götz and Seltmann (2005) and Gronau (2005), the utilization of lifestyle-based mobility groups is seen as an appropriate way to better understand and meet the expectations of today's heterogeneous transport behaviour in the leisure and tourism context. Those concepts rooted in Bourdieu's critic of rational choice models, suggest a more individualised analysis of transport choice resulting in a more adequate integration of individual *habitus* in the analysis of transport behaviour. Instead of categorising individuals simply based on their ability to drive a car, the individual *habitus* towards driving a car is also considered, where lifestyle-based mobility groups are applied. Although such concepts exist for quite a while they have not yet been applied to the specific situation of urban tourism, although the individual *habitus* and related individualised life-styles have been identified as a promising way to deal with consumers in the field of urban tourism.

2.2   Transport Behaviour in Urban Tourism: Impacts of Technological and Product Innovations from the Transport Sector

The concept of sustainable mobility has clearly impacted political decisions in recent years, especially on a European level. After opening up the European transport market, the European Union is now focusing on introducing a more sustainable transport system. The cornerstone of this approach is to improve the competitiveness of environmentally friendly modes, to create integrated transport networks, as well as to create fair conditions of competition between modes. The basic approaches towards this goal include technological solutions and more sustainable behaviour. The European Union stresses the key role of Intelligent Transport Systems (ITS) in ensuring sustainable mobility, for example through their capacity to promote public transport alternatives (European Commission 2008).

Integrated ticketing services are one element of ITS. For over a decade, integrated ticketing has been on the agenda of EU transport policy. Since 2001 all major

European transport policy documents propose integrated ticketing as a high priority measure to help increase passenger intermodality and the attractiveness of public transport and thus encouraging travellers to use more environmental friendly modes of transport (European Commission 2011). These measures result in the fact that within Europe most countries have installed integrated-ticketing systems, at least in their capital cities. To what extent such systems may have also impacted tourist behaviour has unfortunately not yet been studied. One might think of increased tourist mobility or an extended catchment area of tourist activities through improved access to different transport modes by utilising one single ticket. There-fore it might be a promising approach to evaluate studies from the transport sector on their relevance for the tourism sector. Existing strategies from the commuter sector such as integrated ticketing, e-ticketing or intermodal transport offers might impact tourism-related transport demand as well. This debate is also reflected in recent activities of the European Parliament, such as the STOA-Workshop on "Integrated e-ticketing for public transport and touristic sites" in late 2013. Based upon the EU-funded project of the same name aiming at a review of existing systems of urban transport ticketing and their level of integration into tourist sites, experts discussed possible impacts of integrated systems on the various stakeholders, amongst them of course also tourism service providers. Such initia-tives show the increasing interest, also from political stakeholders, for the vast field of transport behaviour, urban context and tourism.

Figure 1 therefore is to be understood as a first attempt towards a systematic overview on possible strategies towards a stakeholder, as well as a spatial-integration process in the field of integrated ticketing for public transport and tourist sites. Once the term integrated ticketing is used one has to refer to the type

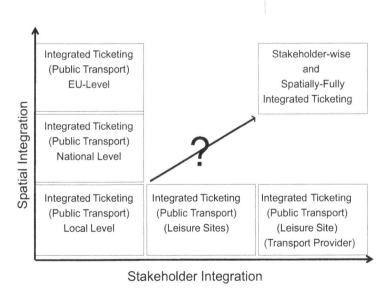

Fig. 1 Integrations levels of ticketing systems

of integration; actually there are two main approaches towards integrated ticketing. One is aiming at spatial integration of one stakeholder group namely transport providers. Resulting in tariff and ticketing systems allowing customers to travel within a given region with several different transport providers by using one single ticket. Depending on the spatial integration level one might therefore have an integrated ticket only within a specific city or region or as in the case of the Swiss *Generalabonemment* for all public transport providers in the national context.

The second integration process refers to different stakeholder groups within one spatial context. Examples might be the various "city-cards" in urban destinations, integrating public transport supply and access to various attractions within the given destination. In contrast to the spatial integration not one stakeholder group is integrated on various spatial levels but various stakeholder groups are integrated at one spatial level. As outlined in the figure above, one might consider a combination of spatial and stakeholder integration when it comes to integrated ticketing systems. Combining spatial as well as stakeholder integration in future might also be a promising approach for the field of urban tourism, especially if one considers that the constant increase of integrated ticketing systems throughout the EU, especially in metropolitan regions, parallels with a steady increase of tourism demand in such regions. Hence the question arises to what extent these trends have an impact on tourism development or vice versa.

Related to the field of integrated ticketing, but in many cases still treated independently, one can refer to the research field of so-called "combined tickets". This ticket innovation was related to the development of large-scale leisure facilities in urban areas at the turn of the millennium, offering visitors of such attractions a special entrance ticket including a discounted public transport ride to the specific attraction. Similar to today's increase in urban tourism, metropolitan regions hosting such large-scale-leisure facilities saw a clear increase of leisure travellers and excursionists with a high share of private transportation already in the past. A study performed in Switzerland resulted in a private car share of 83 %. A further study dealing with modal-split at multiplex cinemas resulted in a share of 82 % (Freitag and Kagermeier 2002). At the time this trend was seen as major threat for the quality of life in urban regions, but also as a threat for the attraction operators, therefore the concept of "combined tickets" was introduced. Such tickets offering attraction visitors a discounted public transport ride have since those days become increasingly popular in metropolitan areas of Germany, for example. Despite the constantly increasing amount of such tickets and the long period they are already on the market, only a few isolated case studies (Gronau 2010; Kagermeier 2002) evaluated the impacts of such products on the mode choice of visitors at the specific site. Therefore no clear conclusion on the effectiveness of such activities can be drawn yet.

Beside the aforementioned fields of already existing and well-established transport products impacting mobility in urban tourism, one has to also include innovative and emerging transport options in an upcoming research agenda. Latest product innovations in the urban context include for example cycle hiring stations, trishawsupply, and new inner-urban car-sharing systems (e.g. "car2go" and "drive now"). These new forms of supply, but also their impact towards a more sustainable transport in the urban tourism context might be a field to look at. Beside the environmental impact, there is also the dimension of a more positive urban-tourist experience, when using such innovative modes; in other words the impact of new forms of transport supply in the urban context on the tourist experience might be topical, as well.

This section on mobility and technology might not be complete without referring to the field of smart cities or smart tourism. The ongoing digitalization of course leaves its traces in the field of urban transport supply, intelligent trip planner systems supporting tourists in their transport mode as well as route choice, providing onsite-information for customers supporting their navigation process through unknown urban places offering convenient e-ticketing-options. On the other hand, such systems provide urban transport suppliers with a wide range of information on transport behaviour of users, including sites visited, common itineraries or preferred ticket options. This information of course might even be considered a sensitive one and the willingness of consumers to provide this information is still questioned in many cases.

2.3   Locals Versus Tourists? Negotiating Identities and Transport Needs

Considering the latest debate on rising resistance of locals towards an overwhelming urban tourism development, as in the in case of Venice (Minoia 2016), Prague (Dumbrovská 2016) or maybe the most prominent case of Barcelona (Fava and Palou Rubio 2016), one might even consider tourists as a threat to urban communities. In this case, especially the field of transportation needs might be a relevant one. While addressing the issue we might come back to Urry's "New Mobilities Paradigm" mentioned earlier in this chapter. By Urry questioning traditional categories such as tourists and locals, one might even question the common separation of local and tourist related demand in urban transport. The blurred tourist–resident categories revealed in the study of Moscardo et al. (2013) suggest that there may be a need for new models of citizenship, which recognise different patterns of obligations and responsibilities for these new categories of population. While Coles (2008) has discussed the ways in which new tourism mobilities in Europe are challenging ideas about the rights and freedoms of citizens, most discussions in the tourism literature either ignore the responsibilities of tourists or present them as a variation of responsible consumers, with a broad global responsibility to be more sustainable (cf. Verbeek and Mommaas 2008). To date, very little tourism research has considered the specific responsibilities and obligations that tourists have towards the communities they visit. Responsible citizenship also brings rights and privileges (Coles 2008) and there has been no explicit discussion in the tourism literature of the responsibilities that destination communities have towards tourists. Hannam argues that an important research topic in tourism is that of "how tourists negotiate their identities and their notions of citizenship in the so-called contact zones at the interstices of different countries where notions of citizenship can become highly contested and multiple identities become increasingly fluid" (2009, p. 108). According to Hannam and Knox, "moving between places physically or virtually can be a source of status and power for many tourists over their life course" (2010, p. 165), therefore the question arises to what extent tourists are willing to take responsibility for destinations they travel to or are willing to negotiate their needs and wants with local communities. In this framework Hannam and Roy outline the opportunity for the field of tourism studies related to Sheller and Urry (2006): "The mobilities paradigma arguably allows us to place travel and tourism at the centre of social and cultural life rather than at the margins." (2009, p. 92).

Even beyond the debate on blurred tourist-resident categories or a possible conflict between these groups, one might consider the opportunities related to tourists as new target groups of public transport supply in the urban context. To what extent, for example might the demand generated by tourists complement instead of compete with existing local demand? Could tourists rather be understood as additional users instead of competitors on scarce public transport resources? Preliminary studies on the "iAmsterdam city card" have shown a rather complementary character of tourist transport behaviour in relation to local use. The main peak times generated through commuter needs are not times of heavy use by tourists. It is right the other way round; tourists tend to use the system mainly in-between the existing peak hours and therefore could be considered as useful additional demand to back up occupancy within times of lower demand (Dominicius 2013). Considering those results further research into mobility patterns of tourists within urban areas, might lay the foundation for specific mobility management measures for tourists through local authorities and transport providers, solving the possible conflict on the scare public transport resources (Hall 1999), in case it really exists. Therefore more detailed analysis including also other urban destinations might give interesting perspectives on this ongoing debate on conflicting needs of tourists and locals.

3 Conclusion

To conclude this chapter, a clear deficit of transport studies in the field of urban tourism has to be stated. This seems quite surprising, keeping in mind that urban tourism in particular faces the need for managing site accessibility. Hence one should perceive the adaption of existing transportation systems to tourist requirements as a highly relevant field. To summarise the identified possible fields of

Table 1 Aspects of transportation in urban tourism research

Aspects	Concepts/trends	Issue	Research field
Transportation and tourism identity	Urry (New mobility paradigm)	Blurring of classical segmentations	Renegotiation of tourists perception of their responsibility for destinations
	Bourdieu (lifestyle concept)	Individual attitudes complement rational choice	New understanding of transport behaviour based on *habitus*
Innovations in transport technology	Intelligent transportation systems (ITS)	Increased accessibility of transportation systems	Change of mobility patterns of tourists due to ITS
	New mobility services ("uber", bike stations, etc.)	Blurring of traditional transport services	Impacts of new transport services on transport behaviour and tourist experience
Tourists versus locals	Hall (locals versus tourists)	Conflict on scare transport resources	Identification of existing fields of possible competition and specific framework conditions

future research Table 1 provides a brief overview.

Following the structure of the chapter the table refers to three main aspects:

• Impacts of main sociological approaches such as Urry or Bourdieu on the field of transportation in urban tourism. Possible fields might be a new understanding of transport behaviour of tourists within urban destinations or the changing attitude of tourists towards their responsibility for visited destinations.
• Impacts of innovations in the transport sector, such as ITS-technologies or new mobility services. Increased accessibility of systems through supporting IT-services, a clear tendency towards more individualised services and diversification of transport service providers will impact transport behaviour as well as mobility patterns of tourists.
• Last but not least possible conflicts evolving from an increased transport demand of tourists in the urban context might be topical. To what extent do various user groups compete on transport supply? What concepts might be implemented to secure accessibility of all users to existing systems?

For all the mentioned fields unfortunately a clear lack of empirical research has to be stated. Beside those fields also various subfields such as the attitude of existing target groups in urban tourism towards different transport options, the impact of a variety of transport alternatives on the visitor experience or the management of attraction sites in relation to their specific accessibility offer can be identified. When considering literature from the transport sector it becomes obvious that there is a huge amount of possible research fields on transport in the urban tourism context. Major trends in the transport sector such as the concept of sustainability, intermodality, integrated ticketing or combined ticketing, have a clear reference to the tourism field, but are rarely reflected in tourism studies. Additionally sociological approaches such as the concept of tourism identities might be a promising field to interrelate transport and urban tourism studies, as well. Finally yet importantly, the emerging field of growing conflicts between local well-being and tourism development could be an interesting arena for transport-related research.

References

Albalate D, Bel G (2008) Tourism and urban public transport: holding demand pressure under supply constraints. Tour Manag 31(3):425–433

Barr S, Shaw G, Coles T, Prillwitz J (2009) A holiday is a holiday: practicing sustainability, home and away. J Transp Geogr 18(3):474–481

Chapmann L (2007) Transport and climate change: a review. J Transp Geogr 15(5):354–367

Coles T (2008) Telling tales of tourism: mobility, media and citizenship in the 2004 EU enlargement. In: Burns PM, Novelli M (eds) Tourism and mobilities: local–global connections. CABI, Wallingford, pp 65–80

Desforges L (2000) Traveling the world-identity and travel biography. Ann Tour Res 27(4):926–945

Dickinson JE, Filimonau V, Cherrett T, Davies N, Norgate S, Speed C, Winstanley C (2013) Understanding temporal rhythms and travel behaviour at destinations: potential ways to achieve more sustainable travel. J Sustain Tour 21(7):1070–1090

Dominicius H (2013) The City Card the best visitor tool. Presentation at the STOA-Workshop on integrated e-ticketing for public transport and touristic sites, Brussels, 16 Oct 2013

Dumbrovská V (2016) Urban tourism development in Prague: from tourist mecca to tourist ghetto. In: Bellini N, Pasquinelli C (eds) Tourism in the city—towards an integrative agenda on urban tourism. Springer, Heidelberg

Duval DT (2007) Tourism and transport—modes, networks and flows. Channel View Publications, Clevedon

European Commission (2008) Action plan for the deployment of intelligent transport systems in Europe (Action Plan No. COM(2008) 886 final). Brussels

European Commission (2011) White paper. Roadmap to a single European transport area—towards a competitive and resource efficient transport system (White Paper No. COM(2011) 144 final). Brussels

Fava N, Palou Rubio S (2016) From Barcelona: The pearl of the Mediterranean to bye bye barcelona. Urban movement and tourism management in a Mediterranean city. In: Bellini N, Pasquinelli C (eds) Tourism in the city—towards an integrative agenda on urban tourism. Springer, Heidelberg

Freitag E, Kagermeier A (2002) Multiplex-Kinos als neues Angebotselement im Freizeitmarkt. In: Steinecke A (ed) Tourismusforschung in Nordrhein-Westfalen: Ergebnisse—Projekte—Perspektiven. Mannheim, MetaGis

Götz K, Seltmann G (2005) Urlaubs- und Reisestile—ein Zielgruppenmodell für nachhaltige Tourismusangebote. ISOE-Studientexte, Nr. 12. Frankfurt am Main

Gronau W (2005) Freizeitmobilität und Freizeitstile. Ein praxisorientierter Ansatz zur Modellierung des Verkehrsmittelwahlverhaltens an Freizeitgroßeinrichtungen. Metagis, Mannheim

Gronau W (2010) The number of 'non-captives' as an indicator of the quality of public transport supply: an alternative quality measure in the context of mobility-management. Int J World Rev Intermodal Transp Res 3(1/2):91–102

Gronau W, Kagermeier A (2007) Key factors for successful leisure and tourism public transport provision. J Transp Geogr 15(2):127–135

Guiver J, Lumsdon L, Weston R (2008) Traffic reduction at visitor attractions: the case of Hadrian's Wall. J Transp Geogr 16(2):142–150

Hall DR (1999) Conceptualising tourism transport: inequality and externality issues. J Transp Geogr 7(3):181–188

Hall CM (2014) Tourism and mobility. Paper presented at CAUTHE conference, Brisbane, 10–13 Feb 2014

Halsall D (1992) Transport for tourism and recreation. In: Hoyle BS, Knowles RD (eds) Modern transport geography. Belhaven, London, pp 155–177

Hannam K (2009) The end of tourism? Nomadology and the mobilities paradigm. In: Tribe J (ed) Philosophical issues in tourism. Channel View Publications, Clevedon, pp 101–113

Hannam K, Knox D (2010) Understanding tourism a critical introduction. Sage, London

Hibbert JF, Dickinson JE, Gössling S, Curtin S (2013) Identity and tourism mobility: an exploration of the attitude–behaviour gap. J Sustain Tour 21(7):999–1016

Kagermeier A (2002) Folgen konsumorientierter Freizeitgroßeinrichtungen für Freizeitmobilität und Freizeitverhalten. In: Gather M, Kagermeier A (eds) Freizeitmobilität – Hintergründe, Probleme, Perspektiven. Mannheim, MetaGis

Lanzendorf M (2001) Freizeitmobilität. Unterwegs in Sachen sozial ökologischer. Mobilitätsforschung, Trier

Larsen J (2008) De-exoticizing tourist travel: everyday life and sociality on the move. Leisure Stud 27(1):21–34

Le-Klähn D-T, Hall M (2014) Tourist use of public transport at destinations—a review. Curr Issues Tour. doi:10.1080/13683500.2014.948812

Lumsdon L, Page SJ (eds) (2004) Tourism and transport: issues and agenda for the new millennium. Elsevier, Oxford, p 180

Minoia P (2016) Venice reshaped? Tourist gentrification and sense of place. In: Bellini N, Pasquinelli C (eds) Tourism in the city—towards an integrative agenda on urban tourism. Springer, Heidelberg

Moscardo G, Konovalov E, Murphy L, McGehee N (2013) Mobilities, community well-being and sustainable tourism. J Sustain Tour 21(4):532–556

Page S (2005) Transport and tourism. Pearson, Harlow

Prideaux B (2000) The role of the transport system in destination development. Tour Manag 21 (1):53–63

Schiefelbusch M, Jain A, Schafer T, Muller D (2007) Transport and tourism: roadmap to integrated planning developing and assessing integrated travel chains. J Transp Geogr 15 (2):94–103

Scott D, Gössling S, Hall CM (2012) Tourism and climate change: impacts, adaptation and mitigation. Routledge, Abingdon

Sheller M, Urry J (2006) The new mobilities paradigm. Environ Plann A 38:207–226

Verbeek DHP, Mommaas JT (2008) Transitions to sustainable tourism mobility: the social practices approach. J Sustain Tour 16(6):629–644

The Participatory Place Branding Process for Tourism: Linking Visitors and Residents Through the City Brand

Mihalis Kavaratzis

Abstract This chapter contributes towards a holistic understanding of city brand formation centring on the goal of harmonising residents' views and internal perspectives of the city with urban tourism goals and externally oriented branding efforts. The main premise is that in order to capture the ways in which place brands actually operate and form, it is necessary to capture and enable negotiations of meaning and change. This is particularly the case in the contemporary tourism environment with its emphasis on interactive and co-created destination brands. The chapter's main proposition is the participatory place branding process, which incorporates a novel understanding of the formation of the place brand and how this might be influenced by destinations. The interrelated stages of this process arc suggested as a valuable tool in destination branding efforts to develop co-created destination brands that incorporate external and internal meanings of the locality while addressing market challenges.

Keywords Place branding • Destination branding • Participatory brands • Place brands

1 Introduction: We Are all 'Yelpers' Now!

Online reviews are very influential in the travel and tourism industry (Munar 2011). In preparation for a trip or when booking a hotel or restaurant, we all increasingly turn to online review websites rather than official websites and even more to user-generated content websites such as Wikitravel and Tripadvisor, travel community sites such as Wayn or Virtualtourist, and the user reviews in booking websites such as Booking.com or Trivago.com. While word-of-mouth has always been influential, the digital technologies available today have made it easier, faster and much more desirable (Oliveira and Panyik 2015) to post comments that can have a significant impact. The contemporary tendency towards reading and posting online reviews and commentary on social media has led to the development of devoted websites

M. Kavaratzis (✉)
University of Leicester School of Management, University Road, LE1 7RH Leicester, UK
e-mail: m.kavaratzis@le.ac.uk

© Springer International Publishing Switzerland 2017   93
N. Bellini, C. Pasquinelli (eds.), *Tourism in the City*,
DOI 10.1007/978-3-319-26877-4_6

and mobile Applications where people can review and 'complain' about hospitality services (a successful such website is Yelp.com), about other people, such as their roommates or the staff at the local post office (e.g. the discontinued application 'Peeple') or even—rather worryingly—engage in anonymous gossiping with strangers about a common acquaintance (e.g. the mobile application 'The Know'). These practices bring with them novel challenges for business owners in the travel and hospitality industry and for destination managers and marketers. While it seems self-evident that a positive review should be embraced, what is the 'right' way to respond to negative comments and reviews?

In August 2014 the news featured a report about the Union Street Guest House in Hudson, New York, which decided to take an aggressive stance: it warned customers signing a wedding party contract—and put a clause in the contract itself—that they would have to pay a fine of $500 for every negative review their guests posted online (Economist 2014). Expectedly, this had the exact opposite effect than what the hotel intended causing "a tsunami of fake reviews, equal parts humorous and hectoring" (Elwood 2015). As CNN reported:

> Hundreds of people took to Yelp.com on Monday to complain about the policy and write mostly fake, eviscerating reviews of the property. At one point Monday there were more than 700 reviews on Yelp, but the company had deleted many reviews by Monday afternoon because they didn't reflect 'first-hand experiences', according to Yelp. 'Trying to prevent your customers from talking about their experiences is bad policy and, in this case, likely unenforceable anyway,' Yelp said.

In another incident also reported in the Economist (2014),

> a property in Tennessee filed a $10 m lawsuit after being branded on TripAdvisor the 'dirtiest hotel in America'. It inevitably backfired. The hotel lost its case and millions of people who had never heard of its grubby reputation then read all about it in the media.

The above examples might be of individual hotels but they speak of the whole tourism sector. Destination brand managers find themselves in similar positions when dealing with the challenges they face. In general, it seems to be better and more effective in our times of online comments for destination branding to engage with stakeholders in a dialogue, to ask and listen to them, to treat them as part of the business/destination experience and as allies in improving it. This does not only refer to external audiences such as visitors but, of course, extends to local residents who might be considered the most important stakeholders of all. However, is this understanding embedded in the way city and destination brands are conceptualised and in the suggested processes of developing the place's brand? What is the right way to embrace user-created content online and "strategically integrate the content they generate into the whole destination branding effort" (Oliveira and Panyik 2015, p. 53)? Before addressing this important question, it is helpful to discuss place and destination branding.

2   Place Branding: A Brief Overview

One of the factors that have made place branding popular is the significance of the image in place management and particularly destination management. Image formulation and image communication have been highlighted in the place marketing literature as crucial elements of a place marketing approach (e.g. Kavaratzis 2004). The image is important because places—whether places of residence, work, leisure, tourism and so on—can be understood through their images or through peoples' perceptions of them. Places are constituted by a plethora of images and representations (Hubbard and Hall 1998) and people encounter and understand places through perceptions that they process to form in their minds an image (Creswell 2004). In this sense, the object of place marketing (and perhaps of all place management) can be usefully considered to be the place's image. The fact that place marketing is based on representations enables us to tackle not the place itself but its meaning in a symbolic and ideological context (Bailly 1994). Also Mommaas (2002) suggests that, to a great extent, it is the image that needs to be planned and not the place itself. This brings all place management closer to the realm of branding, which deals with such image-based and intangible elements (Kornberger 2010). Therefore, and despite challenges related to understanding image formation and its effects on the brand, image becomes a crucial element for place branding efforts.

Another factor of place branding's popularity is the accumulated experience of applying branding-related measures. Much of the development of place branding came as a result of the practice itself. Cities, for example, started promoting themselves for various reasons in various places and eras (Ward 1998) and this has meant that the accumulated experience and achievements kept bringing more and more attention to the practice and methods of place branding, slowly refining and expanding it. A third significant factor is that branding is a very well established and popular activity within general product and corporate marketing and it has proven very effective in the commercial world. The success of all major commercial brands speaks for itself and has triggered the interest of local authorities and tourism planners to look favourably into applying branding principles in their operations (Kavaratzis 2004). However, the differences between places and more mainstream commercial organisations are significant and branding cannot be applied in the same way (Hankinson 2010). The import of approaches, terminologies and methods from the commercial world to the world of place development is not straightforward (Braun 2012). This explains the fact that place branding has been approached from a variety of perspectives and with different aims and intentions.

Several perspectives can be identified in the literature and include the *country of origin* approach (e.g. Papadopoulos and Heslop 2002; Papadopoulos 2004) focusing on the role of the place in product branding; the *public diplomacy* approach (e.g. van Ham 2008; Sevin 2013) examining the relationships between the place's authorities and external stakeholders in order to enhance the place's reputation; the *analytical underpinnings* approach examining the theoretical foundations of place branding (Kavaratzis 2004; Govers and Go 2009) and how this might be put into practice (e.g. Anholt 2007; Braun 2012); the *identity-based* approach (Mayes 2008; Kalandides 2011; Kavaratzis and Hatch 2013) that deals with the way individuals attribute meanings to the place brand. Amongst these, we need to pay particular attention to the *destination branding* approach (Morgan et al. 2002; Blain et al. 2005).

The branding of tourism destinations has gained considerable popularity (e.g. Ritchie and Ritchie 1998; Hankinson 2004; Blain et al. 2005; Gartner 2014; Campelo et al. 2014). A fundamental explanation of its growth is that, as Morgan et al. put it, "the battle for customers in tomorrow's destination marketplace will be fought not over prices but over hearts and minds" (2002, p. 12). Based on definitions of general branding, destination branding is often thought to be a way of communicating a destination's special identity and uniqueness by differentiating its character and offer from that of competing destinations (Qu et al. 2011). Ritchie and Ritchie defined the destination brand as "a name, symbol, logo, word mark or other graphic that identifies and differentiates the destination" (1998, p. 45) also encapsulating a memorable travel experience uniquely associated with the particular destination (Ritchie and Ritchie 1998; Blain et al. 2005). The general aim of destination branding is thought to be to contribute towards a positive destination image (Qu et al. 2011) by consistently reinforcing a mix of brand elements (Cai 2002). Clarke (2000) usefully adds that the destination brand also provides a focus for the integration of producer efforts to work towards the same outcomes, meaning that the brand can be used as a common goal for several activities of various actors in the tourism industry to collectively aim at. This is an important aspect of place branding in general as the brand might function as a strategic guidance for the wider marketing and management efforts stemming from the general branding proposition that brands operate as catalysts for corporate strategies (e.g. Hatch and Schultz 2002). Obviously, this idea starts going beyond the definition of the brand as a name or logo and it is something that will be examined again later in this chapter.

A significant point of criticism of both general place branding and, particularly, destination branding practice (Munar 2011; Oliveira and Panyik 2015) is that their principal expression has been the design of new logos, the development of new slogans and a general focus on visual design. More often than not, the call for the development of a place brand means the designing a new logo (Govers 2013) or an advertising campaign (Ashworth and Kavaratzis 2009). This is an unfortunate situation as it limits the potential of place and destination branding to contribute to place development and it misses out on the contemporary understandings of how place brands form and what they are about. For instance, as Munar (2011) found out, tourists do not use the formal brand elements when they talk about a destination and their experience, particularly in the online environment; "elements such as taglines, slogans or logos are virtually non-existent as part of Tourism Created Content' (Munar 2011, p. 302). The study by Munar (2011) identified several factors that change the locus of control of destination brand creation and found that tourists create three types of content in the digital sphere: narrative, visual and audio. None of the instances investigated in these three types used any form of the official brand elements such the logo or the slogan. For example, almost 4000 reviews of France and Greece in 'IgoUgo' contained zero results of the national brands (Munar 2011). The author gives two explanations for this: (a) that Tourism Created Content is embedded in a culture of anti-commercialism and (b) that today's branding campaigns do not reach their internet-based targeted groups. This chapter adds a third potential explanation, namely the fact that destination branding is not powerful due to these brand elements but due to its potential to provide a platform for information and experience exchange that plays a very significant role in the creation of the brand. Munar goes on to propose a rethinking of destination branding, which has now become "to a larger extent, the expression of the interaction and participation of the end-users" (2011, p. 251), something that this chapter takes further.

3   Place Brands: Looking Back to Move Forwards

It is useful to take a look back at the basics of place branding and the place brand. This 'looking back' allows for detailed consideration of three particular realisations that are important for the argument of this chapter. These realisations are rather old insights but they have obviously not become established parts of the place and destination branding collective understanding. Thus, although they seem basic and rather self-evident, they are useful in order to move towards a refined understanding of the place branding process. This refined understanding relates to the significance of stakeholders in the contemporary tourism environment.

The first of these realisations is the widely acknowledged idea that a place's brand is created in peoples' minds as they encounter all aspects of a place. The place brand is based on what a place 'has', 'does' and 'shows' but it is constructed by each individual separately as it refers to a mental process that occurs in the mind of individual people. It is individuals that know and use various associations with the destination, the combination of which creates the brand. Naturally, different individuals will construct the brand differently as they will have different levels of knowledge, understanding, interest, affection and so on. A very simple and self-evident—although often overlooked—implication of this is that the brand is not constructed in newspapers' pages, billboards or TV commercials; and it is certainly not created in the City Hall's meeting rooms or the consultant's office. Collectively such elements and many more, such as landscape elements, organisational structures, events and other activities and the general infrastructure of the place (Kavaratzis 2004) send messages about the place. These messages become the raw material, which is then processed by each of us resulting in the construction of the place brand. This is where a geographical and spatial understanding (e.g. Lefebvre 1991) is helpful as it indicates the place-making elements

(Kalandides 2011) that will be used for the construction of the place brand (Kavaratzis and Kalandides 2015).

The second realisation relates to the concept of value and brand co-creation (e.g. Gregory 2007; Hatch and Schultz 2010; Warnaby 2009). A place brand has many co-creators who co-construct it through a process that can only be conceptualised as a dialogue (Kavaratzis and Hatch 2013). Through the exchange of ideas, experiences, emotions, opinions and messages these co-creators constantly re-create the place brand. Local authorities, politicians and consultants are simply equal participants in this process. That is why a 'full stakeholders perspective' (Hatch and Schultz 2010) is useful here and indeed the significance of stakeholders and particularly residents has been highlighted (e.g. Bennet and Savani 2003; Houghton and Stevens 2010; Braun et al. 2013). In this sense, it is useful for place branding to conceptualise cities (and destinations) as systems of stakeholder relationships rather than other definitions of place (such as geo-physical or administrative). A 'blurring' of all sorts of boundaries can be observed, much in the way that leads cultural geographers to understand places as open and fluid (Massey 1994; Ingold 2011). The boundaries of tourism destinations cannot be thought to be the physical or administrative boundaries that tourism planners are responsible for. Rather, they need to be thought of as the boundaries set by various stakeholders (including residents and visitors) as they interact and—in their interactions—define what the destination actually is. Therefore, the place brand also needs to follow this constant re-definition of the destination according to stakeholders' relationships.

The third realisation relates to the paradox that can be observed when branding is wrongly treated as a promotional campaign: the brand is called to simplify the place, to give it a clear meaning, to attach to it an easily defined and understood identity that will appeal to everyone. It is called to promote the place as a single entity, as a whole that is identifiable and coherent. Places, however, do not subject themselves to such simplifications (Creswell 2004; Govers and Go 2009; Kalandides 2011). Places do not have a single identity neither a single image (Ren and Blichfeldt 2011; Hjortegraad-Hansen 2010). Places do not even have a clear function as they are simultaneously places of residence, work, visit, leisure, entrepreneurship, financial investment, social interaction, social activism, emotional attachment and many more. In other words, places have multiple meanings and are much 'messier' than expected—fortunately for all of us as citizens but perhaps unfortunately for those of us who desire an easily applicable—perhaps magical—recipe for place branding success.

4 Towards Participatory Branding

The above three realisations logically lead away from the emphasis on 'signs and logos' that we have seen in the definition of destination brands mentioned above. Instead, they point to an emphasis on the role of all stakeholders in place branding. It becomes rather obvious that the brand is not constructed in the logo or other promotional devices but rather in a system of interactions that allow the co-creation of its meaning. Socio-cultural approaches to tourism destinations (e.g. Saraniemi and Kylänen 2011) are useful here in order to understand their complexity and dynamic nature. All places and their brands can be thought to be constructed through social interactions (Kavaratzis and Kalandides 2015) between stakeholders. Particularly for destination brands, these stakeholders are varied (tourism authorities, the tourism and hospitality industry, other forms of governance bodies, relevant sectors such as retail or transportation etc.) and, if the socio-cultural nature of destinations is considered, they include both tourists and residents.

Regarding tourists, an increase of their significance can be observed in relevant literature and this has meant that "the tourist experience today is fully understood as a personal experience in which the person is the main actor" (Goytia Prat and de la Rica Aspiunza 2012, p. 18). In this sense, the tourist experience is formed in an environment that allows all interconnected stakeholders to interact and create their own meanings of their experience. In this environment, "experience is a continuous interactive process of doing and undergoing, of action and reflection, from cause to consequence, that provides meaning to the individual" (Boswijk et al. 2005, p. 2). This 'search for meaning' that we can observe in visitors' motivation and behaviour, particularly in urban tourism, leads to much closer links and more intense interactions with the local community than in the past. Several manifestations of this combine into a higher degree of involvement of local populations in the provision of the tourist experience. This extends beyond the acknowledged significance of locals in destination promotion, their role in the evaluation of the destination brand and their potential as destination 'brand ambassadors' (Braun et al. 2013). Several trends accentuate the role played by locals before, during and after the actual visit. Such trends include the social media frenzy that we have seen in the introduction and extend to the exchange of advice or sharing of place 'stories' by locals via Social Media, which highlights their role in brand 'co-creation'. As Oliveira and Panyik conclude, "the digital domain has emphasised the co-creational process of territorial brands in general and, at the same time, made participation in this process more freely available and more desirable" (2015, p. 69). The chapter "Globetrotters and Brands: Cities in an Emerging Communicative Space" also discusses social media as unique and vital platforms to monitor and communicate with target audiences and, thus, co-create destination brands. In particular, Sevin in his chapter will conclude that social media platforms are useful for monitoring reputation, for creating content and for engaging with target audiences. In this environment, destination branding becomes much more communicative than in the past and the destination brand cannot be considered anymore to be limited to the traditional definition of a symbol, name or logo.

'Sharing economy'-based activities are also important, such as accommodation in private houses (e.g. Airbnb; 'couchsurfing'), in-house dining (where non-professional local cooks prepare and serve in their homes locally-inspired meals) or guided tours by locals who are not professional guides but can show the 'authentic' destination. This changes the destination offer and challenges established understandings of how destination brands form and might be influenced. The example of Airbnb.com is illustrative of some of the impacts that the sharing economy has on destinations. As Turner comments:

> the growth and mainstream adoption of home sharing is leading to fundamental changes in how people travel and experience destinations. These trends are resulting in increased travel, increased spending and an engagement with different parts of the city than travellers have typically visited. [...] Airbnb hosts [...] stay longer and spend more on local businesses (2015, p. 20).

Areas of the city that have traditionally not received the benefits of tourism (such as direct income to local businesses or increased attention from local authorities) are more likely to be part of these benefits as, for instance, "42 % of guest daytime spending remains in the neighbourhoods in which they stay" (Turner 2015). Home sharing allows hosts to benefit significantly in terms of additional income and they use this additional income to pay for everyday essential expenses such as rent, bills or groceries and it helps them to stay in their houses (Turner 2015). Importantly, in terms of community development, it can be argued that home sharing, and, in general the involvement of non-professional locals in tourism provision, allows hosts to come closer to their own community and strengthens knowledge, understanding and appreciation of the identity of the area. In fact, "52 % of hosts say that hosting has positively impacted the way they interact with their community" (Turner 2015).

Naturally, such a major trend within tourism cannot be considered only in positive terms and indeed several aspects of these trends require analysis, clarification and a detailed examination of their consequences. For instance, the authenticity of the tours, dining or other services offered by non-professional locals can be questioned. Or the fact that new areas of the city are now also becoming tourist sites when visitors stay in them can be seen as a negative development as well. On the one hand, one can wonder how long it might take before more traditional tourism businesses open in these areas as well and whether this might be a welcome development. On the other hand, the fact that tourists can now be seen 'everywhere', is something that not all residents are happy or comfortable with. Figure 1 exemplifies this with a sign found in one of Barcelona's less 'touristic' district in 2014. These are tensions that neither tourism planning nor destination branding can afford to ignore as they impact so heavily on the destination and its meaning and there is a need to link the two better together, something that this chapter attempts to contribute to. This is especially necessary as significant challenges emerge to various tourism stakeholders and several actors of the tourism industry have reacted negatively to these trends. Hoteliers are expectedly against platforms of private accommodation such as Airbnb as they lose business and are forced to alter their own offering. Taxi drivers across many countries have demonstrated against platforms such as Uber (which allows private cars to offer transportation services). Professional tourism guides are lobbying for regulations against the tours offered by non-professional guides. These reactions are understandable but there are two crucial questions that need to be asked. First, responding hastily with 'punishing' measures might lead to situations similar to the ones described in the introduction

Fig. 1 A sign illustrating the tensions between residents and tourists. *Source*: the author

and have the opposite effect. Secondly, the role of tourism planners and local authorities comes into question as it might be approached from different angles. On the one hand, the voices that call for fines or strict regulations arguably aim at protecting the interests of established tourism industry participants and not necessarily of the destination as a whole and its future. On the other hand, tourism planning has the responsibility to facilitate the development of tourism in the contemporary environment and, for that, it is necessary to work towards bringing tourism stakeholders closer together. Arguably, the way forward is not to work *against* these trends attempting to 'stop' them by regulating in the opposite directions. Rather, there is a need to work *with* these trends and integrate them in tourism planning by listening to all interested parties and regulating accordingly. This is a goal that the participatory place branding process described below might help to achieve.

5   The Participatory Place Branding Process

All insights and challenges discussed above make place branding a complicated process that only vaguely resembles the branding process described and applied in the commercial world. They point to the urgent need for a turn towards a more

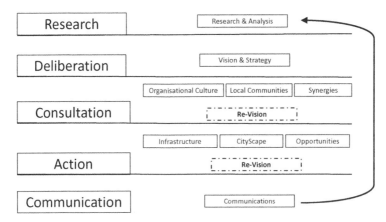

Fig. 2 The participatory place branding process. *Source*: adapted from Kavaratzis and Hatch 2013

inclusive and participatory type of place brands and a place branding process that considers, embraces, facilitates and encourages interaction and fluidity leading to stakeholder engagement. The cumulative experience of place branding practice and the slow progress of relevant theory have developed the know-how for a refined appreciation of place branding so that it can fulfil its role as a place development tool. In an effort to contribute by summarizing and synthesizing the progress made in the field under the light of the developments, practices and ideas discussed above, this chapter suggests a process of place branding implementation that consists of the five interrelated stages of the participatory branding process (Fig. 2).

The first stage is *Research*, which includes extensive investigation of the place's resources and the current and potential perceptions (image or reputation) of the place by internal and external audiences utilizing quantitative and qualitative techniques that help reveal the essence of the place. The second stage is *Deliberation*, in which the core group of stakeholders responsible for the place branding process (local authorities, tourism offices, directly involved sectors, consultants and experts) discuss and draft a proposition for a strategic vision of the future. The third stage is *Consultation*, which consists of extensive discussions with local communities in order to refine the vision and strategy as well as the seeking of synergies and partnerships with sectors and other places that might be mutually beneficial. The fourth stage is *Action*, which consists of measures improving the place's infrastructure, regeneration initiatives, landscape interventions and the opportunities it offers to all audiences for residence, leisure, work, education, investment and quality of life. The final stage is *Communication*, which wraps up all of the above and aims at making all interventions, place features and opportunities known to the wider public.

The process outlined here intends to describe the full complexity of place branding, which stems to a great extent from the need to simultaneously address the needs of different economic sectors, different stakeholder groups and different audiences. In a destination management sense, it is important to keep the process linked to tourism planning. This is possible in several ways. First, the participatory branding process provides space and opportunities for incorporating different interests. If the process is followed, the voices of people who have not been traditionally able to influence tourism planning can be heard, including those affected by the trends discussed above. The stages of research and consultation are especially important here. Secondly, the process allows for officials in different capacities to work together, such as tourism offices, investment agencies, economic development departments, heritage offices, public relations departments and so on. This is very helpful in avoiding the fragmentation of efforts that is currently evident. Following the process allows better planning of common activities and better coordination of separate activities for each step. The stage of seeking out synergies is of particular importance in this sense. Thirdly, the process can be used not only for the development of a general destination brand but also for managing smaller-scale projects. All tourism planning projects affect the destination brand and vice versa. If the process is followed, it is more likely that people will get more engaged and involved in the projects and therefore the whole effort will become more effective.

It is essential to underline that the process is not meant to be linear where one step follows the previous in time or significance. On the contrary, the steps are overlapping and linked and they take place simultaneously. It is also important to note that a co-creational view of the place brand implies that the vision for the place needs to be re-visited at regular intervals in order to cater for changes in the external environment and to account for the effects of the branding process itself as these will demonstrate themselves in the physical and social mosaic of the place. Furthermore, all stages of the process and all activities included are actual branding activities. The process does not imply that research should take place before the start of a branding programme but, rather, that research is in itself a branding activity (i.e. an activity that sends vital messages about the place's brand). In this sense, 'research' projects become initial 'consultation' projects. Therefore, research extends beyond perception and image studies or benchmarking that are commonly asked for in place branding project briefs. The research stage does not necessarily aim at identifying a single identity of the place or a 'unique selling proposition'. Rather, it aims at capturing the plurality of the destination and its brand. Kavaratzis and Kalandides (2015) for example examine the case of Bogota Colombia describing how research using thematic workshops has been instrumental in developing the place branding strategy itself.

6   Place Brands, Tourism and the Local Community

Oliveira and Panyik (2015) suggest that co-created destination brands will be the future's success stories and this chapter argues that the participatory place branding process can be a very helpful tool in that direction as it provides strategic guidance for the brand's co-creation. It particularly captures the way in which place branding becomes a strategic activity that involves all stakeholders or, in line with Pasquinelli (2014), how city branding is a process of collective strategy making. The main conceptual implication of the line of thinking presented here for tourism destination planning is that the place brand is best considered a platform that brings together the destination, its internal stakeholders and its external audiences. To put it simply, like Airbnb, the place brand needs to be thought of as a platform that links visitors' and local communities' experiences and meanings. The participatory place branding process capitalises on this idea and makes it a central element of the efforts of tourism marketers. It is particularly interesting to discuss the implications for the way in which the local community is conceptualised and treated in destination branding. In the participatory destination branding approach, locals are treated as (a) informants (in the Research and Deliberation stages), (b), controllers and legitimators (in the Consultation stage), (c) main beneficiaries (in the Action stage) and (d) target audience (in the Communication stage).

The main practical implication of participatory branding is that the destination branding process, which is very commonly separate to the wider place branding process, needs to be tightly linked to the wider process that constructs the place brand. Therefore, coordination is necessary. The cooperation of tourism marketing offices and other departments that are responsible for place branding is essential although frequently lacking. This is also crucial because the link between locals and visitors means that all activities (even promotion) are addressing both audiences simultaneously, so separation is neither effective nor desirable. Even if there are activities with a clear orientation towards outsiders, such as an advertising campaign, the locals are the ones who will have to 'enact' and realise whatever promise is made by the campaign.

The participatory approach is a promising development for destination branding but there is significant ground to be covered in order to refine and clarify it. On the one hand, there is clearly a need for more research on the ways in which stakeholders engage in destination brand co-creation and on how they perceive this engagement. This research will assist in refining and clarifying the conceptual basis of participatory place branding. On the other hand, the practical challenges of the participatory approach are significant and need to be studied in detail. The use of case studies of places that have used such approaches is necessary and the development of innovative methods and tools that capture the online engagement in greater accuracy. This will assist in providing destinations with practical explanations of the reasons to invest in participatory destination branding.

The main advantage of the participatory approach is that the locals benefit more from the development of the place brand, in the sense that the brand incorporates and highlights issues and areas that have not been beneficiaries of place branding up until now. The place brand 'comes closer' to the residents because it is not seen as imposed from above (the authorities) or from the outside (some highly paid consultant) but based on the reality of the place as this is lived by the place's residents and experienced by its visitors. This is very important as it leads to the feeling of brand ownership by locals and tourists. A brand developed through the participatory process has significantly higher chances than a traditionally developed brand to be 'owned' by its end users. Locals and visitors are much more likely to share the feeling of ownership and participation and it is what lacks when the participatory nature of place branding is ignored. If this is considered and if the participatory place branding process is followed, there is a lot that place branding can do to help places realise their potential for development. If place branding continues to be treated merely as a promotional tool, then there is very little it can do.

References

Anholt S (2007) Competitive identity, the new brand management for countries, regions and cities. Palgrave-McMillan, Basingstoke

Ashworth GJ, Kavaratzis M (2009) Beyond the logo: brand management for cities. J Brand Manage 16(8):520–531

Bailly AS (1994) Urban representations: the imaginary in the service of the economy. In: Ave G, Corsico F (eds) Marketing Urbano international conference. Torino Incontra, Turin

Bennett R, Savani S (2003) The rebranding of city places: an international comparative investigation. Int Public Manage Rev 4(2):70–87

Blain C, Levy SE, Ritchie JB (2005) Destination branding: insights and practices from destination management organizations. J Travel Res 43(4):328–338

Boswijk A, Thijssen JPT, Peelen E (2005) A new perspective on the experience economy: meaningful experiences. Pearson Education, Amsterdam

Braun E (2012) Putting city branding into practice. J Brand Manage 19(2):257–267

Braun E, Kavaratzis M, Zenker S (2013) My city—my brand: the role of residents in place branding. J Place Manage Dev 6(1):18–28

Cai L (2002) Cooperative branding for rural destinations. Ann Tour Res 29(3):720–742

Campelo A, Aitken R, Thyne M, Gnoth J (2014) Sense of place: the importance for destination branding. J Travel Res 53(2):154–166

Clarke J (2000) Tourism brands: an exploratory study of the brands box model. J Vacat Mark 6 (4):329–345

Creswell T (2004) Place: a short introduction. Blackwell, London

Economist (2014) Bad hotel reviews, 5 Aug 2014. http://www.economist.com/blogs/gulliver/2014/08/bad-hotel-reviews

Elwood M (2015) The Yelp effect and why we love to leave online reviews. Conde Nast Traveller, 25 Oct 2015. http://www.cntraveler.com/stories/2015-10-29/the-yelp-effect-why-we-love-to-leave-online-reviews

Gartner W (2014) Brand equity in a tourism destination. Place Brand Public Dipl 10(2):108–116

Govers R (2013) Why place branding is not about logos and slogans. Place Brand Public Dipl 9 (20):71–75

Govers R, Go F (2009) Place branding: virtual and physical identities, glocal, imagined and experienced. Palgrave-Macmillan, Basingstoke

Goytia Prat A, de la Rica AM (2012) Personal experience tourism: a postmodern understanding. In: Sharpley R, Stone PR (eds) Contemporary tourist experience. Routledge, Oxon

Gregory A (2007) Involving stakeholders in developing corporate brands: the communication dimension. J Mark Manage 23(1/2):59–73

Hankinson G (2004) Relational network brands: towards a conceptual model of place brands. J Vacat Mark 10(2):109–121

Hankinson G (2010) Place branding theory: a cross- domain literature review from a marketing perspective. In: Ashworth GJ, Kavaratzis M (eds) Towards effective place brand management. Edward Elgar, Cheltenham, pp 15–35

Hatch MJ, Schultz M (2002) The dynamics of organisational identity. Hum Relat 55(8):989–1018

Hatch MJ, Schultz M (2010) Toward a theory of brand co-creation with implications for brand governance. J Brand Manage 17(8):590–604

Hjortegraad-Hansen R (2010) The narrative nature of place branding. Place Brand Pubic Dipl 6 (3):268–279

Houghton JP, Stevens A (2010) City branding and stakeholder engagement. In: Dinnie K (ed) City branding: theory and cases. Palgrave-McMillan, Basingstoke, pp 45–53

Hubbard P, Hall T (1998) The entrepreneurial city and the new urban politics. In: Hall T, Hubbard P (eds) The entrepreneurial city: geographies of politics, regime and representation. Wiley, Chichester

Ingold T (2011) Being Alive: essays on movement, knowledge and experience. Routledge, Oxon

Kalandides A (2011) The problem with spatial identity: revisiting the 'sense of place'. J Place Manage Dev 4(1):28–39

Kavaratzis M (2004) From city marketing to city branding: towards a theoretical framework for developing city brands. Place Brand Public Dipl 1(1):58–73

Kavaratzis M, Hatch MJ (2013) The dynamics of place brands: an identity-based approach to place branding theory. Mark Theory 13(2):69–86

Kavaratzis M, Kalandides A (2015) Rethinking the place brand: the interactive formation of place brands and the role of participatory place branding. Environ Plan A 47(6):1368–1382

Kornberger M (2010) Brand society: how brands transform management and lifestyle. Cambridge University Press, Cambridge

Lefebvre H (1991) The production of space. Blackwell, Malden

Massey D (1994) A global sense of place. In: Massey D (ed) Space, place and gender. Polity Press, Cambridge, pp 146–156

Mayes R (2008) A place in the sun: the politics of place, identity and branding. Place Brand Public Dipl 4(2):124–132

Mommaas H (2002) City branding: the necessity of socio-cultural goals. In: Hauben T, Vermeulen M, Patteeuw V (eds) City branding: image building and building images. NAI Uitgevers, Rotterdam, pp 34–44

Morgan N, Pritchard A, Pride R (2002) Destination branding: creating the unique destination proposition. Butterworth-Heinemann, London

Munar AM (2011) Tourist created content: rethinking destination branding. Int J Cult Tour Hosp Res 5(3):291–305

Oliveira E, Panyik E (2015) Content, context and co-creation: digital challenges in destination branding with references to Portugal as a tourist destination. J Vacat Mark 21(1):53–74

Papadopoulos N (2004) Place branding: evolution, meaning and implications. Place Brand 1 (1):36–49

Papadopoulos N, Heslop L (2002) Country equity and country branding: problems and prospects. J Brand Manage 9(4):294–314

Pasquinelli C (2014) Branding as urban collective strategy-making: the formation of Newcastle Gateshead's organisational identity. Urban Stud 51(4):727–743

Qu H, Kim LH, Im H (2011) A model of destination branding: integrating the concepts of the branding and destination image. Tour Manag 32(3):465–476

Ren C, Blichfeldt BS (2011) One clear image? Challenging simplicity in place branding. Scand J Hosp Tour 11(4):416–434

Ritchie BR, Ritchie RJB (1998) The branding of tourism destination: past achievements and future trends in destination marketing—scope and limitations, Report of 48th Congress. AIEST, St-Gall, pp 89–116

Saraniemi S, Kylänen M (2011) Problematizing the concept of tourism destination: an analysis of different theoretical approaches. J Travel Res 50(2):133–143

Sevin E (2013) Places going viral: Twitter usage patterns in destination marketing and place branding. J Place Manage Dev 6(3):227–239

Turner M (2015) The impact of home sharing on cities. Cities Today 2015:19–21

Van Ham P (2008) Place branding: the state of the art. Ann Am Acad Polit Soc Sci 61(1):126–149

Ward SV (1998) Selling places: the marketing and promotion of towns and cities 1850–2000. E&FN Spon, London

Warnaby G (2009) Towards a service-dominant place marketing logic. Mark Theory 9(4):403–423

Globetrotters and Brands: Cities in an Emerging Communicative Space

Efe Sevin

Abstract This chapter presents and discusses a new communicative space in which contemporary cities exists. The outset of such a space is the result of two interrelated developments. First, international tourism has become a viable source of income for cities causing thcm to compete with each other for potential visitors. As a result, cities have widely embraced the practice of city branding for promoting themselves as touristic destinations. Second, the rise of social media use in such branding projects brought cities closer to their target audiences—at least in terms of communication. The new communicative space concept, therefore, explains a situation in which target audiences, including residents and potential visitors, interact with each other and contribute to the establishment of the reputation of a city, or its brand.

Keywords Tourism • City branding • Social media • Communicative space

1 Introduction

This chapter explores the new communicative space in which contemporary cities exist and proposes policy recommendations for practitioners to better adapt to contemporary conditions. The 'new' aspect of this particular communicative space stems from the fact that city administrations—let it be through destination management offices or other bureaucratic institutions—feel the need to engage with *new* audiences via *new* media platforms in order to establish their reputations and promote themselves. This need for engagement is caused by three recent developments in urban tourism, local governance, and communication technologies.

First, there is an increasing number of people travelling internationally as tourists. In 2014, over 1.1 billion individuals visited other countries, generating an economy of $1197 billion (UNWTO 2015), following a steady increase in the recent years, including a 4.3 % and 3.7 % increase respectively from 2014 figures.

E. Sevin (✉)
Department of Public Relations and Information, Kadir Has University, Kadir Has Caddesi,
34200 Cibali, Istanbul, Turkey
e-mail: efe.sevin@khas.edu.tr

© Springer International Publishing Switzerland 2017   109
N. Bellini, C. Pasquinelli (eds.), *Tourism in the City*,
DOI 10.1007/978-3-319-26877-4_7

The potential to generate revenue strengthens tourism's role as a substantial source of income. Additionally, the increasing number of arrivals position tourists as stakeholders in urban settings. As temporary residents of a city, they both are influenced by and influence how a city is portrayed internationally. Their travel decisions are affected by the reputation of the cities. Their experiences during their visit change the way their social circles perceive a city. Thus, in addition to being a brief part of the local economy, tourists get involved in establishing a city's brand.

The second development that gave rise to the new communicative space is based on the aforementioned international portrayals of cities. Starting with the earlier works on country of origin impact—the argument that consumer behaviour is influenced by the perception of the manufacturing country—, it has been argued that the image of places has the potential to produce economic, social, and political effects. When Simon Anholt (1998) introduced the concept of *nation brands*, the link between perception of a country and its economic, social, and political successes started to be studied and discussed through this concept. Currently, branding practice include monitoring and manipulating the perceptions of town, cities, regions, nations, and other places of different sizes.

Third, social media has proved to be a crucial platform to disseminate messages and engage with target audiences. Regardless of the specific platform, social media create three noteworthy communication opportunities for cities. First, local governments can produce and distribute multimedia content for relatively smaller budgets. Compared to other advertising venues—such as TV, radio, and billboards—, digital production and advertising processes are less costly. Second, local governments can establish their presence on social media. A Facebook or Twitter account can be used as the embodiment of a city. Through interacting with these official accounts, individuals can access information coming from city officials and institutions. Third, social media can be used to create a social network around a city. Individual users can be encouraged to create their own content about places and share them with other interested users.

The rest of the chapter is composed of four parts to explain the impacts of this new communicative space on cities. The first part starts with a concise working definition of city branding and unpacks the assumptions regarding communication in the process. The second part introduces social media as a unique platform and discusses the changes brought to city branding. The third part provides guidelines for practitioners to make better use of social media platforms. The chapter concludes with suggesting research stream that is based on a reflection on how and to what extent the new communicative space supports city officials in building the reputation of cities and managing the perceptions in the eyes of target audiences.

2 Place Brands, Branding, and Cities

City branding is a relatively young practice and discipline that does not necessarily present universally agreed upon definitions. Thus, it is important to provide working definitions of theoretical concepts used throughout the chapter. In the following pages, two similar yet distinct concepts are used together: city branding and place branding. Place branding is a generic name covering branding attempts that include places, i.e. geographic entities. Specific subfields take the name of the geographic entity that is under study. For instance, if the focus is on the branding attempts of an entire country, the concept of nation branding is used. In the cases where the branding attempts of cities are discussed, the city branding understanding is invoked.

The fundamental understandings behind place brands and place branding are straightforward. The former concept argues that the perceptions of places have social, political, and economic impacts (Govers 2011). Places are—for one reason or another—known for their certain characteristics. Maldives is famous for its pristine beaches, and German engineering is revered. When individuals hear City of Love, more often than not Paris is the city that comes to mind. Thus, an individual might choose Maldives over Germany for a summer vacation or would be willing to pay a higher price for a German product or book a romantic get-away in Paris.

The latter concept, place branding, discusses why and how a place gets to be known by certain characteristics. Is Paris the only romantic city? Is German engineering better regardless of the company in question? Does Maldives only offer sun and sea tourism vacations? Place branding argues that it is possible to change the perceptions of places by using a variety of techniques and tools that resemble corporate marketing and branding processes. The inclusion of 'branding' in the concept has misled numerous practitioners and scholars to assume that place branding was identical to corporate branding (Anholt 2007; Wilford 2009). Yet, despite their similarities, place/city branding has characteristics that are not shared by corporate branding. The chapter by Kavaratzis (2016), for instance, presents participation and deliberation in place branding as one such characteristics.

There is an academic consensus that defines place/city branding as being more than only creating new logos and slogans (Kavaratzis and Ashworth 2006). Therefore, even though establishing new visual identities is still an inherent part of campaigns (Fan 2010), city branding is fundamentally a meaning-making process. A 'city' itself is a social construction of a space that is created by individuals and societies through assigning meanings to specific geographic areas (Boisen et al. 2011, p. 137). The images that appear in the minds of individuals as soon as a city is named are such meanings assigned to these areas. Revisiting the Paris example, naming the city might bring positive images such as those of romance, the Eiffel Tower, and other tourist attractions, as well as negative images such as terrorism threats following the recent attacks in November 2015.[1] City branding monitors these perceptions, strategically chooses desirable images to project to target audiences (Kerr and Oliver 2015), and disseminates messages through a variety of tools and techniques (Kavaratzis 2004). Some of these images are based on what Paris has to offer, while some are actively promoted by the Paris Convention and Visitors Bureau[2] and other related branding campaigns such as #ParisWeLoveYou.[3] Yet, these images do not constitute the entire picture. City brand images are prone to being influenced by messages crafted by unofficial resources. In the case of Paris, individuals' messages of solidarity as well as of fears and concerns following the terrorist attacks become—at least temporary—part of the city's brand image.

Within the contours of this chapter—new communicative space in city branding—, three aspects need further elaboration: components of a city brand, tasks in city branding, and actors involved in campaigns. The brand of a city is "a network of associations in the consumer's mind based on the visual, verbal, and behavioural expression of a place" (Zenker and Braun 2010, p. 5). The brand is influenced by a combination of what a city has to offer—such as its infrastructure, landscape, culture, and inhabitants—and what the branding project wants the city to be known for, or its brand identity (Anholt 2007). Ultimately, the city brand is what stays in the minds of the people, or the perceived identity. This identity is triggered by (i) the 'realities' of a city, i.e. its landmarks, landscape, services (ii) messages communicated by officials, i.e. promotion campaigns, and (iii) messages communicated by unofficial channels, i.e. tourists reviews and social media messages.

City branding is used to cover the entire process in which city brands are monitored, managed, and communicated to the audiences. Thus, branding is a constant process. Brand managers first analyse the perception of the cities. Based on the analysis, a branding strategy is created. Subsequently, appropriate branding messages are disseminated. Prior to the launch of "I Amsterdam", Amsterdam Partners—the entity in charge of city branding—carried out an analysis of how the city was perceived. The results showed that Amsterdam was known as "city of canals" and a place for "sex, drugs, R&R" (Stamp 2012). Brand managers subsequently decided to downplay these aspects and promote the city as a "great place to live and work" (Stamp 2012). Afterwards, the branding campaign started to share messages relevant to the projected identity with target audiences. The motto was chosen to reflect the diverse opportunities offered to visitors, and residents—both

---

[1] These image arguments are based on a Twitter hashtag search done on http://www.hashtagify.me/. On hashtagify.me, the users can enter a search keyword and see the hashtags most frequently used with the search keyword. In the case of Paris, these hashtags included romance, Eiffell Tower, and terrorist attacks.

[2] The website of the bureau is accessible at http://www.parisinfo.com/ Last accessed December 19, 2015.

[3] The website of the campaign is accessible at http://parisweloveyou.fr/ Last accessed December 19, 2015.

current and prospective. The main website for the campaign[4] categorises three different types of target audiences. In addition to visitors (I AMVisiting), the website offers information for people who want to relocate to Amsterdam (I AMLocal) and for businesses that want to use Amsterdam as their base of operations (I AMBusiness). Top attractions listed for visitors list museums (such as *Van Gogh Museum* and *Rijksmuseum*) as well as neighbourhoods (such as *Oud-West* and *Jordaan*) rather than the city's red light district or coffee shops where marijuana smoking is accepted. The I AMLocal and I AMBusiness sections promote the city as a thriving location for businesses and open-minded people and provide detailed information about the bureaucratic processes that need to be followed to complete a relocation to Amsterdam.

Kavaratzis (2004) introduces three categories of communication in city branding. *Primary communication* refers to the activities that include changes in the fields of landscape, infrastructure, and bureaucratic structures (Kavaratzis 2004). By changing the architecture or service industry in a city, the perception of target audiences might be influenced. *Secondary communication* refers to the formal marketing communication, such as advertising and event management (Kavaratzis 2004). *Tertiary communication* refers to 'word of mouth' marketing (Kavaratzis 2004). Brand managers are not the only actors controlling communication in city branding. Residents (Braun et al. 2013), competitors (Alexa 2010), as well as tourists (Munar 2011) also voice their opinions about a given city, therefore, have the potential to influence the perceptions of target audiences. Even though local governments might attempt to control the first two communication categories, tertiary communication is beyond their direct reach.

One of the main differences between corporate and city branding is the actors involved in the process. In corporate cases, there is a clear owner of the brand/company, and an individual or a unit whose task is to manage the said brand. The managers and directors in a company have the right and possibility to manipulate its brands as it wishes. Yet, their equivalent in cities—the political leadership of a city—cannot claim an exclusive ownership of the brand. For instance, "I Amsterdam" campaign was organised by Amsterdam Metropolitan Area's marketing department. Yet, the department does not have the exclusive right to control the brand of Amsterdam. A group of residents that were unhappy with the department's projection of Amsterdam as a place with no problems decided to launch their counter "I Amsterdamned" campaign to voice the issues they face in their day-to-day lives (Braun et al. 2013). In Ankara, residents did not welcome the new logo proposed by the mayor's office which highlighted the religious aspects of the city's landscape and started a guerrilla marketing campaign to bring back the previous logo, escalating the discussion on the new logo onto a debate about politics, secularism, and urban life in the capital (Hayden and Sevin 2012). Thus, residents are—at least should be—included in the branding processes.

---

[4]The website of the campaign is accessible at http://www.iamsterdam.com/ Last accessed February 18, 2016.

International tourism grants outside parties the ability to present their input on what a city means for them (Byrd and Gustke 2011). More and more people have the opportunity to visit a foreign city and form their opinions based on their first-hand experiences. In brief, a city branding campaign requires a "dialogue, debate, and contestation" (Kavaratzis and Hatch 2013, p. 82) among parties and includes engagement with a variety of actors, including but not limited to residents, civil society groups, bureaucrats, and target audiences (Sevin 2011). This approach to city branding is close to the concept of 'co-creation' (Prahalad and Ramaswamy 2004). Co-creation in branding replaces the company-centric view and institutes an active role to consumers who interact with the products, goods, and services to create their own experiences (Prahalad and Ramaswamy 2004). In the case of city branding, co-creation argues that visitors and other outside audiences should be seen as stakeholders as they create their own experience by interacting with the city (Hatch and Schultz 2010). The views of these audiences should be taken into consideration in branding campaigns (Kavaratzis and Hatch 2013).

To sum up, a city brand refers to how a given city is perceived by audiences. City branding is the continuous process of monitoring these perceptions, creating strategies to establish more desirable perceptions, and communicating with target audiences to reach the desired states. Despite the fact that city branding campaigns are mainly undertaken by political and/or bureaucratic authorities, other local and foreign actors also influence the perception of target audiences. Cities are not solely geographic spaces but rather are social constructs built by the perceptions and meanings assigned to them by various actors. The first two of the three developments that gave rise to the new communicative space—namely increasing number of international tourists and introduction of city branding—point out that there are systematic efforts contributing to the meaning-making processes. Moreover, a group that could have been positioned as an external stakeholder—tourists—has become an invaluable part of these branding processes. The next section introduces the third development, social media through a discussion of how communication technologies are used in city branding and how they influence the contemporary urban settings.

3   Completing the New Communicative Space: Social Media

Social media is a generic term used to describe internet-based platforms that allow users to create and exchange content (Gallant and Boone 2011). Prominent examples include social networking platforms (Facebook, Twitter), blogs, review websites (Tripadvisor, Yelp), and video sharing platforms (Youtube, Vimeo). Social media has been well received and adopted in city branding campaigns (Braun et al. 2013; Yan 2011). The widespread acceptance of social media in city branding was supported by the fact that these platforms are relatively cheaper than

Fig. 1 Three developments leading to the new communicative space

traditional advertising outlets (Sevin 2013), and provide the opportunity to reach out to a large number of internet users (Pew Research Center 2013) (Fig. 1).

The new communicative space is complemented by social media giving a new platform to communicate with non-residents. As argued above, increased tourist arrivals and reliance on city branding as a method to establish reputation encourage city marketing professionals to engage with visitors. Social media, within this understanding, presents opportunities for circulating official advertising campaigns and word of mouth, or in other words for secondary and tertiary communication processes (Kavaratzis 2005). More specifically, city branding projects use social media to disseminate their messages directly to international tourists given the financial, logistical, and content-production advantages of these platforms (Fouts 2010; Go and Govers 2010). Similarly, international travellers also make use of social media platforms to disseminate their own experiences and information, as well as to learn from the experiences of other visitors (Munar 2011). Most travellers use social media websites, such as Tripadvisor, and read user reviews before deciding on their final destination (Gretzel and Yoo 2008).

City branding in social media requires a strategic look to reputation. Brand managers have always been expected to monitor the reputation of their cities and engage with a variety of stakeholders to co-create city brands (Kavaratzis and Hatch 2013, p. 72). Social media presents additional platforms for monitoring reputation, creating content, and engaging with target audiences. The next three sections provide concrete examples on the use of social media.

3.1 Monitoring in Social Media

The new communicative space urges brand managers to see the reputation of their cities as a manageable asset. By tracking the views of individuals about a given city, it will be possible to assess where a city stands and how it can be made more attractive for potential visitors, residents, investors, and other stakeholders. Outside social media, tracking can be done by asking people their opinion through surveys (Feinberg and Zhao 2011), and interviews (van Meer and Strous 2012). Social media improves on these non-digital monitoring tools at least in three different aspects. First, data is readily available online. Internet users tend to voice their opinions and share their experiences online without any prompt (Cha et al. 2010). Therefore, the individuals are not limited by pre-written surveys or influenced by the interviews. Monitoring can be done by gathering the user views that are already shared. Second social media enables the users to reflect on their experiences immediately (Marres and Weltevrede 2013). Through sharing photos, writing reviews, or sending tweets, the users express how they view a given city instantly. Last, social media includes metadata (Marres and Weltevrede 2013). In other words, social media can be scraped for information beyond the content shared. For instance, each tweet sent carries over a dozen of other variables in addition to the 140 characters typed. These variables include user characteristics such as location, Twitter username, and device used, as well as tweet characteristics such as number of retweets and favourites. Monitor does not need to be limited to the views expressed by users.

Govers (2015) presents the example of Dubai and its online monitoring from 2008 to 2011. By using the Radian6 platform, Dubai carried out content and semantic analyses, and "scanned +150 million blogs, 90+ million Tweets, 25k+ online mainstream news sites, 420+ video and image sharing sites, hundreds of thousands of discussion boards, Facebook, Friendfeed, and LinkedIn Answer" (Govers 2015, pp. 77–78). Radian6—currently working as a part of Salesforce Marketing Cloud—is a platform that aggregates content from a number of social media platforms and provides user-friendly reports about the reactions of Internet users. Radian6 and other paid services such as Hootsuite, Heartbeat, Keyhole, and Simplfy360 can document information about both the content shared on social media and the attached metadata. It is also possible to move away from paid service and scrap data from social networks directly (for an example with Twitter, cf. Sevin 2014).

Another venue for online brand monitoring is the travel specific websites such as Tripadvisor, Booking.com, and Hotels.com. Existing research on tourism behaviour argues that tourism specific websites influence the travel decisions of potential visitors (cf. Gretzel and Yoo 2008). Therefore, views expressed on these sites are important for city branding professionals. Tripadvisor's dashboard function enables managers to monitor the user reviews (Schaal 2012). Hootsuite incorporated Tripadvisor into its monitoring services in 2013 (Miller 2013).

3.2 Content Creation in Social Media

Social media platforms encourage the cities to pursue more creative communication campaigns that could not have happened outside the digital communication tools. For instance, #ParisWeLoveYou campaign curates the photos and texts shared by users and shares them on their websites. Amsterdam answers questions posed by potential tourists on Twitter. The city of Sun Valley, Idaho built a robot that Internet users can control remotely to skip stones in a lake.[5]

---

[5]Information about Sun Valley's *Skippy the Stone Skipping Robot* can be found here http:// skiptown.visitsunvalley.com/. Last accessed December 29, 2015.

Besides the interactive and multimedia nature of social media, there is a trend of including smartphones. Applications enable visitors to get information about touristic attractions, restaurants, maps, and directions. In addition to generic applications such as Foursquare and Yelp, there are location specific applications such as South Korea's *Visit Korea 3.0* that was created by the Korean Tourism Organization. The application presents an up-to-date digital travel guide. Certain applications make use of the sensors in smartphones to create applications based on contextual awareness (Dickinson et al. 2014). In other terms, smartphones enable location-based data or communicate with other devices for real-time updates. London Bus Checker is such an application that provides information on the public bus system (Dickinson et al. 2014). London Tube is an augmented reality application that shows the closest subway stops in the city.

Social media presents unique opportunities to create innovative content. Yet, it should be noted that creativity is not a perk but rather an expectation in social media. The reason for such an argument is two-fold. First, social media users are exposed to a high volume of messages. Every second, over 20,000 gigabytes of data are transferred over the internet, including over 7000 tweets sent, 6 h of video uploaded to YouTube, and 500,000 of likes shared on Facebook.[6] Users are likely to ignore most of the content that does not catch their or their friends' attention (Nahon and Hemsley 2013). Second, the audiences are not captive. Even if they click on a city branding link, this does not necessarily mean that they are going to consume the content. On average, users spend 15 s on a webpage before moving onto the next (Haile 2014). Creativity, within this perspective, is seen as vital in producing content that will distinguish itself among others and reach social media users.

3.3   Co-creation in Social Media

Social media platforms do not follow a one-way communication understanding. As argued above, there is at least the expectation of engaging with audiences (Smith 2013). In terms of city branding, social media platforms gave cities an online front office (Auer et al. 2012). Therefore, there is a direct—as well as fast and free—link between users and cities. Currently, through Twitter, individual users can directly talk to and interact with places such as San Francisco (@onlyinSF) and Paris (@Parisjecoute) (Sevin 2013). Earlier research has shown that cities fail to benefit from the two-way communication capabilities of social media, and are limited to content dissemination (Ketter and Avraham 2012; Sevin 2016; Yan 2011; Zavattaro 2014). Indeed, digital communication makes it possible to send messages in a relatively cheaper and faster manner compared to non-digital communication methods. A tweet does not require a drastic financial investment and is shared

---

[6]Real time data about internet traffic can be seen here: http://pennystocks.la/internet-in-real-time/ Last accessed February 27, 2016.

instantly with other users. However, it should be noted that social media differentiates itself from earlier digital communication outlets—such as static websites—by enabling interaction through user-generated content. A social media communication campaign can also listen to what other users are saying and engage them.

Co-creation requires an open dialogue. The brand of a city is expected to be sum of all the experiences individuals have had in their interactions. Urban setting should not be seen as an out-of-touch static product that can be marketed. As the increasing number of international tourist arrivals demonstrates, individuals interact directly with cities or have the opportunity to share the experiences of their friends. Therefore, the photos shared on Flickr by a tourist can equivalently help another individual assign meanings to a space as the official advertising campaign. Moreover, it is possible to even argue that the word of mouth on social media is more effective than formal communication channels (Berger 2013). Individuals are more likely to trust the views and ideas of people in their social networks as opposed to professionals that are being paid to represent a city.

Social media removes obstacles in front of collective action (Shirky 2009, p. 159), therefore facilitating engagement and brand co-creation. The Page function of Facebook makes it possible for Facebook users to follow a city and interact with its posts. Hashtags are used to categorise tweets on Twitter, therefore, bringing people who discuss the same subject together. Video and photo sharing websites, including Vimeo, Youtube, and Flickr, have the function to content using labels and allow other users to comment on shared posts.

Co-creation through social media changes the approach to both secondary and tertiary communication in city branding. Given the fact that co-creation in branding happens through individuals creating as well as exchanging and commenting on existing content, tertiary communication increases its importance. More importantly, as individuals learn from each other, secondary communication needs to track and incorporate the messages in tertiary communication. The new communicative space augments the role of tourists and tourism, as well as branding and branding communication in establishing the reputation of cities. The next section outlines concrete recommendation for practitioners to adapt to the new communicative space.

4   Conclusions and Future Research

This chapter unpacks and systemises a phenomenon that is familiar to many of us from our daily lives. The new communicative space is basically the reflection of globalization in urban tourism. We travel more often and further away than the generation before us. International travel is within the grasp of a larger number of people. We are closer to foreign cities than ever. Through social media and/or visits, we experience these places, shape our own views, and to an extent claim stakes in establishing city brands. On the other side of the equation, we observe a rising competition among destinations for the same pool of potential visitors. City officials try to communicate the unique and appealing aspects of their cities to target audiences to attract a higher number of visitors. In the upcoming years, the research and practice in urban tourism need to pay closer attention to the reputation and perception of cities. The field of city branding can be seen as a pioneering approach as it proposes a strategic way of thinking about promotion activities. Instead of focusing solely on promoting tourism in the short run, city branding seeks for ways to build up the reputation of cities. Within the contours of this chapter, social media was introduced as a feasible communication tool that can be used in establishing and monitoring city brands. These digital platforms facilitate engagement and collaboration with target audiences.

The new communicative space paves the way to three significant strains of research. First, the rise of urban tourism situates tourists as new stakeholders for city officials. These temporary residents also experience cities. However, the differences between residents and non-residents should be still acknowledged. It is an acceptable assumption to argue that visitors present their inputs about the reputation of cities, however, as the rebranding of Amsterdam demonstrates, their inputs are not necessarily welcomed—or even compatible—with those of the residents. If the number of international arrivals keeps increasing as it has in the past, there is a need to specifically define the interaction between locals and visitors in terms of city brands.

Second, social media are currently used as platforms to solely disseminate creative messages and are not fully exploited. Yet, they have the potential to be an important development and communication tool for stronger brands through engagement and brand co-creation. There is need for further research on how we can employ different platforms more effectively. For instance, tourism-related information seems to be shared on two types of websites: generic sharing websites, and tourism specific websites. The former type includes prominent tools such as Facebook, Twitter, and Instagram, whereas the latter includes tools that focus specifically on travel related themes such as Tripadvisor or Booking.com. Potential tourists tend to rely on the second group while finalizing their travel decisions (Gretzel and Yoo 2008). In other words, these sites are visited after a travel decision is made and before it is finalised. Generic websites are more frequently visited, even when people are not planning to travel. Therefore, they might have different influences on people's travel decisions.

Third, even though social media have proven to be effective in influencing real-world activity (Shirky 2010, p. 38), they are only tools. Focusing on the capabilities of a given platform is futile regardless of its popularity. It should be noted that the popular social media platforms of the last decade—such as MySpace, ICQ, and MSN Messenger—are no longer used. The usage habits of individuals are more important than the technology itself. Social media can and should "be regarded as a novel form of collective value creation" (Munar et al. 2013, p. 9). Future research questions should be posed at the underlying communication needs and value creation processes.

References

Alexa LE (2010) Urban marketing and its impact over the competition between cities. Manag Mark-Craiova 1(1):39–42

Anholt S (1998) Nation-brands of the twenty-first century. Brand Manag 5(6):395–417

Anholt S (2007) Competitive identity: the new brand management for nations, cities and regions. Palgrave Macmillan, Basingstoke

Auer C, Srugies A, Loffelholz M (2012) The role of social media in public diplomacy: potentials and reality. Presented at the International Studies Association, 1–4 April 2012, San Diego, CA

Berger J (2013) Contagious: why things catch on. Simon & Schuster, New York, NY

Boisen M, Terlouw K, van Gorp B (2011) The selective nature of place branding and the layering of spatial identities. J Place Manag Dev 4(2):135–147. doi:10.1108/17538331111153151

Braun E, Kavaratzis M, Zenker S (2013) My city—my brand: the different roles of residents in place branding. J Place Manag Dev 6(1):18–28. doi:10.1108/17538331311306087

Byrd ET, Gustke L (2011) Using decision trees to identify tourism stakeholders. J Place Manag Dev 4(2):148–168

Cha M, Haddadi H, Benevenuto F, Gummadi KP (2010) Measuring user influence in twitter: the million follower fallacy. Presented at 4th ICWSM, 23–26 May, 2010, Washington, DC

Dickinson JE, Ghali K, Cherrett T, Speed C, Davies N, Norgate S (2014) Tourism and the smartphone app: capabilities, emerging practice and scope in the travel domain. Curr Issues Tour 17(1):84–101. doi:10.1080/13683500.2012.718323

Fan Y (2010) Branding the nation: towards a better understanding. Place Brand Public Dipl 6 (2):97–103. doi:10.1057/pb.2010.16

Feinberg Z, Zhao X (2011) The Anholt–GfK Roper nation brands IndexSM: navigating the changing world. In: Go F, Gover R (eds) International place branding Yearbook 2011 managing reputational risk. Palgrave Macmillan, Basingstoke, pp 63–76

Fouts JS (2010) Social media and immersive worlds: why international place branding doesn't get weekends off. In: Go FM, Govers R (eds) International place branding Yearbook 2010 place branding in the new age of innovation. Palgrave Macmillan, Basingstoke, pp 113–120

Gallant LM, Boone GM (2011) Communicative informatics: an active and creative audience framework of social media. TripleC-Cogn Commun Co-Oper 9(2):231–246

Go FM, Govers R (2010) The E-branding of places. In: Go FM, Govers R (eds) International Place Branding Yearbook 2010 place branding in the new age of innovation. Palgrave Macmillan, Basingstoke, pp 121–131

Govers R (2011) From place marketing to place branding and back. Place Brand Public Dipl 7 (4):227–231. doi:10.1057/pb.2011.28

Govers R (2015) Rethinking virtual and online place branding. In: Kavaratzis M, Warnaby G, Ashworth GJ (eds) Rethinking place branding. Springer International Publishing, Cham, pp 73–83

Gretzel U, Yoo KH (2008) Use and impact of online travel reviews. In: O'Connor P, Höpken W, Gretzel U (eds) Information and communication technologies in tourism 2008. Springer Vienna, Vienna, pp 35–46

Haile T (2014) What you think you know about the web is wrong. Time. Retrieved from http://time.com/12933/what-you-think-you-know-about-the-web-is-wrong/

Hatch MJ, Schultz M (2010) Toward a theory of brand co-creation with implications for brand governance. J Brand Manag 17(8):590–604. doi:10.1057/bm.2010.14

Hayden C, Sevin E (2012) The politics of meaning and the city brand: the controversy over the branding of Ankara. Place Brand Public Dipl 8(2):133–146. doi:10.1057/pb.2012.8

Kavaratzis M (2004) From city marketing to city branding: towards a theoretical framework for developing city brands. Place Brand 1(1):58–73. doi:10.1057/palgrave.pb.5990005

Kavaratzis M (2005) Place branding: a review of trends and conceptual models. Mark Rev 5s(4): 329–342. doi:10.1362/146934705775186854

Kavaratzis M (2016) The participatory place branding process for tourism: linking visitors and residents through the city brand. In: Bellini N, Pasquinelli C (eds) Tourism in the city—towards an integrative agenda on urban tourism. Springer, Heidelberg

Kavaratzis M, Ashworth G (2006) City branding: an effective assertion of identity or a transitory marketing trick? Place Brand 2(3):183–194. doi:10.1057/palgrave.pb.5990056

Kavaratzis M, Hatch MJ (2013) The dynamics of place brands: an identity-based approach to place branding theory. Mark Theor 13(1):69–86. doi:10.1177/1470593112467268

Kerr G, Oliver J (2015) Rethinking place identities. In: Kavaratzis M, Warnaby G, Ashworth GJ (eds) Rethinking place branding. Springer International Publishing, Cham, Heidelberg, pp 61–72

Ketter E, Avraham E (2012) The social revolution of place marketing: the growing power of users in social media campaigns. Place Brand Public Dipl 8(4):285–294. doi:10.1057/pb.2012.20

Marres N, Weltevrede E (2013) Scraping the social?: Issues in live social research. J Cult Econ 6(3):313–335, http://doi.org/10.1080/17530350.2013.772070

Miller D (2013, December 5) HootSuite Now Monitors Yelp, Google+ Local, TripAdvisor. Retrieved from http://socialhospitality.com/2013/12/hootsuite-monitor-review-sites-through-reputology-app/

Munar AM (2011) Tourist-created content: rethinking destination branding. Int J Cult Tour Hosp Res 5(3):291–305. doi:10.1108/17506181111156989

Munar AM, Gyimothy S, Cai L (2013) Tourism social media: a new research agenda. In: Munar AM, Gyimothy S, Cai L (eds) Tourism social media: transformations in identity, community and culture, tourism social science series. Bingley, Emerald, pp 9–23

Nahon K, Hemsley J (2013) Going viral. Polity, Cambridge

Pew Research Center (2013) Social networking fact sheet. Pew Res Cent Internet Am Life Proj. Retrieved from http://www.pewinternet.org/fact-sheets/social-networking-fact-sheet/

Prahalad CK, Ramaswamy V (2004) The future of competition: co-creating unique value with customers. Harvard Business School Pub, Boston, MA

Schaal D (2012, January 24) TripAdvisor analytics tools enable hoteliers to monitor the competition. http://www.tnooz.com/article/tripadvisor-analytics-tools-enable-hoteliers-to-monitor-the-competition/. Retrieved 18 Feb 2016

Sevin E (2011) Thinking about place branding: ethics of concept. Place Brand Public Dipl 7(3):155–164. doi:10.1057/pb.2011.15

Sevin E (2013) Places going viral: Twitter usage patterns in destination marketing and place branding. J Place Manag Dev 6(3):227–239. doi:10.1108/JPMD-10-2012-0037

Sevin E (2014) Understanding cities through city brands: city branding as a social and semantic network. Cities 38:47–56. doi:10.1016/j.cities.2014.01.003

Sevin E (2016) Branding cities in the age of social media: a comparative assessment of local government performance. In Sobaci MZ (ed) Social media and local governments. Public Administration and Information Technology, Springer International Publishing, pp. 301–320

Shirky C (2009) Here comes everybody: the power of organizing without organizations; [with an updated epilogue], Nachdrth edn. Penguin, New York, NY

Shirky C (2010) Cognitive surplus: creativity and generosity in a connected age. Penguin Press, New York

Smith W (2013) Brands must get social media right [WWW Document]. Brand. Strategy Insid. http://www.brandingstrategyinsider.com/2013/03/brands-must-get-social-media-right.html#.VCAz4L65LG6

Stamp J (2012) Rebranding Amsterdam and what it means to rebrand a city. Smithsonian. Retrieved from http://www.smithsonianmag.com/arts-culture/rebranding-amsterdam-and-what-it-means-to-rebrand-a-city-19539392/

UNWTO (2015) UNWTO tourism highlights, 2015th edn. UNWTO, Madrid

van Meer L, Strous B (2012) Communicating destination brand personality: the case of Amsterdam. Presented at the Users of the world, unite! The challenges and opportunities of Social Media, Utrecht, The Netherlands

Wilford H (2009) Cities and their brands: lessons from corporate branding. Place Brand Public
     Dipl 5(1):26–37. doi:10.1057/pb.2008.3
Yan J (2011) Social media in branding: fulfilling a need. J Brand Manag 18(9):688–696
Zavattaro SM (2014) Place branding through phases of the image: balancing image and substance.
     Palgrave Macmillan, New York, NY
Zenker S, Braun E (2010) Towards an integrated approach for place brand management. Presented
     at the 50th European Regional Science Association Congress, 19–23 August 2010, Jönköping,
     Sweden

The Construction of an Emerging Tourist Destination and Its Related Human Capital Challenges

Assya Khiat and Nathalie Montargot

Abstract An emergent destination wishing to develop tourism has to think about its workforce and provide a sufficient volume of workers. This chapter highlights the importance of examining the performance and competitiveness of the tourist sector in an emerging destination, through the impulse of national tourism policies and through a better management of human resources, both on a macro and micro levels. The stakes perceived by the tourism professionals in Algeria are investigated, with a focus on Oran, the second biggest city of Algeria and capital of tourism, on the south shore of the Mediterranean basin. The first part is dedicated to a review of literature that will allow exploring the distinctive issues related to hospitality and the tourism sector. This part will also highlight the way international chains are expanding, focusing on a high quality of service and attaching importance to human capital management, as a key factor for optimizing guest's satisfaction. Then, both a documentary study, exploring the strategy of an emerging destination in matter of tourism development and a qualitative analysis, based on interviews led with professionals of the sector, will be exposed. The results show that the volume of students in tourism and hospitality is widely insufficient to meet the needs, that the capacity of welcoming tourists is above all perceived as a cultural question. As a driver of economic development, managing a city as a tourism destination needs to ensure both sustainable growth and an ability to cope with human capital challenges in the industry.

Keywords Human capital • International chains • Quality standards • Emerging destination • Hospitality

A. Khiat
LAREEM, Oran 2 University, Oran, Algeria
e-mail: assya.khiat@gmail.com

N. Montargot (✉)
LR-ReM, La Rochelle Business School, La Rochelle, France
e-mail: montargotn@esc-larochelle.fr

© Springer International Publishing Switzerland 2017
N. Bellini, C. Pasquinelli (eds.), *Tourism in the City*,
DOI 10.1007/978-3-319-26877-4_8

1 Introduction

The tourism activity increased about 25 % in the last decade and represents now-adays approximately 12 % of the world economic activity. Actually, tourism, one of the largest industries of the world and a key driver for socio-economic progress, is increasing all across the globe. As a matter of fact, the World Tourism Organization (UNWTO) states that "an ever increasing number of destinations worldwide have opened up to, and invested in tourism" and that "many new destinations have emerged in addition to the traditional favourites" (UNWTO 2014, p. 2).

Urban tourism is linked to socio-economic development. "Whether visiting for leisure, business, or to meet friends and relatives, tourists contribute to the local economy and support jobs across the city and beyond" (UNWTO 2012, p. 4). Tourism policy therefore is a very important part of urban development, "it is not just a strategy to provide a competitive product to meet visitors' expectations but a way to develop the city itself and provide more and better infrastructures and bring conditions to residents" (UNWTO 2012, p. 7).

Tourism also appears to be a major sector of job creation. According to the World Travel and Tourism Council (2015), the sector will continue to outperform the wider economy, as it has done for 4 consecutive years, generating 105 million direct jobs in 2014 (3.6 % of total employment). By 2025, the industries will account for 131 million direct jobs, an increase of 2 % over the next 10 years. This greater need for human resources emphasizes the fact "the story of successful tourism enterprises is one that is largely about people—how they are recruited, how they are managed, how they are trained and educated, how they are valued and rewarded, and how they are supported through a process of continuous learning and career development" (Failte Ireland 2005, p. 8).

The purpose of research is based on the construction of an emerging urban tourism destination and its human capital challenges. UNWTO refers to urban tourism as trips taken by travellers to cities or places of high population density. The duration of these trips is usually short (1–3 days) (UNWTO 2012). City tourism is one of the fastest growing travel segments worldwide.

The chapter will be conducted from two perspectives, macro (large-scale social processes) and micro (small groups or individual interactions). This chosen approach can be explained because tourism involves social structures and institutions, as well as companies hiring individuals to meet the customers' needs. Moreover, providing fulfilling employment opportunities to the local population is a fundamental aspect of economic development, as well as a manner to favour key players and meet customers' needs.

In a macro-analysis perspective, governments target to increase the value of their destination in order to strengthen tourist attraction and competitiveness. Tourism may impact positively economic indicators, such as employment, growth, external balances and investments. Moreover, the performance of the sector may generate indirect impacts over other sectors (agriculture, craft industry, culture, construction, building and public works, services, transport...).

The consciousness of the importance of the stakes highlights the tourism development as a vector of economic and social development, and imposes the necessity to adopt a strategic vision. Thus, destinations build strategic plans to achieve their goals. They design and clarify their vision in the short term, middle term and long-term horizons to position their country as a receiving country. They also have to give adequate attention to human resources development, since they "play an important role in stimulating the request, creating a relaxation atmosphere, formulating a buying decision, forming and maintaining the interest, the sympathy for a certain tourism product or holiday destination, hotel or food unit, way of transport of form of entertaining and in determination of tourist coming back" (Gherman et al. 2011, p. 234). The destinations also have to operationalize financial plans in order to support tourism activities and attract important investors, property developers, tour operators and international chains. They also have to define the pertinent instruments of their policies and specify the conditions of their feasibility.

In a microanalysis perspective, people are an organisation's greatest asset (Bolton and Houlihan 2007). Actually, an emergent destination wishing to develop tourism has to think about betting on human capital and provide a sufficient volume of workers, mainly characterised by low skills (Westwood 2004; Di Liberto 2013). In fact, growth in tourism in developing countries means that "the sector has become an important source of employment for those previously dependent on subsistence living so that what is, ostensibly, the same work in a technical sense is constructed in very different ways across social, cultural and economic contexts" (Baum 2007, p. 1396).

The mainstay of the chapter is formed by an analysis concerning the construction of an emerging destination and will emphasise on the importance of human capital as a key resource to develop tourism. Thus, both a documentary study exploring the Algerian strategy in matter of tourism development and a qualitative analysis, based on interviews led with professionals of the sector in Oran, will be presented. Beforehand, a review of literature will allow an exploration of the importance of human capital in the industry and the way international chains are expanding, proceeding and optimising guests' satisfaction.

2 International Chains Expansion and Their Quest for Quality

Whitelock and Yang (2007) state that the globalization of the market is influencing companies, which are seeking for new geographical coverage beyond their domestic market, especially in the emerging destinations. International expansion shows a variety of market entry modes, via a mixture of acquisitions, hotel consortia, mergers, direct ownerships, joint ventures, franchising, management contracts or strategic alliance agreements, affecting at various levels control and coordination processes (Azevedo et al. 2002). Those entry modes have something in common.

They must "achieve effective and efficient control at the same time as ensuring sufficient responsiveness to local market conditions is a challenge for any service firm but particularly so for those that employ multiple market entry methods" (Brookes and Roper 2010, p. 2).

The issue of decentralising decisions in the business units arises. What degree of latitude might be given to the units abroad? Is it pertinent to impose the same model and processes in all the countries or on the contrary would it be wiser to adjust the strategies to the different destinations? Concerning this matter, Child and McGrath (2001) through an extensive review of the literature firmly recommend decentralisation, which is at the same time a better way to achieve agreed goals rather than to impose them top-down, and a manner to get a better understanding of the market realities, especially if the companies lack of experience in the country. International groups are struggling on the ground of the quality of service to position themselves and appear different in the consumer's mind. Therefore, the quality of service must be reached at all levels.

Regarding the literature, the quality of service concept is subjective according to the fact that perception varies and depends on individuals, time and space. Kapiki on his part highlights the fact that "quality service is a management tool that provides companies by a means of monitoring service from the customers' perspective" (Kapiki 2012, p. 54).

The essence of the word "service" is based on an interaction between a customer and a front-line employee, during a human experience lived by the guest through his emotions and feelings. In order to measure service quality and any possible gap between customers' expectations and services delivered, Parasuraman et al. (1994) developed the SERVQUAL scale to assess service quality using five dimensions:

- Tangibles aspects (Physical facilities, equipment, and appearance of personnel)
- Reliability (Ability to perform the promised services dependably and accurately)
- Responsiveness (Willingness to help customers and provide prompt service)
- Assurance (Knowledge, courtesy and ability to inspire trust and confidence)
- Empathy (Caring, individualized attention the firm provides its customers).

In an increasingly competitive market, guests' overall perception of quality is crucial and correlated to employee's behaviours, attitudes, responsiveness and ability to meet the clients' needs (Richard and Gill 2003). Thus, service attitude is a central competency for employees (Jui-Min Li et al. 2009) who must give customers a positive image that strengthen satisfaction (Doucet 2004) and loyalty (Dimitriades 2007). But, in the meantime, "downward pressures on the overall cost of tourism (low cost airlines, aggressive tour operators, electronic distribution, deregulation) encourages the use of low cost labour and, to an extent, may also deflate expectations of service and product quality" (Baum 2007, p. 1396).

Globally, the consumer experience is a multidimensional concept made of people encounters with products, services and businesses (Lewis and Chambers 2000). This experience is related to cognitive and emotional aspects. According to Bitner (1992) and Carbone and Haeckel (1994), to manage a total customer experience, where mechanics and humanics clues are significant. Mechanics are composed of "sights, smells, tastes, sounds, and textures generated by things" (Carbone and Haeckel 1994, p. 13), while humanics are linked to social interactions between and among customers and employees. Humanics are very important, "they are engineered by defining and choreographing the desired behavior of employees and customers involved in the customer encounter" (Carbone and Haeckel 1994, p. 13). At the centre of these humanics, the reception job position plays at the same time a marketing role and a connection towards operational activities. It is a central asset in the tourism industry (Dogor Di Nuzzo 2009).

The ability of welcoming reflects a real will to favour satisfaction and wellness of guests. Reception is also linked to image and reputation. Consequently, the skills necessary to deliver a high quality of service are among the most important factors to be taken into consideration, to increase the competitiveness of a company.

Three dimensions emerge when dealing with reception positions: "(1) the gratitude (to recognise the visitor by concrete gestures); (2) the hospitality (to fulfil its expectations, exceed them and solve his problems) and (3) the mothering (to take care of him at different degrees)" (De Grandpré et al. 2012, p. 1). Moreover, the customer is more sensitive to reception than any other elements of the stay, such as activities or visits (Dulude and Bastien 1998). The moment of encounter is crucial, since a tourist becomes the ambassador of a destination (or not), according to his experience (Servet and Tesone 2005).

3   The Analysis of the Urban Tourism Development in Oran

The documentary and qualitative studies have been conducted in order to give some sense, understanding and interpreting of the professional representations, in a particular urban context. For a better understanding, some background information concerning Algeria and Oran are provided. The ground and the sample as well as the modalities of data collection and processing are detailed below.

Algeria is bordered to the northeast by Tunisia, to the east by Libya, to the west by Morocco, to the southwest by Western Sahara, Mauritania, and Mali, to the southeast by Niger, and to the north by the Mediterranean Sea. Some background information concerning Algeria and Oran, an important coastal city located in the North-West of the country, are useful to understand the particular context.

The analysis of the Fig. 1 shows the evolution of the tourism in Algeria over a 10 years period. The travel departures show 88 % increase, whereas the arrivals show a global increase of 59 %. However, the evolutions show for the departures an increase, dated from 2008, whereas the arrivals are constantly increasing over the period, except for the last year, which sees a reduction of about 400,000 tourists, consecutive to terrorist threats in the country.

The research is firstly based on documentary study to grasp the characteristics of tourism reception in the Oranese region. Choosing this region is understandable by the fact that Oran is the metropolis of the Algerian West, including 26 municipalities whose 14 are coastal zones. Its coast extends over 124 km, approximately 1/10 of

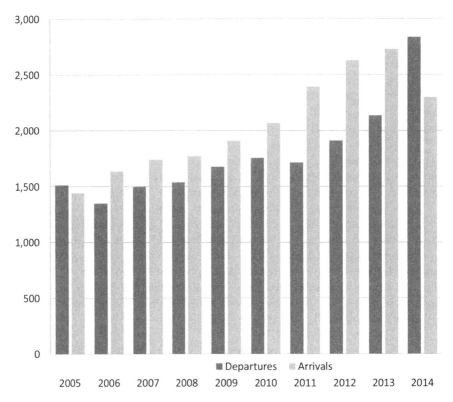

Fig. 1 Algerian Tourism Statistics 2005–2014 (in thousands). *Source*: authors' elaboration on Eurostat 2015

the national coast (Kacimi 2013). The urban area of Oran, on the south shore of the Mediterranean Basin is the second biggest city of Algeria, which counts two million inhabitants nowadays and received more than 14 million tourists in 2012. Oran, a country town of the Oranese province is located at 432 km from the capital, Algiers. The city is considered as the touristic capital and the main commercial and industrial centre of the west part of the country. Its port registers an important traffic with Europe and one can also reach Oran by ferry from the ports of Marseille, Sète, Alicante or Almería, via the national company.

Oran is called the second Paris, a *fiesta* capital and the birthplace of Raï, this rebellious music that has been exported all around the world. The place is known for its liberal mores. The explanation may be historical. Oran was Spanish for 300 years. *Sidi El Houari* the historical district named 'the old Oran' holds to this day the imprint of various occupations experienced by the city (Spanish, Ottoman and French). The hospitality industry is prosperous. With 46 hotels under construction and more than 6000 beds, Oran is ranked first Province (*Wilaya*) of the country in terms of accommodation facilities. The sector generates 30 % of the GDP and employs 5 % of the working population.

Table 1 Sample composition

Travel agents		Front-line employees in hotels	
Number	Characteristics	Number	Characteristics
10	Travel agent managers From 2 to 10 years of experience	12	Receptionists, Front office manager From 1 to 5 years of experience 6 over 12 employed in international chains Hotels from 3 to 5 stars, 45 to 256 rooms

To collect the qualitative information, a questionnaire was developed around several themes including the training, the sense of reception, the perceived quality of service level and its management. Concerning the data collection and sampling, 22 semi-directive interviews were led in the region of Oran, face-to-face, between October 2014 and January 2015, with professionals, travel agents and front-line employees in different hotels, until the saturation point was reached. The average duration of the interviews lasted 30 min. The Table 1 reveals the precise composition of the sample.

The interviews were entirely transcribed and prepared for an analysis of thematic contents. We used *Nvivo 10* software, a qualitative data analysis computer software package. It has been designed for qualitative researchers working with very rich text-based and/or multimedia information, where deep levels of analysis on small or large volumes of data are required to facilitate the work of codification and reduction of the data. The data processing led to the production of results presented now.

4 Findings

On the one hand, the documentary study highlights the Algerian strategy chosen to develop tourism (Sect. 4.1). On the other hand, thematic contents analysis gives four results: an insufficient volume of students currently in training to meet the needs (Sect. 4.2), criteria of recruitment based on a cultural propensity to be welcoming (Sect. 4.3) and the increasing influence of new international chains spreading quality improvement in Oran (Sect. 4.4).

4.1 Algeria Is Setting Up a New Strategy of Tourism Development

Tourism is sensitive to conjunctures. But, beyond political, economic and social concerns, the Arab Spring did not generate noticeable changes in the tourism configurations of the Southern and Eastern Mediterranean Countries (Lanquar

2015). Algeria with more than half a population of 34 million inhabitants is composed of people less than 25 years old. This group faces unemployment challenges for 21 % of them (Banque Africaine de Développement 2011, p. 7). According to Lanquar, "Algeria is one of the few MED 11 countries[1] where tourism suffered greatly from the 2008 world economic crisis: tourist arrivals in 2010 fell sharply and scarcely exceeded the international tourist arrivals of 2005" (2011, p. 119). The economy has grown strongly in the last number of years, mainly thanks to the rise in the world markets of oil and gas prices (98 % of the exportation in 2014) and the strong demand for those natural resources.

Economic growth has been increasing up to 6 % annually. However, Algeria is very dependent on the oil windfall. Especially with the current drop in prices, fluctuations therefore may weaken public finances. The country has finally embarked on the development of its infrastructure, in poor condition in many regions, after more than one decade of serious disrepair. Highways, dams, power plants and desalination of seawater, the realization of ongoing projects abound. Algeria faces several threats, as punctual terrorism continues to hang over and to threaten foreign investment.

Among, its closest competitors, Algeria is ranked at the 147th position in its contribution to the GDP, out of 174 the country is still very far after Morocco (42nd rank) and Tunisia (39th rank). Tourism in Algeria is less developed than in its neighbours. For instance, "Morocco, Tunisia and Egypt, and a lot of tourist arrivals in Algeria have family connections in the country and will stay with family rather than in hotels" (Eurostat 2015). The tourism sector in Algeria is also "in a paradox situation, on one hand we notice a deficit in accommodation capacity, in marketing, a lack of know-how in hostelry, restaurant, etc. On the other hand, we find an attractive image and a shining touristic potential and capacity" (Bouadam 2011, p. 1). So, why is tourism in Algeria underestimated? Kacimi (2013) wanders if it is because of the weakness of the services, the lack of professionalism, the insufficient accommodation facilities, the insecurity in the country and/or a non-achievement of the reforms? (Kacimi 2013).

As a matter of fact, Algeria still suffers from the lack of priority given to tourism and from an insufficient political vision to cluster with other economic sectors such as agriculture, communication and transportation (Lanquar 2015). It was only in 2008 that the national institutions began taken into account the issues, in order to transform Algeria into a "must-visit" worldwide destination, by 2025 (Khiat 2014).

To ensure development, the Algerian government created a project in 2008 to build its vision of tourism. This plan is currently an integral part of the National Scheme of Town Planning (SNAT 2025) and a strategic framework of reference for tourism policies. This plan:

---

[1]Eleven of the southern Mediterranean countries.

- Shows its tourism development vision at different temporal horizons, either in the short (2009), middle (2015) and long term (2025) in order to consolidate Algeria as a receiving country;
- Defines means of its implementation and specifies conditions of its feasibility;
- Insures in a sustainable development framework, the triple balance of social equity, economic efficiency and ecological protection;
- Promotes natural, cultural and historical potential of the country and put them at the disposal of tourism in Algeria in order to push it to the rank of destination of excellence in the Euro-Mediterranean region (National Agency of Investment Development 2015). Algeria also proposes a politico-legal environment favourable to tourism development with measures such as the launch of several projects which adds up 65,540 beds and the encouragement of the Algerian state for investing, by offering advantages to the investors. From then on, mainly French investors are trying to dominate the market, especially those targeting a business clientele.

The improvement of the tourism sector in Algeria can also be reached thanks to several measures related to diversification and quality offers. Safety measures and improvement of the signalling system, roads and infrastructures have been decided. Moreover, a plan to inform the key actors in the industry of a quality approach has been clearly defined. The documentary analysis having allowed a better understanding of the context in which the government intervened and set its goals, the results of the analysis of the interviews led with the professionals is now presented.

4.2   The Volume of Students in Tourism is Insufficient to Meet the Needs

According to the interviewed professionals, the take up of their new job in the tourism sector often seems fortuitous and without direct link with their previous background. For two third of the interviewees, their current job is far away from the tourism world and from front-line positions, as indicated by the professionals interviewed. Career paths may be different. "I am an IT specialist" (Travel agent 2). "I have graduated from the university, thus I am an urbanism engineer specialized in town planning, nothing to do with the service" (Hotel 1). "I studied international trade at the university, I also trained in computing" (Travel agent 1). Generally speaking, their current job position seems to have been learned "on the job" according to the interviewees. The importance of the experience seems determinant, in order to be able to hold the position and deal properly with the clientele. "I worked with my father in the travel agency; I can tell I have learnt the job with him, through his experience" (Travel agent 4).

4.3   Recruitment Criteria Based on a Supposed Cultural Propensity to Welcome Guests

In the opinion of professionals, the criteria of recruitment are for a large part based on social skills. "Welcome first of all is a personal aspect, it belongs to people, we are smiling or we are not" (Hotel 3). The front-line staff competencies are described with some traits and skills "the smile, the appearance, the attention" (Hotel 12). Accordingly, some professionals perceive that the propensity to welcome is truly innate. "It is a question of courtesy, if we are polite; we are appreciated by anybody, no need to study for that!" (Travel agent 3).

However, the natural trait dedicated to welcome customers turns out insufficient to master the front-line positions, "that is why some time of adaptation is needed. Practically, it is necessary that they do their training more than once, many points remain unclear at their level [. . .] there are basics, things to be known before entering in the hospitality industry" (Hotel 3). The culture of the service sounds delicate and historically sensitive, since the image of service sometimes merges with an image of submission. "In Algeria, we still not have this culture of service to others, people think, I am not going to serve him, it is rather embarrassing. We always have this feeling to make something that disturbs, that is against nature, that remembers the past. In fact, it is quite the opposite. It is a quality to be at the service of others" (Hotel 3).

4.4   International Chains Spreading the Quality of Service Delivery Among the Market

The arrival of international chains on the market globally seems to have strengthened the quality of reception, in many ways, since the new entrance of international chains, like Starwood, Hyatt, Hilton or Accor. "When these firms set up in Algeria, people are trained in these hotels. Such as very well-known hotels, the Sheraton or the Meridien, Hilton or Mercure. In those places, people are really trained to new procedures, new tools" (Hotel 5). The necessity for Algeria "to improve the sector" (Travel agent 10) springs from the speeches. The professional wish is to optimize the reception service to upgrade the quality and achieve better financial outcomes. Actually, "when we exceed the expectation of a customer, it is a personal satisfaction and an extra financial return for the industry" (Hotel 11).

Concerning the continuous training, the contents and the learning conditions vary largely according to the operational policies. The duration of the trainings is heterogeneous and often takes place as an extra working time. "Sometimes we have 1 h trainings and sometimes from 8 a.m. till 6 p.m., during several days. The thing is, it is hard to resist, we have our shifts and the training at the same time" (Hotel 1). Unanimously, the first moments at the reception desk are considered crucial and delicate. The opportunity to give a good impression definitely requires professional skills. The first contact with the customer "plays a role at 80 %. If the customer is satisfied with his/her welcome, then we can overtake all other problems. But at the opposite, if a customer is not satisfied, whatever we will do for him/her, we will fail, because we have poorly started the relationship" (Hotel 7).

5   Discussion

The findings highlight the importance of examining the performance and competitiveness of the tourist sector, through the impulse of national touristic policies and through a better management of human resources, on both a macro and micro level. Actually, the implementation of strategies of tourism imposes the implication of all the key economic players to follow the new touristic orientations.

Times have changed and the Algerian government since 2008 has decided to prioritise tourism to develop the country. In a macro-analysis perspective, with an unemployment rate approaching 10 %, the tourism sector could generate hundreds of thousands of jobs, thanks to its domestic tourism (1.6 million Algerians living abroad visited the country in 2012) and thanks to foreign tourists. This tourism development will be possible, provided the fact that valuing the jobs in the industry, offering quality training and fostering behavioural change of the population towards the image of service, are taken into consideration.

The results of the qualitative analysis highlight both the urgency of increasing the volume of tourism students and the necessity of educational and vocational training to improve professional skills in the country. Indeed, training is an important component of success in tourism and hospitality organisations. Therefore, governments and other public institutions play an important role in the improvement of tourism-orientated education. The institutional reforms and the development of pertinent curricula should attract investors and support education in the sector.

Nevertheless, the national orientation towards tourism must be taken into account. For example, in Algeria, the tourism consideration has changed to move on from historical sufferings. "The Algerian government's revolutionary orientation meant that after the revolution and up to 1980s, it opposed tourism. The nature of tourism service towards foreigners, including Algeria's former colonisers implied servitude towards foreigners, which the government viewed as unacceptable both to national pride and to Algerians image abroad" (Gray 2000, p. 400).

Service has always been and probably will always be highly important in the tourism industry. Every viable company must provide an acceptable and effective level of service, in order to retain customers, avoid costs due to poor quality of service, revenues loss and negative word of mouth. If a real cultural dimension of hospitality in the Maghreb is underlined, individual traits or a personal orientation naturally centred on customer relationships are not sufficient, a real orientation towards service, based on hard and soft skills, must be boosted, sustained and professionalised in the industry. Educational and vocational education is thus essential.

6 Conclusion

The aim of this paper was to examine the construction of emerging urban tourism destinations and its human capital challenges. It has been found that the construction of an urban emerging destination needs governmental decisions, plans and measures, which federates the key actors of the sector and attracts investors. The importance of Human Resource Development in the tourism sector is also linked to the global improvement of the quality of service, through learning and performance at individual and organizational levels.

Human capital must respond to the new challenges of emerging urban tourism destinations. From a micro-analysis perspective, the issue of quality of service delivery is central and related to human capital management. Kapiki adds that "a quality service management system is a result-oriented approach. Increasingly, guests are willing to pay more when they visit hospitality properties offering service that meets or exceeds their service expectations" (2012, p. 54). The results show that international standards applied in hotels of international reputation, during the service delivery, are now spreading in the Oranese market. The control of quality needs processes and some forms of measurement, adjustment and inspection activities, to see if the standards are respected on a daily basis. In this way, international chains are pollinating national business units, through processes and good practices, but they also attract professionals and constitute a new benchmark reference for their competitors.

Managing a city as a destination involves addressing many challenges. "Managing urban tourism, however, is no simple task. As metropolitan areas expand rapidly, both the public and private sector face radical changes, as well as significant opportunities" (UNWTO 2012, p. 4). In fact, a positive working environment combined with satisfying job conditions, which encourage loyalty, commitment and engagement, have to be globally considered when setting up management policies.

Avenues of research may consist in studying over time the evolution and degree of maturity of the Oranese urban tourism market, confronted to the difficulties exposed during this preliminary research. To avoid some limits, questioning various actors upstream and downstream, including teachers in the hospitality sector and customers may highlight the phenomenon. Moreover, a comprehensive analysis of strategies and best practice examples in the context of emerging urban tourism destinations around the globe and especially in the Mediterranean Basin, would help understanding the challenges, and the ways chosen to get prepared for the future. An interdisciplinary approach will also enrich the research and provide comparative and complementary views.

References

Azevedo P, Silva V, Silva A (2002) Contract mix in food franchising. Paper presented at the 6th conference of the international society for new institutional economics. Cambridge, MA

Banque Africaine de Développement (2011) Investissements chinois et création d'emplois en Algérie et en Égypte, Note économique

Baum T (2007) Human resources in tourism: still waiting for change. Tour Manag 28:1383–1399

Bitner MJ (1992) Servicescapes: the impact of physical surroundings on customers and employees. J Mark 56(2):57–71

Bolton S, Houlihan M (2007) Searching for the human in human resource management: theory, practice and workplace contexts. Palgrave Macmillan, Basingstoke

Bouadam K (2011) The national strategy of tourism development in Algeria: issues, opportunities and limitations. Rev Appl Soc-Econ Res 1(2):23–37

Brookes and Roper (2010) The impact of entry modes on the organisational design of international hotel chains. Serv Ind J 30(9):1499–1512

Carbone LP, Haeckel SH (1994) Engineering customer experiences. Mark Manage 3(3):8–19

Child J, McGrath R (2001) Organizations unfettered: organizational form in an information intensive economy. Acad Manage J 44(6):1135–1149

De Grandpré F, Leblanc M, Royer C (2012) Etude sur l'accueil touristique au Québec. UQTR, Québec

Di Liberto A (2013) High skills, high growth: is tourism an exception? J Int Trade Econ Dev 22 (5):749–785

Dimitriades ZS (2007) The influence of service climate and job involvement on customer-oriented organizational citizenship behavior in Greek service organizations: a survey. Employee Relat 29(5):469–491

Dogor Di Nuzzo B (2009) L'accueil, un métier: application au tourisme et à l'hôtellerie. Editions Management & Société, Condé-sur-Noireau

Doucet L (2004) Service provider hostility and service quality. Acad Manage J 47(5):761–772

Dulude N, Bastien S (1998) L'assurance qualité: un outil à implenter dans le domaine du tourisme. Téoros 17(3):51–53

Eurostat (2015) Basic figures on the European neighbourhood policy—South countries—2015 edition. Eurostat Compact guide

Failte Ireland (2005) A human resource development strategy for Irish Tourism. Competing through People, 2005–2012. Fáilte Ireland, Dublin

Gherman R, Dincu AM, Dumitrescu C, Toader C (2011) Human resources development in tourism. Agricultural Management/Lucrari Stiintifice Seria I. Manage Agricol 13(4):233–240

Gray M (2000) The political economy of tourism in North Africa. Comp Perspect Thunderbird Int Bus Rev 42(4):393–408

Jui-Min L, Jen-Shou Y, Hsin-His W (2009) From various service typologies: integrating the perspectives of the organisation and customers. Serv Ind J 29(12):1763–1778

Kacimi Z (2013) Place de l'Algérie dans le contexte du tourisme maghrébin. Thèse. Paris, Université IV—Sorbonne

Kapiki S (2012) Quality management in tourism and hospitality: an exploratory study among tourism stakeholders. Int J Econ Pract Theor 2(2):53

Khiat A (2014) De la nécessité de la formation à logique de la compétition dans les métiers du tourisme. In: d. V. Salon International du Tourisme (ed) Oran, Algérie

Lanquar R (2011) Tourism in the MED 11 countries. CASE Network Reports, Apr 2011 (98):161

Lanquar R (2015) Tourism in the Mediterranean. In: Ayadi R, Dabrowski M, De Wulf L (eds) Economic and social development of the Southern and Eastern Mediterranean countries. Springer, New York

Lewis RC, Chambers RE (2000) Marketing leadership in hospitality. Wiley, New York

National Agency of Investment Development (2015) http://www.andi.dz/index.php/en/secteur-du-tourisme

Parasuraman A, Zeithaml V, Berry L (1994) Reassessment of expectations as a comparison standard in measuring service quality—implications for further research. J Mark 58 (1):111–124

Richard S, Gill F (2003) The implications of hotel employee attitudes for the development of quality tourism: the case of Cyprus. Tour Manag 24:687–697

Servet D, Tesone D (2005) Prior experience satisfaction and subsequent fairness perceptions within the service experience. J Hosp Leis Mark 13(4):121–137

UNWTO (2012) Global report on city tourism. AM Reports, vol 6 [pdf]. UNWTO, Madrid. http://dtxtq4w60xqpw.cloudfront.net/sites/all/files/pdf/am6_city_platma.pdf

UNWTO (2014) Tourism highlights. 2014 Edition

Westwood A (2004) Skills that matter and shortages that don't. In: Warhurst C, Grugulis I, Keep E (eds) The skills that matter. Basingstoke, Palgrave, pp 38–54

Whitelock J, Yang H (2007) Moderating effects of parent control on international joint ventures' strategic objectives and performance. Asia Pac J Mark 19(3):286–306

World Travel and Tourism Council (2015) Economic impact of travel & tourism 2015, November. http://www.wttc.org/-/media/files/reports/economic%20impact%20research/economic%20impact_midyear%20update_161115%20(2).pdf

Urban Coastal Tourism and Climate Change: Indicators for a Mediterranean Prospective

Robert Lanquar

Abstract Urban theory ignores generally urban coastal tourism. This tourism, which mixes a wide range of cultural and leisure activities, faces the impacts of climate change, which accelerates sea-level rise and extreme weather events. Indicators identified in the literature concerning urban coastal tourism are not numerous according to their relationships with environmental, economic, social and ethical factors. This chapter is preliminary to a Mediterranean research for MEDCOP 21 projects in order to establish a system of indicators as a tool aimed at urban planners and local authorities for decision-making and prospective research as well to indicate how to evaluate the new smart tourism concept.

Keywords Urban coastal tourism • Climate change • Environmental—social—economic—ethical indicators • Decision-making • The Mediterranean • Smart tourism

1 Introduction

Urban coastal tourism is not only mass tourism. It mixes a wide range of cultural and leisure activities as the 'sea, sand, sun' products and water sports. Urban theory ignores largely the influence of tourism in the development of the coastal cities. Nowadays, and more in the future, these coastal tourism cities will have to face the impacts of climate change, which accelerates sea-level rise and extreme weather events. These cities are more and more connected as using ICT (information and communications technologies). Moreover, with this ICT revolution, indicators and metadata are a central source for taking decisions for the future of a city or a territory. How to develop a system to measure these impacts and serve as a tool aimed at urban planners and local authorities for decision-making and prospective research? How to get account of the transformations that are currently occurring and to recognize the warning signs of the impact of climate change on coastal cities?

R. Lanquar (✉)
La Rochelle Business School, La Rochelle, France
e-mail: lanquarr@esc-larochelle.fr

© Springer International Publishing Switzerland 2017
N. Bellini, C. Pasquinelli (eds.), *Tourism in the City*,
DOI 10.1007/978-3-319-26877-4_9

The measurement of economic performance and social progress shows the limits of indicators such as GDP allowing only the assessment of the added value of an economy and forgetting to take into account other social and environmental values and variables (Lanquar 2012, p. 33). It shows the need to construct new indicators that take into account these new realities, especially after the COP21 of December 2015 that reached a definitive agreement between governments, civil society and companies on the battle against global warming. Then, the main question will be to know if those indicators are adequate all over the world, if it is not necessary to differentiate then in developed countries and in developing countries.

2   The European Blue Growth Strategy and Urban Coastal Tourism

In 2010, Europe has announced a strategy for sustainable coastal and maritime tourism welcomed by the European Parliament, the Council, the Committee of the Regions and the European Economic and Social Committee in the framework of the European Blue Growth. Coastal and maritime tourism is considered as one of the five focus areas for delivering sustainable growth; so it was recommended "a series of actions to boost the sector and support the development of sustainable tourism in coastal destinations... with a view to capitalise on Europe's strengths and enabling it to substantially contribute to the Europe 2020 objectives for smart, sustainable and inclusive growth" (European Commission 2014, p. 1).

To reach this objective, the European Commission invites Member States and regional and local authorities to analyse more deeply the use of ICTs and new tools to measure and determine the state of coastal and maritime tourism. It asks to "invest in quality control initiatives for tourism products and staff" (European Commission 2014, p. 5). Those initiatives are supposed to stimulate innovative management schemes to boost tourism, especially in coastal urban areas. To reach this objective, detailed and accurate instruments are needed to make the tough decisions; indicators on the diverse aspects of tourism sustainable development are one of these tools.

Indicators are information or sets of information contributing to the assessment of a situation by a political authority, a business leader, the civil society, above all by policymakers. There are ways to gauge a situation. Theoretically, indicators as statistical tools for obtaining information from a process involving data collection, processing of collected data, the interpretation of the data, the presentation to make the data comprehensible for all.

3 The Importance of Indicators

A measurable economic factor that changes before the economy starts to follow a particular pattern or trend. Leading indicators are used to predict changes in the economy, but are not always accurate. Indicators are mainly used as a representation of criteria, often non-measured or non-measurable, providing information before taking decision on policies and budgets. In general, the indicators point toward the status or the performance on economic, social or environmental matters. Leading indicators may allow to predict changes in an economy, society or environment. But the academic literature believes they are not always accurate. Control panels may gather them in function of strategic data evaluated as quickly as possible. They are data on operational or structural functions and allowed drawing up policies and budgets. They are necessary in a coastal town where the governance's aim is to manage the daily life of its inhabitants as well as to be prepared for the future of its resident population; moreover, a coastal city receives each year tourists. Sometimes, those tourists, temporary residents, are more numerous than its residents.

As underlined by the European Commission, tourism depends on a healthy environment and the sustainable use of natural and cultural assets, but activities are often concentrated in already densely populated areas (i.e. urban areas), "leading to vast increases in water demand, more waste and emissions from air, road and sea transport at peak periods, more risks of soil sealing and biodiversity degradation (from infrastructure developments), eutrophication and other pressures. In addition, the impacts of climate change exacerbate pressures on these areas and could reshape tourism's geographical and seasonal distribution" (European Commission 2014, p. 6). That is considered as one of the main problem for the future of coastal urban tourism.

The United States Environmental Protection Agency (EPA) has prepared in 2014 a very comprehensive set of indicators on climate change. For this US agency, one important way to track and communicate the causes and effects of climate change is using indicators. The indicators in the EPA 2014 Report relate to the causes and effects of climate change not only to "provide meaningful, authoritative climate-relevant measures about the status, rates, and trends of key physical, ecological, and societal variables" (EPA 2014, p. 1), but also by building analytical tools by which user communities (such as a coastal city) can derive their own indicators.

In tourism, the most well-known indicators are included in the *Travel and Tourism Competitiveness Index* (TTCI), elaborated by the World Economic Forum since 2007. This Index aims to measure the factors and policies that make it attractive to develop the travel and tourism sector in different countries as tourist destinations. The data derive from an Executive Opinion Survey (Survey) and quantitative data from other sources such as UNWTO, WTTC, and the national tourist administrations. Based on variables that facilitate or drive tourism and travel competitiveness, this survey includes:

1. The tourism and travel regulatory framework
2. The business environment and infrastructure
3. The human, cultural, and natural resources.

Only after 2013, TTCI includes climate change as a pillar of this index. The explanation is simple: from 2010, the World Economic Forum fully recognised the global warming and included it in its works and declarations.

Each of the pillars assembles fourteen individual variables:

1. Policy rules and regulations
2. Environmental sustainability
3. Safety and security
4. Health and hygiene
5. Prioritisation of Travel and Tourism
6. Air transport infrastructure
7. Ground transport infrastructure
8. Tourism infrastructure
9. ICT infrastructure
10. Price competitiveness in the travel and tourism industry
11. Human resources
12. Affinity for Travel and Tourism
13. Natural resources
14. Cultural resources.

How can we apply these indicators to measure the impact of tourism in a coastal city in 2015 and after, when climate change influences more and more strategies and policies? In the Mediterranean, more than half of the tourist frequentation concerns these cities. For a town that wants to develop a sustainable, responsible and smart tourism, what are these indicators? How to use them to assess local economic, social and environmental performance in relation with climate change? How can they help to measure the level of well-being and the quality of the public services? How are they linked to the new concepts and models of smart tourism?

4   Common Indicators for the Mediterranean

The objective of the Mediterranean Blue Plan/Regional Activity Centre of UNEP—MAP (Mediterranean Action Plan under the Barcelona Convention) is to raise awareness of stakeholders concerning environment and sustainable development issues. In the context of the Barcelona Convention, the Blue Plan built common indicators as "measures that summarizes data into a simple, standardized and communicable figure and is ideally applicable in the whole Mediterranean basin, but at least on the level of sub-regions and shall be monitored by all contracting parties. A common indicator is able to give an indication of the degree of threat or change in the marine ecosystem and can deliver valuable information to decision-makers" (Blue Plan 2005, p. 2). These common indicators were proposed on the basis of experience already gained by the Blue Plan Contracting Parties through their regular monitoring activities as well as the experience of the EU Mediterranean countries, and then updated for the implementation of EU Directives such as the Marine Strategy Framework Directive adopted in 17 June 2008 and later, the specific European Strategy for more Growth and Jobs in Coastal and Maritime Tourism (ECORIS 2013).

The Blue Plan uses scenarios to forecast the future of the Mediterranean region. In this respect and through its dual functions as an observatory of the environment and sustainable development and a centre for systemic and prospective analysis, the Blue Plan has built a solid basis of environmental and sustainable development data, statistics, and indicators to follow the progresses towards sustainable development in the Mediterranean. With these data, it is possible to show "the main changes in terms of: socio-economic disparities between the two shores, economic weight of the Mediterranean region in the world, poverty and unemployment, contribution of the region to global pollution (climate change), environment degradation costs and the capacity of development to consider the needs of future generations. To that end, the major macro indicators available will be used, taking into account the usual interpretation caveats" (Blue Plan 2005).

The elaboration of common indicators allows preparing and implementing a cost effective integrated monitoring programme of marine and costal quality environment. The same type of indicators may be used for analysing coastal tourism cities. These indicators show the importance of environmental impacts and allow the definition of drivers for development scenarios until 2025, 2030 and 2050 as they were developed by MEDPRO (Lanquar 2013). MEDPRO is the European instrument for the prospective of the East and Southern Mediterranean until 2030. If these scenarios are not focused on climate change until 2013, they have a direct link with this major issue.

5 The Blue Plan Method to Design Indicators

In all, the Blue Plan experts defined or suggested 130 indicators for sustainable development according to a method including a code, an indicator label and the following elements: strategic objective; rationale; definition; unit; objective and/or targeted values; organisational indications; geographical scope; references; international data sources; and precautions for use.

The Blue Plan identified a list of 34 priority indicators, some of them related with coastal cities' tourism (Table 1).

In addition, as reported in the following Table 2, other non-priority indicators allow a more accurate follow-up to fit with the EU Environment Action Programme to 2020 (European Union 2013) and the climate change adaptation and mitigation focus with the financing of the European Investment Bank which provides different supports to tourism SMEs.

Table 1 Indicators for environmental performance of the Mediterranean coastal cities according to the Blue Plan (2013)

Objectives	Measures
Improving integrated water resource and demand management	Index to monitor water demand
Decouple water demand and GDP growth	Water efficiency index
	Water intensity index ratio compared to GDP
Preserve water resources	Exploitation index of renewable water resources
Achieve the Millennium Development Goals (MDGs) for access to safe drinking-water and sanitation	Proportion of the population with access to safe drinking water
	Proportion of the population with access to sanitation
Managing energy demand and mitigating the effects of climate change	Energy intensity, total and per sector
	Proportion of renewable energies in the energy balance sheet
	Proportion of Greenhouse Gas emission
Ensuring sustainable mobility through appropriate transport management	Motorized transport intensity in relation to the GDP
Stabilize or reduce whenever possible the proportion of road transport in the overall volume of traffic by a shift to sea and rail and reduce urban vehicle congestion and pollution noise by promoting low-pollutant public transport	Proportion of public surface transport (urban and interurban)
Promote sustainable tourism: diversify tourism by developing offers that enhance Mediterranean diversity	Proportion of non-seaside beds in total number of holiday beds
Increase benefit and added-value from tourism for local communities and stakeholders in developing countries	International tourism receipts with assessment of effective benefits for destination countries and local populations
Promote a sustainable urban economy	Number of coastal cities with over 10,000 inhabitants engaged in a process Agenda 21 type or in urban renewal programmes
Reduce social disparities	Proportion of urban population with access to a decent dwelling
Improve the urban environment by reducing waste generation and improve air quality	Index for household (residents and tourists) waste generation per capita and number of uncontrolled dumping sites
	Air quality in major Mediterranean urban areas, assessed via a composite index
Promoting sustainable management of sea and coastal areas	Number of local plans
Promote balanced development and integrated management of the coastline. Push back urbanization to prevent artificialisation of coasts. Avoid linear and continuous urbanization	Artificialized coastline/Total coastline (0–1-km and 1–10-km strip)
Reduce pollution from land-based sources	Proportion of coastal urban inhabitants with no access to sanitation

(continued)

Table 1 (continued)

Objectives	Measures
Halt or reduce marine/coastal biodiversity loss	Bring at least 10 % of the marine and coastal surface under some form of protection
	Surface of protected coastal and marine areas
Strengthen solidarity, commitment and financing for a sustainable development at local levels	% Aid allocated
Strengthen reciprocal commitments, solidarity and Euro-Mediterranean cooperation for sustainable development	EU net public financial flows to EU Mediterranean members
Promote implementation of systems to enable funding of SMEs for productive and innovative activities (micro-credit, venture capital, incentives, etc.)	Proportion of bank credit allocated to the private sector—SME
	Proportion of alternative financing volume to bank credit
Strengthen local authorities' prerogatives and capacities	Proportion of local government tax revenue as percentage of total tax revenues (government receipts)
	Proportion of government budget allocated to local authorities
Reinforce territorial and social cohesion. Develop public financial mechanisms to support the least favoured regions	Number of Public financial mechanisms to support the least favoured regions

Source: Blue Plan (2013)

Table 2 Other indicators for environmental performance of the Mediterranean coastal cities

Objectives	Measures
Reduce exposure to floods and drought hazards	Regulation indexes
Protect water resources	Unsustainable water exploitation index
Reduce water pollution	Purification rate of collected wastewater
Tourism carrying-capacity and saturation	Index of density along the coast
Marinas and ports built on sea	Artificialized land use per capita
Biodiversity	Indicator as an instrument to halt or significantly reduce marine and coastal biodiversity loss
Posidonia	Share of the surface area of in the infra-coastal zone of the city
Water quality	Composite indicator to improve coastal water quality
Cultural diversity	Indicator showing this diversity

Source: Blue Plan (2013)

6 Conclusions

Since 2005, the Blue Plan is continually improving its own indicators' set, by opening tracks for the tourist coastal cities facing the challenge of climate change. On June 5, 2015 in Marseille, during the MEDCOP21 Conference, the workshop on *Cities and sustainable territories* highlighted existing initiatives and formulated innovative proposals brought by civil society actors. These proposals intend to enrich a Mediterranean Positive Agenda (Lanquar 2015). The project proposed, with the association *Diplomatie* and *Développement Durable*, is to design an Indicators' System, including the most important climate changes, impacts, vulnerabilities and preparedness, and mitigation responses, and focused on tourism with several goals:

- customisable to be used by a wide variety of stakeholders, public and private, and adapted to the specific needs at each local urban level;
- explanatory for coastal tourism city management, research, and training, allowing to determine what are the actual climate-related conditions, in order to develop effective mitigation and adaptation measures;
- linked with the global climate change indicators, and in this way providing analytical tools by which user coastal tourism cities can derive their own indicators for particular purposes;
- periodically updated and evaluated to identify opportunities for indicator research and development as a part of long-term sustained assessment activities.

Urban populations are growing faster and more than half of the world's population lives in cities. These coastal cities have to face serious issues concerning the climate change. More and more information and communications technologies (ICT) are necessary to resolve their daily problems to "coordinate all activities and services, leading to connected, better informed and engaged citizens" (Buhalis and Amarangana 2013, p. 553) and to find solutions and reinforce initiatives for mitigating and adapting these cities to climate change. Smartness is now the master word to enhance citizens' quality of life and to improve city services and products in order to challenge the stakes of climate change. Smart tourism destinations "exploit synergies between ubiquitous sensing technology and their social components to support the enrichment of tourist experiences" (Buhalis and Amarangana 2013, p. 553). Smart tourism is becoming the objective of coastal cities to drive innovations and measure their efficiency. With the challenges and opportunities of the three-dimensional big data (volume, velocity and variety), indicators are more necessary than ever to analyse a local situation and take better decisions.

References

Blanke J, Chiesa T (2007) The travel and tourism competitiveness index: assessing key factors driving the sector's development. The travel and tourism competitiveness reports. World Economic Forum, Geneva

Blanke J, Chiesa T (2008) The travel and tourism competitiveness index: assessing key factors driving the sector's development. The travel and tourism competitiveness reports. World Economic Forum, Geneva

Blanke J, Chiesa T (2011) The travel and tourism competitiveness index: assessing key factors driving the sector's development. The travel and tourism competitiveness reports. World Economic Forum, Geneva

Blue Plan—PNUE (2005) Regional workshop on indicators for sustainable development strategies and policies in the mediterranean region. Plan Bleu, Nice

Blue Plan—PNUE (2006) Methodological sheets of the 34 priority indicators for the 'Mediterranean Strategy for Sustainable Development' Follow-up Working document. Plan Bleu, Sophia Antipolis

Blue Plan—PNUE (2013, May) Mediterranean strategy for sustainable development follow-up, Main indicators, 2013 Update. Plan Bleu, Sophia Antipolis

Buhalis D, Amarangana A (2013) Smart tourism destinations. In: Xiang Z, Tussyadiah I (eds) Information and communication technologies in tourism 2014. Springer International Publishing Switzerland, Basel

ECORIS (2013) Study in support of policy measures for maritime and coastal tourism at EU level, Final Report, DG Maritime Affairs and Fisheries. European Commission, Brussels, 15 Sep 2013

European Commission (2014) Communication from the Commission to the European Parliament, the Council, the European economic and social Committee and the Committee of the regions, A European Strategy for more Growth and Jobs in Coastal and Maritime Tourism, 0.2. 2014 COM (2014) 86 final, Brussels

European Union (2013) Decision n 1386/2013/EU of the European Parliament and of the Council of 20 November 2013 on a General Union Environment Action Programme to 2020 'Living well, within the limits of our planets. Official Journal of the European Union, Strasbourg

EPA (2014) Climate change indicators in the United States, 3rd edn. U.S. Environmental Protection Agency, Washington, DC

Lanquar R (2012) Le tourisme fait-il le bonheur des nations ?, Editions Espaces, Revue mensuelle de réflexion du tourisme et des loisirs, n° 307, Paris

Lanquar R (2013) Tourism in the Mediterranean. In: Rym A, Marek D, Luc DW (eds) Economic and social development of the Southern and Eastern Mediterranean countries. Springer, Heidelberg-New York

Lanquar R (2015) MEDCOP21. Les Méditerranéens prennent en main leur destin climatique, Editions Espaces, Revue mensuelle de réflexion du tourisme et des loisirs, n° 325, Paris

Rugg G (2007) Using statistics. A gentle introduction. McGraw-Hill, London

World Economic Forum (2013) The travel and tourism competitiveness report 2013. In: Blanke J, Chiesa T (eds) Reducing barriers to economic growth and job growth. World Economic Forum, Geneva

Visitor Streams in City Destinations: Towards New Tools for Measuring Urban Tourism

Göran Andersson

Abstract City destinations are central in the study of tourism. But how can visitor streams related to the destination characteristics and visitor segments be analysed and discussed as a basis for improvement of the destination? This research used statistical data and qualitative information as "knowledge indicators" rather than as "unambiguous facts". The research included analysis of about 100 destination plans, a pilot study of statistics and qualitative destination information about Stockholm, and a literature review. It resulted in the development of the visitor stream concept, which can be used in future research on the integration of various visitor segment streams. A method for analysing visitor streams is suggested: (1) defining "focused destination" and its characteristics, (2) investigating quantitative and qualitative destination information, (3) identifying visitor segments, and (4) analysing streams with new destination tools. The knowledge gained will introduce and address new issues concerning statistics for measuring, monitoring and assessing the actual value of tourism, particularly urban tourism.

Keywords City destination • Destination characteristics • Visitor segment • Visitor stream • Visit statistics

1 Introduction

The city destination of Stockholm, with a population of 2.1 million, provides about 11 million commercial guest nights annually and is ranked as one of Europe's top 10 destinations (Stockholm Visitors Board 2014). Since tourism destinations are the foundation for tourism in general (Swedish Tourism 2010), it is important to conduct economic, effective and sustainable development as proposed by several destination actors in a pilot study on destination planning. How can the destination be developed? One approach could be to study the supply and demand sides of the destination and how these sides interact.

G. Andersson (✉)
Department of Tourism Studies, Södertörn University, Stockholm, Sweden
e-mail: goran.andersson@sh.se

© Springer International Publishing Switzerland 2017
N. Bellini, C. Pasquinelli (eds.), *Tourism in the City*,
DOI 10.1007/978-3-319-26877-4_10

147

First, how could the supply side be studied for the chosen *focused destination?* Connected to this question is knowledge about the destination characteristics and its strengths from the visitor's perspective. For example, city tourism destinations, such as Stockholm, typically have a higher attraction density (e.g. more attractions per square kilometre) than rural destinations.

Second, how could the demand (and also revenue) side of the destination be studied using unique criteria for preliminary visitor segmentation in the city, such as visitor purpose? Connected to this question is how to choose economically strong and reachable *focused visitor segments*, such as city-breakers, using the knowledge about preliminary visitor segments and their relation to the destination characteristics.

Third, how could the interaction *between the supply and demand* sides be studied? Managers of the destination management organisation (DMO) and some tourist companies in Stockholm have complained about the lack of dynamic information concerning visitors' movements and activities while they are visiting the destination of Stockholm.

There seems to be a lack of knowledge about *visitor streams within the destination*, such as the cruise passenger stream in Fig. 1, for instance. The problem, though, is how statistics and qualitative information can be collected and analysed with the limited resources available. Furthermore, the statistics are too static, because they are not connected to other activities within a tourist's whole trip. This will demand *new approaches* to tourism statistics and study techniques. In the end, the knowledge gained will introduce and address new issues concerning

Fig. 1 Cruise passenger stream in Stockholm. *Source*: Adamsson and Ports of Stockholm (2015)

statistics for measuring, monitoring and assessing the actual value of tourism, particularly urban tourism.

The research purpose is to obtain a deeper understanding about how focused destinations can be developed using knowledge of how targeted visitor segments related to destination characteristics can result in visitor streams within the destination.

2   The City Destination

2.1   Focused Destination

To understand destination characteristics, a clear definition of "destination" must be used (Framke 2002). In this article, "focused destination" is defined as a specific geographical place that is targeted to a sufficiently large group of potential visitors, based on the individuals own needs and image thoughts about the site, and where the whole visitor product is provided by a cooperating business and public sector in a sustainable way (Andersson 2013).

Using this definition, one can choose the focused destination and its limited area in the city. Depending on how the analyst formulates the problem, different parts of the city or the whole city can be investigated as a potential focused destination. To be considered a true focused destination, all the criteria in the destination definition above must be fulfilled. Destinations can be divided into local, regional and country levels (UNWTO 2004). The next section presents an example of focused destinations on different levels in a city tourism context, in Stockholm.

The above understanding of what constitutes a "focused destination" is not the only one, however. Framke (2002) found in an investigation of destination articles that there are different destination definitions, but that the knowledge can be divided into two main areas: business understanding and sociological understanding.

2.2   Destination Areas and Levels in Stockholm

Several limited geographical areas that could be considered focused destinations have been found in Stockholm at three destination levels: regional, local and attraction-based destination points.

The *regional destinations* can also be seen at different levels, such as a group of local destinations covering an urban area with a focused regional place image. Examples include Stockholm Town, Roslagen County and Södertörn County. A map of Stockholm Town can be studied in Fig. 2. An alternative to this analysis is a

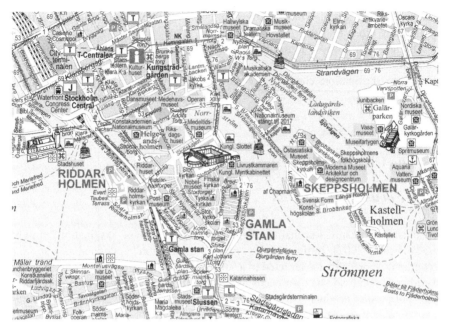

Fig. 2 Regional destination "Stockholm Town". *Source*: Stockholm City Municipality (2016)

group of local and regional destinations covering an urban area with a national place image, such as Greater Stockholm.

Local destinations can be seen as tourism-matured focused places, where both tourism demand and supply are substantial and obvious. It is difficult to find exact figures to describe what constitutes "substantial", but the destination is in general heavily dependent on the economic activity that tourism represents. The criterion "obvious" is based on that local destinations are held as positive images in the minds of key visitor segments, and they are promoted co-operatively by both business and private sectors. From the destinations' character, the following local examples in Stockholm can be found: the amusement island "Djurgården", the old town and the city centre. The local destination "Stockholm centre" has often been marketed by destination organisations as "Beauty on the water" using photos such as the one in Fig. 3.

Within regional or local destinations there are *attraction-based destination points*. These points are based on visitor attractions, which are permanently delimited places but offer a total tourism product for the visitor. In Stockholm, some typical destination points include the "Friends" and the "Globen" event arenas and the "Stockholmsmässan" fair and exhibition arena.

In the pilot study of written destination plans (discussed further in the method section), it was sometimes difficult to delimit local city destination areas within regional city destinations, which was not so problematic at rural destinations. This is because the local city destinations are so close together that visitors often move

Fig. 3 Destination "Stockholm centre". *Source*: Stockholmsfoto.se (2016)

through several of them within a single day. Local rural destinations are generally located farther apart and are less interconnected with other destinations so that visitors are more likely to spend the whole day in one chosen rural destination.

2.3   *Destination Characteristics*

City destinations have their own character. Each city destination has its own natural attributes, cultural attractions, and shopping opportunities (Lucarelli and Berg 2011). Researchers have investigated the character of various destinations. Valls et al. (2014) analysed 82 items from 11 European tourist cities to create the Tourism Innovation Capacity of Barcelona Index. The 82 items were categorised into four fields: basic city facts such as population and GDP; transport connections such as direct flights; tourism competitiveness such as number of museums and tourists; and finally, creative society such as level of research and use of technology. Turner and Reisinger (1999) found 27 destination characteristics in a destination study, such as "historic sites". These characteristics can be considered for use in an analysis of Stockholm.

In a highly competitive world, it is a trend for cities to adopt entrepreneurial and internationally oriented policies in order to increase their competitiveness, which has resulted in the emergence of entrepreneurial cities. Important economic indicators for such competitiveness include tourism-related figures (Shen 2004).

Furthermore, the National Tourism Strategy 2020 project group (Visit Sweden 2012) has proposed that a number of criteria must be fulfilled before a destination can be considered mature for foreign tourism in Sweden. The use of the Internet and the rise of low-cost airlines have spurred competition among European cities over the last decade (Dunne et al. 2007).

2.4 Destination Characteristics in Stockholm

Six typical destination characteristics were found in the written destination plans in Stockholm. The characteristics are useful for understanding the urban destination's tourism potential based on its character. The pilot study on the focused destination plans assessed the characteristics of the destination and the number of visitors it received. The analysis of the plans revealed a connection between the strength of typical characteristics and the number of visitors. The examples of typical characteristics were Visitors attraction cluster, Effective incoming transport system, Accommodation alternatives, Nearness to the city centre, Degree of developed tourism industry and Kind of experience focus.

3 Method

At the start of the pilot study, 100 destination plans were analysed. The plans had been written over a period of 10 years by undergraduate students taking a course at Södertörn University. Statistics and qualitative destination information were also collected, and a literature review was conducted. Further on, as a typical example of city visitor streams, cruise passengers in Stockholm were studied, based on several in-depth interviews and analysis of statistical data and maps. The next step will be to conduct a main case study on regional, local and point-destination levels of Stockholm and their associated visitor streams in order to understand how various streams are integrated in the destination and how the destination can be developed using this knowledge.

4 Statistics

4.1 Tourism Statistics

Typical tourism statistics available for Stockholm include statistics on transport, accommodations, visitor attractions, general incoming tourists and special investing. The Stockholm Visitors Board (2015) has collected a lot of data for the

Stockholm region. For example, in 2014 there were 26.7 million arrivals and departures by air and 10.1 million by ferry. Statistics Sweden (2015) is an administrative agency and its main task is to supply customers with statistics for decision-making, debate and research, and also to coordinate the Swedish system for official statistics. The agency is mainly assigned tasks by the government and different agencies, but it also has customers in the private sector and among researchers. For many years, Statistics Sweden has collected information on guest nights at hotels in Sweden. For example, between 2008 and 2014, Stockholm's guest nights increased by 26 %, but in rural areas the increase is much less. In order to show a typical statistical table from Statistics Sweden (2015) data are extracted from the table about guest nights and presented in Table 1.

The Stockholm Visitors Board (2015) also presents the number of visitors to attractions in Stockholm. The most visited attraction in Stockholm is the House of Culture and Stockholm City Theatre, which had 2.6 million visitors in 2013. Stockholm City Theatre AB was established in 1960 as a municipal limited company. Statistics for 2014 also include the House of Culture—formerly part of Stockholm's Culture Administration—combined with the Stockholm City Theatre AB. The operation is called the Culture City Theatre and is directed by the council; it presents events ranging from theatre, dance, and music performances to debates, literature presentations, and art and design exhibitions (Stockholm City Theatre AB 2016).

Incoming tourism is very important to the Swedish tourism industry as well as the country as a whole (Swedish Agency for Economic and Regional Growth 2014). Therefore, in order to improve knowledge about incoming tourism in Sweden, a national border survey called IBIS is carried out by the Agency. IBIS investigated foreign visitors' main reasons for visiting Sweden (e.g. private trip, business trip) during the period 2011–2013 and also asked questions about the activities the visitors were engaged in and the countries they were visiting from. The top three activities in Stockholm in 2013 were (1) shopping (11.3 million); (2) restaurant visits (10.8 million); and (3) sightseeing (4.5 million). One conclusion that can be made about the statistics at present is that there are a lot of tourism data on specific and focused areas covering rather long periods.

4.2 Producers of City Tourism Statistics

Several organisations produce statistics on Stockholm, from specific tourism statistics to general statistics which can also be used in tourism analyses. Producers of specific tourism statistics on the local and regional levels include the Stockholm Visitors Board, local transport companies, visitor attraction organisations, local meetings industry organisations and privately owned tourism consultancy companies that produce specific tourism reports. Producers of national-level statistics include the authorities for various transports (especially airline, train and ferry

Table 1 Number of nights by region and year in Sweden

	2008	2009	2010	2011	2012	2013	2014
00 Sweden	50,097,388	51,011,006	52,406,034	52,624,008	52,690,482	53,735,774	56,401,219
0010 Greater Stockholm	9,348,127	9,372,903	10,010,623	10,405,413	10,675,264	10,950,741	11,775,137
0060 Sweden exclusive. Metropolitan areas	30,983,561	31,536,625	31,983,468	31,876,681	31,773,530	32,372,825	33,572,010
XXX	X	X	X	X	X	X	X

Source: The Swedish Agency for Economic and Regional Growth and Statistics Sweden (2015)

industries), international meetings industry organisations and the Visit Sweden organisation.

The general statistics that can also be used in tourism at the local and regional levels are produced by the Growth and Regional Planning Administration in Stockholm County and the Municipality of Stockholm, among others. The general statistics that can also be used in tourism, on a national level include those produced by the Swedish Agency for Economic and Regional Growth and various statistics from the national public organisation Statistics Sweden. Despite all these statistics, there is a lack of interconnected statistics and interpretations of data from different sources.

4.3   Statistics on Visitor Streams

There are no available official statistics for detailed tourism streams, defined as a process consisting of the visitor's main activities during travel to, from and within the destination, in Stockholm. Discussions at statistical meetings at the Swedish Agency for Economic and Regional Growth led to the conclusion that there may be insufficient resources available to collect such statistics in detail. However, even if tourism stream statistics are poor, it is still possible to use some types of *statistical indicators*. These indicators represent the streams, but are built on available indirect statistics and qualitative judgements which have been interpreted into stream-oriented conclusions.

5   Targeted Visitor Segments

5.1   Criteria for Visitor Segmentation and Typical Visitor Segments

To understand the demand side, unique criteria can be used for visitor segmentation in the city, such as visitor purpose. For example, Muzaffer Uysal and McCleary (2006) found that there was a relationship between cultural/heritage destination attributes and overall satisfaction with the cultural/heritage experience. An important aspect of visitors' choice of destination is their image of the destination. Dolnicar and Grabler (2004) found that different consumers have different perceptions of various destinations in their minds.

When analysing the destination plans (which were written during at a university course by undergraduate students at Södertörn University) used in the pilot study, the following segmentation criteria were found useful in Stockholm (Andersson 2014): Demographic, Behavioural, Accommodation, Transport, Visitor purpose, Travel length and Season. These criteria, in combination with destination characteristics, have been used to develop the following typical visitor segments in Stockholm (Andersson 2014): City-breakers, Families with children, Cruise passengers, Congress and fair visitors, Conference guests, Active older people, Couples without children, Individual business travellers, Singles, Naturalist city tourists, Car travellers and Free independent travellers.

5.2   Visitor Segment Targeting

An important issue is how the individual visitor selects a specific destination. Each destination has to develop its product and marketing campaigns in order to effectively promote its attributes as benefits to each of its target markets. The challenge is to identify the attributes and benefits that the individual market segments value the most (Reisinger et al. 2009). Therefore, a destination management organisation (DMO) has to select some overall *target* visitor segments, which are economically strong and reachable. Using a specific targeting purpose in tourism marketing, these target segments can be selected based on the destination's characteristics and strengths and on overall visitor segments in the destination. Visit Sweden (2015) has identified some segments, such as "DINKs: double income no kids", "WHOPs: wealthy healthy older people" and "Active family", that can serve as overall segments for city tourism. The overall targeted visitor segments give input to a basic touristic infrastructure in the destination based on a strong destination economy and demand. However, after the DMO's selection of these overall target visitor segments, private companies or public organisations in the destination can also choose special target visitor segments based on their own organisational purposes, such as local sustainability.

6   Visitor Streams

Valls et al. (2013) proposed that identifying destination characteristics related to visitor segments and their holiday can help in the interpretation of contemporary urban tourism flows in Europe, facilitating city strategic planning in order to boost competitiveness. For a specific purpose, such as to stimulate commercial product packaging, destination companies and organisations can choose specific visitor segments as target groups, based on their destination's strengths and weaknesses.

The tourism destination can be analysed from a visitor stream perspective, where the stream can be *defined* as a process consisting of the visitor's main activities during travel to, from and within the destination. The *main activities* typically include transport, accommodation, attraction activities, shopping, restaurant visits and meetings. Depending on visitor stream needs and wants, different activities will be undertaken and in different orders.

There are *different approaches* to studying the stream. The first approach is the "Chosen tourism activity", which gives knowledge about the visitor stream close to one chosen activity and could be used by the interested destination actor in relation to its focused activity. The "Easiest investigation method" is the second approach, which could be used by destination companies or organisations when investigating their own detailed problem questions with a lack of investigation resources. The third approach is "The chronological stream", which could be used by an analyst with enough investigation resources of visitor flows covering the whole destination or at least a substantial and clear part of it. Furthermore, patterns of visitor streams in Stockholm are changing. Therefore visitor stream planning has to be regularly updated. Another complicating factor in the analysis is that comparisons of individual attributes can be misleading because it is the combination of destination attributes that creates the tourist image (Turner and Reisinger 1999).

The analysed visitor segment *stream content* could be: defined visitor segment, visitor data, spatial destination data such as points and routes, time information and tourism product. The visitor segment "cruise passengers" to Stockholm has been chosen, taking a chronological stream approach, which is presented below.[1] After analysing passenger streams, conclusions can be made about the stream route and its main activities; number of visitors and their behaviour at different places and times; positive and negative impacts the stream has on the destination; and what potential decisions could be taken in order to reduce any negative impact. The passenger stream is very concentrated in general concerning routes (15–20 main streets in the centre of Stockholm) and points (three main visitor places, such as the Vasa Museum). For example, the Vasa Museum[2] had more than 1.2 million visitors during 2014. Half of the yearly visitors come during June–August (Authority for Cultural Analysis 2015), and 30 % are cruise passenger groups, which means that of

---

[1]The number of cruise ships in Stockholm during the April–October 2015 season was 247, with 53 turnaround ships, bringing a record high number of 530,000 passengers (Ports of Stockholm 2015). Most of the passengers disembark in Stockholm; about 50 % of them join the sightseeing tours offered by the shipping company and about 25 % make their own arrangements in Stockholm (Anrin 2015). The average number of passengers per ship was 2150, and a bus can take about 20–40 passengers. Every ship often needs about 50–60 buses, and they offer 10–12 different bus routes in Stockholm (Anrin 2015). Every day, one to eight ships (two on average) come to Stockholm from June through August, and every ship stays for an average of 7 h. Passengers can take a sightseeing tour in central Stockholm lasting from 3½ to 5 h, often before noon, according to the official program. This means that during the high season, there could be between 2000 and 16,000 cruise passengers in the centre of Stockholm on any given day. These sightseeing tours mostly use just three or five activity points, which are based on visitor attractions, restaurants, shopping, guided tours, outlooks and exploring independently. This means that a very small city area is used by cruise passengers.

[2]In 1625 the Swedish king signed a contract with a Dutch master shipwright to build Vasa, which was going to be the most powerful warship in the Baltic. In 1628, Vasa foundered in Stockholm harbour before the eyes of a large audience, scant minutes after setting sail for the first time. Vasa was found in 1956 and raised from the bottom of the sea. The new museum was opened 1990 and since then millions of visitors from all over the world have made their way here (Vasa Museum 2016).

the 6000 visitors per day, in general about 1800 are cruise passengers. The result is that the cruise passenger segment influences the logistic situation heavily. In comparison, of all guest nights at hotels in Stockholm, 55,000 visitors on average will stay in Stockholm per day from June through August.

Some important conclusions from this stream analysis are that there is a need to develop commercial products of attraction and sightseeing concepts for cruise passengers, and that local incoming companies and DMOs need to coordinate the marketing in their cruise networks with shipping companies. The boat sightseeing concept has to be developed as a complement to the bus concept in order to improve the destination logistics and to reduce overcrowding in some places. This demands more professional planning of the transport system by the destination actors (see chapter "On the Move: Emerging Fields of Transport Research in Urban Tourism"). When using the boat sightseeing concept it is also possible to take a boat trip around the Stockholm archipelago and experience beautiful nature areas close to Stockholm Town. This connection to nature tourism in Stockholm has also been pointed out by Thurau et al. (2007), who concluded in a study that cruise ship tourists prefer ecotourism opportunities more than was expected, and that marketing and services should be redirected toward sustainable, human-scaled ecotourism excursions.

There are different *types* of visitor streams. The cruise passenger's visitor stream routes and points are predefined and stable. This stream represents the stable visitor streams. Other visitor streams, such as the city-breaker segment, are more flexible and likely to improvise when visiting a destination. The improvised visitor segments have to be analysed and shown using other techniques. It is especially important to analyse parallel visitor streams for the segment, and sometimes even geographically extended visitor points where visitors are more likely to move around individually. However, more research is needed to understand these improvised visitor segments' streams.

A visitor streams analysis model is proposed in Fig. 4.

7 Conclusions

The main investigation still has to be done. However, here are conclusions found so far. The supply side of the destination can be studied through the chosen *focused destination and its character*. City tourism destinations, such as Stockholm, have their own characteristics. The demand side of the destination can be studied through the *identified visitor segments,* which are economically strong and reachable, based on an analysis of the visitor segmentation criteria and the destination characteristics.

Knowledge of the destination characteristics and visitor segments can be used for understanding and presenting visitor streams. The *visitor segment stream* content and the stream's points and routes connected to the main visitor activities have been defined in this chapter. It can be difficult to find relevant and exact data and more general qualitative information at city destinations such as Stockholm and

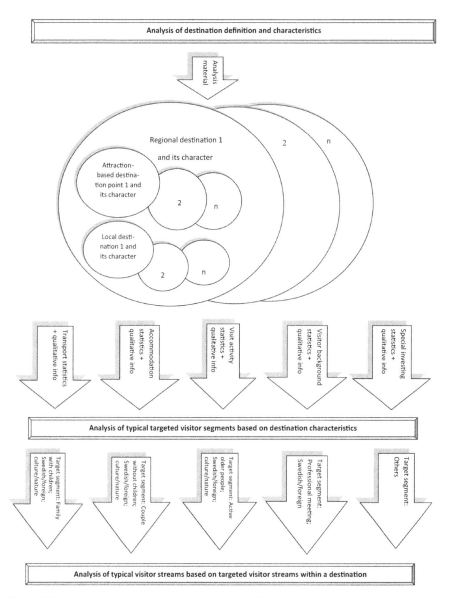

Fig. 4 Visitor streams analysis using statistical and qualitative indicators

their visitor streams. Therefore it is proposed here to use *statistical data and qualitative information* as "knowledge indicators" rather than as "unambiguous facts", which means that the investigator has to triangulate various sorts of knowledge into general guidelines for city visitor streams.

In this paper, a *four-step method* for analysing visitor streams in a city destination is suggested: (1) Defining the focused destination and its characteristics,

(2) Investigating quantitative and qualitative destination information as indicators for visitor streams, (3) Identifying and targeting visitor segments and (4) Analysing streams using new tools for targeted visit segments in the chosen destination. The so-called *chronological stream approach* with a possibility to update the data regularly is recommended when analysing the streams carefully. In order to improve the *presentation*, Geographical Information Systems (GIS) can be used.

Using this method, *three main question* areas can be addressed with the support of a stream analysis. The first question relates to a complete visit product where the visitor streams are located, which offers everything that the visitor needs during the journey. The second relates to destination market planning co-ordinated by the destination management organisation and conducted by individual tourism companies and public organisation. The third relates to destination logistics (such as transports and parking places), which are analysed and developed in detail by involved tourism companies in the stream, and on a general level by public organisations together with the tourism industry.

It is important to compare knowledge about visitor streams in city destinations other than Stockholm. The conclusions at a 2014 tourism statistical conference at the Mid-University in Sweden were that other European cities have almost the same questions about statistical development and tourism interpretation. Even though different *cities have different* important visitor streams for the overall target visit segments, the cities can consider *analysing the segments* in the section "visitor segments". However, there are different *types of visitor streams*. The cruise passenger's visitor stream routes and points are predefined and stable. Other streams are more flexible and likely to improvise when visiting a destination, which demands other sorts of analysis techniques such as analysing parallel visitor streams. In a final analysis step, all the specific streams for the destination's overall target segments can be integrated into one *joint visitor stream*. In this joint stream only the main information is presented in order to be able to conduct the stream analysis efficiently. Finally, there is a need for further development of tourism-related statistical and qualitative stream methods.

References

Adamsson PE, Ports of Stockholm (2015) Photo of cruise passengers in Stockholm harbour. www.portsofstockholm.com/about-us/press-room/. Accessed 1 Dec 2015
Andersson G (2013) Report of the research project "Development of export matured destinations: a literature review of the state of the art 2012". Tourism Studies, Södertörn University, Stockholm
Andersson G (2014) The pilot study "Analysis of visitor target groups at a city destination". Tourism Studies, Södertörn University, Stockholm
Anrin J (2015) In-depth interview about cruise passengers in Stockholm. The managing director of or the tour operator Seascape, Stockholm
Authority for Cultural Analysis (2015) Visit development for central museums 2014. www.kulturanalys.se. Accessed 1 Dec 2015

Dolnicar S, Grabler K (2004) Applying city perception analysis (CPA) for destination positioning decisions. J Travel Tour Mark 16(2–3):99–111. doi:10.1300/J073v16n02_08

Dunne G, Flanagan S, Buckley J (2007) City break motivation: the case of Dublin—a successful national capital. J Travel Tour Mark 22(3/4):95–107

Framke W (2002) The destination as a concept: a discussion of the business-related perspective versus the socio-cultural approach in tourism theory. Scand J Hosp Tour 2(2):92–108

Lucarelli A, Berg PO (2011) City branding: a state-of-the-art review of the research domain. J Place Manage Dev 4(1):9–27

Muzaffer Uysal JH, McCleary K (2006) Cultural/heritage destinations: tourist satisfaction and market segmentation. J Hosp Leisure Mark 14(3):81–99. doi:10.1300/J150v14n03_07

Ports of Stockholm (2015) Press release: record number of cruise passengers visit Stockholm. www.portsofstockholm.com/about-us/press-room/. Accessed 1 Dec 2015

Reisinger Y, Mavondo F, Crotts C (2009) The importance of destination attributes: Western and Asian visitors. Anatolia 20(1):236–253. doi:10.1080/13032917.2009.10518907

Shen J (2004) Urban competitiveness and urban governance in the globalizing world. Asian Geogr 23(1–2):19–36. doi:10.1080/10225706.2004.9684110

Statistics Sweden (2015) Tourism statistics in Sweden. www.scb.se. Accessed 1 Dec 2015

Stockholm City Municipality (2016) Stockholm tourism map. Open data, City planning office, Stockholm City municipality, Stockholm

Stockholm City Theatre AB (2016) The website of the house of culture and city theatre. http://kulturhusetstadsteatern.se/Om-Kulturhuset-Stadsteatern/. Retrieved 12 Feb 2016

Stockholm Visitors Board (2014) Facts about Stockholm's tourism industry 2013. Stockholm

Stockholm Visitors Board (2015) Facts about Stockholm's tourism industry 2014. Stockholm

Stockholmsfoto.se (2016) Photo of "Destination Stockholm centre". www.stockholmsfoto.se/bildarkiv Accessed 12 Feb 2016

Swedish Tourism (2010) National strategy for Swedish tourism. Swedish Tourism Ltd. www.strategi2020.se. Accessed 1 Dec 2015

Swedish Agency for Economic and Regional Growth (2014) Results from the Swedish Border Survey IBIS 2013, foreign visitors in Sweden. Stockholm

Swedish Agency for Economic and Regional Growth and Statistics Sweden (2015) Facts about Swedish tourism 2014. www.tillvaxtverket.se. Accessed 18 May 2015

Thurau BB, Carver AD, Mangun JC et al (2007) A market segmentation analysis of cruise ship tourists visiting the Panama Canal Watershed: Opportunities for ecotourism development. J Ecotour 6(1):1–18. doi:10.2167/joe138.0

Turner L, Reisinger Y (1999) Importance and expectations of destination attributes for Japanese tourists to Hawaii and the Gold Coast compared. Asia Pac J Tour Res 4(2):1–18. doi:10.1080/10941669908722039

UNWTO (2004) Indicators for sustainable development for tourism destinations guidebook. UNWTO, Madrid

Valls JF, Banchini S, Falcón L, Valls G (2013) Repositioning of Barcelona's image in the light of the redefinition of the urban tourism planning model. Rev Turismo Patrimonio Cult 11 (1):89–105

Valls JF, Sureda J, Valls-Tuñon G (2014) Attractiveness analysis of European tourist cities. J Travel Tour Mark 31(2):178–194. doi:10.1080/10548408.2014.873310

Vasa Museum (2016) The Vasa history. http://www.vasamuseet.se/en/vasa-history. Accessed 16 Feb 2016

Visit Sweden (2012) Recommended criteria for export matured destinations. Visit Sweden, Stockholm. www.partner.visitsweden.com/sv/Startsida/Turism-i-Sverige/. Accessed 23 Sept 2015

Visit Sweden (2015) Destination Sweden Brand. Visit Sweden, Stockholm. www.visitsweden.com/sverige/brand. Accessed 5 May 2015

Part II
The Construction of Multiple City 'Products' Through Culture, Creativity and Heritage: Principles, Policies and Practices

Museumification of Historical Centres: The Case of Frankfurt Altstadt Reconstruction

Nebojša Čamprag

Abstract The modernisation of Frankfurt's destroyed Altstadt, followed by the gradual formation of a skyline nearby, were both results of a post-war decision that rejected reconstruction as a common solution. Current planning and image-making in Frankfurt takes a major turn; alongside the dominant image of an important global player, implementation of a certain replica of destroyed medieval city is underway. The focus on this specific case aims to bring understanding to the museumification of urban centres as a phenomenon driven by the interests of competing present-day agendas. The revival of the historical Altstadt in Frankfurt certainly raises some threats, such as commodification of culture, museumification of heritage, production of themed public spaces, and overall touristification. However, this intervention is also an opportunity to soften established negative image of cold financial metropolis, enrich diversity of public spaces, create identification point for local residents, and finally make Frankfurt more visible on tourist maps.

Keywords Frankfurt Altstadt • City image • Urban tourism • Museumification of heritage • Touristification

1 Introduction

As a result of numerous phenomena associated with the era of neo-liberal globalization, many authors generally agree on the opinion that history and past became a convenient resource base for a wide range of high-order economic activities and development strategies (Ashworth and Larkham 1994; Rypkema 2001). Common apprehension of this potential could be illustrated by a twofold relation between heritage and development as defined by Nyström (1999), depending on a strategy mobilised: consumption development strategies use built heritage to create attraction to a city, while production-oriented strategies take heritage as an important element for establishing a milieu of creativity and innovation. In both of the cases,

N. Čamprag (✉)
Faculty of Architecture, Department of Urban Design and Development, Technical University of Darmstadt, Darmstadt, Germany
e-mail: camprag@stadt.tu-darmstadt.de

© Springer International Publishing Switzerland 2017   165
N. Bellini, C. Pasquinelli (eds.), *Tourism in the City*,
DOI 10.1007/978-3-319-26877-4_11

heritage *per se* was perceived as of importance for promoting the development of cities, attracting enterprises, a skilled working force, inhabitants and tourists, as well as for urban branding and marketing (Scheffler et al. 2009; Ebbe 2009; Rypkema 2001). These goals, however, would hardly be possible without the process of historic preservation, which not only aims to ensure identification and protection of major landmarks and monuments, but also holds economic development potential of its own. Thus strategies based on historic preservation offer a range of measurable benefits, such as jobs and household income, job training, city centre revitalisation, heritage tourism, property values, and small business incubation (Rypkema 1999, 2001, 2008; Scheffler et al. 2009; Gražulevičiūtė 2008). Although the relationship between heritage, preservation and development usually refers to the potential of heritage to serve as an important regional development asset, it can, however, also include some negative impacts on the heritage in question (Schröder-Esch 2006, pp. 191–192). The focus of this chapter is a controversial phenomenon that involves the creative mobilization of selected and desired pasts and histories for present-day agendas and interests (Daugbjerg and Fibiger 2011), which is becoming a more usual practice despite its rather contentious nature. Manipulation of the past, inspired by the development potential contained in heritage itself, found its use particularly for the purpose of boosting 'cultural' or 'heritage tourism', today being the most important sector of economy using heritage as a resource (Porter 2008).

1.1 On the Manipulation of the Past

Besides the above-mentioned common belief that historic preservation holds a substantial role in the process of sustaining heritage and thus initiating economic development, this process was recently approached from a new perspective. Especially viewed as 'critical' is the decision of what to preserve and how, an issue upon which the legitimacy of the whole process was questioned (Gražulevičiūtė 2008). Relevant for this critical approach is the issue of the finite nature that characterises tangible heritage, in addition to changing and disappearing of traditional building skills and techniques (Will 2009). In this context, conservation and restoration processes could also be understood as a way towards the partial or complete renewal of components and materials of built heritage. Considering, in addition, the intangible aspects of heritage that imply memories, former customs, local tradition, or even destroyed urban fabric, built heritage could finally be regarded as a convenient medium for manipulation. It ranges from the selection of suitable and non-suitable heritage for preservation, to even some particular examples of the production of new-old built heritage (Huxtable 1997; Roost 2000).

Ashworth (1998) considered that the above described phenomenon is not new, as built heritage of European cities has already been 'filtered' over time both by the processes of eradification and museumification, which created an urban landscape reduced in its original meanings. On the one hand, eradification (or eradication) is a rather common process that involves destruction or disappearance of buildings, urban ensembles and spaces. This process occurs involuntarily when caused by war or natural disasters, but was also often implemented voluntarily due to the needs of modernisation or as requested by particular political or cultural regimes. On the other hand, museumification is a more subtle intervention that involves retention of buildings and urban spaces, however not without deliberate change of their functions or even forms in particular cases. The purpose of this process is in fact transformation of the meaning of a conserved heritage, with the intention to use it as a tourist and economic resource (Ashworth 1998; Gospodini 2002). Such 'filtering' of built heritage is certainly not finite, but rather a dynamic activity, powered by the new generation of agendas and interests.

As Ulbricht and Schröder-Esch (2006) claimed, those aspects of heritage that cannot be marketed easily are usually excluded both from cultural reality and conservation policy. This new-age phenomenon involves disregarding the unwanted elements of the 'real' heritage, and is additionally supported by a fictionalisation of the past through the tourism-related use of culture. As an outcome, the visitors get the picture they expect to see (Ulbricht and Schröder-Esch 2006), which in some cases even involves introduction of 'fake' elements in the heritage milieu of cities (Huxtable 1997; Roost 2000). An extreme example involves the trend of 'copycat architecture', particularly booming in rapidly developing countries, such as UAE or China. Borrowing some iconic landmarks from cities all over the world and inserting them into the new cultural context of the modern Chinese city where they never actually belonged to represents typical example of the creation of 'fake' urban environments. Obsession with the need to attract tourists' attention is unfortunately not limited only to borrowing single elements from the past and/or other cultural meridians, but also involves copying the whole cities, as it was the case with Austrian city of Hallstatt. This centuries-old picturesque town was simply cloned in the frames of a housing development project in the Chinese province of Guangdong, serving as a strong magnet for both tourists and investors.

Having in mind the whole variety of manifestation forms associated with the phenomenon of manipulation of the past, historical physical configuration of modern cities could certainly be questioned as created, developed and transformed by someone for some purpose. This process is characterized by the whole range of selection criteria determining 'appropriateness' of built heritage to be preserved—or borrowed and recreated—from the past and thereby integrated into a city's overall identity (Gospodini 2002; Kelleher 2004; Graham and Howard 2008).

1.2   Touristification of Cities: From Preservation
to Production of Heritage

Contemporary phenomenon of urban history and tradition revival, which occurs in different forms and extents in cities all over the world, can be explained by the post-modern nostalgia for what is lost, which in fact reflects general dissatisfaction with the present. This feeling of loss causes not only romantic revival of traditional values and the growing trend for preservation of the old cities, but also construction of new urban neighbourhoods that often look like the old ones, as previously illustrated by the Hallstatt-copy example. As our world of cities becomes all the more homogeneous, marked by identity crisis of urban public realm, such look back in history could be understood as a wish to return to the origins, nature, and archetypes, as a way to response sudden changes that globalisation imposes (Ellin 2002). Not surprisingly, the new trend gets supporters from a variety of high-end economic activities, ranging from tourism development to intercity competition.

Despite its development potential, many authors argued that lending from the past often proves to be selective, even generally inappropriate in many cases (Huxtable 1997; Roost 2000). In addition to the more common process of museumification, by which urban heritage is being transformed into a tourist or economic resource, some even more extreme cases are emerging, such as already mentioned 'copycat architecture' or 'Disneyfication' expanding from American cities. As an overall misuse of historical architectural interpretation, 'Disneyfica-tion' originates from the big projects of the entertainment industry where a *coulisse* of European city is similarly used in order to construct motives and settings that would attract tourists (Roost 2000). The criticism of such phenomena usually refers to reviving or creating tradition that all too often fails to preserve the past, but develops interest-driven invented tradition[1] instead (Ellin 2002). Their tendency to erase modern chapters and re-evaluate and idealise periods before modern move-ment is considered to be manipulation of the past, in many cases resulting with 'hyper real' surroundings, as a complete falsification of reality (Ellin 2002). Urban neighbourhoods and whole towns created in this way indeed represent a serious threat for the genuine authenticity of urban environments, but at the same time their capability to significantly boost tourism development makes it increasingly com-mon practice. Through a particular case study on Frankfurt in Germany, this chapter aims to examine both the harms and benefits that such an approach can have on cities.

Frankfurt was one of the few cities that opted for change and modernisation of its historical core, right after the fatal destructions as a consequence of the World War II. Rather than plain rebuilding of lost structures, this city gradually managed to re-establish its identity on the basis of its long tradition in trade and banking, and later to become the financial capital of both the country and the European Union.

---

[1]The term 'invented tradition' is coined by Eric Hobsbawm, first mentioned in his book released in 1983 *Inventing Traditions. Mass Producing Traditions: Europe, 1870–1914.*

Thereby established completely new recognisable image of a modern global metropolis with distinguished skyline next to the very centre turn out to be an exception to other European cities. However, what makes this case relevant for the focus of this chapter is a recent turnover in Frankfurt's planning and development directions—the new trend paradoxically enabled re-creation of the lost medieval urban core, seven decades after its complete destruction. The real importance of the initiative to rebuild this long lost historical core is not in its spatial proportions, nor in its architectural values, but rather in pretentious task to influence and soften the negative image of the tough business metropolis, standing in juxtaposition to a range of development agendas. By these means, Frankfurt should become more attractive for new investors, residents, and especially for development directions imposed principally by the agenda of tourism industry.

2   Background on the Museumification of Frankfurt's Centre

Traditionally the most distinguished carriers of urban identity within contemporary cities are old historic cores (Hilber and Datko 2012). Vinken (2008) designated such urban centres as "Traditionsinseln",[2] as well as carriers of a code for natural order and naturalness (Vinken 2008, p. 12). Their sublime features, embodied in unique constellations of stratified historical and cultural imprints are certainly making interventions within urban cores the most delicate urban change being conducted nowadays. Unfortunately, their critical position between the two extremes, involving continuity that preservation imposes and necessary changes to respond development requirements is what finally makes them often exposed to compromising planning decisions.

The current renewal of Frankfurt's historical core in the Altstadt district is not the lonely case of history-inspired construction of the old historical cores; there are many other well-known examples of similar interventions, especially among the cities that suffered destruction during World War II. In Dresden, as an example, a majority of the iconic historic buildings were restored in traditional spirit, as mixtures of historical remains and new elements. The main intention in this case, as Will (2009) describes, was not to disturb the significance and meaning of the place; however the final result that ignored the reality of war damages reached the state of an "idealised work of art" (ibid. 15). Reconstructed imitations alongside the integrated relics of the old Dresden actually undermined their authority as historical witnesses. Such questionable approach towards reconstruction provided at the end a kind of "architectural prostheses" for the "crippled city" (ibid. 15). This substitution cannot offer a replacement for what is lost, although it manages to provide what observers expect to see. Similarly, as the critic Manfred Sack described, the market

---

[2]In English: urban islands of tradition (translated by the author).

square in Hildesheim, destroyed in the war and rebuilt to its previous appearance in the 1990s, could be considered as a representation of not healed but "cloned" square, sending an image "as if nothing had happened" (ibid. 16). The trend goes on with a current reconstruction of the Berlin Palace, where the latest building technology and materials are being used to create a resemblance with the iconic predecessor, also with assignment of the new functions to the traditional typology of a residential castle. This kind of unconstrained heritage interpretation and production is also occurring in the historic core of modern Frankfurt, which generally holds an image of a global city with a distinguished skyline, but its emerging features involve questionable reconstruction and creative replication of the irretrievably lost gothic city. Urban change in all the above examples paradoxically took reverse direction, with the challenge of implementing fake "new old" into the existing and real "old" urban environment that is paradoxically newer in appearance.[3]

Until its nearly complete destruction in 1944, Frankfurt's historical nucleus was a palimpsest of various architectural styles, including Gothic, renaissance, baroque and classicism that held a supreme role in the identity of the whole city. Although its peripheral zones have been rebuilt during the first phases of the post-war reconstruction in the 1950s, the very central area between the Cathedral and City Hall (so-called Dom-Römer area) remained empty for a relatively long time, as it was subjected to constant disagreements (Müller-Raemisch 1996). Besides, centre of gravity for city's post-war development shifted westwards to the neighbouring financial district (Bankenviertel), where dynamic formation of the high-rise cluster commenced, followed by the rise of the early skyline. The deadlock situation within Altstadt itself temporarily ended at the beginning of the 1970s, when the massive concrete block of the Technical City Hall (Technisches Rathaus) was finally erected in the demolished and cleared central area. At the same time, underground car parking, railway station (U-Bahn), and a modern block of the Historical Museum on the southern side were constructed. After 40 years of discussions, the first historical 'reconstruction' on the site followed in 1983, when Samstagberg houses were rebuilt[4] as partially modern buildings that respected the historical structure and the scale of the plot, but were in fact serving as a buffer zone between the Römerberg Square and developments that followed (Schembs 2005). A few years later, modernisation of the site continued, when the elongated, modern structure of the Schirn Art Gallery (Schirn Kunsthalle) was introduced. All these interventions further deepened the after-war rupture in the city's spatial development, as they represented an absolute contrast to the previous delicately fragmented structure of the former medieval city.

During the 1980s, the initially negative connotation of the high-rise in Frankfurt started to change. The emerging skyline gradually turned into a point of

---

[3]Ada Louise Huxtable (1997) introduced the concepts of 'real' and 'fake' in urban environments.
[4]The reconstructed houses are: Großer Engel, Goldener Grief, Wilder Mann, Dachsberg/Schlüssel, Großer und Kleiner Laudenberg and Schwarze Stern.

identification for local residents, and was later even used as one of the main cornerstones of the marketing and branding strategies of the city. Although the developed city image of a financial metropolis indeed attracted new businesses and investors, Frankfurt still lacked assets suitable for urban tourism development, also attributable to the chaotic postmodern situation within its historical core. An idea to recover the traditional, historic appearance of the city was thus gradually gaining in importance, while the main reasons to legitimate the need for its redevelopment were the low quality of the existing urban space, and the lack of reference to the historic centre (DomRömer Gmbh 2015). The city municipality saw an outstanding opportunity to finally redevelop the attractive Dom-Römer area in 2007, when the rental period for the Technical City Hall expired. On the basis of the winning urban competition entry in 2005 by Architekten KSP Engel and Zimmermann the idea of reviving the old city structures, based on their historical streets and plots outlines, adapting it to the present-day functional requirements emerged. Directions set to 'historicise' the Altstadt caused another review by the city municipality concerning the now-inadequate postmodern Historical Museum building, proposing thus a new one, which would better fit into the newly planned urban environment. Both Technical City Hall and the old Museum building were finally torn down in 2011, which thereby marked the beginning of the new chapter in the striving for a complete makeover of the former historical urban core.

3   Reinvention of Frankfurt's Altstadt

The site of the so-called DomRömer project, also known as 'Frankfurt's New Old City'[5] (DomRömer Gmbh 2015) occupies around 7000 m^2 in the very heart of Frankfurt's former historical city centre. For this purpose specifically, the City of Frankfurt, as the major investor of the project, founded DomRömer GmbH in July 2009 (DomRömer Gmbh 2015), which was authorised as the legal entity responsible for development, planning and project implementation of the area between the Cathedral and City Hall, as well as for marketing and sale of the newly created houses, apartments and commercial space. These decisions were welcomed by the Tourism + Congress GmbH in charge of promotion of a positive image of Frankfurt worldwide, recognising DomRömer project as an important chance for urban recognisability and tourism development in the city that suffers from having an image of a "cold" financial centre (Marketingplan 2012, 2011; Frankfurt für Alle 2009).

After the post-war structures have been demolished, the process of new-old town district recreation started with division of the area into approximately 30 small plots. In its current state of development (Fig. 1), the project involves 15 reconstructions of both the most famous and well-documented historical houses, formally

---

[5]In original text "Neue Frankfurter Altstadt" (translated by the author).

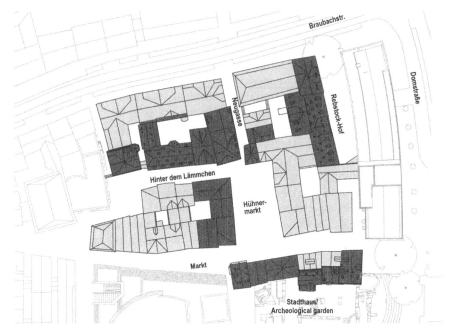

Fig. 1 Master plan of the DomRömer area in 2016 according to DomRömer GmbH and Schneider + Schumacher Architekten. Historical reconstructions are showed in *dark grey*. *Source*: Author's representation

named 'creative replicas' (schöpferischen Nachbauten),[6] and twenty new designs inspired by their historical predecessors (Neubauten). The use of archaic architectural language, both within the reconstructions and historically inspired new designs, along with the compact rows of houses and reconstruction of historical urban public spaces, should all contribute to the anticipated revival of the traditional image and atmosphere of the historic urban core (Fig. 2). Once completed by the end of 2017, the whole newly developed Altstadt is at the same time planned to become a magnet for new residents, visitors and tourists through the optimal balance between the three most attractive urban activities: residential, work and leisure.

Besides being an enormous influence on the image of the whole city, the DomRömer project could also be considered as a trigger for further historically inspired redevelopment occurring in its immediate environment. The Archaeological Garden (Archäologische Garten) next to the site is an open-air installation,

---

[6]Fifteen iconic historical houses that will be reconstructed are: Klein Nürnberg, Goldenes Lämmchen, Alte Esslinger, Esslinger (all in Hinter dem Lämmchen Street, numbers 8, 6, 4, 2); Zür Flechte (Markt 20); Rebstock-Hof (Braubachstr. 19), Braubachstr. 21; Goldene Waage, Grüne Linde, Neues Rotes Haus, Rotes Haus, Goldene Schere, Eichhorn, Schlegel, and Würzgarten (all at Hühnermarkt Square, numbers 5, 13, 15, 17, 22, 24, 26 and 28).

Fig. 2 DomRömer project visualisation: Christmas market on the Hühnermarkt square © HHVISION. *Source*: DomRömer GmbH

containing remains of the oldest structures of the city from Roman times and Middle Ages, discovered during the excavations for an underground parking garage in the 1950s (DomRömer GmbH 2011, p. 6). On the one hand, presence of this site represented a challenge for the recreation of old urban structures, while on the other contained genuine potential on its own that needed to be harnessed. Therefore, the site was planned to get closer to the public through the integration with a completely new facility for congresses and exhibitions, named Townhouse on the Markt Square (Stadthaus am Markt). The winning design, inspired by traditional forms, materiality, and dense parcelling, respected both the morphology and character of Frankfurt's historic city. Aside its main tasks to provide adequate protection and the attractive museum-like presentation of the archaeological remains (DomRömer Gmbh 2015), this building also ensured a major public function and thus diversity in the emerging tourist district.

The final project that influences the general appearance of the Altstadt area to a large degree is also the new building of Frankfurt's Historical Museum on the Römerberg Square. The former massive concrete structure that ignored the surrounding built environment was replaced by a new building of traditional forms and materiality. It was introduced in accordance with the historical layout of the former old city, and at the same time re-established final parts of the historic Saalgasse Street. With the completion of these diverse projects, Altstadt is supposed to get its reconstructed appearance inspired by tradition, as an alternative to the well-established reputation of Frankfurt as a predominantly financial metropolis.

4   The Museumification of Altstadt as a Development Strategy

Reconstruction of Frankfurt's historical centre was originally initiated by a group of citizens in need of an embodiment of common memory and for a strong point of identification. Some well organised citizens' initiatives, such as "Pro Altstadt" and "Altstadt retten" (saving Altstadt) were active from the initial phases of the reconstruction project, keeping a close watch on its progress and generally opposing any proposals for modernisation of the historical core. Several city officials and marketing and tourism policy creators also welcomed and supported this initiative, advocating for a more diverse city image, which would finally make the city an attractive location for investments and tourism development. Reinvention of the historical core with a 'romantic' approach to the filtration of architectural heritage finally aimed to revive the old city from collective memory, with all the desired features that tickled the imagination of both inhabitants and visitors. Indeed, semi-fictional, tradition-inspired reconstruction of the Altstadt could be considered as an important asset for city marketing and urban identity building, but also as an opportunity to resolve still problematic post-war situation in Frankfurt's city centre by the means of urban planning and design. However, different professionals having disparate agendas remain divided upon the issue, where some of them saw strengths and opportunities in the project's implementation, while others pointed to possible threats, rather taking the critical perspective. Several planning professionals from the City Planning Office, as an example, retained their critical positions describing the complex ironically as a mixture between "new buildings and new buildings"[7] involving objects based on history and tradition, whose market value was constructed around the idea to buy oneself a piece of authenticity.

Some disputable aspects of this project indeed may not be overlooked, involving problematic and constrained use of archaic architectural language, or voluntary production of themed public spaces. Through such implementation of new-old architectural heritage, the phenomena of filtration and museumification eventually provide not only what future visitors and residents expect to experience, but also directly respond to their user preferences. This implies that all the features that rendered the medieval core of Frankfurt out-dated were simply left out during the reconstruction. These features were indeed unsuitable to fulfil the needs and functions of a modern city long before its destruction in the turmoil of the war;

---

[7]In October 2012, at the time when project implementation was in its initial phase, the author interviewed two planners from the City Planning Department in Frankfurt. The aim was to find out what was the general opinion of the professionals regarding realisation of the DomRömer Project.

however, although the way built facilities are used today significantly changed in comparison with some historical epochs, it remains rather questionable which is the tolerable extent of changes that will not invalidate the claims of authenticity. Similarly, filtration of unwanted layers of disruption by the post-war planning, with the exception of some important infrastructural improvements, could also be regarded as arguable. These interventions promote not only a sort of artificial built environment, but unfortunately encourage the creation of conflicting situations. After all, conflicts between proper reconstruction and contemporary building laws, regulations and technology, the burning issue of historical epoch to be reconstructed, as well as conflicts between historical use and contemporary needs are only some of the issues Frankfurt's emerging new-old historical core faces.

Besides all the critical issues connected to the Altstadt reconstruction, the still incomplete revival of the historic city already found its place in the strategic marketing planning and branding of Frankfurt, as well as in plans for future cultural production. Moving the already romanticised Christmas market to the new scenery of an "old" city, introduction of new exhibition spaces, several museums and restaurants, as well as creation of the image of an old European city is a picture that tourists certainly wish for. Therefore, the main beneficiary of the reconstructed Altstadt in both of the cases will certainly be tourism business, where the newly built old city should not only compensate for the lack of historic image of the city, but would also serve as a stage for culture commodification through themed history- and tradition-inspired events (Fig. 2). Once implemented, the new-old Altstadt will undoubtedly make a significant contribution to the whole city, although the remaining question is the exact impact of these consequences. Since Frankfurt suffers from its reputation of a cold financial city, revived historical core could indeed provide a particular reinforcement of the existing homogeneous but inflexible city image, and finally offer necessary diversity. On the other hand, the paradox of reviving the folklore-inspired urban ambiance could also have some less desired effects. They could involve the Frankfurt example to get into the focus of debates among the urban planning professionals worldwide, and an unfortunate distraction from some other significant development efforts. Also interesting could be the effects of the criticised and disputed 'addition' from the perspective of the activities associated with the city's established reputation of an important global player.

5   Discussion and Conclusions

Heritage today is grasped as an asset, which functions by mobilising selected and desired pasts and histories in the service of present-day agendas and interests (Daugbjerg and Fibiger 2011). In the previous praxis of top-down policies and strong nation-states, aspects of heritage that could not be marketed easily or did not have much relevance for political identity building were usually excluded both from cultural reality and conservation policy. Today, however, this outstanding authority for deciding what is to be preserved was taken over by the powerful tourism industry, becoming the most prominent economic sector of contemporary cities in which heritage is exploited as a resource. What makes the tourism era more advanced in the mobilisation and manipulation of heritage is its justification of fictionalisation of the past, found in the tourism-related commodification of culture. A typical example is the growing response to what the visitors expect to see (Ulbricht and Schröder-Esch 2006), which supports the current praxis of introducing 'fake' elements into the heritage milieu of cities (Huxtable 1997; Roost 2000).

Clear eradication of unwanted design elements and functions in Frankfurt's Altstadt imposes the idea of museumification occurring in this historic district. Through adaptations of urban memory to contemporary demands of real-estate market and tourism trends, the initiative creates a somewhat fake urban landscape of selected and re-invented traditional background (Huxtable 1997; Ellin 2002). However, concerning the wider context of goals and interests shared by the tourism and urban policies in Frankfurt, reinvention of the lost urban district could also be approached from another perspective. Expected benefits that initiated such an activity stem from a certain duality that generally characterises not only Frankfurt as a city, but its development strategies as well. They are constructed around the main aim of promoting diversity in order to oppose any negative connotation that an image of a solely business-focused city can develop. Urban branding and marketing efforts are thus setting disparate foci, mobilising different strategies for achieving corresponding goals, and finally producing the two distinguished city images. The alternative one, upon which most of the future development directions are constructed, aims to present Frankfurt as an attractive city to visit and discover.

Although contrasting duality of Frankfurt's strategies inevitably creates conflicts, their common goals set on promoting diversity are supposed to bridge the deficiencies and target as many interest groups as possible. Therefore, an intervention based on false interpretation of history in Frankfurt's urban core does not enjoy support by many professionals, but is also not openly contested by them, due to its importance for the overall urban policy. From a wider perspective, the tourism city emerging in Frankfurt is not only a fake urban landscape created around fictionalisation of its past, but also a useful development tool that targets exactly those elements of the overall city image upon which the goal of desired diversity and attractiveness depends. Finally, reconstruction of the historic Altstadt in Frankfurt indeed represents a typical example of manipulation of the past through museumification of urban heritage, but it also serves as a strong evidence of power that tourism policies hold in the overall urban framework. Which are further directions these policies could take, how beneficial or harmful their influence will be, by which means will tourism policies continue to shape cities in the future, and what could be the most feasible ways of better integration of tourism policies into overall urban development strategies are only some of the emerging questions for the future research agenda.

References

Albert Speer und Partner GmbH, Polytechnische Gesellschaft e.V. and der Stiftung Polytechnische Gesellschaft Frankfurt am Main (2009) Frankfurt für Alle—Handlungsperspectiven für die international Bürgerstadt Frankfurt am Main. AS&P, Frankfurt

Ashworth GJ (1998) The conserved European city as cultural symbol: the meaning of the text. In: Graham B (ed) Modern Europe. Place, culture, identity. Arnold, London, pp 261–286

Ashworth GJ, Larkham JP (1994) Building a new heritage: tourism, culture and identity in the new Europe. Routhledge, London

Daugbjerg M, Fibiger T (2011) Introduction: heritage gone global. Investigating the production and problematics of globalized pasts. Hist Anthropol 22(2):135–147

DomRömer Gmbh (2011) DomRömer Zeitung—Informationen zum Wiederaufbau der Frankfurter Altstadt, Frankfurt am Main, 2010–2012, April/May 2011

DomRömer Gmbh (2015) The official website of the DomRömer project. Accessed 29 Mar 2015

Ebbe K (2009) Infrastructure and heritage conservation: opportunities for urban revitalization and economic development. Cultural Heritage and Sustainable Tourism Thematic Group, The World Bank Urban Development Unit

Ellin N (2002) Postmoderni urbanizam (Postmodern urbanism). OrionArt, Belgrade

Gospodini A (2002) European cities and place-identity. Discussion Paper Series 8(2). University of Thessaly, Department of Planning and Regional Development, pp 19–36

Graham B, Howard P (2008) Heritage and identity. In: Graham B, Howard P (eds) The Asgate research companion to heritage and identity. Ashgate, Farnham and Burlington, VT, pp 1–15

Gražulevičiūtė I (2008) Cultural heritage in the context of sustainable development. Aplinkos tyrimai, inžinerija ir vadyba/Environ Res Eng Manag 37(3):74–79

Hilber L, Datko G (eds) (2012) Stadtidentität der Zukunft. Jovis Verlag GmbH, Berlin

Huxtable AL (1997) The unreal America: architecture and illusion. The New Press, New York, NY

Kelleher M (2004) Images of the past: historical authenticity and inauthenticity from Disney to time square. CRM Journal, Summer:6–19

Müller-Raemisch H (1996) Frankfurt am Main: Stadtentwicklung und Planungsgeschichte seit 1945. Campus Verlag, Frankfurt/Main, New York, NY

Nyström L (1999) City and culture: cultural processes and urban sustainability. The Swedish Urban Environment Council, Kalmar, Sweden

Porter BW (2008) Heritage tourism: conflicting identities in the Modern World. In: Graham B, Howard P (eds) The Asgate research companion to heritage and identity. Ashgate, Farnhamp and Burlington, VT, pp 267–281

Roost F (2000) Die Disneyfizierung der Städte. Leske + Budrich, Opladen

Rypkema D (1999) Culture, historic preservation and economic development in the 21st century. Paper presented at leadership conference on conservation and development, Yunnan Province, China, September 1999

Rypkema D (2001) The economic power of restoration. Paper presented at restoration & renovation conference, Washington, DC, 15 January 2001

Rypkema D (2008) Heritage conservation and the local economy. Glob Urban Dev 4(1), August 2008, pp 1–8

Scheffler N, Kulikauskas P, Barreiro F (2009) Managing urban identities: aim or tool of urban regeneration? In; URBACT Tribune. URBACT, pp 9–13, November 2009. http://www.urbact. eu/file/10907/download?token=iYk_AUPe. Accessed 24 Nov 2015

Schembs H (2005) Das war das 20. Jahrhundert in Frankfurt am Main. Wartberg Verlag GmbH & Co. KG, Gudensberg-Gleichen

Schröder-Esch S (2006) Defining and applying 'heritage' in the context of development issues: experiences from the Interreg project HERMES. In: Schröder-Esch S (ed) Practical aspects of cultural heritage—presentation, revaluation, development. Bauhaus Universität, Weimar, pp 189–202

Tourism + Congress GmbH Frankfurt am Main (2011) Marketingplan 2012—Die Touristische
  Vermarktung der Stadt Frankfurt am Main. Frankfurt, November 2011
Ulbricht JH, Schröder-Esch S (2006) Introduction: the political dimension of heritage. In:
  Schröder-Esch S, Ulbricht JH (eds) The politics of heritage and regional development strate-
  gies—actors, interests, conflicts. Bauhaus Universität, Weimar, pp 7–15
Vinken G (2008) Zone Heimat—Altstadt im Modernen Städtebau. Deutscher Kunstverlag, Berlin,
  München
Will T (2009) R@MIT in Dresden—the European city between restoration and transformation. In:
  Pham N, Heinen M (eds) The European city in transformation. DRESDEN, Delft, pp 14–19

Heritage and Urban Regeneration: Towards Creative Tourism

Maria Della Lucia, Mariapina Trunfio, and Frank M. Go

Abstract The question of how cities can capitalise on cultural legacy hybridisation to activate effective and sustainable urban regeneration has still not been fully answered. This chapter presents a conceptual framework based on public–private participation in cultural legacy hybridisation, designed to interpret the determinants and forms of urban regeneration and consider their possible implications for urban tourism. The framework's application to a multiple case study analysis, focusing on three small and medium-sized Italian cities, has validated its interpretative capacity. In Pompei public investment in culture has proved to be almost entirely unproductive; in Trento public-driven regeneration has allowed for value creation through cultural heritage hybridisation; in Lecce stakeholder engagement in communities of practice is the driver of socio-economic value and innovation. Urban tourism in these cities is closely connected to the nature of their urban regeneration: cultural tourism in Pompei, its combination with creative tourism in Trento and innovative forms of tourism in Lecce.

Keywords Heritage • Urban regeneration • Hybridisation • Stakeholder engagement • Creative tourism

1 Introduction

Culture and creativity have finally become part of the political and theoretical debate as engines of socio-economic development and regeneration. European, national, regional and urban political agendas (KEA 2006, 2009; European

M. Della Lucia (✉)
University of Trento, Trento, Italy
e-mail: maria.dellalucia@unitn.it

M. Trunfio
University of Naples "Parthenope", Naples, Italy
e-mail: mariapina.trunfio@uniparthenope.it

F.M. Go
Erasmus University, Rotterdam, The Netherlands
e-mail: fgo@rsm.nl

© Springer International Publishing Switzerland 2017
N. Bellini, C. Pasquinelli (eds.), *Tourism in the City*,
DOI 10.1007/978-3-319-26877-4_12

Commission 2010; CSES 2010; OECD 2009; Sacco 2011, 2012) focus increasingly on these assets in the move towards both economic development and well-being (Tavano Blessi et al. 2015). The literature includes culture in the 'new orthodoxy' to enhance the competitive advantage of cities, and culture-driven urban regeneration is considered to be the engine of a new urban entrepreneurialism (Miles and Paddison 2005). The shift of post-industrial societies towards the symbolic economy (Zukin 1995) over the last 10 years has accelerated the repositioning of culture in the value chain for the development of new, culture-based approaches to urban regeneration (among the others, Hall 2004; Lazzeretti 2004; Hutton 2009; Scott 2010; Sacco et al. 2013; Della Lucia and Franch 2014; Go and Trunfio 2014; Sacco et al. 2014; Della Lucia et al. 2016). To be effective and positive, these processes also require social changes: intangible innovations manifest on the level of social practice and innovations that create social value (Choi and Majumdar 2015).

Urban tourism is involved in this transformation as a lever of urban regeneration with the potential to capitalise on urban heritage and its hybridisation with creativity to contribute to both communities' development and well-being in terms of employment, accessibility, knowledge and social innovation, higher quality public spaces: all changes that both meet social needs and improve a society's skills, relationships and capacity to act (Caulier-Grice et al. 2012).

Home of the Roman Empire and a major centre of the Renaissance, Italy is internationally known for its rich and valuable cultural legacy, including 47 cultural UNESCO World Heritage Sites, art, architecture, festivals, food and other forms of local culture. The hybridisation of the country's rich cultural resources—and, indeed, traditional cultural tourism—provides an opportunity to enhance and extract value from the Italian cultural legacy, which is facing the challenges posed by the need for innovative forms of cultural tourism. This paradigm shift requires not only the promotion and preservation of cultural resources but a social change in which communities and visitors interact and participate in cultural experiences.

This chapter contributes to the debate by drawing on the most recent literature and empirical analysis on culture-led urban regeneration (Della Lucia and Franch 2014; Della Lucia et al. 2016) to design a preliminary conceptual framework of cultural legacy hybridisation through stakeholder engagement which shapes different paths of urban regeneration and diverse forms of urban tourism. This framework is tested through a multiple case study design focused on three small and medium-sized Italian cities (Pompei, Trento and Lecce) to identify the possible connections in these cities between cultural legacy hybridisation, public–private stakeholder engagement, socio-cultural innovation and tourism. The main questions that drive the analysis are: how can cities capitalise on stakeholder engagement to hybridise cultural legacy with urban creativity? What effects may these processes have on socio-cultural innovation and urban tourism?

The first part of the paper outlines the theoretical debate on heritage, urban regeneration and creative tourism. It provides a framework for interpreting the hybridisation process of cultural legacy carried out by public and private actors, applied in the case study analysis in the second part. The conclusion sketches the theoretical and practical implications of the study.

2   Heritage and Urban Regeneration

A city's history, cultural capital, creative industries and local atmosphere define its tangible and intangible—both artistic-cultural and professional-productive—urban heritage. This cultural legacy can be exploited to create and capture urban value while maintaining a strong link with an authentic sense of place (Hall 2004; Scott 2006). The challenges defined by the combination of globalisation, the ICT revolution and the experience economy, may encourage cities to reconcile the local and global dimensions of culture (Lazzeretti 2004) and to put themselves at the heart of complex internal and external networks in order to innovate their cultural legacy.

These divergent forces mean that culture-led urban regeneration is marked by both continuity with urban heritage (cultural legacy) and the latter's profound transformation. Innovative policy-making is thus required to complement the strengths of a city's legacy, to overcome its weaknesses or even make up for its absence (Della Lucia and Franch 2014; Della Lucia et al. 2016). Iconic buildings and events are currently among the most important cultural catalysts available to urban policy makers to increase the vibrancy of cities by attracting creative people and lifestyles to them, target markets flexibly with thematic strategies and enhance image-making and brand building/positioning (Roche 1992; Evans 2003; Richards and Wilson 2006; Getz 2008, 2010; Trueman et al. 2008). Their development, which often requires sizable public investment, may also entail the risk of serial reproduction and the loss of a city's authenticity (Smith 2007).

The reconciling of past/tradition and future/innovation, that is recognised as crucial to sustainable and successful culture-led regeneration (Della Lucia and Franch 2014), requires participatory and inclusive development processes which entail a balance between public-driven processes and stakeholder engagement. These processes foster the enhancement of urban heritage value through creativity and knowledge which originate in other sectors of local economy. The nature and scale of this innovation can be interpreted within the Culture 1.0 to Culture 2.0 to Culture 3.0 evolution paradigm (Sacco 2011), which has transformed culture from a domain that absorbs public resources devoted to it for the benefit of society as a whole (Culture 1.0) to a value generating activity. Culture 2.0—the culture industries and the creativity-intensive non-cultural industries (architecture, fashion, design, advertising)—and emergent Culture 3.0—transversal linkages throughout economies and societies, fostered by culture-led creativity—are the drivers of this shift.

3 Urban Heritage and Creative Tourism

Urban tourism is often seen as one of the most important drivers of the creation and capturing of value through culture-led regeneration processes. Traditional cultural tourism builds on continuity with urban heritage (Richards 2014); event tourism, iconic building tourism and architourism are new forms of tourism which introduce profound changes in urban heritage (Klingmann 2007; Ockman and Fraust 2007; Getz 2008). The "cloning" of innovative urban tourism forms by following exogenous prescriptions and copying ideas from other cities through "policy tourism" has led to the tourism commodification phenomenon criticised as "McGuggenisation" (McNeill 2000), "Dubaisation" (Al Rabadya 2012), "festivalisation" (Quinn 2006) and "eventification" (Jakob 2012).

Creative tourism is one of the most important manifestations of heritage hybridisation in urban contexts (Richards 2011, 2014; Richards and Marques 2012; OECD 2014). It builds on contemporary creativity, innovation and intangible content to meet local communities' needs for cultural and creative expression and contemporary visitors' demands for meaning and authentic experience (OECD 2014). Although it still only accounts for a small part of cultural tourism, creative tourism may encourage a shift from mass cultural tourism and the serial reproduction of culture (Richards and Wilson 2006) to new, place specific tourism models based on intangible culture and local creativity.

A city's ability to transform its intangible endowment into a tourist offer that has a distinctive symbolic value thus becomes crucial for urban competitiveness, as does its capacity to use these products to attract sustainable segments of cultural tourism (OECD 2014). Developing successful creative tourism forms involves collaboration with a wide, dispersed value network rather than with a narrow value chain: different creative content and lifestyles need to be combined in the tourism experience, both in the city and at a distance, or even virtually, via new technology. The locations, functions and roles of both cultural and non-cultural industries best shape the range of creative tourism products (Richards and Wilson 2006) which can harness local creativity and provide experiential attractions. Although creative tourism may assume many different forms, three broad and interconnected categories emerge (Richards 2014): the cultural events or creative performances typical of advanced tourism products; clusters or cultural districts which are an expression of creative spaces; creative strategies and policies that promote the hybridisation of culture with place specific resources. The construction of creative experiences requires an understanding of the relationship between urban systems and businesses, but this understanding is often missing, from both practice and the literature. Innovative policies mobilised around a strong urban vision are thus still often needed to create and capture the value of urban context by hybridising tourism through creativity (OECD 2014). They include creative content development, linking creativity and place, knowledge and capacity building, network and cluster formation.

4 Case Study and Research Methodology

Italy's rich heritage resources (13,000 libraries, 4500 museums and monuments, 50,000 archaeological and architectural sites and 51 UNESCO sites; Grossi 2015)—the role of which in shaping national identity and brand image is crucial—, and its powerful cultural and creative industries, should make culture and creativity central to its national and local development strategies (Sacco 2012). However, Italian urban policies have usually focused on traditional cultural heritage. Cultural restoration projects, public cultural organisations (national museums), and cultural tourism and local products have been the main levers of urban development. On the other hand, public institutions, even city managers and operators are still sceptical about the need to hybridise cultural legacies with the creative economy, and how this can be achieved (CSES 2010; Sacco 2011). The exceptions to this pattern are mostly large or medium-sized cities which have implemented urban regeneration projects based on the innovation of their unique cultural legacies and the related offer.

Building on the core assumptions that the hybridisation of cultural heritage with creativity and stakeholder engagement are key drivers for the effectiveness and sustainability of urban regeneration, a conceptual framework combining public–private participation in cultural legacy hybridisation has been designed to define and interpret different models of urban regeneration and their possible implications for urban tourism. The matrix drawing urban regeneration models combines two dimensions (Fig. 1):

- Public–private stakeholder engagement, assumed to be the driver of cultural heritage hybridisation. It is low when a public actor plays a primary or exclusive role in activating and leading heritage exploitation/hybridisation, including managerial innovation; it is high when diverse (private/public, internal/external) stakeholders participate in, and add value to, these processes;
- Heritage hybridisation, assumed to be the source of socio-cultural innovations. It is low when continuity with the past/cultural legacy prevails and is displayed in heritage conservation and/or value creation through traditional cultural tourism; it is high when the past meets contemporary creativity through cross-fertilisation

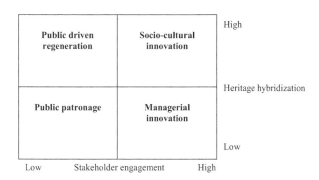

Fig. 1 Urban regeneration models

		High
Public driven regeneration	**Socio-cultural innovation**	
		Heritage hybridization
Public patronage	**Managerial innovation**	
		Low

Low   Stakeholder engagement   High

of cultural legacy with the cultural and creative industries and/or other sectors, also allowing for forms of creative tourism to emerge.

Four models of urban regeneration processes may be envisioned within this framework:

- *Public patronage* (low stakeholder engagement and low heritage hybridisation) occurs when cultural organisations (museums, archaeological sites, libraries, theatres, etc.) are managed from the top down by political bodies (State, Superintendencies, Municipalities, etc.) which invest public funds in heritage conservation. As culture is not included within an integrated development strategy or city plan, this form of urban regeneration may be equated with the pre-industrial model of Culture 1.0/2.0 in which cultural resources receive public funds without generating economic value for the city (Sacco 2011). In this model, urban tourism preserves continuity with the past through traditional forms of cultural tourism.
- *Managerial innovation* (high stakeholder engagement and low heritage hybridisation) occurs when cultural organisations are managed by private actors who build on managerial competences to improve organisational effectiveness and heritage conservation, accessibility, fruition and promotion. ICTs, digital marketing, new organisational models are among the main levers and traditional cultural tourism benefits from these innovations.
- *Socio-cultural innovation* (high stakeholder engagement and high heritage hybridisation) occurs when culture is the engine of widespread urban economic transformation and social change, led by public–private partnerships. This model may be equated with the post-industrial model of Culture 3.0 (Sacco 2011) in which culture generates extensive value through its transversal linkages throughout economies and societies, fostered by culture-led creativity. Forms of creative tourism take place within this model of urban regeneration, including cultural events based on creative content, cultural clusters or districts and hybridisations of culture with place specific resources. Both residents and visitors benefit from the enhanced standards and services in the urban area.
- *Public driven regeneration* (low stakeholder engagement and high heritage hybridisation) occurs when policy makers integrate culture into their urban strategy and planning, fully recognising it to be one of the main drivers of urban development. This public driven regeneration model may potentially benefit from complementarities of culture with other public policies (knowledge, technology, tourism); however synergies with other stakeholders operating in these fields remain weak. This form may be equated with the industrial model of Culture 2.0 (Sacco 2011) in which cultural resources generate—mainly economic—value, but there is still considerable potential for cross-fertilisation with other sectors. In this model of urban regeneration cultural tourism is combined with emerging forms of creative tourism.

This framework has been tested through a multiple-case study (Yin 2014) focused on three small and medium-sized Italian cities (Pompei, Trento and Lecce) to provide preliminary insights into new phenomena in context (Creswell 2007). It examines how stakeholder participation in cultural legacy hybridisation shapes different urban regeneration models and related forms of urban tourism. Both the methodological choice of cases and the issues investigated draw on appropriate sources of case study methodology (Yin 2014; Xiao and Smith 2006; Baxter and Jack 2008). The cases are small and medium-sized cities (urban level) within a single country (national level), Italy (Xiao and Smith 2006). The selection criteria were the heterogeneity of the cities in terms of socio-cultural context, cultural legacy, urban regeneration projects, stakeholder engagement and tourist flows. This heterogeneity enables us both to validate the interpretative capacity of the conceptual framework and to evaluate and compare the drivers and forms of urban regeneration of these cities—including possible implications for urban tourism—effectively.

4.1 The City of Pompei

The city of Pompei (pop. 25,397)—located in the Campania region of south-west Italy, where family expenditure on culture is only 54 Euro per month (Grossi 2015)—has a significant cultural legacy: a unique archaeological site which was designated a UNESCO cultural heritage in 1997. The site comprises the ruins of the ancient Roman city of Pompei—with its villas, frescos and everyday objects—which were buried by the eruption of Vesuvius in 79 A.D. Since their discovery in the eighteenth Century, the importance of the ruins has been recognised and the ancient city is an important tourist attraction. This archaeological site is, in fact, the second most visited (more than 2.6 million annual visitors) in Italy, after the archaeological circuit of Rome (the Colosseum, the Roman Forum and the Palatine hill) (MIBACT 2015). However, as is all too common in Italy, this significant cultural catalyst has not fostered the socio-economic development of the urban area.

The *public patronage model* seems to be shaping the regeneration of Pompei. Public actors (State, Ministry of Cultural Heritage and Tourism and Special Superintendency for the Archaeological Heritage of Naples and Pompei) have invested heavily in site safety and restoration (105 million Euro, *Grande Progetto Pompei* DL n. 34/2011) but have failed to design an integrated urban strategy (Go and Trunfio 2012) which would allow private actors to exploit this unique cultural legacy through heritage hybridisation and socio-cultural innovation, thus developing the whole municipality and fostering new entrepreneurship. The consequence of this failure is that the archaeological site concentrates more than 2.6 million visitors, participating in traditional forms of cultural tourism, but city tourism represents only 4% of total visitors—almost 101,000 in 2014 (Istat 2015)—who spend only one night in the municipality. Those benefiting from the attractiveness of the archaeological site are, instead, international tour operators, cruise liners and the neighbouring destinations of Sorrento, Naples, Capri.

4.2   The City of Trento

The city of Trento (pop. 115,000), set in the northeast of Italy, is the provincial capital of the autonomous province of Trento, whose special status under Italian law has always allowed it considerable autonomy in formulating and funding development policies. This Alpine city has a significant but not outstanding cultural legacy which has been complemented (since the Sixties) with far-sighted investments in knowledge (scientific and technological research centres, university, technological districts, etc.) and culture (cultural catalysts, events, iconic buildings) through innovative public-driven policies and projects.

In the last decade, the municipality of Trento has reinforced these investments with its strategy to reposition itself as a cultural city, thus exploiting its cultural and artistic heritage—both religious and secular. Today, the historic buildings which house cultural activities—restored in the Eighties to provide local communities with educational and leisure opportunities—have become tourism marketing tools. Heavy investment in two iconic museums—both publicly owned and funded, both entirely in keeping with the city's past—best testifies to this strategy: the Mart, a gallery of modern and contemporary art designed by Mario Botta, and the Muse, a science museum designed by Renzo Piano (Della Lucia 2015).

The city of Trento represents a *publicly driven regeneration model*: the integration of culture into urban public planning is evident in the fertilisation of the traditional, and fragmented, Alpine economy by the post-industrial economy. The main cultural and creative institutions, associations and industries are concentrated in the city, which also holds hallmark cultural events and provides services and amenities. The success of this public-driven urban regeneration is evident from the number of visitors, not only to the Muse—just two and a half years after its opening, it is among the top ten museum in Italy—but also to the leading hallmark cultural events of the city—the Festival of Economics and the Trento Film Festival—which represent the achievements of the most dynamic sectors of the cultural and creative industries in the area. Creative tourism is thus the main driver of urban tourism in Trento. Other positive effects are new entrepreneurship in the culture and creative industries (e.g., publishing and audio-visual), new urban experiences and projects (e.g., sustainable mobility, smart city initiative, see http://smartcities.ieee.org/) and heightened urban symbolic meaning (Trento's historical identity has been combined with its Alpine and knowledge/innovation identity). Due to the related increase of cultural consumption on the part of both residents and visitors, families spent more on culture in Trento province than anywhere else in Italy—165 Euro monthly (Grossi 2015). However, a possible excess of faithfulness to its historical identity/heritage and/or past path dependence on the leading role of public institutions is limiting the city's openness to the rich cross-fertilisation which stakeholder engagement often stimulates, locally and internationally. The formation of trust-based relationships with other local stakeholders, both inside the culture sector and in other sectors, would facilitate the creation of the critical mass of partnerships necessary for effective socio-cultural innovation in urban culture-led regeneration.

4.3   The City of Lecce

Lecce (pop. 93,302) is the provincial capital of the province of Lecce in Apulia, south-east Italy, a region with an average family expenditure on culture of 61 Euro monthly (Grossi 2015). Situated in an agricultural—olive oil and wine—and industrial area—ceramics and the quarrying of 'Lecce stone', Lecce is an art city nicknamed "the Florence of the South". Due to its unique cultural heritage (*Leccese* baroque) and socio-cultural atmosphere, the city is an attractive tourist destination both as a cultural city *per se* and as the main urban area serving the province's seaside destinations; a strong local sense of place and belonging has produced, and maintains, Lecce's clear urban identity.

The visionary cultural project 'Reinventing Eutopia'—which made Lecce a candidate for the European Capital of Culture 2019, competing with Cagliari, Perugia, Ravenna, Siena and Matera (which won)—clearly demonstrates the city's ability to engage stakeholders in hybridising urban cultural legacy with creativity in order to promote development through community engagement and entrepreneurial participation (Lecce 2014). The staging of cultural events and activities during its period as an Italian Capital of Culture in 2015 (jointly with Cagliari, Perugia, Ravenna and Siena) reinforced this enthusiasm by creating opportunities for cultural exchange through peer-to-peer communities of practice in cultural fields—"laboratories of change and experience" (Lecce 2014).

Lecce's regeneration is characterised by a *socio-cultural innovation model* in which public–private partnerships interpret cultural hybridisation as the engine for widespread urban economic transformation and social change. The creativity labs are the main facilitators of culture co-creation and hybridisation, through actors' engagement in communities of practice (Wenger 2010). These labs are complex spaces where culture and creativity combine on a social and technological platform shared by private and public stakeholders. For example, Lecce's 'Urban Opened Creative Lab' engages technical staff and a wide range of the city's cultural, social and economic actors in working groups tasked with the definition of future visions of the city, and the promotion of hybridisation between diverse sectors. This platform enables stakeholders to balance their interpretation of local heritage with their perspective on the need to integrate technological, market and organisational change and social innovation in order to co-create a desirable value proposition (Go and Trunfio 2011).

5   Conclusions, Limits and Future Research

The question of how cities can capitalise on cultural legacy hybridisation to activate effective and sustainable culture-led regeneration processes has not yet been fully answered, although both academics and policy makers widely recognise that such processes undoubtedly offer opportunities for development and innovation. This contribution proposes a conceptual framework based on public–private participation in cultural legacy hybridization to design and interpret the determinants of urban regeneration, the forms that it can assume, and the possible implications for urban tourism. The framework defines how the significance of a city's cultural legacy; the nature and level of its hybridisation with the culture and creative industries and other sectors (cultural legacy versus cultural catalysts versus cross-sectoral fertilisation and innovation) and the nature and level of stakeholder engagement (public patronage versus innovative policy making versus private–public stakeholder engagement), all play their part in shaping regeneration processes.

By applying this framework to a multiple case study analysis focused on three small and medium-sized Italian cities, this chapter tries to shed some light on the patchy Italian cultural scene. Its determinants interpreted the urban regeneration models in the three cities in our study, all of which demonstrate different drivers and models of regeneration. Pompei is an example of almost completely unproductive traditional public investment in the restoration of cultural heritage, largely because it fails to engage stakeholders in heritage exploitation. In Trento regeneration is led by innovative policy making which has allowed for the hybridisation of cultural heritage with other assets—knowledge and tourism in particular—but many more opportunities to widen the range and depth of hybridisation through stakeholder engagement are yet to explored. Lecce is an experimental lab of socio-cultural innovation where communities of practice allow creativity and knowledge to be integrated within local contexts, thus innovating cultural legacy and defining new models of cultural co-creation.

Urban tourism in all three cities is closely connected to their urban regeneration model. Pompei—with its public patronage model—is dominated by traditional forms of cultural tourism—visitors concentrated in, and visiting only, the archaeological site; in Trento, the public driven regeneration model is fostering the combination of traditional cultural tourism with creative forms of urban tourism connected to iconic buildings and cultural events; Lecce's socio-cultural innovation model allows the city to experiment with innovative forms of tourism by building on synergies and cross-fertilisation between individual and sectoral creativity.

The study has both theoretical and managerial implications. The theoretical framework integrates the heretofore scattered knowledge crucial to interpret the different models of cultural-led urban regeneration and define possible forms of urban tourism. These forms—shaped by both a synthesis of cultural legacy and innovation and the (im)balances of public–private stakeholder engagement—can be connected to the models used to incorporate culture into urban regeneration processes (DCMS 2004), and to paradigmatic phases of cultural economy evolution (Sacco 2011). From the managerial viewpoint, this framework invites policy makers and entrepreneurs to take up the challenge of showing that heritage cross-fertilisation can drive extensive socio-cultural urban innovation and thus enhance urban sustainable development and well-being. The two dimensions of the matrix are levers, which can be used to change and manage urban regeneration paths and lead to the realisation of Culture 3.0 (Sacco 2011), with socio-cultural innovation fostering transversal linkages throughout economies and societies, thus encouraging culture-led creativity and developing new forms of tourism. The benefits of this transition include the emergence of strong symbolic meaning, which empowers people to participate in cultural co-production and fosters capacity building, cognitive skill building, psychological wellbeing and the evolution of motivations and learning patterns.

The results of this exploratory and comparative study are revealing but preliminary. Diverse questions arise from the analysis: what levers are needed to enable public and private actors to drive the shift from public patronage to socio-cultural innovation? How could social and sectoral interactions be encouraged to promote the development of forms of creative tourism? Can creative tourism improve a city's image and its sustainable development? Future research will try to answer these questions by carrying out a qualitative analysis involving representative stakeholders from the three cities, in order to identify the drivers of shifts from hard to soft power (Nye 2004), and to assess the role of social media and technological platforms in the strengthening of stakeholder engagement, on both the demand and the supply side.

References

Al Rabadya R (2012) Creative cities through local heritage revival: a perspective from Jordan/ Madaba. Int J Herit Stud 18(3):1–16

Baxter P, Jack S (2008) Qualitative case study methodology: study design and implementation for novice researchers. Qual Rep 13(4):544–559. http://www.nova.edu/ssss/QR/QR13-4/baxter. pdf. Accessed 5 Mar 2015

Caulier-Grice J, Davies A, Patrick R, Norman W (2012) Social innovation overview: a deliverable of the project TEPSIE—The theoretical, empirical and policy foundations for building social innovation in Europe. European Commission—7th framework programme. European Commission, DG Research, Brussels

Choi N, Majumdar S (2015) Social innovation: towards a conceptualisation. In: Majumdar S, Guha S, Marakkath N (eds) Technology and innovation for social change. Springer India, Mumbai, pp 7–34

Creswell J (2007) Qualitative inquiry and research design: choosing among five approaches. Sage Publications, Thousand Oaks

CSES (2010) Study on the contribution of culture to local and regional development—evidence from the structural funds. European Commission, Brussels

DCMS (2004) Culture at the heart of regeneration. DCMS, London

Della Lucia M (2015) Creative cities: experimental urban labs. Int J Manag Cases 17(4):156–172

Della Lucia M, Franch M (2014) Culture-led urban regeneration and brand building in Alpine Italian towns. In: Go FM, Lemmetyinen A, Hakala U (eds) Harnessing place branding through cultural entrepreneurship. Palgrave Macmillan, New York, NY, pp 122–140

Della Lucia M, Trunfio M, Go FM (2016) Does the culture of context matter in urban regeneration processes? In: Alvarez M, Yüksel A, Go FM (eds) Heritage tourism destinations: preservation, communication and development. CABI Publishing, Wallingford, pp 11–21

European Commission (2010) Green paper on unlocking the potential of cultural and creative industries. European Commission, Brussels

Evans G (2003) Hard-branding the cultural city—from Prado to Prada. Int J Urban Reg Res 27 (2):417–440

Getz D (2008) Event tourism: definition, evolution, and research. Tour Manag 29(3):403–428

Getz D (2010) The nature and scope of festival studies. Int J Event Manag Res 5(1):1–47

Go FM, Trunfio M (2011) E-services governance in public and private sector: a destination management organization perspective. In: D'Atri A, Ferrara M, George JF (eds) Information technology and innovation trends in organizations. Springer, Wien, pp 11–19

Go FM, Trunfio M (2012) A paradigm shift from tourism destination management to democratic governance of place branding. J Travel Tour Res Spec Issue Destination Manag 12:4–17

Go FM, Trunfio M (2014) A cultural hybridization approach to reinterpreting the integration-diversity dichotomy: the case of Guggenheim's master branding Bilbao. Eur J Cross Cult Competence Manag 3(2):158–174

Grossi R (2015) Cultura, identità ed innovazione. La sfida per il futuro. XI Rapporto annuale Federculture. Il Sole24ore, Milano

Hall P (2004) Creativity, culture, knowledge and the city. Built Environ 30(3):256–258

Hutton TA (2009) The new economy of the inner city: restructuring, regeneration and dislocation in the 21st century metropolis. Routledge, London

Istat (2015) Movimento turistico nel 2014. http://www.istat.it/it/archivio/176210. Accessed 15 Oct 2015

Jakob D (2012) The eventification of place: urban development and experience consumption in Berlin and New York City. Eur Urban Reg Stud 20(4):447–459. doi:10.1177/0969776412459860

KEA (2006) The economy of culture in Europe. Directorate-General for Education and Culture, Brussels

KEA (2009) The impact of culture on creativity. Report for the European Community. Directorate-General for Education and Culture, Brussels

Klingmann A (2007) Brandscapes: architecture in the experience economy. The MIT Press, Cambridge

Lazzeretti L (2004) Art cities, cultural districts and Museums. An economic and managerial study of the cultural sector in Florence. Firenze University Press, Firenze

Lecce (2014) Lecce 2019 reinventing Eutopia. Application for the title of European capital of culture 2019. http://www.lecce2019.it/2019/bidbook.php?setLanguage=eng. Accessed 28 Sept 2015

McNeill D (2000) McGuggenisation: globalisation and national identity in the Basque country. Polit Geogr 19(4):473–494

MIBACT (2015) Musei, monumenti ed aree archeologiche statali. http://www.statistica.beniculturali.it/Visitatori_e_introiti_musei_14.htm. Accessed 28 Sept 2015

Miles S, Paddison R (2005) Introduction: the rise and rise culture-led urban regeneration. Urban Stud 42(5/6):833–839

Nye J (2004) Soft power. The means to success in world politics. PublicAffairs, New York, NY

Ockman J, Fraust S (2007) Architourism: authentic, escapist, exotic, spectacular. Prestel, London

OECD (2009) The impact of culture on tourism. OECD, Paris

OECD (2014) Tourism and the creative economy. OECD, Paris

Quinn B (2006) Problematising "festival tourism": arts festivals and sustainable development in Ireland. J Sustain Tour 14(3):288–306

Richards G (2011) Creativity and tourism. State Art Ann Tour Res 38(4):1225–1253
Richards G (2014) Creativity and tourism in the city. Curr Issue Tour 17(2):119–144. doi:10.1080/13683500.2013.783794
Richards G, Marques L (2012) Exploring creative tourism. Spec Issue J Tour Consum Pract 4 (2):1–11
Richards G, Wilson J (2006) Developing creativity in tourist experiences: a solution to the serial reproduction of culture? Tour Manag 27(6):1931–1951
Roche M (1992) Mega-events and micro-modernization. Br J Sociol 43(4):563–600
Sacco PL (2011) Culture 3.0: a new perspective for the EU 2014–2020 structural funds programming. European Expert Network on Culture, Brussels
Sacco PL (2012) Culture and the structural funds in Italy. Expert Network on Culture, Brussels
Sacco PL, Ferilli G, Tavano Blessi G, Nuccio M (2013) Culture as engine of local development processes: system-wide cultural district I: theory. Growth Change 44(4):555–570
Sacco PL, Ferilli G, Tavano Blessi G (2014) Understanding culture-led development: a critique of alternative theoretical explanations. Urban Stud 51(13):2806–2821
Scott AJ (2006) Creative cities: conceptual issues and policy questions. J Urban Aff 28(1):1–17
Scott AJ (2010) Cultural economy and the creative field of the city. Geogr Ann Ser B Hum Geogr 92(2):115–130
Smith MK (2007) Space, place and placelessness in the culturally regenerated city. In: Richards G (ed) Cultural tourism: global and local perspectives. The Haworth Press, Binghampton, pp 91–119
Tavano Blessi G, Grossi E, Sacco PL, Pieretti G, Ferilli G (2015) The contribution of cultural participation to urban well-being. A comparative study in Bolzano/Bozen and Siracusa, Italy. Cities 50:216–226
Trueman M, Cook D, Cornelius N (2008) Creative dimensions for branding and regeneration: overcoming negative perceptions of a city. Place Brand Public Dipl 4(1):29–44
Wenger E (2010) Communities of practice and social learning systems: the career of a concept. In: Blackmore C (ed) Social learning systems and communities of practice. Springer, London, pp 179–198
Xiao H, Smith SLJ (2006) Case studies in tourism research: a state-of-the-art analysis. Tour Manag 27(5):738–749
Yin RK (2014) Case study research: design and methods, 5th edn. Sage Pubblication, Thousand Oaks
Zukin S (1995) The cultures of cities. Blackwell, Malden

Building Košice European Capital of Culture: Towards a Creative City?

Kamila Borseková, Anna Vaňová, and Katarína Vitálišová

Abstract This chapter aims to identify the most important success factors leading to the reinvention and development of Košice as a creative city. The catalyst shifting Košice from an industrial city to a modern creative twenty-first century city was the award of the title European Capital of Culture in 2013. Changes in its cultural infrastructure produced various events that created a new development impulse in the city's cultural life. Implementation of project Interface, realisation of investment projects, organisation of hundreds of events and revitalisation of urban spaces and places began the overall transformation of the city, increasing its attractiveness for citizens, tourists, entrepreneurs and investors.

Keywords Culture • Creative city • Creative tourism • Revitalisation • Attractiveness

1 Introduction

A number of authors, including Florida (2005), Maitland (2007), Richards and Wilson (2006, 2007), and Rogerson (2007), discussed the role and importance of creativity. Creativity as the crucial concept in different social and academic fields reflects an advancement of creativity in society. It was preceded by broadening notions of culture (Richards 2011; Richards and Wilson 2007) and it reflects the 60 year voyage from the culture industry, through the cultural industries to creative industries (O'Connor 2010). According to Richards (2011, p. 1240), "as in many other disciplines, creativity has increasingly become a focus of attention for tourism scholars in recent years. Although the concept of creativity remains elusive to define, it has been integrated into tourism in a range of different forms, via creative people, products, processes and places. The growth of creative approaches to tourism can also be linked to the various strategies to create distinctive places, including the promotion of creative industries, creative cities and the creative class". The integration of spatial development and the creative approach, both

K. Borseková (✉) • A. Vaňová • K. Vitálišová
Faculty of Economics, Matej Bel University, Banská Bystrica, Slovakia
e-mail: kamila.borsekova@umb.sk; anna.vanova@umb.sk; katarina.vitalisova@umb.sk

© Springer International Publishing Switzerland 2017   193
N. Bellini, C. Pasquinelli (eds.), *Tourism in the City*,
DOI 10.1007/978-3-319-26877-4_13

based on quality human resources, bring a set of new activities known as creative tourism into the tourism destination. It includes the activities directed toward an engaged and authentic experience, with participative learning in the arts, heritage, or the special character of a place, and it provides a connection with those who reside in this place and create this living culture (Creative Cities Network 2006).

2 Creative Tourism and Creative City

Early links between tourism and creativity were made through the analysis of creative activities in tourist destinations (Zeppel and Hall 1992). While cultural tourism is seen as inflexible relying mostly on built heritage and culture, creative tourism uses intangible resources and thus allows a higher level of flexibility and dynamism. Creativity, mostly dependent on human capital, is seen as a renewable and sustainable resource that does not require a lot of investment for maintenance and preservation as do museums and monuments (Richards and Wilson 2006, 2007).

Creative tourism is defined by Richards and Raymond (2000, p. 18) as "tourism which offers visitors the opportunity to develop their creative potential through active participation in learning experiences which are characteristic of the holiday destination where they are undertaken". Tourists are becoming experimentally involved in order to engage with the real cultural life of destinations in an authentic and memorable manner (Hung et al. 2014; Creative Cities Network 2006). According to Landry creative tourism provides an opportunity for tourists to get under the skin of the place through ordinary activities, like seeing people go to work, queuing, buying drinks or food, chatting on the sidewalks and the like (2010, p. 37).

Thanks to the active participation of tourists in creative tourism, interacting with locals and their culture, they are becoming co-producers of the experience they consume (Prebensen 2014; Richards 2012, 2013; Tan et al. 2015). Joint creation of experience by consumers and producers (Binkhorst and den Dekker 2009) enhances authenticity and innovation, which can impact on the competitive advantage of destinations (Miles and Green 2010; Richards and Wilson 2006). Despite the differences in definitions, Richards sums up the common elements of creative tourism. Participative and authentic tourist experiences foster creativity through contact with local people, their habits and culture. Passive consumption is replaced by the co-creation of creative tourism destinations and an emphasis on living and intangible culture rather than a static, intangible cultural heritage (2011). On the other hand creative tourism requires a greater level of innovation (Richards and Wilson 2006) and relies on creative governments (Florida 2002) and the development of creative communities (Smith 2009). The creative sector can provide wider and more sustainable benefits for the destination and provide dynamism while releasing the creative potential of the inhabitants, visitors and places (Richards and Wilson 2007).

Cultural and creative industries (CCI) are the engines of development and economic growth in many regions and countries. According to a survey by the International Confederation of Societies of Authors and Composers (CISAC) the global CCI revenue is $2250 billion, which corresponds to 3 % of the world's GDP. Global CCI generates 29.5 million jobs, and occupies 1 % of the world's active population.[1]

According to UNWTO (2015) tourism is a key to development, prosperity and well-being through the creation of jobs and enterprises, export revenues and infrastructure development. The development of the world tourism sector is significant, from 25 million international tourists in 1950 to 1133 million in 2014. Currently tourism contributes directly or indirectly 9 % of world GDP and 9 % of world employment. Its share of world's exports is 6 %.

Cultural and creative industries as well as tourism are significant contributors to the future development of cities, regions and nations. So according to Richards and Marques (2012) creative tourism is therefore a key development option for various cities and destination regions. Firstly, it responds to the need for tourism to re-invent itself as well as to the need for destinations to do something different in a saturated market. It can also meet the desire of tourists for more fulfilling and meaningful experiences.

Creative tourism is a form of networked tourism, which depends on the ability of producers and consumers to relate to each other and to generate value from their encounters. Creative tourists are "cool hunters" in search of creative "hot-spots" where their own creativity can feed and be fed by the creativity of the places they visit. The interconnection of cultural and creative industries with tourism offers a space for modern, creative and innovative ways of urban development.

Cities and urban areas have always been places where human creativity flourished; "urban creativity can be seen as an umbrella concept that combines different dimensions of creativity from economic and social creativity to technological creativity or innovation" (Girard et al. 2012, p. 24). Urban creativity refers to several concepts, including creative industries, creative tourism and creative cities.

A creative city is a place where people think, plan and act with imagination (Landry 2000). The concept of a creative city is often associated with the process of creative and innovative thinking (Landry 2000; Kalandides and Lange 2007), while other authors include the concept of creative people or a so-called creative class (Florida 2005), cultural organisations, and creative and cultural activities are the key preconditions for creative city development (Bradford 2004; UNCTAD 2008; Smith and Warfield 2008).

Several authors see creative cities as very dynamic and turbulent places. According to Bradford (2004) creative cities are dynamic locales of

---

[1]The study analyses 11 cultural and creative industry sectors: advertising, architecture, books, gaming, movies, music, newspapers/magazines, performing arts, radio, television and visual arts. See more at http://www.worldcreative.org/

experimentation and innovation, where new ideas flourish and people from all walks of life come together to make their communities better places to live, work and play. Hall (2000) considers creative cities as places of great social and intellectual turbulence.

The idea of a creative thinking process can be applied to a range of social, economic and environmental problems in creative cities (Kalandides and Lange 2007) with strong flourishing arts, culture and creative diversity. Cities worldwide are using culture and creativity to brand themselves (Richards 2001) and culture and creativity have become crucial factors in urban development strategies (McCann 2001). The role of creativity in urban development could be seen as a factor of socio-economic vibrancy (Ray 1998). Montgomery (2007) suggests that successful cities of the new economy will be the ones that have invested in their capacity for creativity and that understand the importance of locality and cultural heritage.

3   Key Aspects of the Creative City and Competitive Advantage

A number of features and factors distinguishing the creative city have been described in various studies (e.g., Hall 2000; Hamilton et al. 2009; Landry 2000; Wu 2005) and elaborated into various creative city indices (for example the European Creativity Index elaborated by KEA 2009; Florida 2002, 2005; the Hong Kong Creativity Index 2004). Cities attractive for creative activities seem to have some common characteristics: these cities are authentic and unique, with a strongly perceived local identity, human diversity and a diversity of cultural heritage. Creative cities tend to have a tradition of creativity, innovation and cluster development. Both hard and soft infrastructure is involved. Creative cities are supposed to be open to new ideas, and different life styles. Creative cities are often described as open cities and cool cities at the same time (Baycan 2012). The creative city is represented both as a clarion call for imaginative action in the development and running of urban life and as a clear and detailed toolkit of methods by which our cities can be revived and revitalised (Landry 2000).

In sum it seems that all cities are creative places by their nature as they are resourceful, productive, innovative, original, imaginative and dynamic (Moore-Cherry 2015). To be competitive, cities need however to set objectives about how to use all of their resources, i.e., economic, political, and most of all, cultural resources efficiently and effectively. Cities have to be able to maintain existing, or attract new inhabitants, entrepreneurs and tourists. Cities have always been the centres of culture and civilisation and the hubs of creation. But today they face enormous challenges (infrastructural, economic, social and environmental) and dramatic changes are taking place. There has to be a paradigm shift in the way cities are managed (Suciu and Ivanovici 2009). Support for and targeted building of creative and cultural industries is not enough.

Cities need to build competitive advantage. Creation, building and exploitation of competitive advantage is influenced by several factors. Generally authors are agreed on the crucial role of human resources in terms of their knowledge, skills and creativity (Kitson et al. 2004; Porter 1999; Ulrich and Lake 1991). Other factors of competitive advantage are social and institutional capital (the scope, depth and orientation of social networks and institutional forms); cultural capital (the range and quality of cultural facilities and assets); knowledge and creative capital (the presence of an innovative and creative class); infrastructural capital in terms of the size and quality of public infrastructure (see Kitson et al. 2004 for more details); financial resources and prices (Ulrich and Lake 1991); infrastructure and location (Maier and Tödtling 1997; Porter 1999; Ulrich and Lake 1991); cooperation, partnership (Michael 2003; Poon 2002; Saxena 2005; Soteriades 2012) and integration with regional clusters (Porter 1999).

The importance of factors of competitive advantage was empirically tested within our research aimed at identifying and exploiting competitive advantage on the regional level, from both theoretical and practical viewpoints. The theoretical aspects were tested by experts dealing with the issue of competitive advantage, using the Delphi method, with a two round questionnaire survey. The practical aspects were tested on a panel of practitioners from regional authorities from all Slovak NUTS 3 regions, using structured interviews. The data collected were evaluated by a Friedman test using an SPSS program. The most important factor according to our research results on both the empirical and theoretical aspects is the quality of human resources. Other important factors are the knowledge infrastructure in terms of education, academic and research institutions; the innovative environment, including the innovativeness of businesses and their potential for generating new ideas and innovation; and the creative potential and infrastructure in terms of the presence of a creative class and creative urban places suitable for a wide spectrum of creative activities such as concerts, theatres, exhibitions and other kind of events. It turns out that the factors that impact on building creative cities and the factors that determine competitive advantage are very similar.

4   Making Košice a Competitive Creative City and Attractive Creative Tourist Destination

The following case study is based on empirical research from three projects. One was an international EU 7th Framework Programme project on the functioning of local production systems in crisis conditions. This project looked at the creative and tourism local production systems for Slovakia and four other EU and non-EU countries. Other two national projects, which are ongoing, focuses on Slovak creative industries that deliver the crucial intangibles to the public sector in the

Fig. 1 Political map of Slovakia. *Source*: R.G.T. Press

context of innovation and smart growth[2] and Marketing in regional and local development.[3] The data was gathered during a study visit to Košice in 2015 and 2016. As the 2013 European Capital of Culture it provided an excellent experimental site to study the development of a creative city intended to attract creative tourists from all over the world.

Košice is the second largest city of Slovakia, situated in the eastern part of the country, only 20 km from Hungary, 80 km from Ukraine and 90 km from Poland (Fig. 1). The city is divided into four districts and has almost 250,000 inhabitants. It is the administrative centre of the Košice Region. The city plus its conurbation has almost 390,000 inhabitants. The city has a strong tradition in steel production, currently represented by the company US Steel Košice which is the biggest employer in eastern Slovakia with more than 12,000 employees and an annual production capacity of 4.5 million tons. Besides steel the IT sector is growing, as evidenced by the IT Valley cluster. The transport infrastructure, including road, rail and an international airport, is well developed and Košice is the most important transport hub in eastern Slovakia. The education sector includes primary and secondary schools, three universities and a college. Košice is an old city, with a rich culture and heritage. St. Elizabeth's church, with its landmark dome is the easternmost Gothic cathedral in Europe. The city's historical centre is the largest urban preservation area in the country. Since 1924, on the first Sunday in October Košice has

---

[2]Project VEGA 1/0680/14 Creative industries as a key source of the public sector's intangible assets in the context of innovation and smart growth.
[3]Project KEGA 007UMB—4/2015 Marketing in regional and local development.

hosted the International Peace Marathon, Europe's second oldest and of the world's oldest marathon.

Following a presentation of the project *Košice Interface 2013*, the city won the title European Capital of Culture, in competition with nine other Slovak cities. The main aspects that were highly valued in the proposal were the European dimension of the project; the involvement of the citizens; the benefits of the project for the city, country and Europe; long term sustainability; originality; clearly defined structures; funding and resources, and project presentation.

The Interface project was based on the long-term transformation of the city through culture. The project was defined as a set of tools, procedures and measures enabling the user to interact and enter into cultural processes, understood in their broadest sense. The aim of the project was to engage the cooperation of all stakeholders who could contribute to transform the cultural, social and economic environment. The transformation was encouraged by creativity, new ideas and projects, but also by increasing and deepening public interest in culture and art.

"Supporting creativity" was a main message of the project and a new vision of Košice, which until then had been known mostly for its rich history and well developed heavy industry. Thanks to the Interface project and the title of 2013 European Capital of Culture (ECoC), Košice created a new perspective for its development. The project's slogan was "Use the city" in the sense of stimulating interest in becoming an active part of the cultural and social processes in the city. Košice could become an environment favourable to the development of cultural interaction and the slogan should encourage citizens in its unlimited use.

Investment projects were the basis of the European Capital of Culture concept and the Interface project was oriented on the significant development and revitalisation of the city's cultural infrastructure. Changes in cultural infrastructure have led to the implementation of various events and thus to a new development impulse to the cultural life of the city. The main reasons why Košice was awarded the ECoC title were:

- The wide participation of citizens and independent artists in creating projects and formulating a new vision and philosophy of urban renewal;
- Well-developed European cultural cooperation and an intensive exchange of experience between the project team, artists and foreign partner cities from twelve countries;
- The creation and operation of new suitable city spaces for the independent art scene;
- The creation of a grant system for supporting independent artists, cultural organisations and new culture production in the city;
- Having good cultural, transport and technical infrastructure;
- Having clear and transparent institutional and financial rules;
- Possessing personal and expert capacities; experience in organising big events and professional management structures;
- The cultural heritage of Košice and the whole Eastern region of Slovakia, which has 10 of the 15 Slovak cultural sites listed by UNESCO, including the famous

vine region Tokaj, and two nature sites. The European Commission also appreciated that support for the whole ECoC project was coordinated by an association of legal entities called Coalition 2013+ founded in 2010. The coalition involves more than 40 members and includes institutions and organisation from the private, public and non-profit sectors actively contributing to the project's implementation and future sustainability.

From 2008 Košice started to prepare the necessary infrastructure for the implementation of ECoC activities. The investment activities were aimed at the reconstruction of the cultural and historical heritage of Košice, using modern information technologies. Two types of investment project were undertaken. These either involved the recovery and modification of facilities that were originally used for cultural purposes, or were innovative projects involving the revitalisation and reconstruction of buildings and spaces that originally served a different purpose. Previously abandoned and unused places and spaces have become cultural resources for the city. The revitalisation of buildings and spaces was the basis for the realisation of cultural events and at the same it was a tool for the overall planned transformation of the city. The noninvestment activities were based on a mix of cultural, dance, musical and literature events. A space was created for young artists, creative people and their performances.

During the main project implementation year of 2013 huge investments were made in culture. Altogether more than 71 million Euros, were invested in 20 capital investment projects in cultural and public infrastructure. Investments were made by the city of Košice (49,670,721.06€), Košice self-governing region (11,979,931€), Ministry of Culture (5,178,447€) and NGOs projects (4,422,770€). Construction investment created directly and indirectly 771 new jobs (Evaluation Report of ECoC 2013).

Altogether more than 600 projects were undertaken between 2009 and 2013. The largest and the most costly projects were the transformation of abandoned military barracks into a modern and multifunctional Kulturpark, and the refurbishment of an abandoned and defunct swimming pool at the Kunsthalle exhibition centre. As both spaces are in the city centre, in order to bring culture to the outskirts and suburbs of the city, the project SPOT was completed. This involved transforming a group of old heat exchangers and small heating plants in different residential districts into a network of community art centres.

In 2013 there were 25 key events plus an additional 60 large scale events and around 300 accompanying small scale events. There was a significant increase in tourism in 2013 with 151,512 visitors staying, including 67,141 international visitors. This was a 17 % increase on 2012 and a 31 % increase on 2009. The number of overnight stays (285,494) represented a 10 % increase on 2012 and a 30 % increase on 2009. During the critical ECoC events the city's accommodation capacity was 98 % full (Ex-post Evaluation of the 2013 European Capitals of Culture).

It is a positive fact that the number of events organized in the following year, 2014, was even higher, almost 500. For comparison, in 2012 only 110 events were

Fig. 2 Interconnection of
success factors for the
development of a creative
city and creative tourism

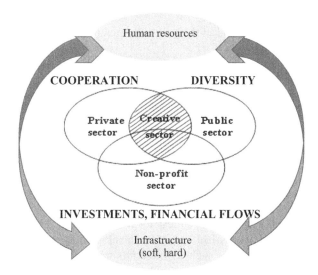

organised, and in 2010 and 2011 there were only 94 organised events. The ECoC
and the implementation of the Interface project had a very positive influence on the
city's image, the level of cooperation among sectors and stakeholders, the investments and financial flows, and the tourism and culture environment. The interconnection of success factors for the development of a creative city and creative
tourism is sketched in Fig. 2.

The ECoC competition, the implementation of project Interface and the cultural
and creative activities managed by coalitions of stakeholders from public, private
and non-profit sectors were important in initiating the modern economic and social
development of Košice. The building and reconstruction of the cultural infrastructure, the concentration of the 'creative class', networks, partnerships, and the
financial and political support, have all contributed to transforming Košice into
creative city, attractive for domestic and creative tourists. The investments during
the 5 years of preparation for the ECoC and the year of ECoC implementation
created suitable conditions (such as new public spaces, new types of cultural events,
leisure time infrastructure) for the support and development of creative tourism.

5   Conclusion

The title European Capital of Culture contributed to the long-term development of
Košice. The program ECoC impacts on the cultural system and the program of the
city. ECoC brings new ideas and opportunities to the city and thereby generates new
and creative types of activities that extend the possibilities of cultural industries and
of employees in the sector. The ECoC program can contribute to the creation of new
networks and the improvement of existing ones. Networking in the cultural sector

creates opportunities for the development of cooperation and partnerships which may be reflected in the long-term functioning of the city's cultural sector (Garcia and Cox 2013).

The benefits for Košice can be measured in quantitative and qualitative terms. The qualitative benefits include the investment of more than 71 million Euros in the city and its urban infrastructure and the increase in the number of facilities offering cultural products, services and events, including the Kulturpark, Kunsthalle, and SPOT community art centres. Investment projects created directly or indirectly 771 new jobs. There is also the increase in the number of guests and overnight stays compared to previous years. This increase was noticeable in 2012, and there was an additional 30,000 increase in guests in 2013. In 2014 it dropped by over 7000, but it still represented a substantial increase in visitors compared to before the ECoC program. The direct cause of the rise in visitors is the increase in organised events—with 385 in 2013 and almost 500 in 2014. In fact, "In Košice there was a great effort made to set tourism on a new development route, not only based on traditional cultural tourism such as museums and galleries but also towards new modern experimental forms of culture such as street art and festivals" (Šebová et al. 2014, p. 667).

Among the qualitative benefits of the ECoC program are the improved image and the enhanced prestige of the city. This effect is related to cultural influences of the program. The improvement in the city's image is a well-established objective of the ECoC program, either seen as transforming the image of the city relative to other industrial cities or those with inferior images, or as increasing its national and international profile. Improving its image is indirectly connected with increasing tourist attendance, because a more attractive city attracts more investments, more attention, and so in the longer run more tourists (Palmer et al. 2004).

The change in the perception of the city by its residents was also evaluated when the impact of ECoC was assessed (for more details see McAteer et al. 2014, Ex-post Evaluation of the 2013 European Capitals of Culture). The survey aimed to investigate citizens' views on changing the city's image, the improvement of urban living conditions and the individual benefits of ECoC implementation. Also investigated was whether citizens felt that the new investments were implemented. Even in 2012 Košice residents noticed the new investments and projects, and their awareness increased over time as the activities continued. Investments in urban infrastructure were appreciated by 80 % of respondents. Residents also perceived an improvement in the city's image and 40 % of respondent's sensed that the projects created new jobs. Another positive element was that the percentage of citizens confirming the statement that every citizen of Košice will be or already has benefited from the ECoC grew between 2013 and 2014 by almost 20 %. This shows that by 2014 people had noticed that there were more activities, investments and events being organised in the city. Further proof of a positive perception of the ECoC program and its investment projects is that 58 % of citizens considered Košice a better place than before its implementation.

The changing image of Košice was also reflected by its inclusion in a list of places worth visiting. One of the most prestigious tour guides, the Lonely Planet, included Košice in its Top 10 destinations for 2013. Besides the improvement in the city's image, one may argue that the most important qualitative benefit is the revitalisation of its cultural and creative infrastructure, including the creation of modern, functional urban places and spaces suitable for the development of cultural and creative industries and the overall transformation of an industrial city into a creative city. This new approach is made sustainable by the integration of the needs of both residents and tourists. The ECoC title acted as a catalyst for new urban development with a focus on economic restructuring and tourism. Through the synergy effect it brought a significant development to the city by increasing its attractiveness for citizens, tourists, entrepreneurs and investors.

References

Baycan T (2012) Creative cites. Context and perspectives. In: Girard LF, Baycan T, Nijkamp P (eds) Sustainable city and creativity: promoting creative urban initiatives. Ashgate, Burlington, VT, pp 15–53

Binkhorst E, den Dekker T (2009) Agenda for co-creation tourism experience research. J Hosp Mark Manag 18:311–327

Bradford N (2004) Creative cities: structured policy dialogue backgrounder. Canadian Policy Research Networks: Background Paper F/46

Creative Cities Network (2006) Towards sustainable strategies for creative tourism. Discussion report of the planning meeting for 2008 international conference on creative tourism. http://unesdoc.unesco.org/images/0015/001598/159811E.pdf. Accessed 1 Dec 2015

Florida R (2002) The rise of the creative class. Basic Books, New York

Florida R (2005) Cities and the creative class. Routledge, New York and London

Garcia B, Cox T (2013) European capitals of culture: success strategies and long-term effects. http://www.europarl.europa.eu/RegData/etudes/etudes/join/2013/513985/IPOLCULT_ET (2013)513985_EN.pdf. Accessed 22 Feb 2016

Girard LF, Baycan T, Nijkamp P (2012) Sustainable city and creativity: promoting creative urban initiatives. Ashgate, Burlington, VT

Hall P (2000) Creative cities and economic development. Urban Stud 37(4):639–649

Hamilton L, Arbic A, Baeker G (2009) Building the creative economy in Nova Scotia. http://www.novascotiacan.ca/pdfs/report.pdf. Accessed 10 Nov 2010

Hudec et al (2015) Evaluation report of European capital of culture 2013. http://krvam.ekf.tuke.sk/index.php/aktivity-katedry/na-stiahnutie. Accessed 22 Feb 2016

Hung WL, Lee YJ, Huang PS (2014) Creative experiences, memorability and revisit intention in creative tourism. Curr Issue Tour. doi:10.1080/13683500.2013.877422

Kalandides A, Lange B (2007) Creativity as a synecdoche of the city—marketing the creative Berlin. In: HKIP & UPSC conference: when creative industries crossover with cities, Hong Kong, 2–3 April 2007

KEA 2009: KEA European Affairs (2009) The impact of culture on creativity. A study prepared for the European Commission. June 2009. http://www.acpcultures.eu/_upload/ocr_document/CEKEA_CultureCreativity_CreativityIndex_2009.pdf. Accessed 15 Jun 2016

Kitson M, Martin R, Tyler P (2004) Regional competitiveness: an elusive yet key concept? Reg Stud 38(9):991–999

Landry C (2000) The creative city. Earthscan, London

Landry C (2010) Experiencing imagination: travel as a creative trigger. In: Wurzburger R, Aageson T, Pattakos A, Pratt S (eds) A global conversation. How to provide unique creative experiences for travelers worldwide. Sunstone Press, SantaFe, pp 33–42

Maier G, Tödtling F (1997) Regional and urban economics. ELITA, Bratislava
Maitland R (2007) Conviviality and everyday life: the appeal of new areas of London for visitors. Int J Tour Res 10:15–20
McAteer N et al (2014) Ex-post evaluation of the 2013 European capitals of culture. http://ec.europa.eu/programmes/creative-europe/actions/documents/ecoc-2013-full-report.pdf. Accessed 20 Jan 2015
McCann P (2001) Urban and regional economics. Oxford University Press, Oxford
Michael EJ (2003) Tourism micro-clusters. Tour Econ 9(2):133–145
Miles I, Green L (2010) Innovation in creative services. In: Gallouj F, Djellal F (eds) The handbook of innovation in services: a multi-disciplinary perspective. Edward Elgar, Cheltenham, pp 178–196
Montgomery J (2007) The new wealth of cities: city dynamics and the fifth wave. Ashgate, Aldershot
Moore-Cherry N (2015) Creative cities. In: Davies WKD (ed) Theme cities: solutions for urban problems. Springer, London, pp 359–379
O'Connor J (2010) The cultural and creative industries: a literature review, 2nd edn, Creativity, culture and education series. Creativity, Culture and Education, London
Palmer R et al (2004) European cities and capitals of culture—study prepared for European Commission—part I. http://umea2014.se/wp-content/uploads/2013/01/Rapporten_del_1.pdf. Accessed 22 Feb 2016
Poon A (2002) Tourism, technology and competitive strategies. CAB International, Oxford
Porter ME (1999) Competitive advantage of nations. Free Press, New York, NY
Prebensen NK (2014) Facilitating for enhanced experience value. In: Alsos GA, Eide D, Madson EL (eds) Handbook of research on innovation in tourism industries. Edward Elgar, Cheltenham, pp 154–180
Ray C (1998) Culture, intellectual property and territorial rural development. Sociol Ruralis 38:3–20
Richards G (2001) The market for cultural attractions. In: Richards G (ed) Cultural attractions, European tourism. CABI, Wallingford, pp 31–53
Richards G (2011) Creativity and tourism: the state of the art. Ann Tour Res 38(4):1225–1253
Richards G (2012) Tourism, creativity and creative industries. Paper presented at the conference: creativity and creative industries in challenging times, Tilburg University, Tilburg
Richards G (2013) Cultural tourism. In: Blackshaw T (ed) Routledge handbook of leisure studies. Routledge, Abingdon, pp 483–492
Richards G, Marques L (2012) Exploring creative tourism. J Tour Consumption Pract 4(2):1–11
Richards G, Raymond C (2000) Creative tourism. ATLAS News 23:16–20
Richards G, Wilson J (2006) Developing creativity in tourist experiences: a solution to the serial reproduction of culture? Tour Manag 27:1408–1413
Richards G, Wilson J (2007) Tourism, creativity and development. Routledge, London
Rogerson C (2007) Creative industries and tourism in the developing world: the example of South Africa. In: Richards G, Wilson J (eds) Tourism, creativity and development. Routledge, London, pp 229–239
Saxena R (2005) Relationships, networks and the learning regions: case evidence from the Peak District National Park. Tour Manag 26(2):277–289
Šebová M, Džupka P, Hudec O, Urbančíková N (2014) Promoting and financing cultural tourism in Europe: a case study of Košice, European Capital of Culture 2013. Amfiteatru Econ 16 (36):665–669
Smith M (2009) Issues in cultural tourism. Routledge, London
Smith R, Warfield K (2008) The creative city: a matter of values in creative cities, cultural cluster and local economic development. Edward Elgar, Cheltenham, pp 287–312
Soteriades MD (2012) Tourism destination marketing: approaches improving effectiveness and efficiency. J Hosp Tour Technol 3(2):107–120

Suciu M, Ivanovici M (2009) Creative economy and macroeconomic stability during the financial stability. 10th international conference. Finance and economic stability in the context of financial crisis, West University of Timisoara, Bucharest

Tan S, Tan SH, Luh DB, Kung SF (2015) Understanding tourist perspectives in creative tourism. Curr Issue Tour. doi:10.1080/13683500.2015.1008427

Ulrich D, Lake D (1991) Organizational capability: creating competitive advantage. Acad Manag 5(1):77–92

UNCTAD (2008) Creative economy report 2008. http://unctad.org/en/Docs/ditc20082cer_en.pdf. Accessed 20 Dec 2015

UNWTO (2015) Tourism highlights 2015 edition. http://www.eunwto.org/doi/pdf/10.18111/9789284416899. Accessed 22 Feb 2016

Wu W (2005) Dynamic cities and creative clusters. World Bank Policy Research Working Paper No. 3509

Zeppel H, Hall MC (1992) Arts and heritage tourism. In: Weiler B, Hall MC (eds) Special interest tourism. Wiley, London, pp 47–69

The Role of Fashion for Tourism: An Analysis of Florence as a Manufacturing Fashion City and Beyond

Luciana Lazzeretti, Francesco Capone, and Patrizia Casadei

Abstract The aim of this chapter is to contribute to the academic debate on the fashion city definition and foster some economic implications for tourism. First, two main approaches in the debate are discussed: a supply-side perspective, which defines a fashion city as a 'manufacturing fashion city' based on its physical image and presence of a garment industry, and a demand-side perspective, which deploys the term 'symbolic fashion city' in line with its virtual image and new information and communication technologies. The city of Florence is then examined; traditionally defined as a city of art, Florence is also a creative city characterised by the presence of a significant fashion- and design-manufacturing cluster. Our analysis includes the re-emergence of Florence as a widely recognised major fashion city in both Italy and abroad. The chapter concludes with a discussion of the role the fashion industry plays in cultivating the image of the city, fostering local competitive advantage, and increasing its appeal as a tourist destination.

Keywords Fashion city • Fashion and design industries • Creative industries • Tourism

1 Introduction

Creative industries have long been at the centre of heated academic and political debate, and are increasingly regarded as leading sectors for promoting economic development in Europe and abroad (UNESCO 2013; Barrowclough and Kozul Wright 2008; Power 2011). Recently, the European Commission (2010) expanded the definition of creative industries to include eno-gastronomy, green economy, experience economy, creative tourism, and businesses such as fashion and design (Lazzeretti and Capone 2015).

The current debate on creative tourism focuses on the shift from conventional models of cultural tourism to new models based on intangible culture and contemporary creativity (Capone 2016; Richards 2013; Lorentzen and Hansen 2009).

L. Lazzeretti (✉) • F. Capone • P. Casadei
University of Florence, Florence, Italy
e-mail: luciana.lazzeretti@unifi.it; francesco.capone@unifi.it; patrizia.casadei@unifi.it

© Springer International Publishing Switzerland 2017   207
N. Bellini, C. Pasquinelli (eds.), *Tourism in the City*,
DOI 10.1007/978-3-319-26877-4_14

Richards and Wilson (2006) argued that in contrast to most cultural tourists, creative tourists are increasingly looking for more engaging, interactive experiences; such experiences are thus crucial for destination management and local competitiveness. Fashion and design have also been increasingly regarded by tourism leaders, planners and trade promoters as important elements for the promotion of creative cities, a trend which supports the idea of a new type of creative tourism oriented more towards symbolic contents, where fashion and tourism progressively converge and enrich each other through the creation of memorable images and identities for contemporary urban environments (Breward and Gilbert 2006; Jansson and Power 2010).

A highly reciprocal relationship exists between fashion branding and tourism development strategies: on the one hand, a 'fashionable' tourist city can be perceived as more attractive for specialised firms and creative professionals; on the other hand, tourism experiences, which include fashion and luxury shopping in addition to cultural and creative activities, can result in increased recognition of the fashion identity of a city (Chilese and Russo 2008).

A changing importance of the locations of fashion design, production and consumption can be observed in the long-term trajectories of the main fashion capitals. Fashion cities act as tourist 'honey pots', alongside museums and galleries, and the experience of places traditionally associated with fashion has greatly contributed to the growth of urban tourism (Gilbert 2006).

According to a creative economy approach, a fashion city may be defined as a type of creative city characterised by a high concentration of creative industries, such as fashion industries, as well as by a large number of designers, public and private cultural institutions, and a fashion cluster that may appeal to tourists.

The aim of this chapter is to contribute to the debate on the fashion city definition via a 'manufacturing' perspective, and to investigate the implications of this perspective for tourism. Although many studies have addressed the fashion city debate, the majority of academic researchers have mainly focused on the symbolic content of cultural fashion products and city images, neglecting the impact of local industries and industry clusters on promoting city images and fashion industries, respectively. We focus here on Florence, traditionally defined as a city of art, but also as a creative city characterised by the presence of a prominent fashion- and design-manufacturing cluster. This cluster is identified by its cultural institutions (e.g., the University of Florence, Polimoda, fashion museums), small and medium-sized enterprises, and multinational firms like Gucci, Ferragamo and Prada.

The chapter is organised as follows. In the next section, we review the literature on the 'fashion city' concept from both a supply- and demand-side perspective. In Sect. 3 we analyse the re-emergence of Florence as a major fashion city according to a manufacturing perspective. In Sect. 4, we identify and examine geographical fashion and design industry clusters. The last section discusses how fashion affects the image of the city, contributes to the fostering of local competitive advantage, and increases tourist appeal.

2   Towards a Definition of the Fashion City: From Manufacturing to the Symbolic Production of Fashion

In recent decades, the process of globalisation and the growing relevance of intangible business activities have positioned cultural and creative industries— together with the concept of a 'creative city'—in an increasingly prominent role within processes of innovation, growth and economic development (Power and Scott 2004). In particular, recent trends of globalisation, such as the phenomena of market saturation and low-cost overseas manufacturing, have profoundly affected the fashion industry. As a result, it has been transformed from traditional manufacturing to a design- and innovation-oriented industry that generates symbolic elements in contemporary cities (Jansson and Power 2010; Williams and Currid-Halkett 2011). The growing emphasis on its 'design-intensive' nature has led to the fashion industry being defined as a key component of cultural and creative industries and a significant element for both the promotion of the cultural and creative economy and for the future of creative cities (Boontharm 2015; Scott 2000).

Within this framework, the idea of the 'fashion city' has received increasing attention as an important tool for the development, growth and regeneration of global and not-so-global cities (Jansson and Power 2010; Pandolfi 2015). Local governments, policy makers and academics across a number of disciplines have all been devoting more attention to this phenomenon. New York, London, Paris, Milan and Tokyo are usually defined as 'world fashion capitals' in which creative talent and the production, trade and consumption of fashion converge; they are also frequently the hosts for internationally acclaimed premier fashion events that serve as significant showcases for designers, products and symbolic images from all over the world (Donvito et al. 2013; Gilbert 2013).

A complex sequence of manufacturing systems, economic factors and cultural images seems to have contributed to the material and symbolic development of the world fashion capitals. In fact, the history and formation of these global centres of fashion have been heterogeneous, undergoing a varying process that has combined production and consumption and integrated material and symbolic content (Scott 1996, 2000). These fashion cities have combined their flexible manufacturing bases with distinctive industrial structures, and have also developed fashion-related institutions critical in enabling local manufacturers to adapt to new competitive pressures. In particular, the emergence of a fashion media system (e.g., advertising, magazines, fashion weeks, fashion news) has played a key role in the establishment of these global centres, acting as one of the most powerful determinants in creating a 'symbolic economy' for fashion (Breward and Gilbert 2006; Jansson and Power 2010).

The Garment District in New York is revealing in this regard, having reinvented itself from an apparel-manufacturing hub to a fashion capital in large part due to the establishment of globally renowned fashion weeks, the rise in importance of fashion magazines, and the development of apparel-related institutions such as prestigious design schools (Rantisi 2004). In Northern Italy, the emergence of Milan as a world fashion capital was not merely the result of the agglomeration of textile and clothing manufacturing firms (including some of the world's largest fashion and design multinationals) located in the area; it was, in fact, also associated with the presence of a strong fashion publishing industry and fashion-related promotional events and institutions that have progressively combined powerful symbols, images and connotations of Milan with fashion (D'Ovidio 2015; Merlo and Polese 2006). Another example of this trend is the fashion capital of Paris, whose status has always been attributed to its peculiar industrial structure, highly specialised craft workers, clustering of elite designers, and the structure of its couture system. However, it has been widely observed that Paris has an established history of cultural representation through a fashion media system that has participated in determining its prestige as a major fashion hub for many years (Gilbert 2006).

The reshaping of cultural, social and economic borders within the ever more globalised and interconnected world has led to the emergence of so-called 'second-tier' or 'not-so-global' fashion cities (e.g., Antwerp, Auckland, Stockholm, Toronto), which have become increasingly visible in a progressively polycentric fashion world. These more peripheral fashion centres can usually compete internationally by supporting creative talent, encouraging design-intensive innovation, and promoting the growth of their cultural and creative industries (Larner et al. 2007; Rantisi and Leslie 2006). The growing importance of fashion as a means for urban economic development and regeneration, in addition to the proliferation of new fashion centres, has raised the essential question of what is fundamentally required to transform second-tier cities into global fashion centres. In an attempt to determine what factors the city of Los Angeles would need to become an elite fashion capital, Scott (2002) emphasised the importance of having a 'flexible' manufacturing basis, highly skilled specialists and training, and research institutes. In addition, international promotional systems, evolving place-based fashion traditions, and strong links between fashion and other cultural industries have been regarded as fundamental components needed to establish a major fashion centre.

This list, however, seems to apply more to the formation of traditional world fashion capitals, since recent economic trends have led to the emergence of more innovative types of fashion cities wherein the physical manufacturing of garments has become less important than the symbolic production of fashion. In fact, the geographical clustering of craftsmanship and flexible manufacturing, which have traditionally been central elements of world fashion cities, are increasingly threatened by the relocation of fashion manufacturing to lower-cost regions and the emergence of the new system of 'fast fashion'. There is growing evidence that peripheral cities are now importing rather than producing fashion, and have been adopting symbolic value in order to promote themselves as fashion centres (Gilbert 2013; Kawamura 2005).

As a consequence, local governments have begun focusing their attention on the crucial role of fashion as an identity creator and strategic asset. To that end, they have sought to reposition cities, especially those less globally recognised, as attractive destinations for investors and tourists by disseminating symbolic images, narratives and myths aimed at creating distinctive identities for urban centres in the wider global economy (Leslie and Rantisi 2009). Specific 'brand channels' such as international fashion weeks, trade fairs, media events, flagship stores, shopping malls and fashion museums have been regarded as among the most important tools for establishing the image and reputation of contemporary fashion centres, as well as for increasing awareness of cultural events, attracting international investments, and promoting tourism (Jansson and Power 2010; Santagata et al. 2009).

For example, the development of the Belgian city of Antwerp as a fashion city was not based on major trade activities or fashion industry development, but was instead the result of a prolonged city branding process which prioritised cultural events and organised tourism in order to provide new experiences for visitors. In particular, it was centred on the fascinating cultural event 'Mode 2001 Landed-Geland' and on the opening of the 'Mode Natie', a multifunctional building that houses the Fashion Academy, the MoMu Fashion Museum and the Flanders Fashion Institute, and whose aim is to promote Belgian fashion at the national and international level. This example is especially significant for understanding how fashion has become a crucial element of urban identity via cultural regeneration and, as a result, a significant feature of the tourism industry as well (Martínez 2007). Similarly, the city of Auckland in New Zealand has revamped its international image by establishing a symbolic connection with some of the global fashion capitals, including London, Tokyo and New York, a tactic which has in turn resulted in additional investments and increased tourism (Larner et al. 2007). These are but two of many examples of local government strategies involving increased investment in the symbolic value of fashion as a means for urban regeneration. In the future, the idea of the fashion city may be reinvented not as a perfect replication of established world fashion capitals, but as a unique combination of existing manufacturing and symbolic content.

Considering all of the aforementioned points, one symbolic example that should be taken into account is Florence, which is an internationally renowned heritage-driven artistic and creative city, characterised by the strong presence of cultural and creative industries such as those specialised in fashion and design. Distinguished by a leading manufacturing system with highly skilled craftsmen, internationally recognised promotional events, prestigious fashion and design schools, and evolving place-based fashion traditions, Florence appears to have all the elements required to enhance its role as a prestigious fashion hub and to stand out among the major fashion cities in the world.

In the next section, we analyse the relevance of fashion for the city of Florence, from its establishment as a major fashion hub in the mid-twentieth century to the present, where the importance of fashion is mainly perceived in terms of the city's strong manufacturing industry, internationally famous high-fashion houses (e.g., Gucci, Salvatore Ferragamo and Prada), and the *Pitti Immagine*: a globally eminent institution dedicated to the promotion of fashion fairs and related events.

3   The Re-Emergence of Florence as a Major Fashion City

Many studies have addressed the city of Florence from either a historical perspective (e.g., the creative 'Renaissance era') or, more recently, a perspective based on a set of elements regarded as fundamental to wider conditions of creativity, which have led Florence to be recognised internationally as a heritage-driven 'creative city'. Within this framework, fashion can be considered a significant means for connecting the Florentine heritage-based tradition with new forms of creativity and innovation based on a strong manufacturing tradition, entrepreneurial culture, and resilient network of public and private cultural institutions, as well as educational centres (Lazzeretti 2004; Bellini and Pasquinelli 2007).

The image of Florence is strongly associated with the history of Italian fashion. In 1951, Giovanni Battista Giorgini (1898–1971) established the first Italian fashion show in the city, which has traditionally been linked to the official birth of Italian fashion and to the emergence of Florence as a fashion capital. Later, fashion designers abandoned the Florentine catwalks, moving first to Rome and then, in the 1970s, to Milan, which achieved and still retains the status of Italian fashion capital. Although the city of Florence has historically lost its prestigious and central role in fashion, it is still characterised by the presence of an internationally acknowledged manufacturing system specialising in the production of fashion and supported by a local concentration of skilled craft artisans. In addition, international high-fashion houses deeply rooted in the Florentine area, as well as a dense network of excellent fashion-related private and public institutions, contribute to producing a highly vibrant and creative atmosphere and promoting the fashion culture within the city (Santagata et al. 2009).

Florentine leather manufacturing has long been regarded as an international epicentre for traditional craftsmanship, expertise and creativity, and the overall fashion sector, which also contains a significant shoe and textile-clothing cluster, is considered a fundamental component of the Florentine economy (Randelli and Lombardi 2014). Alongside the Parisian *haute couture* and the Milanese ready-to-wear, Florentine leather goods are included among those cultural products whose acknowledgment and authenticity are strongly associated with the distinctive image and identity of places and industries (Scott 1996). Florence is globally recognised as being a strategic location for a continuous exchange of experience, knowledge and ideas between skilled craftsmen, fashion designers, and artisans.

Beyond serving as the home for many internationally celebrated Florentine fashion designers and high-fashion houses (e.g., Gucci, Salvatore Ferragamo, Emilio Pucci), Florence's leading manufacturing system and rich artistic, historical and cultural heritage has attracted many young fashion designers (e.g., Edgardo Osorio and Yojiro Kake) over the years. Florence's long-standing fashion tradition and the vitality of its manufacturing sector also influenced the establishment of international academies that specialise in fashion and design, such as Polimoda, in addition to professional schools for more technicians, such as *Alta Scuola di Pelletteria Italiana*.

The main promotional fashion events in Florence are organised by *Pitti Immagine*: an institution dedicated to the promotion of fashion through a variety of cultural initiatives. *Pitti Immagine* also organises some of the most significant fashion fairs in the world: *Pitti Immagine Uomo*, *Pitti Immagine W*, *Pitti Immagine Bimbo*, *Pitti Immagine Filati*, *Fragrance*, and *Modaprima*. In recent years, many other fashion-related events, such as Vogue Fashion's Night Out, have been organised to reinforce the importance of the fashion culture for the city of Florence.

The historic centre of Florence hosts a famous fashion district containing flagship stores for a number of major international luxury fashion brands like Prada, Burberry and Céline (located in exclusive locations such as the Via de' Tornabuoni) and many artisanal workshops (*botteghe*) offering unique items; stores and shops such as these generate a distinct and creative atmosphere that attracts international tourists and business visitors alike. On the outskirts of Florence are an increasing number of retail outlets (e.g., Barberino Designer Outlet, Fashion Valley Outlet Village, The Mall) that help reinforce the association between Florence and fashion culture, and which further generate increased tourism and positive economic activity for the region. It has been noted that the presence of these premium brand outlets, in addition to characteristic Florentine art and culture, has been a powerful motivator for Chinese tourism, which has undergone exceptional growth in Tuscany in recent years. Art, culture, fashion and the city have been merged in the Salvatore Ferragamo and Gucci museums, which are mainly dedicated to 'cult' products developed by these highly symbolic Florentine fashion houses. This type of merger is also evident in the *Galleria del Costume di Palazzo Pitti*, a unique Italian fashion museum associated with fashion events often held in the city. Also worth noting is the Capucci museum, which exhibits 'sculpture-dresses' designed by fashion designer Roberto Capucci for the Venice Biennale in 1995. In recent years, these museums have attracted a large number of tourists increasingly interested in experiencing the fascinating history of the Florentine fashion tradition and internationally renowned high-fashion brands. Also in recent years, customisable 'fashion tours' to museums, designer headquarters, artisanal workshops, retail districts and premium outlets have been organised to guide tourists toward a more firmly rooted understanding of Florentine fashion culture; these tours have partially contributed to renewing the myth and narrative of Florence as a fashion city (Pratt et al. 2012; Scuola Superiore Sant'Anna 2014).

In recent years, fashion seems to have been increasingly adopted as an identity and image creator for the city of Florence with the main purpose of exploiting its traditionally strong competitive advantage in the fashion industry (Capone and Lazzeretti 2016). The city's quick rise in the Top Global Fashion Capital Rankings (GLM 2013)—from the 31st to the 11th position in just 4 years (2011–2015)—is further proof that Florence is experiencing a rebirth as a major fashion city.

4   Fashion Industry Clusters in Florence

In this section, we analyse the presence of geographical clusters operating in the fashion and design industries. We identify local geographical clusters in the metropolitan area of Florence, pointing out the presence of famous firms that cluster around the city of Florence. Several studies have analysed the city of Florence and its creative industries, but the relationship between fashion, fashion design and creative industries within a creative fashion city remains underinvestigated. Recently, D'Ovidio (2014) examined the spatial localisation of fashion industry firms in the city of Milan, while Carlei and Nuccio (2013) investigated the spatial concentration of the clothing industry in the nation of Italy as a whole.

In our study, we define a 'fashion city' as a local creative system characterised by a concentration of fashion and design industries, creative clusters, and fashion designers, an approach that departs from the prevailing literature on the topic (Lazzeretti 2013). This definition is particularly relevant since fashion and design industries tend to agglomerate for creative inspiration, product and process innovation, cross fertilisation of ideas, knowledge and learning, face-to-face interactions and local social ties (Currid-Halkett 2007; Hauge 2007; Jansson and Power 2010). They also tend to localise within urban settings, where concentrations of support institutions, specialised services and skilled professionals sustain their activities (Leslie and Rantisi 2009). Moreover, fashion is considered highly dependent on other creative industries such as music, media, and Information and Communication Technologies. Within artistic cities, an intense interrelationship exists between fashion, museum clusters and fashion events (Sedita and Paiola 2009). Fashion is also usually supported by a strong network of designers who tend to concentrate in specific cities and produce the attractive and intangible 'cultural milieu' so important to contemporary economic development (Williams and Currid-Halkett 2011).

Different studies analysing the city of Florence have led to its international recognition as an art and heritage-driven 'creative city'. As described in more detail above, several efforts have been made to promote fashion in the city based on the following key attributes:

(a) A leading world centre for leather craftsmanship and production, the home of many internationally celebrated designers (e.g., Gucci, Salvatore Ferragamo and Emilio Pucci), the epicentre of a dense network of accomplished fashion and design education centres (e.g., Polimoda and European Design Institute) and private and public local institutions;
(b) Fashion museums (e.g., Salvatore Ferragamo, Gucci, *Galleria del Costume di Palazzo Pitti* and Capucci museums), a famous fashion district and outlets (e.g., Barberino Designer Outlet, Fashion Valley Outlet Village and The Mall), internationally renowned promotional fashion events (e.g., *Pitti Immagine* and *Modaprima*) and an increasing number of organised 'fashion tours'.

Following a method for mapping cultural and creative industries at an international level (Boix et al. 2014), we identified clusters of fashion and design firms in the city of Florence. Location quotients (LQs) were calculated for the clustering of fashion and design firms at the provincial level in Italy.

The fashion industry was analysed using the statistic-economic activities *Textile*, *Clothing* and *Leather* (NACE codes 13, 14 and 15), while for design we analysed the economic activity *Design* (NACE 74.1), which includes fashion design related to textiles, wearing apparel, shoes, jewellery, furniture and other interior decoration and other fashion goods as well as other personal or household goods, but also industrial design; graphic designers; activities of interior decorators. Therefore, as data are not available for fashion design alone, we focused on design in general, hypothesising that if there is a co-location of these two activities, then the two activities are likely interrelated. The source for our data was the 2011 ISTAT Census of Industry and Trade.

The results were georeferenced on the maps presented below (Fig. 1). A threshold of 0.3 % for the weight of fashion and fashion-design industry was used to exclude minor locations. Milan and Florence emerged as the most concentrated hotspots for these two industries. Milan registered a LQ of 1.09 in the fashion industry and a LQ of 2.08 in design. These values are fairly high as large provinces usually have diversified structures of specialisation; moreover, Milan emerged as a significant hotspot in both industries. Similar results were also observed by Carlei and Nuccio (2013).

Florence registered an LQ of 2.90 in the fashion industry and a LQ of 1.45 in design. Both indices are very high, but the LQ in the fashion industry nearly reached 3, which indicates that there are three times the number of firms operating in these activities in the province as compared to the national average.

These results illustrate that there are over 6000 fashion and design firms in Florence, 800 of which specialise only in design (14 %); while in Milan, there are

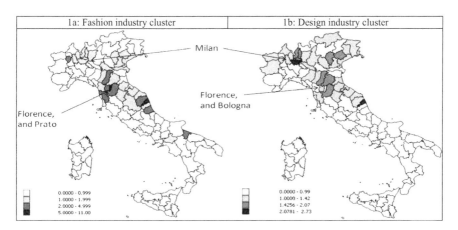

Fig. 1 Fashion and design industry clusters in Italy, 2011. *Source*: our elaborations based on ISTAT (2011)

Table 1 Most significant fashion clusters

Provinces	Firms	LQ in fashion and design	LQ in design
Milano	7264	1.097	2.085
Firenze	5959	2.901	1.450
Fermo	2711	7.500	2.731
Vicenza	2689	1.702	1.476
Padova	2616	1.396	1.223
Modena	2446	2.059	1.683
Varese	2403	1.624	1.380
Treviso	2329	1.448	1.692
Bergamo	2019	1.040	1.257
Bologna	1960	1.008	1.688
Como	1846	1.798	2.064
Pisa	1805	2.331	1.174
Macerata	1752	2.784	1.372
Pistoia	1604	2.819	1.088
Venezia	1584	1.051	1.120
Monza	1537	1.018	1.807

Provinces with LQ > 1 for both sectors
Source: Our elaborations based on ISTAT (2011)

more than 7200 firms, over 3500 of which specialise in design (54 %) (Table 1).
Thus, both cities emerge as important hotspots in the fashion and fashion design
industries in Italy, but with several differences between them. Milan is based on a
strong fashion design specialisation (54 %), and is therefore more similar to other
European fashion cities that specialise in the production of symbolic cultural
products. In contrast, Florence emerges more as a manufacturing fashion city,
characterised by the dominant local manufacturing industry (86 %). Florence represents a mix of clusters of fashion, design, creative and cultural industries that
together help to create the local urban fabric of the city.[1]

5   Conclusions

The aim of this chapter was to contribute to the academic debate on the fashion city
definition and to present some implications for tourism.

Two typologies of fashion cities resulted from the literature review. The first,
called the 'manufacturing fashion city', is based mainly on the supply-side perspective, which is related to the physical image of the city and its garment industry;

---

[1]The analysis is more significant if we include the provinces near Florence. For example, in Prato
there are over 6000 firms specialising in textile-clothing, but only around 100 are specialised in
design. Prato has a typical manufacturing structure not oriented toward design (3 %).

the second is named the 'symbolic fashion city' and is more oriented toward symbolic production and ICTs.

Historically, major fashion cities were based on strong local manufacturing systems, which later developed through the creation of attractive cultural and intangible images and identities that contributed to a symbolic economy of fashion. Recent globalisation trends have highlighted the increasing importance of symbolic aspects of fashion and, at present, many fashion cities are increasingly reliant on fashion and design, rather than on local manufacturing systems.

The fashion city of Florence is mainly characterised by the physical presence of important fashion firms and clusters, and by cultural institutions that configure a creative cluster. The global image of the city is also derived from its internationally renowned fashion houses (e.g., Gucci, Prada and Salvatore Ferragamo). Accordingly, both the physical and symbolic dimensions of Florence are equally important and should be further integrated.

The results of this study reveal that a significant synergy exists between artistic-cultural heritage and fashion industries, and this can generate new market niches for tourism, such as shopping tourism, fashion industry tours, fashion museum tours and fashion itineraries.

However, private and public local institutions have not yet taken advantage of the full potential of fashion as an image and identity creator for the city. There is a lack of events and attractions specifically aimed at guiding tourists in the discovery of the Florentine fashion culture, and there is still enormous potential to reinforce this image and stimulate further synergy between Florentine culture, fashion and tourism.

The promotion of Florence as a fashion city should be included within the wider agenda of combining the cultural heritage-based image of the city with a new identity based on dynamicity and modernity in which fashion, as creativity and culture, can stimulate innovation, creativity and economic development. However, policy-makers and industries should be required to make greater efforts to exploit this unique and privileged opportunity.

Finally, it is both interesting and informative to compare Florence to other manufacturing fashion cities in Italy—especially Milan, the Italian fashion capital. Since the 1970s Milan has been considered better suited than Florence to maintain the prestigious role of Italian fashion capital, due in large part to its strong textile and clothing manufacturing system, specialised ready-to-wear industry, internationally acknowledged designers (e.g., Armani and Versace), place-based design and cultural fashion traditions, and powerful fashion media system that heavily supports its status.

As far as fashion-related tourism is concerned, the establishment of Milan as a fashion capital has led to significant growth in the retail sector and the gradual transformation of the city into a famous shopping destination. Tourists and business visitors alike are attracted to Milan's famous *Quadrilatero Della Moda*, a district occupied by the flagship stores of some of the most important fashion and design brands, as well as many emerging creative and artistic fashion-related boutiques and craft shops. Additionally, Milan Fashion Week, one of the world's premier ready-to-wear fashion events, has become a crucial element in promoting the international image of the city, attracting foreign visitors, and generating tourism with the concurrent development of a business visitor industry (e.g., accommodation and restaurants). Beginning in the 2000s, Milanese fashion, with its prestigious fashion weeks and shopping districts, has been included as a strategic asset in the tourism agenda, becoming part of the local government's plans to promote cultural events and reposition the city as a globally appealing tourist destination.

Although the increasingly transnational and globalised nature of the fashion industry presents a challenge to the prestigious role of Milan as a world fashion capital, it seems that the city has at least in part understood the contemporary relevance of promoting the symbolic production of fashion by sustaining the culture of fashion through its fashion weeks and shopping districts. In this respect, Florence can in the future unlock its full potential as a fashion city, either for local economic development or global tourist appeal, or both.

Further research on other manufacturing and symbolic fashion cities is needed to validate these conclusions, especially those cities that use the symbolic culture of fashion to help generate tourism and in which the future dynamics of manufacturing fashion cities in an increasingly globalised fashion world can be empirically tracked.

References

Barrowclough D, Kozul Wright Z (eds) (2008) Creative industries and developing countries: voice, choice and economic growth. Routledge, London and New York, NY

Bellini N, Pasquinelli C (2007) The political economy of competing regional images: the case of Tuscany's brands. MAIN Lab, Working Paper 2007/04

Boix R, Capone F, De Propris L, Lazzeretti L, Sanchez D (2014) Comparing creative industries in Europe. Eur Urb Reg Stud. doi:10.1177/0969776414541135

Boontharm D (2015) Creative milieux of fashion and reuse in Tokyo, Bangkok and Singapore. J Urban Des 20(1):75–92

Breward C, Gilbert D (2006) Fashion's world cities. Berg, Oxford

Capone F (ed) (2016) Tourist clusters, destinations and competitiveness. Routledge, Abingdon

Capone F, Lazzeretti L (2016) Fashion and city branding: an analysis of the perception of Florence as a fashion city. J Glob Fash Market 7(3):1–15

Carlei V, Nuccio M (2013) Mapping industrial patterns in spatial agglomeration: a SOM approach to Italian industrial districts. Pattern Recogn Lett 40:1–10

Chilese E, Russo, AP (2008) Urban fashion policies: lessons from the Barcelona catwalks. EBLA, Working Paper 200803. University of Turin

Currid-Halkett E (2007) How art and culture happen in New York. J Am Plann Assoc 73 (4):454–467

D'Ovidio M (2014) Il punto di vista. Moda e manifattura a Milano. in 24° Rapporto della Camera di Commercio di Milano, pp 76–88

D'Ovidio M (2015) Moda e manifattura a Milano. In: Camera di Commercio di Milano (ed) Milano Produttiva. Guerini e Associati, Milan

Donvito R, Aiello G, Ranfagni S (2013) Creative networks in Florence and Paris: empirical results on project networks. J Glob Scholars Market Sci 23:379–393

European Commission (2010) Green paper on cultural and creative industries: unlocking the potential of cultural and creative industries. EU Commission, Brussels, COM(2010) 183

Gilbert D (2006) From Paris to Shanghai: the changing geographies of fashion's world cities. In: Breward C, Gilbert D (eds) Fashion's world cities. Berg, Oxford

Gilbert D (2013) A new world order? Fashion and its capital in the twenty-first century. In: Bruzzi S, Church Gibson P (eds) Fashion cultures revisited: theories, explorations and analysis. Routledge, London and New York, NY

Global Language Monitor (2013) London edges New York for top global fashion capital. http://www.languagemonitor.com/fashion/sorry-kate-new-york-edges-paris-and-londonin-top-global-fashion-capital-10th-annual-survey. Accessed 20 Mar 2015

Hauge A (2007) Dedicated followers of fashion: an economic geographic analysis of the Swedish fashion industry. PhD Thesis, Uppsala University

ISTAT (2011) Census of industry and services. Rome

Jansson J, Power D (2010) Fashioning a global city: global city brand channels in the fashion and design industries. Reg Stud 44(7):889–904

Kawamura Y (2005) Fashion-ology: an introduction to fashion studies. Berg, Oxford

Larner W, Molloy M, Goodrum A (2007) Globalization, cultural economy and not-so-global cities: the New Zealand designer fashion industry. Environ Plann Soc Space 25(3):381–400

Lazzeretti L (ed) (2004) Arts cities, cultural district and museums. Firenze University Press, Florence

Lazzeretti L (ed) (2013) Creative industries and innovation in Europe. Routledge, London

Lazzeretti L, Capone F (2015) Narrow or broad definition of cultural and creative industries: evidence from Tuscany, Italy. Int J Cult Creat Ind 2(2):4–19

Leslie D, Rantisi D (2009) Fostering a culture of design. Insights from the case of Montrèal, Canada. In: Pratt A, Jeffcutt P (eds) Creativity, innovation and the cultural economy. Routledge, Abingdon

Lorentzen A, Hansen CJ (2009) The role and transformation of the city in the experience economy: identifying and exploring research challenges. Eur Plann Stud 17(6):817–827

Martínez JG (2007) Selling avant-garde: how Antwerp became a fashion capital (1990–2002). Urban Stud 44(12):2449–2464

Merlo E, Polese F (2006) The emergence of Milan as an international fashion hub. Bus Hist Rev 80 (3):415–447

Pandolfi V (2015) Fashion and the city: the role of the 'cultural economy' in the development strategies of three Western European cities. Eburon, Delft

Power D (2011) Priority sector report: creative and cultural industries. Europa Innova Paper 16 EC. The European Cluster Observatory, Luxemburg

Power D, Scott A (2004) Cultural industries and the production of culture. Routledge, London

Pratt A, Borrione P, Lavanga M, D'Ovidio M (2012) International change and technological evolution in the fashion industry. In: Agnoletti M, Carandini A, Santagata W (eds) Essays and researches. International Biennial of Cultural and Environmental Heritage, Florence

Randelli F, Lombardi M (2014) The role of leading firms in the evolution of SME clusters: evidence from the leather products cluster in Florence. Eur Plann Stud 22(6):1199–1211

Rantisi NM (2004) The ascendance of New York fashion. Int J Urban Reg Res 28(1):86–106

Rantisi NM, Leslie D (2006) Branding the design metropole: the case of Montréal, Canada. Area 38(4):364–376

Richards G (2013) Tourism development trajectories: from culture to creativity? In: Smith M, Richards G (eds) Handbook of cultural tourism. Routledge, London

Richards G, Wilson J (2006) Developing creativity in tourist experiences: a solution to the serial reproduction of culture? Tour Manag 27(6):1408–1413

Santagata W, Borrione P, Barrére C (2009) Fashion true excellence and great international visibility. In: Santagata W (ed) White paper on creativity: towards an Italian model of development. EBLA-CSS, Torino

220 L. Lazzeretti et al.

Scott AJ (1996) The craft, fashion, and cultural-products industries of Los Angeles: competitive dynamics and policy dilemmas in a multisectoral image-producing complex. Ann Assoc Am Geogr 86(2):306–323

Scott A (2000) The cultural economy of Paris. Int J Urban Reg Res 24:567–582

Scott A (2002) Competitive dynamics of Southern California's clothing industry: the widening global connection and its local ramifications'. Urban Stud 39(8):1287–1306

Scuola Superiore Sant'Anna (2014) Città di Firenze, A report for investors: fahion and lifestyle. Florence Council, Esse-Emme

Sedita S, Paiola M (2009) Il management della creatività. Carocci, Roma

UNESCO (2013) Creative economy report. Widening local development pathways. UNESCO, Paris

Williams S, Currid-Halkett E (2011) The emergence of Los Angeles as a fashion hub: a comparative spatial analysis of the New York and Los Angeles fashion industries. Urban Stud 48:3043–3066

Does Recurrence Matter? The Impact of Music Festivals on Local Tourist Competitiveness

Matteo Caroli and Alfredo Valentino

Abstract Despite an increasing interest in recurrent events, we still lack a comprehensive view of their drivers and their consequences for the host location. This chapter seeks to redress this shortcoming by analysing the effects of recurrent events on national and international tourist flows and on the differentiation of demand targets at host locations. Through a qualitative approach based on six recurrent European music festivals we contribute to the growing literature and shed additional light on the effects of recurrent events. A theoretical framework is proposed to explain the impact of recurrent events on tourist flows and demand targets.

Keywords Recurrent events • Territorial competitiveness • Regional development • International tourism

1 Introduction

This chapter investigates recurrent events as a potential marketing tool to enhance the touristic attractiveness of the location where they are hosted. There is a well-established literature on how events, and in particular itinerant ones (e.g., the 1988 Summer Olympic Games in Seoul, the 2010 FIFA World Cup in South Africa, the 2002 Winter Olympic Games in Salt Lake City, the 2003 MTV Europe Music Awards in Edinburgh), can benefit the territorial development of the host country. Some scholars show how these events rapidly boost economic growth in the host country (Bojanic and Warnick 2012; Gil and de Esteban Curiel 2008; Hede 2007; Kim et al. 2010; Monga 2006); others demonstrate their ability to develop culture and arts (Fredline and Faulkner 2002; Harcup 2000; Roche 2000; Burbank et al. 2001; Gratton and Henry 2001; Deccio and Baloglu 2002); still others examine the impact on urban renewal, education, and tourism (Pugh and Wood 2004; Thomas and Wood 2004; Whitford 2004a, b; Reid 2006; Stokes and Jago 2007; Getz and Andersson 2008; Ziakas and Costa 2011). By contrast, Kang and

M. Caroli (✉) • A. Valentino
Department of Business and Management, Università Luiss Guido Carli, Rome, Italy
e-mail: mcaroli@luiss.it; valentinoa@luiss.it

© Springer International Publishing Switzerland 2017   221
N. Bellini, C. Pasquinelli (eds.), *Tourism in the City*,
DOI 10.1007/978-3-319-26877-4_15

Perdue (1994) point to a lack of collaborative endeavour and embeddedness, which undercuts the positive effects in the long run.

Prior research gives little emphasis to recurrent events. The latter tend to be smaller than the itinerant events, but with greater local embeddedness and stronger ties with local stakeholders. Festivals and the like have been defined as "traditional events staged to increase the tourism appeal to potential visitors" (Uysal and Gitelson 1994). Previous studies have shown how recurrent events strengthen local identity and enhance distinctive resources in a specific area: an empirical study of the Ravello Festival by Simeon and Buonincontri (2011) shows that this music festival has improved local competiveness, becoming the distinctive symbol of the host town for subsequent editions.

Some scholars have investigated the impact of recurrent events on the image of the host location and their influence on the seasonality of tourism (Kaplanidou and Vogt 2007; Kaplanidou et al. 2013). Seasonality is a constant problem for the tourist industry, as it makes for uneven demand, while supply is by nature relatively fixed (Connell et al. 2015). Recurrent events can be seen as a strategic tool to reduce seasonality (Ritchie and Beliveau 1974) or as factors distorting temporal tourist imbalances (Goulding 2008). Yet, surprisingly little research has been done on the relationship between visitor attractions and seasonality, although, as Leask (2010) observes, this may reflect the general paucity of work on attractions.

While scholarly attention to itinerant events has grown considerably, there has been no parallel increase in explicit attention to recurrent events. With some laudable exceptions, there has been little effort to understand the motivations for such events or to gauge and explain their impact on territorial development. Little research has been devoted to the question of whether they can improve the seasonal adjustment of a territory. And we still lack insight into how they may stimulate international and national tourist flows.

This relative neglect is especially surprising in light of the broad diffusion of recurrent events. It implies that potentially important drivers and consequences are still being overlooked.

In this chapter these gaps are addressed with an analysis of the effects of recurrent events on international and national tourist flows and on the differentiation of demand targets in the host country. In particular, through a qualitative approach based on six annual Italian and European music festivals, we contribute to the scanty literature on the effects of recurrent events, proposing a theoretical explanatory framework.

2 Recurrent Events as a Factor in Host Location Competitiveness

Recurrent events impact on the competitiveness of the host location (Delamere 1997; Getz and Andersson 2008; O'Sullivan and Jackson 2002). The magnitude of the impact varies over the life cycle of the event, generally being greater during the phases of full development and early maturity (Beverland et al. 2001; Getz 2000). It also depends on the rank or status that the event attains, i.e., 'local', 'regional', 'national', 'international' or, theoretically, even 'global'.

First of all, recurrent events form part of what is offered to visitors as well as residents of the host area. This is of great significance in the market for cultural tourism, and especially in towns or smaller cities and in peripheral areas. If the organisation and content of the event are such as to attract the target group of tourists, then simply attending it is one of the main reasons for deciding to lodge in the host town.

There are additional reasons why a recurrent event can enhance the competitiveness of the local territory:

- It increases the location's visibility and reputation, reinforcing or helping to innovate its competitive positioning. The Festival of Literature in Mantua and the Rossini Opera Festival in Pesaro are fine examples of cultural events that have contributed greatly to the renown and tourist position of their host cities. Moreover, recurrent events can also have a substantial impact in other markets. For example, Verona's Vinitaly fair, now the biggest wine fair in Europe, is an important factor in the positioning of the Veneto region (and, for that matter, of Italy) in the global wine industry.
- It stimulates cooperation among the different actors that take part in the development and implementation of the event. By cooperating, they share a vision of the future development of their territory and learn how to work together to realise it. The actors can be both private and public and have different degrees of institutional importance. Cultural events are usually planned and managed by local organisations, but they can benefit significantly from the advocacy and possibly the sponsorship of national or even international organisations.
- It even can serve as the hub or core component of complex tourist products, developed by the organisers by other actors, or by the destination management office. As a consequence, it increases the value of the experience generated by tourist products. It also increases the importance of the host location as a distinctive feature of the product itself. Moreover, recurrent events can generate other 'side initiatives', widening the target during the main event and/or developing other events at other times of year.

3   Methodology

A theory-building research method from multiple case studies is adopted (Eisenhardt 1989; Yin 2011). This method is designed to develop theory when a phenomenon has not been well explored through data using replication logic (Eisenhardt 1989; Yin 2011). Multiple case studies work as a set of experiments to confirm or disconfirm the theory posited (Eisenhardt 1989; Yin 2011).

Following a theoretical sampling approach in which cases are chosen for theoretical and not statistical reasons (e.g., Eisenhardt and Graebner 2007), we select six European recurrent events that satisfy the following criteria: (1) at least 10 years of activity, (2) a predominantly musical theme and (3) international appeal. Moreover, we take festivals that can be defined as 'home-grown', 'tourist-tempter', or 'big-bang' (O'Sullivan and Jackson 2002). A 'home-grown' festival is essentially small-scale, bottom-up and organised by one or more volunteer organisations promoted by local stakeholders. A 'tourist-tempter' festival is aimed specifically at attracting visitors to stimulate local economic development. A 'big-bang' festival is essentially a marketing tool to promote a myriad of related activities in a definite geographical area, typically a city. This distinction is an important step towards understanding how recurrent festivals can significantly influence the development of rural or urban areas. Urban areas tend to vaunt a multiplicity of infrastructures that are an important incentive for tourists. Thanks to infrastructure, tourists get to these places readily and easily access their many offers. Thus, the 'big bang' festivals can draw more tourists thanks to the wide range of attractions available. In rural areas (as in home-grown festivals) the lack of infrastructure and transport services means that the festival itself is the prime attraction for visitors. People come to a rural area just to attend the festival, and only subsequently do they begin to discover the place and its additional attractions. Accordingly, we have opted to study festivals organised both in major tourist centres like Budapest and Turin and also in rural and small towns such as Glastonbury and Ravello.

Finally, we search for polar-type cases based on the size of the venue. Polar-type sampling emphasises subjects that are more 'transparently observable' and is appropriate when the purpose is to determine the main factors in success and failure (Eisenhardt 1989). Accordingly, we select festivals hosted in small towns or villages (marginal country areas) along with a number in medium-sized and large cities. The idea is to more clearly spotlight the impact of recurrent events on the attractiveness of the location, as suggested by Eisenhardt and Graebner (2007).

4   Data Collection and Analysis

Our primary source of data is semi-structured questionnaires filled out by festival visitors. Every festival committee administers such questionnaires, which provide general information on the visitors and the reasons for their trip. The questionnaires allow a structured examination of the cases and potential replication of the analysis in future study (Yin 2011). Additional data on festivals come from their websites and interviews with organising committee members. Triangulation of data reduces the risk of retrospective and personal interpretation biases and makes the theory more robust.

Within-case and cross-case methods are used. First, individual case studies using the questionnaires and other data sources are built. Each author developed his own, independent view of the case, and we resolved any discrepancies in the course of follow-up with participants and agency members. This was followed by cross-case analysis to identify common patterns (Eisenhardt 1989). As usual in qualitative case research, we do not make a priori hypotheses. Following Miles and Huberman (1985), we first analyse each case study and then compare them to identify common issues and unique features. Case comparisons are facilitated by tables and graphs.

4.1 The Case Studies

Six festivals for the case studies were identified: Ravello, Exit, Umbria Jazz, Glastonbury, Traffic Music, and Sziget. As noted, the events selected have in common the theme, i.e., the music. Three are held in Italy, three in other European countries such as Serbia, UK and Hungary. Three are in small towns (Ravello, Exit, Glastonbury) and three in cities (Traffic, Sziget, Umbria). It is worth giving a brief description of each festival studied with a focus on the venue, the host location.

The Ravello Festival is one of Italy's best-known and popular summer festivals. Ravello is a small hill town on the Amalfi coast in the Campania region. It has been held yearly since 1953, when the mayor decided to promote tourism and the local economy by means of a music festival dedicated to Richard Wagner, who visited the town in 1880. Originally a 2-day event devoted only to Wagner's music, today the Festival runs for almost 2 months and embraces a variety of genres—pop and jazz as well as classical, though the core is still Wagnerian. The target is a niche market of cultural tourists who are drawn by the combination of classical music, the arts, and natural beauty. The town's geographical position, far above the sea, is something of a disadvantage by comparison with the other towns along the Amalfi coast, but it makes up for this by its cultural, natural, and historic attractions and extraordinary panorama. The success of the festival stems from the perfect fusion between Ravello's material and intangible characteristics and musical genres, in line with the 'Ravello lifestyle'. The festival's relationship with the host location is strong, crucial to its success.

The Exit Festival is a major summer music festival, held annually at the Petrovaradin Fortress in the city of Novi Sad, Serbia. It has won awards as *Best Overseas Festival* at the UK Festival Awards in 2007 and *Best Major European Festival* at the EU Festival Awards, 2013. The festival was organised for the first time in 2000 in the university park as a student manifestation for democracy and freedom in Serbia. Since then it has grown in popularity and size, but its characteristic social mission remains unchanged: to help youth in the Balkan countries. Now run by a non-profit organisation, it hosts world-renowned music performers and groups. Although Novi Sad itself is not a major tourist destination (just a few historic buildings, such as the Fortress and a Cistercian monastery, and the nearby National Park of Fuksa Gora), every year it attracts over 100,000 young people from scores of countries thanks to the Exit Festival.

The Glastonbury Festival of Contemporary Performing Arts is a 5-day event held at Pilton in Somerset, six miles east of Glastonbury, England. It is primarily a contemporary music festival, but usually it also includes other arts, such as dance, theatre and circus. It is the world's largest, and the most sustainable, greenfield music festival. And although attendance has been reduced since 2002 because of security issues, it still draws an average of 100,000 spectators every June for the performances of well-known artists from all over the world. The host location is famed chiefly for religious tourism, with the presence of many churches and cathedrals, the destination of pilgrimages from many European countries; it is also known for its traditional pastoral economy, which represents the main connection with the Festival, which was originally inspired by the hippie culture and maintains the goal of protecting the local environment and minimising the event's environmental impact.

The Umbria Jazz Festival is one of the world's leading jazz events. It has been held annually since 1973, at first as an 'itinerant' event in the Italian region of Umbria and then, since 1982, as a 'permanent' one in the regional capital, Perugia. The 10-day event is organised in the medieval centre of the city, perfectly blending jazz, history and culture. The festival attracts jazz buffs and general tourists drawn by the reputation of the event. Perugia itself is one of Italy's major cultural attractions, full of medieval buildings, churches, and historic monuments. It is also known for its academic culture and has Italy's longest-standing university for foreign students.

The Traffic Music Festival is a free music event (especially pop-rock and dance) held annually in Turin since 2004. It is ordinarily a 4-day event combining music with cultural conferences, shows, book presentations, and exhibits. It is targeted to a young audience, somewhat different from the city's typical tourists. Turin is known worldwide as the former capital of the Kingdom of Sardinia, famous for the residences of the House of Savoy, and as the one-time hub of Italy's auto industry. It is rich in historical, especially Baroque, architecture, and as such constitutes an international destination for cultural tourism, mainly for a middle-aged target.

Finally, the Sziget Festival is one of Europe's most popular music and cultural festivals, a week-long event held every August since 1993 in Budapest on Obudai-Sziget island in the Danube. Originally a student event, organised by local students as a summer hangout for music lovers, it quickly gained popularity; by 1996 total attendance was around 150,000, and this was doubled by the turn of the century. The Sziget Festival twice won the European Festivals Awards (2012 and 2015), and according to the international press it is the principal European alternative to the Burning Man Festival (in Nevada). Of course, the host city has played an important

Table 1 The characteristics of festivals and host locations

	Host location	Host location size (inhabitants)	Tourism in the host location	Age of the festival	Type of festival	Governance
Ravello festival	Ravello—Italy	2500	Cultural	62	Classic music	Public–Private
Umbria Jazz	Perugia—Italy	165,668	Cultural—wine and food	33	Jazz music	Public–Private
Traffic festival	Turin—Italy	892,649	Historic and cultural	11	Pop-rock and dance music	Public
Exit festival	Novi Sad—Serbia	388,490	Cultural	15	Rock and electronic dance music	Private
Glastonbury festival	Pilton—England	1030	Religious	44	Contemporary music	Private
Sziget festival	Budapest—Hungary	2,551,247	Cultural	23	Rock music	Private

role in the success of the festival. History, architecture, and culture make Budapest one of loveliest and most-visited of European capitals.

Table 1 summarises the main characteristics of each of the recurrent events chosen and their locations.

5   Theoretical Framework and Propositions

5.1   *International Audience in Recurrent Festivals*

A wide variety of marketing tools are available for locations to increase their tourist flows. Some scholars have shown that one such instrument is recurrent festivals. Recurrent events extend the tourist base of the host location beyond its ordinary geographical boundaries (see Fig. 1).

We focus on the behaviour of international tourists. According to our data, in a time frame of 5 years the international flow of visitors to a destination during a recurrent event increases substantially, outpacing the growth of the local tourist

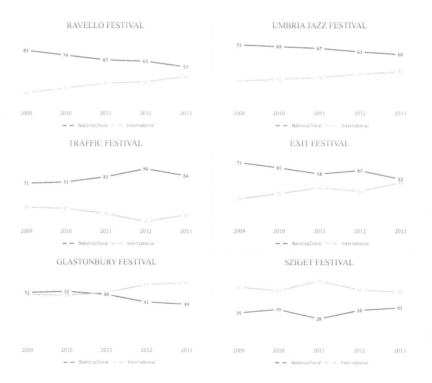

Fig. 1 National/local and international tourist flows over 5 years (2009–2013) for each festival (in %)

flow. We explain this by reference to the evolution of recurrent events and marketing actions to strengthen their competitiveness. In the long run, a festival committee will undertake marketing and strategic actions to attract a steadily increasing international tourist flow. The expansion of international tourism through a festival produces two substantial competitive advantages. First, it improves the international image of the event itself and of the host location. And second, it benefits the tourist industry in the host venue, because international tourists tend to stay longer than domestic tourists in any destination they choose to visit. A successful recurrent festival contributes to the development of the destination's story and image and can become part of the complex experience offered to tourists.

For example, the Ravello Festival was conceived as a traditional event to celebrate classical music and aimed primarily at a niche target living in Campania and nearby regions. Following the introduction of a special section dedicated to Wagner's main operas, there was a considerable increase in the flow of attendees from abroad, especially from Russia and Germany. In the last 3 years the share of foreign tourists has gained about 10 % points, and during the festival itself it is estimated to be 20 times greater than local tourism. A similar pattern is found for the Exit Festival in Serbia. Its main purpose is to stimulate active participation of the young people of Novi Sad in social life. Over the years, however, the Festival has steadily upgraded its programme. The result has been to increase the inflow of tourists from abroad, especially Europeans (from the UK, Germany and all the former Soviet countries) and Americans. In the last 4 years the international share has increased from 35 to 48 %. The Exit Festival has served to restore a positive image for a host location that had finally emerged from a long and bloody war. The Sziget Festival, originally a student-based event, is now one of the most popular music festivals in all of Europe. Another interesting case is Glastonbury, where the percentage of international tourists has grown over the years and since 2011 actually exceeded that of national and local tourists.

Proposition 1 *In the longer run recurrent events improve international tourist flows more than national and local flows.*

5.2   Festivals as Strategic Tools for Differentiating Tourist Demand Targets

When someone is looking for a festival, location may be an important factor in the choice. Locations usually have a clear tourist target, based on their specific natural and cultural features. These features form part of the territorial vocation: vocation is at the basis of a place's perceived image. Sometimes, however, these features are affected by seasonal factors. To overcome the seasonality of demand, a location may create new attractions in the off-season. It may also find it advantageous to seek out and attract new demand segments, different from those served mostly during the high season (Wrathall and Gee 2011).

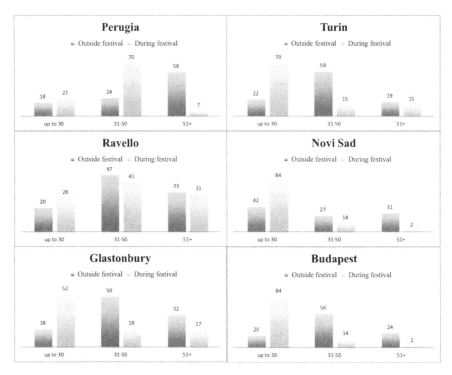

Fig. 2 The distribution of the average demand target in each location during the festival and outside the festival period, by age of tourists

Looking at our case studies, it is clear that recurrent festivals can play an important strategic role in attracting new demand targets. While in some cases they serve to strengthen the strategic positioning of the host location, they can also be a tool to differentiate demand, drawing new, non-traditional demand targets in specific periods and locations. In other words, recurrent events help to develop a new image of the host location by attracting new demand targets. These new tourists, who come expressly for the festival, visit the local attractions together with the traditional visitors (Fig. 2).

A good example is Turin. Not generally one of the top destinations for young people, during the Traffic Festival the city is filled with young tourists, especially in the neighbourhoods nearest to the festival location itself. That is, the Festival is playing an important role in helping to position Turin in the youth tourism market. Another significant example is the Glastonbury Festival, which is held in a seaside town that typically attracts local families with children and religious tourists. During the festival period (in June), the percentage of middle-aged visitors declines in favour of a younger group, aged between 16 and 30 years old. Or take the Sziget Festival: typically, 56 % of tourists in Budapest are between 31 and 50, but during the festival this share drops to 14 %, and the percentage of under-30 tourists soars from 20 to 84 %.

Thus, we can say:

Proposition 2 *Recurrent festivals are attractors of new demand targets with respect to the usual tourist flow.*

6   Conclusions

Our findings contribute to the scanty literature on the touristic impact of recurrent events and help to place the marketing literature. We argue that recurrent events are a powerful tool for enhancing the international attractiveness of tourist destinations and differentiating touristic demand in the host place. They capitalise on the local tradition and the culture and on some of the key capabilities and material assets of the location. Recurrent events can thus strengthen the destination's positioning or help to reshape it. They can influence the way in which the location tells its story and stimulate the involvement of the various actors, of the entire local community and some specific places. At the same time, festivals generate new demand flows, in some cases off-season flows, which are particularly important to sustainable tourist demand. At the beginning of their life cycle, recurrent events will be targeted principally to the local or regional market, but as the years go by they have the potential to achieve higher rank and status, possibly reaching national or international markets.

The successful management of recurrent events can also generate substantial effects on the destination's 'supply side'. They stimulate investment in the improvement of other components of the tourist services and attractions provided (above all accommodations) and transportation.

Given their economic and strategic importance, destination management offices (DMOs) need a strategy to back the institution of a certain number of recurrent events (consistent with the destination's size, of course) and their long-term development. More and more, DMOs are directly involved in the organisation and operation of fairs and festivals. According to a 2015 survey of 326 DMOs in 36 countries by DestinationNEXT, within the next few years this is expected to become one of these offices' most important activities. The DMO should perform three key tasks: (i) stimulate the local public authorities to guarantee the best framework for the recurrent event; (ii) stimulate private investment to sponsor the event and improve other components of the tourist services and attractions offered; and (iii) develop cooperation among various actors, which can be instrumental to success. In some cases, the DMO can also supply the event's organisers with the competences needed for effective and efficient management, including the pre- and post-performance phases. In our view, therefore, an interesting subject for future work is the possible role of DMOs in developing recurrent events, marketing them as a component of the destination's tourist offer and exploiting them to attract tourism.

Future research should also focus on the medium- and long-term impact of recurrent events on the development of the other tangible supply-side components of the tourist industry, the destination's image and brand equity, and tourist flows. Finally, it is important to verify whether the magnitude of the relevant effects changes across the various phases of an event's life cycle.

Acknowledgements The authors thank Marina Emanuela Canino for her invaluable assistance with data collection.

References

Beverland M, Hoffman D, Rasmussen M (2001) The evolution of events in the Australasian wine sector. Tour Recreat Res 26(2):35–44

Bojanic D, Warnick R (2012) The role of purchase decision involvement in a special event. J Travel Res 51(3):357–366

Burbank MJ, Andranovich G, Heying CH (2001) Olympic dreams: the impact of mega-events on local politics. Lynne Rienner Publishers, Boulder, CO

Connell J, Page SJ, Meyer D (2015) Visitor attractions and events: responding to seasonality. Tour Manag 46:283–298

Deccio C, Baloglu S (2002) Non-host community resident reactions to the 2002 Winter Olympics: the spillover impacts. J Travel Res 41(1):45–56

Delamere TA (1997) Development of scale items to measure the social impact of community festivals. J Appl Recreat Res 22(4):293–315

Eisenhardt KM (1989) Building theories from case study research. Acad Manage Rev 14 (4):532–550

Eisenhardt KM, Graebner ME (2007) Theory building from cases: opportunities and challenges. Acad Manage J 50(1):25

Fredline E, Faulkner B (2002) Variations in residents' reactions to major motorsports events: why residents perceive the impacts of events differently. Event Manag 7(2):115–126

Getz D (2000) Festivals and special events: life cycle and saturation issues. In: Gartner WC, Lime DW (eds) Trends in outdoor recreation, leisure and tourism. CABI, Wallingford, pp 175–185

Getz D, Andersson T (2008) Sustainable festivals: on becoming an institution. Event Manag 12 (1):1–17

Gil AR, de Esteban Curiel J (2008) Religious events as special interest tourism: a Spanish experience. Revista de Turismo y Patrimonio Cultural 6(3):419–433

Goulding P (2008) Managing temporal variation in visitor attractions. In: Fyall A, Garrod B, Leask A, Wanhill S (eds) Managing visitor attractions. Elsevier Ltd, Burlington, VT

Gratton C, Henry I (2001) Sport in the city: the role of sport in economic and social regeneration. Routledge, New York

Harcup T (2000) Re-imaging a post-industrial city: the Leeds St Valentine's Fair as a civic spectacle. City 4(2):215–231

Hede A (2007) Managing special events in the new era of the triple bottom line. Event Manag 11 (1–2):13–22

Kang YS, Perdue R (1994) Long-term impact of a mega-event on international tourism to the host country: a conceptual model and the case of the 1988 Seoul Olympics. J Int Consum Mark 6 (3–4):205–225

Kaplanidou K, Vogt C (2007) The interrelationship between sport event and destination image and sport tourists' behaviours. J Sport Tour 12(3–4):183–206

Kaplanidou KK, Karadakis K, Gibson H, Thapa B, Walker M, Geldenhuys S, Coetzee W (2013) Quality of life, event impacts and mega event support among South African residents before and after the event: the case of the 2010 FIFA World Cup. J Travel Res 52(5):631–645

Kim SS, Park JY, Lee J (2010) Predicted economic impact analysis of a mega-convention using multiplier effects. J Convention Event Tour 11(1):42–61

Leask A (2010) Progress in visitor attraction research: towards more effective management. Tour Manag 31(2):155–166

Miles MB, Huberman AM (1985) Qualitative data analysis. Sage, Newbury Park, CA

Monga M (2006) Measuring motivation to volunteer for special events. Event Manag 10(1):47–61

O'Sullivan D, Jackson M (2002) Festival tourism: a contributor to sustainable local economic development? J Sustain Tour 10(4):325–342

Pugh C, Wood EH (2004) The strategic use of events within local government: a study of London Borough councils. Event Manag 9(1):61–71

Reid G (2006) The politics of city imaging: a case study of the MTV Europe Music Awards Edinburgh 03. Event Manag 10(1):35–46

Ritchie B, Beliveau D (1974) Hallmark events: an evaluation of a strategic response to seasonality in the travel market. J Travel Res 14(2):14–20

Roche M (2000) Mega-events and modernity: olympics and expos in the growth of global culture. Routledge, London

Simeon MI, Buonincontri P (2011) Cultural event as a territorial marketing tool: the case of the Ravello festival on the Italian Amalfi Coast. J Hosp Mark Manag 20(3–4):385–406

Stokes R, Jago L (2007) Australia's public sector environment for shaping event tourism strategy. Int J Event Manag Res 3(1):42–53

Thomas R, Wood EH (2004) Event-based tourism: a survey of local authority strategies in the UK. Local Gov 29(2):127–136

Uysal M, Gitelson R (1994) Assessment of economic impacts: festivals and special events. Festival Manag Event Tour 2(1):3–10

Whitford M (2004a) Event public policy development in the Northern Sub-Regional Organisation of Councils, Queensland Australia: rhetoric or realisation? J Convention Event Tour 6 (3):81–99

Whitford M (2004b) Regional development through domestic and tourist event policies: gold coast and Brisbane, 1974–2003. J Hosp Tour Leis Sci 1(1):1–24

Wrathall J, Gee A (2011) Event management: theory and practice. McGraw-Hill, North Ryde, NSW

Yin RK (2011) Applications of case study research. Sage Publications, California

Ziakas V, Costa CA (2011) Event portfolio and multi-purpose development: establishing the conceptual grounds. Sport Manag Rev 14(4):409–423

Enhancing the Tourism Image of Italian Regions Through Urban Events: The Case of Steve McCurry's *Sensational Umbria* Exhibition

Luca Ferrucci, Silvia Sarti, Simone Splendiani,
and María Cordente Rodríguez

Abstract The study analyses the case of the *Sensational Umbria* photography exhibition by Steve McCurry, held in Perugia in 2014. The event proved to be of particular interest, not only for its success in terms of visitors number and impact on the media, but in particular for the innovative use of a photo exhibition for the purpose of promoting tourism in the region. The paper, after a theoretical introduction on the relationship between tourism events and destination image, offers an analysis of the event from different perspectives: economic impact, visitor satisfaction, and effect on the media. The methodology has been twofold, involving both desk analysis and a survey conducted by administering a questionnaire to 455 visitors. The results that emerge illustrate a situation that, while generally positive, leaves margins for improvement, especially in terms of greater involvement by local stakeholders.

Keywords Tourism development • Destination image • Event evaluation

1 Introduction

The growing competition between tourist destinations and the shifts in modes of tourism consumption, which see tourists increasingly looking for symbolic and experiential meanings, are the factors behind the increasing strategic importance of

L. Ferrucci (✉) • S. Splendiani
Department of Economics, University of Perugia, Perugia, Italy
e-mail: luca.ferrucci@unipg.it; simone.splendiani@unipg.it

S. Sarti
Institute of Management, Sant'Anna School of Advanced Studies, Pisa, Italy
e-mail: s.sarti@sssup.it

M.C. Rodríguez
Department of Business, University of Castilla-La Mancha, Cuenca, Spain
e-mail: maria.cordente@uclm.es

© Springer International Publishing Switzerland 2017
N. Bellini, C. Pasquinelli (eds.), *Tourism in the City*,
DOI 10.1007/978-3-319-26877-4_16

destination brands. They represent the set of values that current and potential tourists associate with a destination, which may prove to be the defining factor in the process of choosing a tourist destination. For this reason, a strong brand can be a strategic asset in the competition between territories, as well as a strategic source of destination attractiveness (Aaker 1991; Beerli and Martin 2004; Cai 2002; Konecnik 2004; Morgan and Pritchard 2004).

However, destination brand management is a complex activity, that requiresa coordinated action of multiple stakeholders, which are all responsible—at varying levels—for the process of destination brand image formation (Hankinson 2007; Laws et al. 2002; Pencarelli and Splendiani 2010). In addition, the image of a territory is the result of its history (Anholt 2006; Yeoman et al. 2005), which can only partly be influenced by destination branding policies promoted by the Destination Management Organisation (DMO).

The image of Umbria, subject of this chapter, developed over time in a different manner from other Italian regions. Umbria is a small landlocked region in central Italy where cultural heritage and tourism resources are spread throughout the territory. It lacks three highly important attractions for travellers to Italy: the sea (beach tourism), the mountains (mountain tourism) and those cities known internationally, able to attract major foreign tourist flows like Rome, Florence or Venice. Tourism data for 2015 saw about 2,394,771 arrivals and 5,919,632 overnight stays (an increase of 3.19 % in arrivals and 0.88 % in overnight stays on to 2014), placing Umbria in the lower half of the national ranking in terms of tourist number. Considering that, the tourism development strategies realized in the Umbria region have followed three main directions in the last few years.

The first regards the organisation of cultural events, which are important tourism motivators capable of enhancing destination competitiveness (Bellini 2004; Ferrucci and Bracalente 2009; Getz 2008; Lazzeroni et al. 2013; Prentice and Andersen 2003) and reducing the seasonality of tourism demand. Umbria has been a pioneer in this field, offering a range of internationally recognised cultural events, such as the "Festival of the Two Worlds" (since 1958), "Umbria Jazz" (since 1973) (Bracalente et al. 2011) and "Eurochocolate" (since 1993) (Chirieleison et al. 2013). The second one is the creation of museum networks, with the aim of enhancing a heritage system that involves several small museums working together to preserve and promote their resources. Umbria was the first Italian region to create such a museum network. The third direction is the reorganisation of the regional tourism offering through the presentation of thematic packages, which are better able to promote tourism resources to different segments of the market that are attracted to specific tourist products (e.g., The Way of St. Francis for religious tourists, or Olive Oil and Wine Roads for gastronomic tourism).

2 Using Events to Enhance the Destination Image

Event tourism represents an important field of the tourism strategies adopted by the Umbria region. This indicates the existence of a strong relationship between events policy and regional tourism planning, which constitutes a strategic use of events (Crowther 2010; Markusen and Gadwa 2010; Stokes 2008; see Caroli and Valentino 2016). In particular, *Sensational Umbria* by Steve McCurry—the photo exhibition that is the subject of this research—was organised by the Umbria Region with the precise aim of promoting the image of the destination. *Sensational Umbria* included about 100 images of the region, taken by the renowned photographer Steve McCurry during his journey around Umbria. The exhibition provided an insight into the region, depicting its major cities and small villages, tourist attractions and celebrated cultural events, as well as its traditions and values.

One of the main reasons behind the decision to analyse the case of *Sensational Umbria* regards the many positive effects that the exhibition was intended to create. It has been established that events can generate benefits beyond the purely economic, i.e., cultural, social and environmental benefits (Herrero et al. 2006; Reeves 2002; Wood 2005). However, the analysed event had a number of specific features that make it unique in terms of the multiple benefits attributed to it. The specific characteristics of the exhibition included:

- A universal visual language, capable of overcoming cultural barriers (language, habits and customs), which was intended to communicate a message to an undifferentiated audience;
- An experiential form of communication, as it was designed (location, layout, lights, etc.) to engage the senses of the visitor;
- A high level of visitor engagement, as visitors could also be photographers, using their smart phones and social networks to share their media;
- Features associated with low cost of replication and economies of scope, rather than characteristics of obsolescence. In this context the reproducibility of the exhibition refers to both the possibility to be conveyed online, and through social media, and the possibility for it to be physically moved and replicated at low cost.[1] Moreover, the exhibition does not risk obsolescence, as the value of a photo can increase, rather than decrease, over time.

In addition to these characteristics, the role of the artist should also be noted, as it is crucial in determining the success of the event. Indeed, if the photographer is internationally famous, the exhibition may benefit from two effects. The first involves increased visibility, ensured by the author's ability to attract a loyal audience, as well as wider coverage in the media. The second is a reputational

---

[1]The *Sensational Umbria* exhibition travelled beyond regional and national borders; it was presented in Marseilles, in Milan during Expo 2015, at the Italian Institute of Foreign Trade in New York, and at the European Parliament in Brussels.

effect, involving the positive impact that the artist exercises on the brand of the exhibition, and consequently on the brand of the territory (if, as in this case, the exhibition is dedicated to a territory).

Finally, the communicative value of the exhibition lies in its potential effects, which can be widespread and remain valid over time. The first effect regards the visitors, who personally experience the exhibition, and may therefore promote the event through word of mouth. The second is the impact on traditional media (newspapers, television, radio), which is to be evaluated according to the reach of the media and the frequency of references. The final, and certainly not the least important aspect, regards the impact of social media networks, which can be crucial, especially if properly organised.

3 Evaluation of the Value Generated by the *Sensational Umbria* Photo Exhibition

This study aims to evaluate the performance of the *Sensational Umbria* exhibition from a variety of perspectives:

- Economic balance, considering the costs and revenues of the exhibition, indicating the main items in order to highlight the deficit incurred by the region;
- Direct effect on visitors by means of a survey conducted during the exhibition. Primary data was gathered from a sample of 455 respondents, in order to study the main characteristics of visitors and their overall level of satisfaction;
- Impact on traditional media; exposure in a range of media (newspapers, television and radio) was reviewed to study the press coverage, according to two parameters, i.e., the frequency and reach of communication;
- Impact of the web and social networks; in order to analyse Internet traffic, the performance of the official website was reviewed, along with coverage on other websites, and data relating to social networks.

3.1 Research Methodology

Empirical research was conducted following two different methodologies: desk analysis and a visitor survey. The first one, aimed at measuring the economic balance and the resonance of the event in the media, involved the study of official reports and documents at the Umbria Region. The second one, the survey, was conducted by means of a questionnaire featuring 27 open and closed questions. This self-assessment questionnaire was submitted to 455 respondents between August 2014 and January 2015. The selection of respondents was conducted randomly among visitors, in an attempt to cover the widest possible spectrum. The questionnaire was divided into three sections: general information about the *Sensational*

Table 1 Summary of financial statements

Description	Expenses		Revenues	
	€	%	€	%
Photo reportage	150,000	26.6		
Photo purchases	85,668	15.2		
Art direction (exhibition + catalogue)	101,613	18.0		
External equipment	73,600	13.0		
Sistema Museo: management and promotion	153,240	27.2		
Tickets			204,036[a]	73.9
Bookshop			71,956[b]	26.1
	564,121	100	275,992	100

[a]Net of the portion of ticket revenue due to the artist (10,000€)
[b]Net of the portion of catalogue revenue due to the artist (42,619€)

Umbria exhibition such as familiarity, overall evaluations, future behaviour, motivation for the visit; information about the visitors including socio-demographic profile and cultural habits; information about the stay of visitors who were not resident in Perugia.

3.2 Cost and Revenue Analysis

Firstly, a balance sheet analysis was conducted,[2] considering the main budget items in terms of expenses and revenues. The *Sensational Umbria* photography exhibition attracted 42,304 visitors on 252 opening days (from March 29th, 2014 to January 11th, 2015), averaging 186 visitors per day. A large part of the revenue was derived from the sale of exhibition catalogues, which amounted to 5,014 catalogues sold. Ticket sales made up the rest of revenues. A summary list of the main expenses and revenues is presented in Table 1.

The economic balance of the exhibition presents a coverage rate of about half (48.92 %). The remaining expenses, approximately 288,000€, were financed by regional funds. This appears acceptable when considering the "Advertising Value Equivalency" (AVE), i.e., the ability to generate the same number of impressions, in both traditional media and online. In addition, the non-monetary value generated by cultural activities and the positive effects for the local community must also be considered.

---

[2]The analysis of the budget is not detailed, but merely indicative, and is intended to illustrate the main costs and revenues involved in the exhibition, in order to outline the magnitude and rate approximate coverage.

3.3   Visitor Analysis

A survey was conducted that highlighted the direct effect of the exhibition on visitors. The analysis of the questionnaires provided the visitor profiles, presenting their socio-cultural and geographic characteristics, preferences, overall level of satisfaction, future behaviours, and reasons for visiting the exhibition.

The visitor profile that emerges is predominantly female (60.8 %), single (40.9 %), aged between 26 and 45 (44.7 %), with a university degree (61.6 %), and a career as a manager/businessperson/professional (25.5 %). The most frequent monthly salary was <1000€ (30.9 %), which may be due to the high number of students in Perugia and in this sample (21.5 %). With regard to nationality, visitors were mainly Italian (87.1 %), with 33.7 % resident in Umbria, and a further 31.2 % from neighbouring regions (Marche: 5.3 %, Tuscany: 6.5 %, Emilia Romagna: 8.8 %; Lazio: 10.6 %). Foreign visitors made up 12.9 % of the total—3.5 % were from Romania, 1.8 % from the USA and 0.7 % from the United Kingdom. The results indicate that the attractiveness of the exhibition to foreign tourists was limited, and that the event had little impact on the urban economy, considering the high percentage of visitors from the neighbouring regions that were probably day trippers.

The most frequently reasons to stay in Perugia indicated by respondents— considering that more than one reason could be indicated—were visiting the *Sensational Umbria* exhibition (30.6 %), and visiting Perugia's historical, cultural, natural and gastronomic heritage (23.5 %). Other possible reasons were less frequent, such as visiting friends and relatives (8.3 %), relaxing, leisure and shopping (6.1 %), education and training (5.5 %), business trips (3.5 %) and religious tourism (0.4 %).

In the case of visitors who are not resident in Perugia, the average length of stay was 2 days; however, a high number of visitors (48.8 %) only spent 1 day. The majority of respondents that were not resident in Perugia stayed in a hotel (44.1 %), followed by the home of friends or relatives (19.3 %) and bed and breakfasts (17.2 %). 29.4 % of visitors declared an interest in knowing other small cities in Umbria, such as Assisi (52.2 %). Those who decided to visit other parts of Umbria, apart from Perugia, visited two places on average. This means that the economic effects of the exhibition were spread across the entire region thanks to visitor consumption.

Secondly, the survey examines levels of satisfaction with the exhibition and organisation. An analysis of the questionnaires reveals that most respondents were already familiar with the photographer Steve McCurry. About 75 % declared that they knew the artist: 45.1 % were visiting a McCurry's exhibition for the first time, although they already knew the artist, and 29.9 % had previously attended other exhibitions by McCurry. The rest of the visitors (25 %) were not informed about the artist and had never visited his exhibitions before. With regard to how visitors first heard about the exhibition, most of them found information through printed media, mainly newspaper or magazines (30.8 %) and billboards (30.1 %). It also emerges that the use of personal sources of information is relevant, with recommendations from family or friends (23.9 %) followed by the web (22.4 %) and social networks (11 %). On average, visitors consulted 1.3 sources of information.

With regard to levels of satisfaction, visitors generally agreed or strongly agreed with the statements "this is one of the best exhibitions I could have visited" (44.1 %) and "I am satisfied with this experience" (86.6 %); and disagreed or strongly disagreed with the statements "the photos were good but the quality of services wasn't adequate" (74.4 %) and "there are not enough photos to justify the exhibition" (65.1 %).

Regarding future behaviour, on average visitors agreed or strongly agreed about the possibility of visiting a new McCurry exhibition (86.7 %), recommending someone to visit the *Sensational Umbria* exhibition (85.4 %), or other exhibitions in Perugia (76.3 %).

However, the most positive future behaviour that emerges from the survey is the intention to visit a new exhibition by McCurry (4.2/5), followed by the intention to recommend *Sensational Umbria* (4.1/5), with the possibility of visiting other exhibitions in Perugia a less preferred option (3.9/5). This is especially important in terms of positive word of mouth.

Finally, with regard to overall levels of satisfaction, it emerges that 43.7 % of respondents declared they were very satisfied with the exhibition (giving the maximum score on a scale of 1–5). 94.2 % of those surveyed gave a score of 3 or higher.

3.4   Impact on Traditional Media and Social Networks

Desk analysis was conducted in order to assess the value created in terms of communication and branding, taking into consideration all traditional means of communication: daily, weekly, monthly national/regional newspapers, press agencies, national/regional TV, and radio. From this analysis of traditional media it emerges that the number of impressions was satisfactory, as the reach of the media was. As shown in Fig. 1, much of the coverage was at the national level.

Figure 2 focuses on newspapers, highlighting the different trends observed in the regional, national and foreign press.

With regard to the impact on the web and social networks, articles dedicated to the *Sensational Umbria* exhibition were found in 19 online newspapers/magazines and 69 websites or blogs.

The official website www.sensationalumbria.eu registered 56,393 visitors, with 213,126 page views, from the launch date until the end of the exhibition

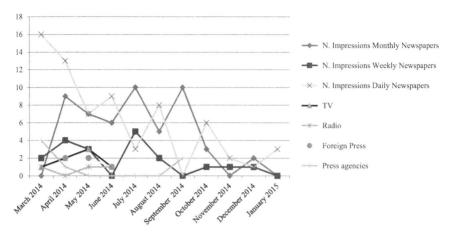

Fig. 1 Traditional media

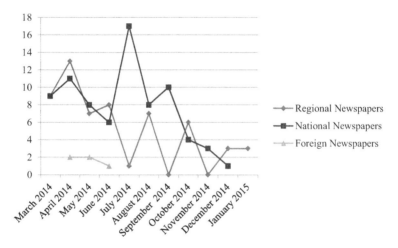

Fig. 2 Newspaper trends

(March 23rd, 2014–January 11th, 2015). The average length of each page visit was impressive, at more than 2 minutes and 20 seconds. Figure 3 describes the monthly trend of visits to the official website.

The positive level of traffic on the website is the result of successful social media marketing policies. The importance of a planned social media strategy was a key element identified from the beginning by the Umbria region. These policies were well organized, thanks to the simultaneous use of the main social media tools, in particular continuous content marketing activity. Particularly good results also emerge regarding Facebook and YouTube performance. Table 2 summarises the social media strategy and the main results achieved.

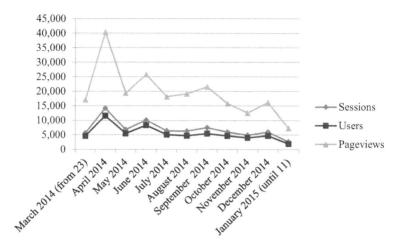

Fig. 3 Trends of main website indicators

Table 2 Social media metrics

Metrics	Facebook	Twitter	YouTube	Instagram	Pinterest	Google+
Activity Input	650 posts	2590 tweets	96 videos (36 self-produced)	248 pictures	35 board + 626 pictures	Replication of Facebook posts
Interaction	10,244 likes	1162 followers	22,151 views, 55 members, 91 likes, 108comments, 178 shares	804 followers, 6866 likes and 184 comments	136 followers	134 followers and 71,279 views

4 Conclusions

Steve McCurry's photo exhibition *Sensational Umbria* proved to be an innovative way to promote the region. It was potentially more effective than traditional tourism promotion initiatives, such as mass media advertising. This innovation is part of a long tradition in the promotion of cultural events that has had a profound impact on the evolution of the Umbria region as a tourist destination. The aim of this chapter was to evaluate the event according to the perspectives of analysis of the economic balance, visitor satisfaction, and impact on the media.

While the survey results reveal many positive aspects, a number of critical issues remain, such as a lack of involvement by operators. They have chosen not to invest resources in this exhibition despite having been involved by the regional government. Their prevailing attitude was a passive, "rent seeking" approach, awaiting the arrival of tourists without making a contribution through the adoption of co-marketing strategies. It would have been opportune to develop better supporting marketing strategies to accompany the exhibition (such as tourist packages, discounts, gifts for clients, etc.), as this would have provided more positive promotional effects.

This is a consequence of the lack of a vocation for strategic cooperation between small tourism and commercial operators active in the same city. This individualist attitude tends to prevail over the propensity for cooperation, according to the economic logic of free-riding.

Another critical factor is the low percentage of tourists among the visitors, in particular those from abroad (only 12.3 %). The exhibition mainly attracted local and regional visitors, who were already familiar with the places shown in the pictures. It can be assumed that tourists prefer to visit Umbria in person: a more emotionally engaging activity than a visit to a photo exhibition. As a result, it displays a limited capacity to attract extra-regional tourists. The exhibition might have been more attractive to this segment of tourists if co-marketing initiatives had been planned (such as joint ticket offers that covered the exhibition and some of the places represented in the images).

This work is intended as a reflection on the communication policies of destinations and their use as tools for the valorisation and promotion of tourism-oriented areas. In the light of this investigation, future research might focus on the evaluation capabilities of communications policies, from an integrated and "holistic" perspective. An isolated instrument—such as an exhibition—can not generate economic spillovers for the territory, unless it is integrated in a comprehensive destination management strategy, which is capable of uniting the valorisation of tourism resources (cultural, enogastronomic, etc.) with relationships with, and the backing of, both public and private stakeholders.

References

Aaker DA (1991) Managing brand equity. The Free Press, New York, NY
Anholt S (2006) Nation-brands and the value of provenance. In: Morgan N, Pritchard A, Pride R (eds) Destination branding. Creating the unique destination proposition. Elsevier, Oxford, pp 26–39
Beerli A, Martin JD (2004) Factors influencing destination image. Ann Tour Res 31(3):657–681
Bellini N (2004) Territorial governance and area image. Symphonya Emerg Issues Manag 4 (1):14–26
Bracalente B, Chirieleison C, Cossignani M, Ferrucci L, Gigliotti M, Ranalli G (2011) The economic impact of cultural events: the Umbria Jazz music festival. Tour Econ 17 (6):1235–1255. doi:10.5367/te.2011.0096
Cai LA (2002) Cooperative branding for rural destinations. Ann Tour Res 29(3):720–742
Caroli M, Valentino A (2016) Does recurrence matter? The impact of music festivals on local tourist competitiveness. In: Bellini N, Pasquinelli C (eds) Tourism in the city—towards an integrative agenda on urban tourism. Springer, Heidelberg

Chirieleison C, Montrone A, Scrucca L (2013) Measuring the impact of a profit-oriented event on tourism: the Eurochocolate festival in Perugia, Italy. Tour Econ 19(6):1411–1428. doi:10. 5367/te.2013.0269

Crowther P (2010) Strategic application of events. Int J Hosp Manag 29(2):227–235

Ferrucci L, Bracalente B (eds) (2009) Eventi culturali e sviluppo economico locale. Franco Angeli Editore, Milano

Getz D (2008) Event tourism: definition, evolution, and research. Tour Manag 29(3):403–428

Hankinson G (2007) The management of destination brands: five guiding principles based on recent developments in corporate branding theory. J Brand Manag 14(3):240–254

Herrero LC, Sanz JA, Devesa M, Bedate A, Del Barrio MJ (2006) The economic impact of cultural events. Eur Urban Reg Stud 13(1):41–57

Konecnik M (2004) Evaluating Slovenia's image as a tourism destination: a self-analysis process towards building a destination brand. Brand Manag 11(4):307–316

Laws E, Scott N, Parfitt N (2002) Synergies in destination image management: a case study and conceptualisation. Int J Tour Res 4(1):39–55

Lazzeroni M, Bellini N, Cortesi G, Lofredo A (2013) The territorial approach to cultural economy: new opportunities for the development of small towns. Eur Plan Stud 21(4):452–472

Markusen A, Gadwa A (2010) Arts and culture in urban or regional planning: a review and research agenda. J Plan Educ Res 29(3):379–391

Morgan N, Pritchard A (2004) Destination branding, creating the unique destination proposition, 2nd edn. Butterworth-Heinemann Eds, Oxford

Pencarelli T, Splendiani S (2010) Il Destination Brand e le politiche di Destination Branding. In: Pencarelli T (ed) Marketing e Management del turismo. Edizioni Goliardiche, Trieste

Prentice R, Andersen V (2003) Festival as creative destinations. Ann Tour Res 30(1):7–30

Reeves M (2002) Measuring the economic and social impact of the arts. Arts Council England, London

Stokes R (2008) Tourism strategy making: insights to the events tourism domain. Tour Manag 29:252–262

Wood EH (2005) Measuring the economic and social impacts of local authority events. Int J Public Sect Manag 18(1):37–53

Yeoman I, Durie A, McMahon-Beattie U, Palmer A (2005) Capturing the essence of a brand from its history: the case of Scottish tourism marketing. Brand Manag 13(2):134–147

Rediscovering the "Urban" in Two Italian Tourist Coastal Cities

Chiara Rabbiosi and Massimo Giovanardi

> *Per quest'anno non cambiare: stessa spiaggia stesso mare*
> *[For this year please don't change: beach and sea will be*
> *the same]*
>
> (E. Vianello, 1962)

Abstract This chapter appreciates the role of tourism within the more holistic framework of urban policy in the context of coastal cities. Through an investigation of two medium-sized Italian cities (Rimini and Pesaro), the study addresses the paucity of literature on regeneration strategies conducted in coastal areas where tourism has already reached a mature stage of development. The idea of a "culture city" emerges as the most appropriate pathway to innovation, change and progress in line with the several, albeit often criticised, examples of culture-led regeneration in urban studies. The discourse analysis of the strategic plans of each city emphasises the different role that the sea and the seaside play in each location. Rimini explicitly includes these factors as pivotal cultural resources, which is evident in the innovative concept of "sea wellness". Pesaro, on the other hand, does not attribute a specific role to the sea and the seaside; they are instead simply juxtaposed with a vibrant city centre that appeals to business and cultural tourists.

Keywords Urban tourism • Culture • Heritage • Seaside • Strategic planning

C. Rabbiosi
Department for Life Quality Studies (QuVi)—Center for Advanced Studies in Tourism
(CAST), University of Bologna, Bologna, Italy
e-mail: chiara.rabbiosi@gmail.com

M. Giovanardi (✉)
School of Management—University of Leicester, Leicester, UK
e-mail: m.giovanardi@le.ac.uk

© Springer International Publishing Switzerland 2017
N. Bellini, C. Pasquinelli (eds.), *Tourism in the City*,
DOI 10.1007/978-3-319-26877-4_17

1   The Complexity of Tourism and "the Urban"[1]

The question of how to pursue alternative paths of development that transcend the problems linked to tourism is certainly not new for destination and city managers. The broad concept of "alternative" approaches to hyper-touristification gained remarkable coverage in the literature on tourism studies between the 1980s and 1990s (see Weaver 1991), and a similar effort is still animating the work of contemporary tourism scholars examining other paradigm shifts, such as the one towards sustainability (e.g., Jamrozy 2007; Buckley 2012). In addition, tourism has begun to assume unprecedented significance as a means for resolving political as well as socio-economic problems of cities and regions affected by the processes of deindustrialisation. As such, it has become a pivotal item on the urban policy agenda (Hoffman et al. 2003).

Cities can be considered as complex and dynamic entities (see for example Comunian 2011). This might be not only due to their rich array of "soft" assets (skills and knowledge, symbols and images, rituals and traditions), but also due to the presence of multiple agents—human and non-human—contributing to the constant redefinition of built environment and infrastructure (ibidem). Tourism takes on a particular role in contributing to the complexity of this urban scenario since it is able to influence not only the pace of change but also its trajectory and implementation (Spirou 2011). Of course, as Pearce contends, "the complexity of urban tourism has no doubt helped delay research in this field, because the need to disentangle it from other urban functions makes it more difficult to study than in many other settings" (2001, p. 928). However, this complexity can also be emphasised as a source of richness, especially with respect to the contribution that physical and symbolic urban assets have on "spatial strategy-making" (Albrechts 2004, 2006). In line with Healey, the urban complexity and its manifestations can be appreciated by endorsing a relational approach to spatial planning, which encourages place managers to "grasp the dynamic diversity of the complex co-location of multiple webs of relations that transect and intersect across an urban area" (2007, p. 3).

With this in mind, we focus on two medium-sized Italian neighbouring cities, Rimini and Pesaro. The two cases have been sampled because of their similarity in terms of size, geographical location and socio-economic development. Hence, different visions and paths for future development are likely to stand out more clearly in the analysis. In both cities, the local economy has mainly developed within Fordist-like scenarios of, respectively, mass tourism at the seaside and industrial production of goods and commodities. In these two cities' recent strategic plans, traditional and novel development paradigms are combined and re-interpreted according to themes that are generally acknowledged as successful formulas for urban and tourism planning, with the issue of cultural tourism acquiring particular prominence in the future envisioned by policy-makers.

---

[1]Massimo Giovanardi is author of the Sects. 1 and 5, and Chiara Rabbiosi of Sects. 2, 3, and 4. Conclusions have been drawn by the authors together.

2 The Post-Fordist Shift in Coastal Cities

Both Rimini and Pesaro are located along the Adriatic coast and have a main source of revenues and jobs provision in seaside tourism, especially during summer seasons. This includes not only tourism at beach areas and facilities; Roman and Medieval heritage assets also characterise the two cities, although these have played an ancillary role in tourist product development and promotion. Both cities are now struggling to find "their own place" in a scenario of increased regional competition, and they are attempting to attract and maintain human and physical capital. In doing so, the cities are also considerably questioning their identity by evaluating what can be saved from their past in order to make them more economically appealing.

By the end of the twentieth century, attracting a range of exogenous resources—people, businesses, and investments—had become the most urgent means to revitalise urban local economy (Cochrane 2007; Gordon and Buck 2005; Harvey 1989). Indeed, cities cannot stand as economic actors on their own, but they can stimulate the agglomeration of demand, that is to say consumption immersed in a continuous circular flow of economic relations on the global scale (Amin and Thrift 2002). In this context, "culture" started becoming a major component of urban entrepreneurialism (Zukin 1995, Evans 2003), and social and demographic changes were increasing the demand for cultural facilities (Uriely 2005). In this scenario, the regeneration policies of cities have taken a variety of paths, ranging from rehabilitating historic neighbourhoods, branding space with cultural amenities, stressing the role of creative clusters, promoting cultural infrastructure (museums, thematic and heritage parks, etc.) and cultural events and festivals (Miles and Paddison 2005; Patel 2012). The rehabilitation of cultural heritage as expressed both in its tangible and intangible counterparts has also become an essential element of this framework (Zukin 2012). So-called cultural tourism (Robinson and Smith 2006) has become an essential corollary of culture-led urban regeneration. Cultural tourism has also been presented as an alternative to mass tourism and established as the "good tourism" that is respectful of sites and populations (Cousin 2008). The specific policies encouraging the development of cultural tourism projects can be understood as a way to generate economic resources by exploiting urban heritage sites and by inviting visitors to engage in practices of cultural consumption.

In this shift, coastal cities have been generally redeveloped through the regeneration of their waterfronts. Urban waterfronts are highly exploitable spaces because they are interfaces between the built environment and water. At the same time, they provide empty space to be re-filled with various amenities, especially in those cases where access to water coincide with hubs for transportation and industry, such as in port cities such as New York, Barcelona or Genova. Much has been written about the regeneration of industrial waterfronts (for a summary, see Brownill 2013). However, little research has focussed either on those coastal cities where tourism had already developed in the framework of a Fordist economy during the twentieth century or on coastal cities which were neither major ports nor major beach resorts. The former applies to the case of Rimini, once known as one of the most famous European destinations for mass tourism at the seaside, and the latter refers to the case of Pesaro, a nearby coastal city whose economy was based on a combination of manufacturing industries (e.g., furniture) and its service sector (e.g., tourism). To fill this gap, the question of how to design innovative tourism policies by keeping the *seaside* as a valuable resource is addressed in this present chapter through a critical investigation of the discourses mobilised by these two cities during the elaboration of their vision in the 2000s through strategic planning. The study is performed by analysing the two strategic plans, which put into discourses the paths for future development of the two cities.

3 A Critical Discourse Approach to Strategic Planning

Both Rimini and Pesaro started practising a collaborative approach to planning in the 2000s that culminated in two strategic plans containing the visions for the two cities' future urban regeneration. Gaining a renewed international interest, strategic planning should be located in the wider stream of relational spatial planning (Healey 2007; Davoudi and Strange 2009). In this view, policy-makers are supposed to address the theme of urban regeneration by fostering the integration and coordination of different sectors and by encouraging the participation of a variety of public and private stakeholders. Participation of individual citizens is also explicitly encouraged.

Strategic planning is not universally defined, but it instead generally focuses on a limited number of key issue areas. Strategic planning takes a critical and strategic view of the environment in terms of strengths and weaknesses evaluated against a background of opportunities and threats. Strategic planning maximises public engagement and develops a long-term vision for the place, together with a set of strategies and tactics within different policy areas. In short, strategic spatial planning designs plan-making structures and develops new ideas and frameworks for managing spatial change. As an ultimate element informing all the resolutions, strategic planning usually identifies a vision, consisting in a set of images that project a desirable future for the city. In addition, "[t]his 'created future' has to be placed within a specific context (economic, social, political, and power), place, time, and scale with regard to specific issues and a particular combination of actors. It provides the setting from the process but also takes form, undergoes changes in the process. All this must be rooted in an understanding of the past" (Albrechts 2004, p. 750).

This present chapter aims to analyse the two cities' strategic plans, and it seeks to identify how tourism is framed in the creation of new urban development policies that intend to reach the desirable future outlined by the plans. This study is exploratory in nature and relies on an interpretivist paradigm in which researchers are engaged with an "empathic understanding of human action rather than with the forces that are deemed to act on it" (Bryman 2012, p. 15). Accordingly, cities are considered mainly as sets of narratives (see Lichrou et al. 2008) and discourses.

In this view, language is considered to be the medium to construct the social world; thus, discourse analysis is adopted as a significant analytical approach of this article (see Lucarelli and Giovanardi 2014). Discourse analysis is increasingly seen as a useful approach to understanding a range of issues in planning, including power, knowledge, ideology, persuasion, social difference and institutional framing (Lees 2004). Planning texts can be seen as concrete realisations of discourses and discursive strategies (MacCallum and Hopkins 2011) between language use, the ways in which planning problems are framed and how potential solutions are justified.

4 Setting the Stage: Rimini and Pesaro in Brief

The city of Rimini (about 145,000 inhabitants at the end of 2013) stands at the core of the so-called Romagna Riviera, a conurbation that includes European coastal beach resorts that were among some of the most profitable during the second half of the twentieth century. The development of mass tourism after World War II rapidly contributed to triggering industrial development (Battilani and Fauri 2009), and it created a remarkable divide between the coast and Rimini's inner region. After many decades of reliance on a model based on mass tourism at the seaside, nightlife services, and the provision of facilities, policymakers have looked into alternative sources of local development since the 1990s. These include business tourism-oriented services and cultural heritage. The construction of new exhibition and congress centres in the first decade of the 2000s has coupled with pioneering efforts in the conservation and management of heritage sites.

Pesaro (about 94,000 inhabitants at the end of 2013) is located along the same coast as Rimini, but it is about thirty kilometres away. Pesaro's economic development has unfolded as less dependent on tourism than Rimini, although seaside tourism is undoubtedly well developed in the area, with well-infrastructured beaches and a wider array of hospitality services. If Rimini is generally considered a *tourist city*, Pesaro is more generally considered an *industrial city*, hosting one of the most important furniture districts in Italy. In addition, Pesaro is the birthplace of the composer Gioachino Rossini and hosts an international opera festival.

5 Future Visions of Tourism in Pesaro and Rimini

5.1 Introducing Strategic Planning

Rimini introduced its strategic plan in the mid-2000s. Officially launched in July 2007 with horizon 2027, Rimini's Strategic Plan[2] was promoted by the

---

[2]http://www.riminiventure.it; the final document of Rimini's Strategic Plan can be downloaded form the website. Accessed 28 Dec 2015.

Municipality of Rimini, the Province, the Chamber of Commerce, and the Rimini Bank Foundation, a charity organisation linked to the leading Rimini bank. In 2008/ 2009, eight working groups were created to discuss the future of Rimini. The groups were composed of a variety of public and private stakeholders, such as public administrations, unions, trade associations, and a variety of third-sector represen- tatives. The spirit of this strategic plan was expressed in the slogan *Il Piano strategico, cambia la tua città* ("The strategic plan changes your city"), stressing the role of local actors as active participants in the planning process. In 2011, the vision emerging from the participatory phase was established and ready to be implemented. Simultaneously, the *Piano Stretegico Valmarecchia*[3] was launched, focussing on the Rimini hinterland Marecchia River Valley. This second strategic plan is generally acknowledged as aiming to extend the "catchment" area of Rimini's Strategic Plan, although it is formally independent from it.

Pesaro, the other city of this study, released its own Strategic Plan at the beginning of the 2000s, under the framework of horizon 2015. The title of the plan's main document is "Pesaro future with a view. Strategic plan of a *city of quality*" (emphasis in original).[4] The process was commenced by the local munic- ipality in 2001, while the analysis and definition of its aims were developed between October 2001 and June 2002. Six working groups were organised in order to elaborate a shared vision for the future of the city, an effort that was guided by the slogan "Pesaro, city of quality". Both public and private actors officially took place in the planning process, including the Province government, professional organisations, banks, foundations and third-sector organisations (Martufi 2012). The participatory character of strategic planning in Pesaro during the mid-2000s has been highlighted in scholarly work (Albrechts 2006), and the focus on strategic planning in the area was progressively extended through a provincial strategic plan released in 2011, which goes beyond the administrative boundaries of the munic- ipality. The table below illustrates the policy areas identified by each of the strategic plans (see Table 1).

5.2 Tourism in an Idyllic Scenario of Culture-Led Development

The two strategic plans feature several elements in common. As illustrated in Table 1's second row, many of the policy areas identified by planners are very similar, such as the foundational role of knowledge, innovation, business attraction and internationalisation. In particular, both Rimini and Pesaro project a desirable future for themselves, by articulating a main overarching discourse that underscores

---

[3]http://www.fiumemarecchia.it. Accessed 28 Dec 2015.

[4]http://www.pianostrategico.comune.pesaro.pu.it; the final document of Pesaro's Strategic Plan can be downloaded from the website. Accessed 28 Dec 2015.

Table 1 The main policy areas of the two strategic plans

	RIMINI	PESARO
Main policy areas as illustrated in each plan	1. A new relationship with the sea 2. Mobility as a major challenge 3. A business system made of people and innovation 4. The quality of a reassembled and cohesive region (*territorio ricomposto e coeso*) [a] 5. Culture that shapes and informs people and creates a new image	1. Attracting enterprises 2. City of culture 3. City promotion and internationalisation 4. Information and new technology 5. Local welfare 6. Local environment (*territorio*)
Common policy areas (compared)	– Culture that shapes and informs people and creates a new image – A business system made of people and innovation – The quality of a reassembled and cohesive region	– City of culture – Attracting enterprises (includes mobility infrastructure) – Local welfare and Local environment
Specific policy areas	– A new relationship with the sea – Mobility as a major challenge	– City promotion and internationalisation – Information and new technology

[a] The original term *territorio* has in Italian, as in French, a different meaning than the English term of territory. *Territorio* corresponds to a wider conception of space as theorised among cultural geographers. We have translated *territorio* with the most appropriate English words according to the different nuances that the term takes in the strategic plans

the redeeming role of culture. Thus, Pesaro's Strategic Plan identifies culture as the "point of departure" for appreciating a renovated interest in "a new humanism" as a key theme, as illustrated by the following excerpt:

> The theme of culture is a point of departure in so far as it represents the shared acknowledgement of the existence of a Pesaro model. The identity of this model is already recognised and can further become a multiplier of local resources, not only from the economic point of view. The idea is to propose Pesaro as a "new humanism" (nuovo umanesimo), the physical and spiritual place of the resolution between economic development and environmental defence, technological progress and arts promotion, mass civilisation and the centrality of human beings. To consolidate this model, the creation of a cultural heritage network has been created. This network will be able to connect and capitalise also on heritage that is not within the city but that can be considered part of this system because of proximity. The relationship between the industrial district and planning, applied arts, and the relationship between tourism and culture have been identified as important actions for the reinforcement of a Pesaro model that has also to keep alive the theme of formation and creation of spillover effects in terms of quality of culture (programme document of Pesaro's Strategic Plan, p. 9).

Two elements emerge as particularly connected with "culture" here, and they can be intended as the two specific embodiments of a re-envisioned idea of what tourism should be in this specific context: the ability of culture-led development to foster *territorial cohesion*, and the ability of culture to be crystallised in *cultural heritage*.

From one perspective, tourism is contextualised within a scenario where the redeeming role of culture works as an enabling factor for an augmented territorial cohesion in a transition from fragmentation (e.g., "resolution") to connectedness ("network", "connect", "relationship"; "system"). This supporting discourse on "networked cities" is featured within the areas of business attraction ("infrastructure"; "encouraging migrants integration") and culture ("take advantage of a *system* of culture") in Pesaro's Strategic Plan. A similar role of culture as a "glue" also stems from Rimini's Strategic Plan which identifies culture as an engine that "gives shape and informs people and creates a new image" (Rimini's Strategic Plan, pp. 106–114), thus avoiding a homologation of culture. This hints at a kind of interconnectedness that puts particular emphasis on the role of social capital ("people"), a major element of territorial cohesion. This expression of culture also sketches an envisioned cultural milieu that would soften the contrasts between residents and tourists without rejecting the centenary tradition of Rimini as a tourist city. Indeed "Rimini [is], a cultured and kind land of history, traditions and hospitality" (Rimini's Strategic Plan, p. 108).

From a second perspective, cultural heritage emerges as another key thematisation of culture-led development. This perspective on tourism as embedded in a hopeful celebration of "culture" and "heritage" renders an urban setting that recalls a fashionable "renewed optimism about cities [...]" as "exciting and creative places in which to live and work" (Gordon and Buck 2005, p. 6). This indeed results in an ideal host city matching new trends in tourism (Richards 2014). Cultural heritage is identified with giving a new meaning to the historic city centre in Pesaro's Strategic Plan, while it takes a more nuanced acceptation in Rimini's Strategic Plan. Besides hospitality (see previous paragraph), cultural heritage includes the regeneration of Rimini's inner city neighbourhoods, the city's Roman remains (as part of the project of events to celebrate 2000 years of the Tiberius bridge "Rimini Fluxus") and the changing role of the seaside (see next section).

The desirable form of tourism, then, is seen as an inherently cultural one, namely as something that goes beyond the traditional dominant model of mass tourism that prevailed during the previous decades. This targeted understanding of tourism is evident in the following quotes from Pesaro's Strategic Plan: "Pesaro aims to promote cultural, urban tourism and not only seaside tourism. [Cultural and urban tourism is] a quality tourism that is already an important part of tourism turnover in Italy today. This kind of tourism will increase on the basis of the growth of a more demanding and sophisticated tourist demand." (Pesaro's Strategic Plan, p. 23). Cultural tourism is thus seen as a leverage for shaping a networked society that is free of conflict in which movements of flows, objects, ideas and people can lead the way towards change and progress.

By linking it to territorial cohesion and cultural heritage, tourism is seen through a more holistic perspective that transcends a view that confines it within the realm of mass tourism at the seaside. This shared attitude in the two strategic plans intends to incorporate "forgotten" aspects of each city into a more varied provision of tourism supply. However, the two plans articulate this view in two different ways, as illustrated by the following section.

5.3   The Relationship with the Seaside: Connectivity or Complementarity?

Both Rimini and Pesaro stress the role of culture as the main engine for future developments and cultural tourism as key driver of this, but the cities do so in different ways. Rimini explicitly includes the seaside as a crucial ingredient of its envisioned future by shedding new light on it. Indeed, the first policy area identified by its plan is termed "A new relationship with the sea" (Rimini's Strategic Plan, see pp. 81–85). In contrast, in Pesaro's Strategic Plan, the sea or the seaside are never stand-alone elements, not even in specific regard to tourism, which is simply a sub-theme under the "culture city" policy area or the "internationalisation" policy area (in this case, tourism is entirely "business tourism"). Rimini, on the other hand, recognises itself a seaside city by re-elaborating the role and the meaning that the sea and seaside may possess for the city's future, a process commonly started after the "eutrophication crises" of the 1990s (Becheri 1991).

The difference between Pesaro and Rimini in their relation to the sea and seaside is articulated along three dimensions that appreciate (i) the built environment; (ii) land use and (iii) urban space as *practised* by social actors. Regarding the first, it is possible to argue that Pesaro's Strategic Plan conceives the historical centre and the waterfront area by simply juxtaposing them, while Rimini's Strategic Plan identifies the fracture between them and suggests a way to recompose it. This fracture is physical since the Marina section and the city centre appear to be heavily disjointed due to the intrusive presence of the railway, splitting the urban fabric into two parts. This fracture is also symbolic since Rimini's tourist resort evokes noisy, over-crowded, leisure-based seaside tourism. According to the vision emerging in Rimini's Strategic Plan, instead, the beach will no longer be just a site "for fun", but it will assume the new identity of an active agent. This vision is developed through the idea of "sea wellness" in Rimini's Strategic Plan (p. 81; pp. 131–132). Seaside tourism is therefore upgraded, and it becomes part of the same ideology of the "culture city".

Transforming the seaside area is thus changing how the beach can be used and the alternative types of tourism that the beach itself will enable. In this appreciation, Rimini identifies the sea and the seaside as "the grounding element of a new concept of well-being" (p. 81), and it stresses the "value" that this new awareness for seaside tourism has "on the other types of tourism [. . .], bringing benefit also to the city and its residents" (p. 132). In fact, while Pesaro addresses primarily business and cultural tourists and scarcely mentions the sea, the Rimini plan assigns the sea as one of the relational hubs of the city's life including residents, tourists and city-users alike. To sum up, Rimini does not reject its "mass tourism identity" but strongly stresses the fact that there is *also* (and has always been) another city rooted in an ancient civilisation and hospitality culture, and that these two "souls" can be genuinely connected.

6   Conclusions

This paper has offered a critical assessment of the discourses developed by two medium-sized Italian coastal cities during the discussion of their future by engaging in collaborative strategic planning. With both cities in need of updating their competitive profile, Rimini and Pesaro have sought to re-assess their traditional background of mass tourist and industrial areas and redefine the role held by tourism within the contemporary scenario. This paper has argued, in fact, that little has been said on the regeneration strategies put forward by those coastal cities in which tourism had already developed in the framework of a Fordist economy during the twentieth century, and few studies thus far have focussed on coastal cities which were neither major ports nor major beach resorts. The idea of a "culture city" emerges in both cases as the most appropriate pathway to innovation, change and progress by scripting the story of cohesive and networked places that resonates, to a large extent, with the several cases of culture-led regeneration featured in the urban studies literature. Yet this redeeming role of culture takes different appreciations according to the specific character and history of the two places, with the role of the sea and the seaside being the main factor.

The study has shown the ambiguous relationship between the two coexisting models of a "seaside city", understood as a legacy of the entrepreneurial spirit of the past and a "culture city" imbued with a renewed awareness for the value of cultural urban assets (Smith and Robinson 2006, p. 5). In the case of Pesaro, we witnessed planners' distancing of themselves from the sea and seaside, explicitly detaching Pesaro from the "Rimini model" based on the mass provision of beach attractions and hospitality services. This can be seen as a means of differentiation that is supposed to bring along a competitive advantage in relation to Rimini itself, which the planners of Pesaro regarded as a "negative" benchmark. Thus, the result is a dominant discourse about the need to entice a more sophisticated tourist demand that is associated with cultural and urban tourism. In Rimini, conversely, the leitmotif of the sea and seaside as implied in (and embedded within) this culture-led regeneration process gives shape to a less predictable formula for development in which traditional assets of the city (the beach culture, the hospitality culture) are rediscovered and channelled into more innovative pathways, as illustrated by the notion of "sea wellness".

It is hard to deny that in both cities, overcoming a simplistic model of the provision of mass seaside tourism reveals novel possibilities for conceiving alternative types of tourism. Business tourism and Meeting Incentives Conferences and Events (MICE) illustrate a common path that has already been undertaken by both cities, particularly by Rimini that has been investing significantly in enlarging its exhibition centre and congress and in attracting major national conferences since the 2000s. This approach to tourism development, of course, would be not conceivable if the beach facilities of Rimini and Pesaro were located outside of a true urban context that includes a variety of other physical and symbolic resources (e.g., archaeological sites, shopping facilities, cultural attractions such as libraries, etc.). Yet the case of Rimini is particularly original since the sea and the seaside are not "distanced" and blurred in a more general overarching discourse on culture; instead, these factors maintain a very important role to play.

On the one hand, several academic commentators have identified cultural tourism as a harmless and distinctive resource that is respectful for the landscape and the local population and, as such, is a preferable path to sustainable tourism. Moreover, cultural tourism is presented in both the plans of Rimini and Pesaro as a tool to amalgamate the interests of different stakeholders and different departments of the local governments. However, this does not mean that any discourse based on culture-led regeneration, especially when this comes too close to an unquestioned faith or an ideology, should be uncritically celebrated. In the cases presented, the *sea* and *seaside* more specifically emerge as particular ambiguous environmental and cultural constructs to be further investigated. Scholars should be encouraged to remain critical and conscious of the meaning-attribution process through which some urban resources are regarded as "cultural" while others are not. In other words, the mechanisms and the key actors that convert local assets into acknowledged legitimate forms of culture which are expected to drive future urban development should not be taken for granted. Some local resources, in fact, might be downplayed and will never reach the status of a "cultural attraction" that is so craved at the moment.

References

Albrechts L (2004) Strategic (spatial) planning re-examined. Environ Plann B Plann Des 31 (5):743–758

Albrechts L (2006) Shifts in strategic spatial planning? Some evidence from Europe and Australia. Environ Plann A 38(6):1149–1170

Amin A, Thrift N (2002) Cities: reimagining the urban. Polity, Cambridge

Battilani P, Fauri F (2009) The rise of a service-based economy and its transformation: seaside tourism and the case of Rimini. J Tour Hist 1(1):27–48

Becheri E (1991) Rimini and Co—the end of a legend? Dealing with the algae effect. Tour Manag 12(3):229–235

Brownill S (2013) Just add water: waterfront regeneration as a global phenomenon. In: Leary ME, McCarthy J (eds) The Routledge companion to urban regeneration. Routledge, London, New York, NY, pp 45–55

Bryman A (2012) Social research methods. Oxford University Press, Oxford

Buckley R (2012) Sustainable tourism: research and reality. Ann Tour Res 39(2):528–546

Cochrane A (2007) Understanding urban policy: a critical introduction. Blackwell, Malden, MA

Comunian R (2011) Rethinking the creative city: the role of complexity, networks and interactions in the urban creative economy. Urban Stud 48(6):1157–1179

Cousin S (2008) L'Unesco et la doctrine du tourisme culturel. Civilisations 57(1):41–56

Davoudi S, Strange I (eds) (2009) Conceptions of space and place in strategic spatial planning. Routledge, New York, NY

Evans G (2003) Hard-branding the cultural city—from Prado to Prada. Int J Urban Reg Res 27 (2):417–440

Gordon I, Buck N (2005) Introduction: cities in the new conventional wisdom. In: Buck N, Gordon I, Harding A, Turok I (eds) Changing cities. Rethinking urban competitiveness, cohesion and governance. Palgrave Publishers Limited, New York, NY

Harvey D (1989) From managerialism to entrepreneurialism: the transformation in urban governance in late capitalism. Geogr Ann Ser B Hum Geogr 71(B1):3–17

Healey P (2007) Urban complexity and spatial strategies: towards a relational planning for our times. Routledge, New York, NY

Hoffman LM, Fainstein SS, Judd DR (eds) (2003) Cities and visitors: regulating people, markets, and city space. Blackwell, Malden, MA

Jamrozy U (2007) Marketing of tourism: a paradigm shift toward sustainability. Int J Cult Tour Hosp Res 1(2):117–130

Lees L (2004) Urban geography: discourse analysis and urban research. Prog Hum Geogr 28 (1):101–107

Lichrou M, O'Malley L, Patterson M (2008) Place-product or place narrative (s)? Perspectives in the marketing of tourism destinations. J Strateg Mark 16(1):27–39

Lucarelli A, Giovanardi M (2014) The political nature of brand governance: a discourse analysis approach to a regional brand building process. J Public Aff. doi:10.1002/pa.1557

MacCallum D, Hopkins D (2011) The changing discourse of city plans: rationalities of planning in Perth, 1955–2010. Plann Theory Pract 12(4):485–510

Martufi F (2012) Percorsi, risultati e incertezze nella pianificazione strategica a Pesaro. Prisma Economia Società Lavoro IV(2):125–137

Miles S, Paddison R (2005) Introduction: the rise and rise of culture-led urban regeneration. Urban Stud 42(5/6):833–839

Patel K (ed) (2012) The cultural politics of Europe: European capitals of culture and European Union since 1980. Routledge, London

Pearce DG (2001) An integrative framework for urban tourism research. Ann Tour Res 28(4):926–946

Richards G (2014) Creativity and tourism in the city. Curr Issue Tour 17(2):119–144

Robinson M, Smith M (eds) (2006) Cultural tourism in a changing world. Politics, participation and (re)presentation. Channel View Publication, Cleveland

Smith MK, Robinson M (eds) (2006) Cultural tourism in a changing world: politics, participation and (re)presentation. Channel View Publications, Bristol

Spirou C (2011) Urban tourism and urban change: *cities in a global economy*. Routledge, London, New York, NY

Uriely N (2005) The tourist experience. Ann Tour Res 32(1):199–216

Weaver DB (1991) Alternative to mass tourism in Dominica. Ann Tour Res 18(3):414–432

Zukin S (1995) The cultures of cities. Blackwell, Cambridge, MA

Zukin S (2012) The social production of urban cultural heritage: identity and ecosystem on an Amsterdam shopping street. City Cult Soc 3(1):281–291

Part III
City Tourism Performance and Urban Wellbeing: Tensions, Risks and Potential Trade-Offs

Venice Reshaped? Tourist Gentrification and Sense of Place

Paola Minoia

Abstract This chapter is aimed to explore the role of tourism in reshaping historical cities, particularly into forms of cosmopolitan consumption. New mobility paradigms seem to merge production and consumption patterns of tourists and residents, all influenced by similar gazing and performing places. The iconic case of Venice shows patterns of staged authenticity, reconstructed ethnicity, and economy of subordination. Drivers to visit Venice include experiences in a setting that is densely characterised by cultural heritage; however, the tourist monoculture and cosmopolitan consumption have depleted the original elements of this attraction: traditional places, residents, livelihoods, material and immaterial cultures. Culture markets and international events, architectural and environmental restoration, together with private forms of transport in the fragile lagoon ecosystem, have transformed the historical city and its unique lifestyle into a place for cosmopolitan consumption, involving tourists together with new residents, sometimes integrating wealthy long-term residents in this overall tourism gentrification. Deprived of great part of what is considered to be the old and conservative block of residents, the gentrified residents acquire spaces for their cultural activities and political acts in their 'saving Venice' projects. Two gentrifying groups are described in this chapter: super rich with their philanthropic associations, and intellectuals. Despite clear differences in their causes and agency, both share common visions over leisurely uses of the lagoon city, artistic production and consumption of its heritage. Sustainability questions could instead propose to start from local memories to reconstruct Venice as a complex urban space with more inclusive sense of place.

Keywords Gentrification • Tourism • Authentication • Cosmopolitan consumption • Right to the city • Sense of place

P. Minoia (✉)
University of Helsinki, Helsinki, Finland
e-mail: paola.minoia@helsinki.fi

© Springer International Publishing Switzerland 2017   261
N. Bellini, C. Pasquinelli (eds.), *Tourism in the City*,
DOI 10.1007/978-3-319-26877-4_18

1 Orientalism and Authenticity as Gentrifying Modes

When we think of Venice it is natural to think of a hyper-tourist city (Costa and Martinotti 2003). Massive tourism in Venice is still growing and has reached 25 million visitors in 2014 with great impacts on the city. However, this chapter will discuss about specific phenomena in gentrification that have interested Venice as well as other tourist cities, where a periodical presence of small but powerful groups of educated urbanities promote new place experiences in selected neighbourhoods (Gotham 2005; Miro' 2011; Zukin 2009). While the chapter is theoretically based, the analysis is qualitative involving participant observation in the historic city and its lagoon and discourse analysis of books, blogs and other media.

Like other tourist centres, Venice is interested by increasing global mobility of people, beyond holidays' or short business travels' spheres, and in constant condition of move corresponding to chosen cosmopolitan lifestyles, merging tourism gazing and residential practices. In fact, these mobilities have great influence upon the residential spatiality as well, giving value to specific elements, which they recognise and promote through *authentication* processes (MacCannell 1973).

Temporary and recursive mobility is not new, but culturally rooted in the Romanticist era of travels. During the nineteenth century, they were constitutive of living practices for Western artists and writers in search for oriental inspiring experiences, such as Byron, Chateaubriand, or Goethe among others involved in the *Italian Grand Tour* (Ujma 2003). These were experiences of cosmopolitanism of a *niche* expressing specialised consumptions rarely interacting with those of locals. Specific services were in place to serve their needs, while local residents mostly neglected their presence.

Now with a wider generalisation of welfare and easier travel opportunities, the search for status recognition passes through voluntary, often leisurely experience of replacements for many more people. While the previously recalled romantic writers searching for orientalism challenged themselves as pioneer in culturally unexplored areas, the new cosmopolitans establish part of their lives in areas where to follow the aspiration of being part in glamorous bohemian locations. Places are seen for their residential setting and for their consumption offer, rather than for their employment potentials.

Besides the higher numbers of people involved, linked in globalised networks potentially aiming for high social and cultural class self-segregation, there are other characteristics differentiating these postmodern travellers from earlier romantic travellers. What can be observed from a geographical point of view is the caused impact in terms of consuming and reproducing places, together with wider cultural influence over long-term residents.

Still a sort of *orientalism* can be recognised, if we consider Said's (1978) definition as a general patronising attitude of the cosmopolitan groups towards the societies of their transitional residences, which are seen as static and less developed. More than in other western tourist cities, the orientalist gaze seems to fit well in Venice, for the exotic charm of its landscape with no cars but wooden boats in waterways and a labyrinth of streets with buildings like in a medina.

It is thus interesting to scrutinise how these new presences are relevant not only for their specific forms of consumption but also for their space narratives and the very production of new space territorialities. Their influence in Venice is neglected by local leaders compared to the phenomena of mass tourism that obscure other ongoing urban processes; or in some cases, it is welcome as a way to reactivate the city. In Venice, besides a continuous marketing of its spectacular heritage in the city centre, one can recognise a new development turn in peripheral neighbourhoods and lagoon islands, which corresponds to the gazing and performing needs of these new cultural elites. No matter their awareness of the structural problems of Venice and its lagoon, their interest is to reproduce patterns of staged authenticity, back to an idealised landscape of the city. These transnational presences produce cultural, political, economic impacts and inequalities, in the way their speculative liveli-hoods contribute in deepening gentrifying forces at the expenses of local ethnicities, although these are closely present in their ideal and narrated landscape. New cosmopolitan identities are created, with new sense of place for Venice; but in reality, poor and low-middle classes of locals have no choice than move out of the city centre, and possibly become daily commuters involved in *servient* economies (Veijola and Valtonen 2007) exploiting the city landscape (Quinn 2007). Tourist gentrification is therefore, a force producing different outcomes: excluding working classes from the right to the city, delocalising productions and services, and reorganising the daily commuters' mobility (Lefebvre 1967; Harvey 2008).

On the other side, other social groups take the lead in the evolution of a new *sense of place* for Venice. This geographical concept (Tuan 1977; Massey 2005) does not only pertain to the psychological sphere of the residents, but also implies personal and political engagement. Moreover, globalisation and tourism marketi-zation have diversified the category of residents in the historical cities, more and more involved in tourism gentrification processes (Gotham 2005).

Explanations of these new trends cannot be solely seen within the tourism discipline, as new forms of tourism. Instead, we need to refer to *the new mobilities paradigm*, as Sheller and Urry (2006) have named the spatial practices created by globalisation and wider generalisation of welfare. Social studies need nowadays to focus on issues of movements, in reaction to the *sedentarist* theories, which locate "bounded and authentic places or regions or nations as the fundamental basis of human identity and experience and as the basic units of social research" (*ibid.*, pp. 208–209).

Within this new mobilities paradigm, Duncan (2012) has focused, more specif-ically, on a sort of *transnationalism* confusing spaces of tourism with places of living, and addressed by new merging visions from tourism, migration and urban studies. An interesting perspective looks at new trends that, instead of turning towards the end of tourism, promote tourism everywhere; or at least, this is what seems to correspond to the current development of Venice.

Urban research intersects this area of study, particularly through the analysis of gentrification. What Lees (2003) has discussed for instance about the super-gentrification in New York, with higher classes' intrusion at the expenses of low-class and middle-class residents, can also be applied to Venice.

The new cosmopolitanism presented in the Naked City by Zukin, again speaking of New York, is also relevant here to understand the new lifestyles that are imported and the processes of authentication that give them authority and power over other classes of residents and their forms of life: "Claiming authenticity becomes prevalent at a time when identities are unstable and people are judged by their performance rather than by their history or innate character. Under these conditions, authenticity differentiates a person, a product, or a group from its competitors; it confers an aura of moral superiority, a strategic advantage that each can use to its own benefit" (2009, p. XII). Not the attachment to history or tradition, then, is what counts, but rather, uniqueness and innovative, creative authenticity that "has a schizoid quality" (*ibid.*) and is made up of bits and pieces of cultural references: fictional qualities for cultural users of the city, who consume its art, food, and images and also its real estate. Thus, authenticity becomes a tool, along with the economic and political power, to control not just the look but also the use of real urban places.

Similar urban developments have occurred in other cities, and particularly in suburbs where residents have imposed rigid landscape policies responding to their desires of aesthetic relations with places, and alleged authenticity's defence. It is the case, for instance, of the neighbourhoods described in *Paris bourgeois-bohème* by Corbillé (2013), and of Bedford, a suburb 40 km from New York City described by Duncan and Duncan (2010).

More in line with the temporality of the residence, typical of super- or tourist gentrification, McWatters (2009) has also introduced the very intriguing concept of *landscape nomadism*, involving the idea of people repacking when in need to find their utopian landscape elsewhere. Like for Zukin, it is important here to base the motivations for staying upon ideas of preservation of the alleged authenticity, which make them oppose to the additional growth of tourism in the areas where they have decided to base their various residences. Quite often, in fact, these mobile elites express their cosmopolitanism by gathering in different locations in the world, where they have properties: in Paris, London, Venice, New York, Montecarlo or in luxury *riads* of Marrakech (Martin 2013). Within these *world cities* (Pacione 2005; Ashworth and Page 2011) they select specific neighbourhoods. Their *authenticity* ideas involve a romanticised image of landscape: a mix of natural paradise and social utopia formed by social status, exclusivity and elitism. However, while the concept of landscape nomadism is important to explain the temporary phase of one's move and the importance of this new type of mobility in one's life experience, it does not clarify the strong impacts it has on places and their identities.

These *new mobilities* can be ascribed to the tourism zone, as in the same way, they use gazing and performing to exercise power (Urry 2002; Coles and Church 2007; Larsen and Urry 2011). The *new mobilities* do not challenge, but on the contrary, further increase the 'touristicization' of the city, intended as commodification of surely marketable material and immaterial cultures and lifestyles. These are groups of recursive visitors, owning second or multiple homes and acting under the influence of a tourist gaze which they apply also in their new residential spaces. The capillarity of their intrusive presence is seduced by the idea of pioneering 'unbeaten tracks'. Their elitist and critical look makes them culturally and politically strong and more influent towards the longer-term residents; and more so than other short-term tourists, who have superficial relations with the city and are rather manipulated by market operators. Instead, these mobile class members are influent as their gazing and performing styles get transposed to the locals, who are themselves flattered by their attention and weakened by their cultural hegemony.

For permanent residents, living in the city is constantly conceptualised as practices are referred to mental models of living in this special city; but at the same time, distinctive living pattern that were common only few decades ago, start to be out of use and forgotten. One example is the everyday use of boats for internal city mobility and transportation of goods that is nowadays challenged by the absence of mooring rights, since the few available spaces are rigidly assigned to a few; this allows people to circulate but not to stop, and makes boats useful for touring but not as ordinary means of transport. Because of an international attention *vis-à-vis* to the practical residential challenges, staying in Venice becomes less natural than it used to be; and on the contrary, because of structural conditions that constantly challenge their living downtown, for a great number of residents it requires daily confirmations and hard choices, and seems to be more and more a matter of resistance and defence of idealised identities, also passing through continuous sharing of international causes for specific safeguarding issues, e.g., against the large cruise ship access or the motorboats waves (*moto ondoso*) causing erosion to the city foundations. However, while these causes mainly involve the protection of physical environmental and heritage capitals, they rarely address less recognisable local economies, cultures, traditional knowledge or public services, such as e.g., ensuring basic commerce, securitising fishing rights, protecting creative glass productions, creating children playgrounds and spaces for elderly, supporting disabled residents, other vulnerable migrants, and so forth. Who has remained to fight for these? As a matter of fact, the right to the city has been denied for a large majority, as proved by the demographic trends showing a loss of more than 120,000 inhabitants over the last 50 years, bringing their number down to 55,000 in 2016. The generational breakup impedes the transmission of traditional knowledge in Venice. The *new residents* flow is a niche phenomenon and does not fill the gap in quantitative terms, but nonetheless contributes to its new *urbanicity* character. Questioning about the consequences of this gentrification phenomenon helps demonstrating that it is far less liberal than it pretends to be, and that, on the contrary, that it exercises a powerful pressure towards the limitation of the city life and a support of planning in line with the tourist monoculture.

2 New Residents and Their Reflected Power Over Venice

More and more, wealthy outsiders move into Venice, where they say they can live peacefully and with their respect of privacy in a seducing urban context. To quote Zukin, we imagine that also in the Venice landscape they let their own experiences being "seduced by appearances" (2009, p. 21). Venice is no more a local city with old traditions and intimate character, but more and more a world city with cosmopolitan identity.

Compared to other migrants, the new cosmopolitan presences are not silent. New mobile citizens share their thoughts about Venice and their discovery of *new self* in Internet blogs and other mass media. Magazines present the lifestyle in the hidden, *non-tourist* but *private* city with "charming residences, walled gardens, off-guide restaurants, disappearing artisans, and secret museums" (Zambon 2012, p. 69). Often, while declaring their love for the city and its traditions, these new residents happen to even blame previous inhabitants for what they judge as cultural disinterest, political laziness, corruption etc. Blogs posted by foreign residents (e.g., http://theveniceexperience.blogspot.fi, http://iamnotmakingthisup.net) sharing opinions on quality of living in Venice and urban dysfunctionality are well followed also by locals who consider these voices as *super-partes* and neutral. Fictional books, like the Brunetti saga based in Venice written by Donna Leon, an American author living in the lagoon city since the 1980s (http://www.donnaleon.net), do confirm these ideas of a charming city in contrast to the capabilities of its human capital; however in this case, while the large world-wide popularity of the books has become an added driver for international tourist arrivals, these stories are unknown by the majority of the local residents. They are not translated into Italian, nor is the German TV-series, based on the books, proposed by any Italian channel, for a veto posed by the writer who prefers a quiet living in her Venice neighbourhood. Besides these and other publications using Venice as a romantic and decadent scene, other voices are publicly raised through the media, showing concern for a city that seems to die under endogenous forces. Some campaigns are local but also advocated in English, so to gather the *new Venetians* and other international forces in the city's causes.

However, not all *new Venetians* are the same. Yet, there are distinctive patterns of living the city. Two types with distinctive interests over the city and interactions with either globalised or local networks, can be recognised.

2.1 Super-Rich Gentrification

> *In front of the continuous Venetian exodus (...) a new wave of persons has arrived in Venice, to stay, love her and live her (...) They are themselves Venetians, by right (...) those that have arrived for their choice, are even more Venetians than those born in Venice* (Falomo and Pivato 2012, p. 8).

In their book "Venetians by choice", Falomo and Pivato have collected 18 interviews to a particular class of new settlers, which reveal an elitist rather than democratic vision of the right to the city. The introduction contains a blame addressed to the *old* Venetians: "And why—and this is the question that I have in my heart—many desire Venice and make all their possible to possess her, while those who were born there, and have got this happy destiny, now abandon her, do not care of her (. . .) do not want her anymore?" (2012, pp. 7–8) Not only these words reveal a gendered relation between the city as a feminine body and the new residents, acting through a sort of masculinity possession power; they also express a divide between the new residents and 'the others', the original residents, in most cases from low and middle-classes, without even questioning the reasons behind an exodus that is caused by the lack of working options, insufficient residential services and high cost of living. In contrast, one of the new *ideal* Venetians, for the writers, is the well-known designer Philippe Starck, whose aesthetic relation with the *ideal* landscapes of the Northern lagoon is represented by its lonely wanders using his private boat; or Michel Thoulouze, founder of Canal Plus and now a fine winemaker in St. Erasmo; or even the President of the Biennale foundation, despite he was lodging in luxury hotel rooms and moving by water taxis: typically tourist services, rather than residential ones. Their financial and globalised cultural positioning entitles them to perform in ways that obscure more traditional knowledges situated in the lagoon. More into the city, but still outside the overcrowded St. Mark complex, other old neighbourhoods appear glamourised by the new bohemians: for instance, the former poor, industrial (now recuperated and gentrified) island of Giudecca. The idea of this previously insane neighbourhood increases the authenticity value of Giudecca, in a way that may remind of Harlem's rejuvenation and estate speculation of the past decade. Instead of letting the city change on the basis of local productive economies and the needs of the working population, there is much more powerful interest to preserve a spectacular image of the historical heritage, which whatever change would only harm.

Authenticity ideas are based on some iconic images of the city, out of the massive tourism trails: lagoon landscapes with little traffic of traditional boats; few islands with rare gardens; empty narrow streets where to wander; warm social relations with the remaining local residents, casual meetings in the street, invitations for *ombre e cicheti* (wine and appetisers); traditional professions, outdoor markets, small shops, etc. Rare presences there are seen as making the authentic sense of place for the new Venetians, and they are valued for their possibility to enjoy an exclusive consumption of the city.

One objection against this *old authentic Venice* vision is the lack of memory and the ill-correspondence to specific historical periods. During the golden era of the Venice republic, the traffic was quite heavy in canals and the lagoons, as portrayed for instance in some famous Canaletto paintings. Even more recently, until just a few decades ago, the lagoon was more intensively exploited for fish farming and picking; it was not just an empty mirror of the sky, but a productive space, filled with wooden poles, nests and boats. Streets were not that empty either and had more open stalls for manufacturers and sellers. Venice was indeed more inhabited and lively that nowadays.

However, not all new super-rich residents claim they live in isolation; some of them instead use their social relations with *old* Venetians, as a proof of their genuine care for Venice. For instance, the actress Emma Thompson stated in an interview (available in youtube) how much she felt having *earned* Venice, since she got local friends. One question is, how many do really relate to Venetians beyond their provision of services to them (like Starck's fishermen from Burano), or security (like Elton John getting introduced to the neighbours in his condo) or gatekeeping to cultural happenings? And which language do they use?

A few super-rich are also engaged in philanthropy, particularly in causes for restoration of historical buildings. Frances Clarke, founder of the committee Venice in Peril, was nominated Venetian of the year 2006. Other US philanthropists formed various foundations, e.g., Save Venice (http://www.savevenice.org) active since 1971 in preserving works of art and architecture; however, web coverage of their charity events reveal a strange combination of charity and dispossession, for the exclusive use that donors can make of these rehabilitated spaces. Buildings become stages for luxury parties gathering affluent members of international networks; and the idea of Venice as a year-round carnival stage is also present. These rehabilitations, combined with other important acquisitions of buildings and islands by corporations through purchases or long-terms tenancies, further contribute to the shrinking of public goods. After rehabilitation, they all conflate into the tourist and leisure economies, seemingly the only rentable uses nowadays. Restored heritage can eventually host art exhibitions (e.g., the Prada Foundation in Ca' Corner della Regina) or the lagoon environment.

These acquisitions by individual or corporate capital also contribute to changes in place identity. Specific projects over places are reflected into narratives that also change memories, also through new toponymy. Recently, the Marriott has started branding its resort in Sacca Sessola island by renaming it as *Isola delle Rose* (Roses' islands), supposedly more attractive for its customers' targets and with no respect for its identity and history.

For causes that fit rather well in their ideal, frozen landscapism, capitalist gentrifiers have also established alliances with other associations. Would the lagoon become endangered, it is hard to believe they would still maintain a close linkage with it; and most probably, for these landscape nomads it would be the *time to repack* (McWatters 2009).

2.2   Intellectual Gentrification

Other evident presences in the city are those of artists, academics, intellectuals and other cultural elites who have moved into Venice to enjoy its active cultural and international environment, so peculiar for a small-sized city. Compared to the super-rich, these groups show clearer political interest and participate in collective projects for the city, with a new sense of community and responsibility (Popke 2003) over Venice. Coalitions around specific claims, particularly against the sale off of buildings or islands from the public authorities to the private sector, make them quite lively actors and position them closer to some progressive components of the city. These sales are quite common nowadays to fill deficits in public budgets and more and more involve goods and areas that are important for residents. A recent example is the wide participation in a competitive bid to purchase the island of Poveglia thanks to crowdfunding organised by a local association (http://www. povegliapertutti.org) with the aim to preserve it for public use and to counteract the restriction of common goods; other coalitions are formed around similar causes, e.g., to rescue the historical building Villa Herion in Giudecca or St Andrea island from privatisation. Participation in local causes is a strong place attractor, enforcing integration and sense of place. This type of activism goes through social networks and cultural associations aggregating a rather homogenous class of intellectuals and attracting sympathising foreigners, however with minor participation of people born in Venice and practically no representation of local working classes.

As a result of this reduced social representation, new projects in recuperated places involve design products, art exhibition and city gardening, creating new interests for leisurely use of spaces, including boating and cultural industries rather than other productive uses, and again linked to global and tourist markets. Thus, apart from minor cases, in general monuments' restoration is again seen as a form of protection, immobility and exhibit, rather than inclusion in public structures for e.g., vocational, educational or recreational needs of elderly, youth and disadvantaged groups. Romantic ideas about the city correspond to strong idealisation of believed past conditions, and disincentive urban plans supporting working residents' needs. Rehabilitation projects do not attempt to restore local production processes, either traditional or innovative, but remain related to the appearance of a frozen, spectacular and historical heritage city, that any change would only harm. Instead, globalisation of economies and consumptions and the myopia of local rulers, who have failed to take care of the traditional professions and livelihoods, have caused disappearance of local productions and even of the basic small retails, substituted by expensive boutiques and a capillary presence of supermarket chains. These consumption places are more adapted for customers of any origin, as they do not require particular linguistic or cultural interaction with local sellers as pre-packed goods are easily available on shelves.

Again, lower social classes are forgotten, both in terms of political representation and livelihoods' protection. Fishing and handcraft have lost their place in the Venice lagoon and city centre, especially for structural reasons that are beyond the responsibilities of the new urbanities; but these problems would therefore need to be addressed by specific protection and social movements' claims, as locals' spatial knowledge and sense of place is getting lost. However, unfortunately the importance to save their presence and weak economy assets is probably underestimated, and too seldom recalled.

The new residents' interest to preserve the environmental safety of the lagoon is instead more effective, as their environmentalism mostly appears *neutral* towards other political causes regarding the inner society. Protests against the *moto ondoso* and pollution produced by tourist ferries endangering the traditional sailing or against the big ships crossing the Canale della Giudecca are highly relevant and immediately understood by the new residents. They do not challenge but, again, fit rather well in their ideal landscape.

So, despite clear differences with the super-rich residents, these types of networks still belong to the tourism gentrification processes. The memory of past uses of the city space guides their authentication of places and new forms of living. They share visions, albeit politically different, over leisurely rather than productive, uses of the urban and lagoon spaces, enjoying the lifestyle of a rather homogenous urbanity.

3 Reshaping Venice as a City Beyond Utopic Landscapes

Is Venice depicted as a true home? Housing is hardly affordable by low and middle classes, and this is a fundamental reason for the progressive suburbanisation of Venice that has brought people and activities out of the historical city. The new inhabitants, basically more affluent, are clearly not fast tourists and claim deep relations with the city and its inhabitants (although most of the time these are daily commuters). However, mostly these presences do not re-energise labour markets beyond the tourism economies and are even indifferent to the functioning of public residential services such as schools, community centres or social supports.

Is the historic city of Venice a world city? Areas that were used as factories, residences, associations' homes, monasteries, etc. have become spaces for arts, design, social gatherings, branded shopping, restaurants and wine bars, to keep alive the circuit of the new residents and their consumption interests. As mentioned before, Venice presents a lot of commonality with other gentrified cities, e.g., New York (Newman and Wyly 2006) and other world cities, because it is stronger in its global links than as a gateway for the surrounding region; but at the same time, its vitality is too exclusively flattened on tourism, leisure and art consumption services. This extreme specificity challenges the very nature of Venice as a city, according to Ashworth and Page's (2011) definition based on multifunctionality and tourists' invisibility. Settis also describes Venice as a dying city. He recalls the need to maintain a social and anthropological diversity and particularly its *civic capital*: "rooted in long-term mechanisms of intergenerational transmission (...) it includes the notion of 'civic culture', a collective sense of values, rights and social memory having cultural, political and economic dimension" (2014, p. 107). More-over, for Settis "the right to the city shall be linked to the social function of property (...) and job right (...) strictly united by juridical, ethical, economic and functional links" (2014, p. 109).

In fact, the tourist gentrification of Venice cannot only be seen as an outcome of coincident will expressed by wealthy bourgeoisies. As pointed out by Gotham (2005), we cannot only assume that demand-side factors left alone drive the process, but we need also to consider the production-side perspective and recognise the role of the local institutions in the tourist gentrification process. Political willingness of the local government would be determinant in guaranteeing protection and reactivation of place-based cultures and livelihoods, against corporative interests and the tourist consumption loop. However, as a matter of fact, Venice has lacked a real governance of the city development. The latest administrations have mostly valued Venice as an economic profitable resource rather than a complex living environment; not only they have overlooked the impacts of big events like the Carnival and Biennale festivals, of the cruise ships going to the Venice Terminal and of other mega infrastructures, but they do not show active role in residence rights in the historic centre. As said, rehabilitation has advanced in form of occasional, mostly privately funded projects targeting the physical capital while the social components have been marginalised. The vacuum of regulations in favour of traditional activities has increased the vulnerability of resident groups and their livelihoods. Instead, during the past two decades free market principles have been followed dogmatically by local administrations. The liberalisation of retails has modified completely the commerce in the city and caused the closure of a pre-existing network of small shops, manufacturers and workshops. New regula-tions of fishing and fish markets contributed to an irreversible decline of most traditional, family-run cooperatives; while liberalisation of B&B and the failed control of illegal hospitality have eroded the real housing offer. The internationalisation of the housing market has made housing impossible to afford for most wages.

More recently, a few residents have started showing resistance to this process of depletion of traditional knowledge and livelihoods. Exercises of place memories have taken place, recalling past traditions and uses of public spaces with old pictures, music and movies shared in Facebook, theatre performances, interviews to old people in newspapers, etc. New civic networks have also been created with a more advanced interest to intervene in the urban political discourse, letting local voices to fill the governance gap and asking for more determined protection of housing rights. One example is the *Gruppo 25 Aprile*, a civic platform for Venice and its lagoon constituted in 2014, in which active residents reclaim the centrality of the right to the city in the governance discourse for Venice: "Like native Indians in America (in the nineteenth century) we now risk being forced out of our environment (...) Forced out of the lagoon, to live on the other side of the bridge (the mainland)" (http://gruppo25aprile.org/for-our-many-foreign-friends/). This idea of an emptying city is well represented through the metaphor of the empty niche in a wall of Venice (Fig. 1), for the group asks the city rulers to engage more

Fig. 1 "What happened to the character that had been positioned in the stone niche? Where are the residents? If saving Venice only means to preserve that piece of wall, we would have failed". *Source*: http:// gruppo25aprile.org/2015/02/

to preserve all urban components of the city, through more inclusive residential, employment and social service policies, and through proactive support to endangered cultures and livelihoods. Venice needs to be reshaped to regain social complexity and inclusiveness and go back to being a city. Basic commerce, fishing rights, artisan business, creative productions, knowledge centres, city gardens, playgrounds, spaces for elderly and migrant groups: who would not like to repopulate Venice if these conditions are met, despite the tourists?

4 Conclusions

Is it too late to recuperate the soul and nature of Venice as a place to live? How can a true re-appropriation of the right to the city occur despite mass tourism and the new cosmopolitan gentrifiers imposing their lifestyles? As Massey (2005) put it, no city can claim having unique sense of place or single essential identity but necessarily reflects plurality of dynamic identities that are socially produced, negotiated and represented. Representation and recognition of the right to the city for of all social and ethnic components are thus fundamental, including long-term residents who still maintain local memories and attachment, together with the new residents. Venice is perhaps more fragile than other cities, but shares common experiences with other historical centres in Europe, like Barcelona and Berlin, where social movements have been created moving from anti-tourist resentments into constructive urban preservation projects with residents' protection aims. Analysing these cases together may open new research ideas on cosmopolitan urban assemblages that can both feed critical urban theories and help finding elements for inclusive governance, aiming to more socially just and ecologically sound urbanism.

References

Ashworth G, Page SJ (2011) Urban tourist research: recent progress and current paradoxes. Tour Manag 32(1):1–15

Coles T, Church A (2007) Tourism, politics and the forgotten entanglements of power. In: Church A, Coles T (eds) Tourism, power and space. Routledge, New York, NY, pp 1–42

Corbillé S (2013) Paris bourgeoise, Paris bohème: La ruée vers l'Est. Presses Universitaires de France, Paris

Costa N, Martinotti G (2003) Sociological theories of tourism and regulation theory. In: Hoffman LM, Feinstein SS, Judd DR (eds) Cities and visitors. Regulating people, markets and city space. Blackwell, Malden, pp 53–71

Duncan T (2012) The 'mobilities turn' and the geography of tourism. In: Wilson J (ed) The Routledge handbook of tourism geographies. Routledge, Abingdon, pp 113–119

Duncan JS, Duncan NG (2010) The aestheticization of the politics of landscape preservation. Ann Assoc Am Geogr 92(2):387–409

Falomo C, Pivato M (2012) Veneziani per scelta. I racconti di chi ha deciso di vivere in laguna. La Toletta, Venezia

Gotham KF (2005) Tourism gentrification: the case of New Orleans' Vieux Carre (French Quarter). Urban Stud 42(7):1099–1121

Harvey D (2008) The right to the city. New Left Rev 53:23–40

Larsen J, Urry J (2011) Gazing and performing. Environ Plan D Soc Space 29(6):1110–1125

Lees L (2003) Super-gentrification: the case of Brooklyn Heights, New York City. Urban Stud 40 (12):2487–2509

Lefebvre H (1967) Le droit à la ville. L'homme et la société 6:29–35

MacCannell D (1973) Staged authenticity: arrangements of social space in tourist settings. Am J Sociol 79(3):589–603

Martin JJ (2013) Countess Marta Marzotto in Her Moroccan Home. Wall St J 21.08.2013

Massey D (2005) For space. Sage, London

McWatters MR (2009) Residential tourism: (de)constructing paradise. Channel View Publications, Bristol

Miro' SV (2011) Producing a "successful city": neoliberal urbanism and gentrification in the tourist city. The case of Palma (Majorca). Urban Stud Res 2011:1–13

Newman K, Wyly E (2006) The right to stay put, revisited: gentrification and resistance to displacement in New York City. Urban Stud 43(1):23–57

Pacione M (2005) Urban geography. Routledge, London

Popke EJ (2003) Poststructuralist ethics: subjectivity, responsibility and the space of community. Prog Hum Geogr 27(3):298–316

Quinn B (2007) Performing tourism in Venice: local residents in focus. Ann Tour Res 34 (2):458–476

Said EW (1978) Orientalism. Vintage, New York, NY

Settis S (2014) Se Venezia muore. Einaudi, Torino

Sheller M, Urry J (2006) The new mobilities paradigm. Environ Plan A 38(2):207–226

Tuan YF (1977) Space and place: the perspective of experience. University of Minnesota Press, Minneapolis

Ujma C (2003) Rome. In: Speake J (ed) Literature of travel and exploration. An encyclopedia, vol 3 R to Z index. Taylor and Francis, New York, NY and London, pp 1024–1028

Urry J (2002). The Tourist Gaze 2.0. Sage, London

Veijola S, Valtonen A (2007) The body in tourism industry. In: Pritchard A, Morgan N, Ateljevic I, Harris C (eds) Tourism and gender: embodiment, sensuality and experience. CABI, Wallingford, pp 13–31

Zambon E (2012) Venezia privata. La Repubblica DCasa 1:69–74

Zukin S (2009) Naked city. The death and life of authentic urban places. Oxford University Press, New York, NY

Websites

http://gruppo25aprile.org
http://iamnotmakingthisup.net/about
http://www.me-de-a.com/project/docu-film-lagunemine/
http://theveniceexperience.blogspot.fi/#sthash.0apn8AkX.dpbs
www.donnaleon.net
www.povegliapertutti.org
www.savevenice.org
www.youtube.com/watch?v=zm68ZJLp8V8

Urban Tourism Development in Prague: From Tourist Mecca to Tourist Ghetto

Veronika Dumbrovská

Abstract Prague has become a significant tourist destination in Europe over the past 25 years. This development has been rapid and unbalanced. This chapter will deal with the changing socio-spatial patterns of tourism in the historic centre of Prague, with a particular focus on the Royal Way. Based on a combination of qualitative and quantitative research methods (such as in-depth interviews with local residents, an analysis of retail outlets on the Royal Way, and an analysis of secondary statistical data on tourism and economic development in Prague), the changing business activities in the historic centre of Prague and their impact on the local community and tourism itself will be analysed. The findings will show that privatisation, restitution, as well as the absence of tourism management have had a profound impact on tourism in Prague, and have contributed to the creation of a tourist ghetto on the Royal Way.

Keywords Touristification • Tourist trap • Royal Way • Transformation • Prague

1 Introduction

Urban tourism has become one of the most significant types of tourism over the last two decades as the number of tourists in urban destinations has started to increase and the tourist industry has grown, and continues to grow. Centres of cities have been changing under the pressure of tourism industries and the formerly residential function has been forced out. Urban tourism precincts have evolved in these locations, sometimes spontaneously, sometimes pre-planned (Spirou 2008).

These processes intertwine with worldwide socio-economic changes. Globalisation, decentralisation and deindustrialisation have caused the crisis of inner cities. In response, city planners and policy makers have tried to find other economic rationales for urban growth (Spirou 2008); "in the 1980s some cities managed to

This article was supported by Charles University in Prague, project GA UK No. 814116.

V. Dumbrovská (✉)
Faculty of Science, Department of Social Geography and Regional Development, Charles University in Prague, Albertov 6, 128 43 Prague, Czech Republic
e-mail: veronika.dumbrovska@natur.cuni.cz

N. Bellini, C. Pasquinelli (eds.), *Tourism in the City*,
DOI 10.1007/978-3-319-26877-4_19

275

make a smooth transition from industrial wasteland to tourist mecca" (Fainstein and Judd 1999, p. 12). The transition of society from an industrial to a post-industrial (consumer) one, facilitated by increased discretionary income and leisure time, caused the growth of demand for tourism (Roberts 1999). Together with the development in transport and informational technologies, cities have become proper destinations for the postmodern consumption of leisure time (Selby 2004). As Ashworth states "...only cities have the critical mass of such resources to attract and satisfy tourism demands" (2009, p. 209).

Prague entered the world tourist market in 1990 after the fall of the communist regime in Czechia (formerly Czechoslovakia[1]). Before 1989, urban tourism in Prague was mostly limited to visitors from the former socialist countries, which constituted 90 % of foreign visitors (Hoffman and Musil 1999). A central planned economy and significant restriction on private ownership stalled the development of the tourist industry in Prague. The historic centre of Prague was strongly protected and development focused on outer parts of the city. This conservation of the historic centre has had significant consequences for urban tourism today. On the one hand, the historic centre has preserved the original character of its fourteenth-century layout (Hoffman and Musil 1999), and on the other, neglecting urban development in the historic centre has led to the dilapidation of some historical buildings.

The Velvet Revolution in 1989 gave rise to a new political regime and profound changes in society and the economy. In the early 1990s the processes of transformation from central planned economy to capitalist system were launched. "The main pillars of transformation were privatisation of state assets and liberalisation of prices" (Sýkora 1999, p. 81). According to Sýkora there were three major outcomes of transformation "which influenced urban development in Prague: (1) new societal rules based on democratic policy and market principles; (2) a vast number of private actors operating in the city (including property owners); (3) an openness of local economic systems to international economic forces" (1999, p. 81). The aim of this chapter is to assess the changing socio-spatial aspects of tourism development in Prague and its impact on local residents as well as on tourism itself.

2 Study Design

2.1 Research Area

The research was conducted in the historic centre of Prague, which was designated as an Urban Landmark Reservation in 1971, and in 1993 was inscribed on the UNESCO World Heritage list. The area covers 894.94 ha and includes historic

---

[1]Czechia (geographical name for the political entity, the Czech Republic) was established in 1993 as one of the successor states of former Czechoslovakia (The Czech and Slovak Federative Republic).

districts of Prague: Old Town, Josefov, Lesser Town, Hradcany, New Town and Vysehrad. Particular attention was focused on the so-called Royal Way, the most visited part of Prague (see Kádár 2013; Dumbrovská and Fialová 2014). This route is 2.4 km long and connects the most remarkable sights in Prague on both sides of the river Vltava: Municipal House, Old Town Square, Charles Bridge, Lesser Town Square and Prague Castle.

2.2 Data Collection and Methods

The research was based on a combination of qualitative and quantitative methods. Primary as well as secondary data were used. In the first stage, secondary statistical data on tourism (number of hotels, beds, and tourists) in Prague were analysed. This part of the research was included in order to obtain an overall view of the development of tourism in Prague. In the second stage, the contemporary situation of tourism development in the historic centre of Prague was analysed, based on a survey (or mapping) of the retail outlets in the most visited part of Prague, the so-called Royal Way. The survey was carried out in summer 2015. In the third stage, in-depth interviews were conducted with residents living (or who used to live) in the historic centre of Prague. Fifteen interviews were undertaken, involving ten women and five men between the age of 40 and 60. The gender distribution of the sample was based on the fact that primarily women take care of the household and family and thus they are more sensitive to the changes of essential retail outlets, which was confirmed by the research. The age range was chosen based on two premises. Firstly, respondents should be in the economically active age to gauge the aspects associated with daily activity and leisure time spent in the historic centre. Secondly, respondents should have lived in the centre of Prague before 1989 to be able to compare the situation before and after the Velvet Revolution and identify the changes after the Revolution. The aim of the survey was to capture the experience of local residents with the changes the historic centre of Prague has undergone due to tourism development and how they have dealt with it. The interviewed residents comprise mainly middle income or slightly higher income groups. Seven respondents work in the public sector (secondary school teacher, primary school teacher, after school child carer, school counsellor, office worker at the post-office, personal assistant a Ministry, researcher) and eight of them work in the private sector (singer, architect, actor, self-employed in the building industry, private medical doctor, lower manager in a business company, restaurant owner, plumber). Every respondent has more than one child, five on them live in a household with their adult children, nine respondents live only with their partner, and one lives alone.

The fourth stage involved a questionnaire survey with Prague residents in pre-selected locations, which was undertaken by students of the University of Business in Prague on behalf of the Czech Tourism Authority in January 2015. Two locations were selected: the firsts in the most touristic part of Prague, i.e. the Old Town Square, and the second in a more residential part of Prague, i.e. Stromovka (a large park in the inner city). The questionnaire survey aimed to assess the satisfaction of local residents with tourism development in Prague. This survey is a part of broader research interests dealing with the overall local residents' satisfaction with tourism development in tourist-attractive locations of Czechia. Respondents of the survey were local residents living within 30 km of the survey area and spending a minimum of three days per week in the locality. In total, 100 questionnaires were undertaken in Prague (50 in Old Town Square and 50 in Stromovka). The selection of respondents in each location was based on predetermined quotas by age and sex (25 men and 25 women).

3   Key Findings

3.1   Economic Transformation and Tourism Development in the Historic Centre of Prague

Tourism in Prague has evolved rapidly. In the 1990s structural transformation started market-led changes in the city environment. The most important mechanisms at the urban level were restitution and privatisation (mostly the so-called small privatisation).[2] According to Sýkora (1994), 70 % of total housing stock in Prague 1 (the central historic district) returned to their original (pre-communist era) owners. The liberalisation of prices and bad condition of buildings led in many cases to an immediate sale of the property, often to foreign capital. The small privatisation between 1991 and 1992 had a profound impact on the functional changes of retail outlets and services in Prague's historic centre. Sýkora states that "nearly 2,500 shops, restaurants and smaller enterprises found new owners or tenants in the small privatisation auctions. . ." (1994, p. 1156). Due to an increasing tourist demand induced by the opening of the state borders to western countries, the supply side (mostly) in historic centre of Prague began to transform in favour of the tourism sector. "Tourism in general and accommodation in particular have attracted more foreign investment than other branches of the economy and triggered a dramatic cycle of hotel building and their reconstruction" (Hoffman and Musil 1999, p. 184). By 1996, the number of beds in collective accommodation had increased by more than 300 % and the number of collective accommodation establishment rose from 111 units in 1989 to 385 in 1996. The number of foreign tourists in collective accommodation increased in the same period by 80 % (Statistical Yearbook of the Czech and Slovak Federative Republic 1990–1992, Statistical Yearbook of the Czech Statistical 1993–1997). If we include tourists in private accommodation units and tourists visiting friends and relatives, the real number of visitors was almost twice as high. "On the one hand, the huge inflow of commercial

---

[2]"The aim of small privatisation was to sell small state-own businesses by mean of public auction into private hand." (Sýkora 1994, p. 1156).

investment facilitated the physical and economic revitalisation of the dingy city centre; on the other hand, however, it led to rather negative consequences, including population decline, traffic overload, and conflict with the historical heritage bodies" (Ouředníček and Temelová 2009, p. 17).

According to interviews with local residents, the changes in functional structure of retail outlets were evident immediately after the revolution. They predominantly state that within 5 years of the end of the communist regime the historic centre of Prague had changed dramatically. The former resident-used facilities like cinemas, cafeterias, bookstores and other essential stores (e.g. grocers, butchers, bakers, ironmongers, etc.) have been fading away and new facilities that serve tourist demand have started to appear. "The urban changes in post-communist Prague [...] have been influenced especially by internationalisation and globalisation." (Sýkora et al. 2000, p. 63). On the one hand, a profound impact of globalisation in the form of large international/global chains (such as McDonalds, KFC, Ritz, Hilton, Billa, etc.) can be observed, and on the other hand, small businesses owned by immigrants from south-eastern Europe have started to emerge (especially from Bulgaria and the former Yugoslavia, Čermáková 2012); "a significant factor contributing to foreign ownership has been the difficulty Czech entrepreneurs have had in borrowing money at reasonable rates" (Hoffman and Musil 1999, p. 184).

Alongside the market liberalisation, the other significant effect associated with the increasing level of international tourism in Prague was an increase in prices. Most of the interviewed residents perceive tourist inflation as constraining. For instance, the residents are ceasing to dine in local restaurants because of price increases.

On the other hand, transformation and the subsequent marked economy have had a positive impact on the overall condition of historic buildings. Foreign investment in the historic centre of Prague and raising revenue from the rental of ground-floor parts of buildings to cafés, restaurants and small shops has allowed for repairs of historical buildings in the city centre. This particular change was perceived by all respondents as the most significant one.

3.2   The Tourist Ghetto on the Royal Way

The processes of touristification of Prague's city centre that started in the 1990s have intensified over time and brought negative effects because of the overwhelming concentration of tourism in the historic core. In 2015, there were 168 retail outlets, 121 restaurants, and 44 accommodation establishments concentrated on Prague's Royal Way. More than 90 % of these facilities could be assessed as tourist-oriented according to the type of goods and services they provide and their price level. Most of the retail outlets consist of souvenir shops, jewellery (mostly Czech garnet) and crystal (mostly labelled as Czech crystal). Other tourist facilities comprise 19 exchange offices, 5 Thai massage services, 3 museums of chocolate, 2 museums of torture, 2 wax museums and 1 Ghosts and Legends Museum.

Local residents, especially women, perceived the overall touristification of Prague's historic centre as insulting their (Czech, Prague) culture. They complained about the type of goods offered on the Royal Way, which are according to most of the respondents mostly kitschy or of fake authenticity.[3] One respondent, who used to live in Lesser Town Square, states that the Royal Way looks like Disneyland, where everything is made only for tourist enjoyment.

The questionnaire survey, as well as in-depth interviews, shows that the perceived level of tourist activity in the historic centre is very high. Despite this fact, residents expressed mostly positive or neutral attitudes to tourists (88 % of questioned respondents). 27 % of them even argued in favour of increasing the number of tourists and 35 % prefer to maintain the current amount.

The in-depth interviews showed that residents perceive tourists and tourism as part of the historic centre. As one resident stated: "At first I had a problem with too many tourists around my home, but then I looked at the building and I realise that they only want to see this beauty" (respondent living in Old Town Square). Most of the residents also stated that this is the price they are willing to pay for living in the centre. There are disadvantages (noise, overcrowding, higher prices), but also advantages (walking distance to culture entertainment, work, and school).

3.3   How the Residents Deal with the Pressure of Tourism Development

The interviews and questionnaire survey show that local residents do not revolt against tourism development and, in most cases, they display positive or neutral attitudes to tourists (see also Pixová and Sládek 2016). Residents use several practices to cope with the overall tourism intensity in their neighbourhood. The concept of coping mechanism comes from outdoor recreation studies (see Manning 1999). Popp (2012) transferred this concept to urban destination. She investigated how tourists cope with negative crowding in Florence. She conducted interviews with German individual tourists staying in the city for longer than average. She states that these tourists use temporal and spatial coping mechanism to avoid crowding. The residents in Prague in the historic core act in a similar way; they primarily use four types of spatial displacement, which are also temporally defined.

Micro-spatial displacement is used by residents for their daily movement, particularly between home and work. They choose less busy side-streets along the beaten track area. They also cross the area in the early morning or later evening hours when tourist traffic is lower.

Intraspatial displacement represents a displacement within the city but outside the tourist area. Residents use this mechanism especially for their leisure activities.

---

[3]Souvenirs and foods labelled as 'Czech' in many cases originate in other countries, such as Russia, and do not have a connection to Czech tradition (e.g. matryoshka).

Most female respondents mentioned these areas in conjunction with babysitting. They usually took their children to gardens or parks in the city centre, where playgrounds are situated. This coping mechanism is granted on the basis of two premises. Firstly, there are quite a lot of green areas in the city centre and, secondly, tourism is highly concentrated (or gated) in a relatively small area.

Interspatial displacement illustrates movement outside the city. A lot of interviewees own a second home in the countryside. They leave Prague almost every weekend from May to September (depending on the weather) and for a longer time during a summer holiday. Second home tourism is a widespread phenomenon in Czechia and represents a significant part of Czech lifestyle (Fialová and Vágner 2014). Interaction with tourist crowding is thus limited to the working day and off-season periods, when the tourism intensity in Prague is significantly lower.

Total displacement represents (in this case) permanent relocation of resident out of the tourist areas. Three interviewed residents have move out of the very city centre within last 10 years, but only one of them stated that tourism development was a reason for moving. This respondent lived in Lesser Town Square for more than 50 years and does not own a second home. She mentioned primarily noise during night-time hours, inappropriate tourist behaviour, as well as tourist overload and congestion.

Crowding studies also identify relative attitudes to crowding according to visitor expectation and previous experiences (Vaske and Donnelly 2002). As urban environment, especially in capital cities, is characterised by higher population density, the tolerance of local residents to overcrowding could be higher than in the case of rural areas.

4   Discussion and Conclusion

The historic centre of Prague and the Royal Way in particular have evolved over the last 25 years into a tourist ghetto. The processes, which have had a profound impact on these changing socio-spatial patterns, started in the 1990s with the structural transformation of the country. Although similar processes of touristification have occurred in western cities, the changes that took place in Prague were intensified by the rapid transformation of the economic, political and social system as well as the effort to make the market competitive internally and externally as soon as possible. The unwillingness of the state to interfere with the market, given the negative experience with the long period of central-planned economy, and the increasing tourism revenues have led to uncontrolled development of tourism in Prague's historic centre. Although local residents do not have a negative attitude towards tourists, the direct and indirect effects of tourism development constrain their everyday movement and quality of life, mainly the higher noise during night-time hours, overcrowding, tourist inflation, and increased phenomena such as crime, vandalism, strip clubs and brothels, etc. Higher tolerance of local people to relatively high tourism intensity in the historic centre of Prague (see Dumbrovská and

Fialová 2014) could be explained by three interrelated circumstances. Firstly, there is quite a large amount of green space in the city centre. Secondly, many respondents own second homes in the countryside, which allows them to "escape" from crowded city. And thirdly, tourism in Prague is gated in a relatively small and easily recognisable area. The creation of a tourist ghetto in Prague could thus have posed a rational division of territory where local residents have a choice to cope with it. This is what Hoffman and Musil have called "tourist Prague and Prague for locals" (2009, pp. 14–15). On the other hand, the creation of a tourist ghetto implicates disruption of the visitor-resident relationship and thus the separation of Prague's tourism from local culture. This could lead to erosion of the sense of place and the identity of the historic core (Simpson 1999) and thus to a loss of competitiveness of the destination. Prague's historic centre as a tourist destination has already reached the stage of consolidation in its tourist area life cycle (Butler 1980) and future development is questionable. Systematic and integrated management of the area is a necessary prerequisite for successful future development of tourism in Prague. A tourism development programme should be implemented in Prague's overall strategic plan and land-use planning document to be able to manage tourism in the historic core in relation to other urban functions and users. Separately developed tourism could lead to degradation by tourist overuse, and thus to the tourist trap effect, i.e. the self-destructiveness of unregulated tourism. The tourism industry devalues its own capital (cultural as well as environmental qualities of the destination) and thus the preconditions for sustainable development in the destination (Pásková 2012).

References

Ashworth GJ (2009) Questioning the urban in urban tourism. In: Maciocco G, Sereli S (eds) Enhancing the cities: new perspectives for tourism and leisure, vol 6, Urban landscape and perspectives. Springer, London, pp 207–220

Butler RW (1980) The concept of a tourist area cycle of evolution: implications for management of resources. Can Geogr 24(1):5–12

Čermáková D (2012) Podnikání migrantů v Praze: případová studie Královská cesta (Migrants' entrepreneurships in Prague: a case study of royal way). In: Ouředníček M, Temelová J (eds) Sociální proměny pražských čtvrtí. Academia, Praha, pp 116–135

Czech Statistical Office (1993–1997) Statistical yearbook of the Czech Republic. Český spisovatel, Prague

Dumbrovská V, Fialová D (2014) Tourist intensity in capital cities in Central Europe: comparative analysis of tourism in Prague, Vienna and Budapest. Czech J Tour 3(1):5–26

Fainstein SS, Judd DR (1999) Global forces, local strategies and urban tourism. In: Judd DR, Fainstein SS (eds) The tourist city. Yale University Press, New Haven, CT, pp 1–17

Federative Statistical Office, Czech Statistical Office, Slovak Statistical Office (1990–1992) Statistical yearbook of the Czech and Slovak Federative Republic. SNTL, Prague

Fialová D, Vágner J (2014) The owners of second homes as users of rural space in Czechia. AUC Geographica 49(2):21–28

Hoffman L, Musil J (1999) Culture meets commerce: tourism in postcommunist Prague. In: Judd DR, Fainstein SS (eds) The tourist city. Yale University Press, New Haven, CT, pp 179–197

Hoffman LM, Musil J (2009) Prague, tourism and the post-industrial city. A great cities Institute Working paper, GCP-09-5, pp 2–24

Kádár B (2013) Differences in the spatial patterns of urban tourism in Vienna and Prague. Urbani izziv 24(2):96–111

Manning RE (1999) Studies in outdoor recreation—search and research for satisfaction. Oregon State University Press, Corvallis, Oregon

Ouředníček M, Temelová J (2009) Twenty years after socialism: the transformation of Prague's inner structure. Studia Universitatis Babes-Bolyai-Sociologia 1:9–30

Pásková M (2012) Environmentalistika cestovního ruchu (Tourism Environmentalism). Czech J Tour 2(1):77–113

Pixová M, Sládek J (2016) Touristification and awakening civil society in post-socialist Prague. In: Colomb C, Novy J (eds) Protest and resistance in the tourist city, Contemporary geographies of leisure, Tourism and mobility. Routledge, London, pp 73–89

Popp M (2012) Positive and negative urban tourist crowding: Florence, Italy. Tour Geogr 14 (1):50–72

Roberts K (1999) Leisure in contemporary society. CABI, Wallingford

Selby M (2004) Understanding urban tourism: image, culture & experience. I.B. TAURIS, London

Simpson F (1999) Tourist impact in the historic centre of Prague: resident and visitor perceptions of the historic built environment. Geogr J 165(2):173–183

Spirou C (2008) The evolution of the tourism precinct. In: Hayllar B, Griffin T, Edwards D (eds) City spaces—tourist places: urban tourism precincts. Elsevier, Oxford, pp 19–38

Sýkora L (1994) Local urban restructuring as a mirror of globalisation processes: Prague in the 1990s. Urban Stud 31(7):1149–1166

Sýkora L (1999) Changes in internal spatial structure of post-communist Prague. Geojurnal 49:78–89

Sýkora L, Kamenický J, Hauptmann P (2000) Changes in the spatial structure of Prague and Brno in 1990s. AUC Geographica 1:61–76

Vaske JJ, Donnelly MP (2002) Generalizing the encounter–norm–crowding relationship. Leis Sci 24(3–4):255–269

From Barcelona: The Pearl of the Mediterranean to Bye Bye Barcelona

Urban Movement and Tourism Management in a Mediterranean City

Nadia Fava and Saida Palou Rubio

Abstract Nowadays large cities, by modifying their internal functioning and capacity for external projection, are becoming powerful nodes of tourist attraction. Barcelona is undergoing just such a process both intensively and paradigmatically as it has experienced continued growth in tourism supply and demand over the past 20 years. Since the mid-nineties, Barcelona has become a renowned international destination and indisputable reference point for urban tourism which, in turn, has generated a significant transformation of its economy, society and urban development; none of which are exempt from criticism or contradictions. In a venture to create a tourist model for the city, the Barcelona City Council introduced the City of Barcelona Strategic Tourism Plan in 2008. At the heart of this strategic plan was an attempt at dialogue between the administration itself and all the other players involved, including the city's residents, about how tourism development could be regulated, the measures required and what the image of the city to be presented internationally should be.

Keywords Urban tourism • Touristic model • City image • Social movements • Barcelona

1 Introduction

At the end of the 1980s Nash (1989) warned that tourism was a destructive and invasive activity for host destinations to such the degree that they adapted to the needs of the industry. These postulates have since been discussed and advanced

This article was published as part of the CIMAR Research Project "La Ciudad y el Mar. La Patrimonialización de las Ciudades Portuarias" (The city and the sea. The patrimonalisation of port cities) financed by the Spanish Ministry of Economy and Competitiveness (HAR2013-48498-P).

N. Fava (✉) • S. Palou Rubio
University of Girona, Girona, Spain
e-mail: Nadia.Fava@udg.edu; Saida.Palou@udg.edu

over the decades by various authors and from different perspectives, not the least from the critical and discerning social science perspective. The philosopher Marina Garcés, during her lecture *Demarcar Barcelona: el turismo extractivista* at the *Centre de Cultura Contemporània de Barcelona* in May 2014 said that, in the case of Barcelona, tourism is an extractive industry, which drains the city of its resources.

From the end of the nineteenth century in Spain, as in other European countries, public administration considered urban tourism as an economic activity grounded in an international projection of the city's image, but one which was to be basically handled by the private sector. In the last 20 years Barcelona has experienced continued growth in tourism supply and demand. Since the mid-nineties, Barcelona has become a renowned international destination and an indisputable reference point for urban tourism, generating a significant transformation of its economy, society and urban development, none of which are exempt from criticism or contradictions.

The territorial hyper-concentration of tourism in specific areas in the city causes explicit inconveniences for local residents and thus raises important challenges in terms of management. Tourist saturation problems are especially problematic in the *Barri Vell* and in districts close to the main historical monuments such as the *Sagrada Família* and *Park Güell*, which are historical hubs where much of the supply and demand of the whole tourist industry is concentrated. For example in the *Barri Vell* district, hotels and restaurants now occupy 30 % of the productive area.

It is calculated that the city currently receives around 30 million visitors per annum, most of who converge on its most central neighbourhoods. Barcelona's hotel infrastructure is comprised of more than 600 establishments with an annual occupation rate of over 60 %. These figures are particularly high if we consider that Barcelona is a city with a surface area of around 100 km^2 and a registered population of 1.6 million.

Today, as a consequence of the increasing number of urban movements calling for better regulation of this activity, it would appear that the Catalan Government is becoming increasingly concerned with the public management of tourism in that it should not just be an economic growth venture, but rather one that must also be compatible with the social well-being of its inhabitants. Internationally, urban tourism experts are searching for instances where public administration of urban tourism is minimising its negative effects while maximising its positive impacts and it would seem that the City of Barcelona Strategic Tourism Plan is an example of just that.

2   Tourism: Conflict, Coexistence and Symbiosis

In Budowski's (1976) landmark article, the 1970 environmental awareness concerns and their conflict with mass tourism emerged. Budowski classified the relationship between nature conservation and tourism into three different categories: conflict, coexistence and symbiosis, which even now are meaningful conceptual frames for understanding the relationship between territory, nature and urban landscapes, and tourism (Rämet et al. 2005).

During the twentieth century Barcelona had a rational coexistence with the slowly increasing tourist phenomenon, but from the nineties onwards this would require a new kind of management, one capable of organising a more inclusive, creative and democratic tourism and city, where tourism could be seen as shaping the image and the content of the city. The documentaries *Barcelona: La Perla del Mediterráneo* (1912) and *Bye Bye Barcelona* (2014), filmed a century apart, exemplify the rapid change from coexistence to conflict in Barcelona's tourism.

In early 1908, the *Sociedad de Atracción de Forasteros* (SAF) was founded in Barcelona to promote international tourism through its magazine *Barcelona Atracción* and would go on to become the platform for the dissemination of the city's modernisation projects. Although SAF attempted to entice tourists to Barcelona as a way of earning foreign currency, tourism was not only viewed from a purely economic perspective because the arrival of foreigners was also perceived as an attractive way to foster cultural exchanges that would modernise the customs and the economy of the country. Moreover, during the Franco era attracting tourists from northern Europe and the United States was an implicit way of diffusing a positive image of Spain around the world.

The SAF-backed *Barcelona: La Perla del Mediterráneo, is* an 8-min promotional documentary based on the Catalan capital. The tourist experience is illustrated through an urban itinerary beginning with the industrial port, then moving on to four men dining in an outdoor restaurant at the top of Montjuic overlooking the Mediterranean Sea and all that is Barcelona. *Barcelona: La Perla del Mediterráneo* reveals a sunny, walkable, bourgeois city with its port, its monuments, *Rambla, Sagrada Familia, Park Güell,* but most of all the quality of its open public spaces and their relationships with urban and natural landscapes. This is exemplified by the images of *Passeig de Gracia, Park Güel[l]* and the magnificent panoramic views; all of which could be associated with the cosmopolitan policies of the *Lliga Regionalista.* This party wanted to place the Catalan capital firmly within the Mediterranean's economic and cultural system and tourism was to be one of the driving forces.

A century later, Eduardo Chibás' 58-min documentary *Bye Bye Barcelona*, illustrates the same bright, accessible, Mediterranean city, where Barcelona is still 'waving' at its tourists, all the while drifting away from its citizens. *Bye Bye Barcelona* focuses on the city's conflicts of interests; its key premise being to compare the tourist masses with the single voice of its citizens clamouring for a more liveable city.[1]

---

[1]It is worth remarking that in the documentary, the deafening groundswell from the grassroots is always associated with the images of the masses, but this disappears completely when we listen to the interviews.

The film documents the same urban spaces as those in *Barcelona: La Perla del Meditterráneo* but they are continually shown as being crammed with tourists, umbrella-wielding tourist-guides and trolleys, rather than local residents. The panoramic views, the link with the natural and cultural landscape, appear to be disappearing behind the forest of souvenirs shops. The film-maker questions if it is possible to reconcile the urban, social and cultural policies. He seems to be in favour of a tourism administration able to consider multiple factors from a more holistic and relational approach.

Barcelona today is a compact city featuring high residential density and mixed land uses, as well as being rich in tourist attractions. However, tourist activity is mostly concentrated in specific areas of the city such as the *Rambla, Sagrada Familia, Barri Gòtic* and the port, which in turn tends to generate social tension resulting from the clash between how tourists and tourist activities make use of its open public spaces and the requirements of the city's own residents. For instance, in the past decade, traffic congestion problems and general criticism of tourism have been especially severe, particularly in the *Ciutat Vella* district.

While both documentaries illustrate the same Barcelona, they have diverse points of views, ranging from coexistence to conflict, on Barcelona's tourism and the visitors it attracts, unveiling both its advantages and drawbacks. Both also pose the question about a more inclusive perspective in urban and tourist policies to generate a more symbiotic link.

3 The City of Barcelona Strategic Tourism Plan

During the 2-year period 2008–2010, the Barcelona City Council introduced an innovative Strategic Tourism Plan, which provided an opportunity to transform a touristic model in crisis. The City of Barcelona Tourist Plan's aim was to strengthen Barcelona's appeal as a tourist destination and to reinforce its position worldwide. It also promoted a tourism model which would strengthen the balance between the needs of the local residents and those of the tourists, the tourist industry and the local economy, as well as local and global culture, all the while preserving the city's identity and values so as to encourage local creativity in a diverse, inclusive and dynamic society.

In order to deal with the negative impacts of tourism, the Barcelona City Council and the Barcelona Tourism Consortium—the body that promotes the city—took the decision to undertake a critical and strategic reflection process aimed at improving relations between the local population and tourism. The Strategic Tourism Plan for Barcelona, implemented between 2008 and 2010, was an unprecedented and daring project that made use of the active participation of over 1000 representatives from the city's tourism sectors and public institutions and had as its main objectives: determining the impacts that tourism generates on the city considering its various manifestations, both qualitative and quantitative; reflecting on the tourism model in

Barcelona; framing the development of tourism in Barcelona in line with sustainable growth; and positively engaging citizens in the city's tourism project.

The Plan was divided into two work phases: an analysis and diagnosis phase and a proposals phase. The former entailed a significant effort to X-ray the reality of Barcelona as a tourist destination in both a holistic and rigorous way, which was basically achieved via two channels: data and knowledge generation and opinion polling. The second phase, dedicated to proposals, entailed compiling a wide range of actions aimed at tackling the main problems deriving from tourism. Four strategic challenges were established to be assumed responsibly by public institutions, tourism sectors and local residents: fostering the territorial decentralisation of tourism; creating new governance structures for tourism; generating complicity between society and public institutions; and promoting competitive leadership as a destination.

The Strategic Plan employed an active methodology based on reflection-action, which means that proposed actions were implemented immediately as decisions were taken. In this respect, it is worth highlighting the Plan's push to create a moratorium on hotels in the *Ciutat Vella* in 2010 in order to stop the compulsive growth of this sector in that area of the city.

Among the most significant actions to be launched once the strategic plan was completed it is worth mentioning the creation of routes around peripheral districts of the city, a strategy to promote simultaneously local heritage sites and the decentralisation of tourism in the centre. However, these new routes in the outlying districts of the city are not yet effective because they were not accompanied by a strict policy of decentralising the hotel business, which, despite the moratorium in 2010, remains concentrated in central areas of the city.

Another significant action stemming from the City of Barcelona Strategic Tourism Plan has been the creation of a tourism management structure within the City Council, a novel move within the municipal government. This unit is responsible for planning tourist activity and taking steps to improve its quality; thus, for example, it proposes policies for regulating public spaces (such as limiting the capacity of *Park Güell*, one of the iconic tourist attractions in Barcelona).

The Strategic Tourism Plan for Barcelona might be considered to be entering a new phase of reflection and tourism management in which the aim is to regulate the industry and make tourism sectors, public institutions and citizens jointly responsible for tourism development in the city.

4 Barcelona Tourism Model in Discussion

Anton Clavé and González (2007) affirm the paradox that the more successful tourism is in a specific location, the nearer to imbalance and to its end as a business it will be. It is often thought that mass tourism can be the beginning of the end for the destination and it will eventually become a victim its own success. The supposed relationship between a greater tourist presence and the degradation of the resource is an association which, as a common denominator, normally implies the belief that massification is linked to high volumes of tourists with low purchasing power. The researchers, however, advise that this is not always the case:

> It is true that limiting the number of tourists visiting a destination means that the income obtained per unit is higher, but an increase in quality is not inversely proportionate to the number of visitors. To give an example, the appearance of low-cost airlines has been associated with a profile of a tourist that is also 'low-cost'. However, statistics consistently show that part of the saving made on the price of the flight is actually transferred to spending at the destination. Not to speak of the many cities that did not previously feature on the tourist map that have managed to consolidate themselves as tourist destinations thanks to low-cost companies connecting their airports (Anton Clavé and González 2007).

The authors agree that there is an ideological reason for the phobia surrounding the massification of tourist destinations, which could be rooted in the history of tourism itself, and which goes hand in hand with reaching social milestones like paid holidays and the welfare state, as well as with other values related to the popularisation of the phenomenon. In any case, it is undeniable that mass tourism has had a negative impact on the city of Barcelona in the sense that is complicates the coexistence of the use of public spaces and innovation in the productive sectors of the city. In fact, for more than a decade the trivialisation of the public space as a consequence of mass tourism has become one of the most criticised aspects of the phenomenon. For example, with regards to the transformations of the urban spaces and their commercialisation, Muñoz (2005) talks about the progressive trivialisation of the urban landscape. The manipulation of history in 'branded cosmopolitanism' and 'consumer romanticism', the simulation of environments as a new iconographic discourse, the construction of a landscape, the simulation of an atmosphere and the directing of the functions of the city have given rise to what Muñoz has identified as its 'urbanalisation'.

Criticism of the trivialisation, or urbanalisation, of the urban landscape has become one the most controversial questions. Lahuerta (2004), another of the most critical voices against the Barcelona model, even suspects that the administrators of the city conceive of it as a sleeping, anaesthetised, static and tranquil body upon which alterations and operations—which consist of preserving the facade of buildings and emptying out their interiors—can be carried out.

The Barcelona touristic model has been the object of many debates and much criticism, some of which even question whether or not a model exists. In fact, the voices that criticise tourism in Barcelona demonstrate that traditionally this phenomenon has developed without any model or criteria and has simply followed the impulse of the market and the interests of the private sector accompanied by the connivance of the public sector. What is certain is that we can characterise Barcelona as a destination that has developed some successful tourism promotion policies, but until the middle of the 2000s the need for tourism planning and management was not considered. It is, therefore, a model based on growth, diversification and the concentration of supply and demand; a model that is simultaneously admired internationally and criticised internally, at least by a large proportion of Barcelona society.

5 Urban Tourism and Social Movements

While urban tourism related to different aspects such as urban regeneration, social theory, visitor perception, transport, sustainability, marketing place among others, has remained a consistent theme in the expansion of tourism research since the 1980s (Ashworth and Page 2010), there is less literature available on urban tourism and urban social movements (USM). In Barcelona, from the beginning of the twenty-first century, tourism has generated a new type of discourse by USM that is contributing to generating discussion on the city's future. It was at the beginning of the 1990s, when scholars and professional began to first speak about the "Barcelona model", describing it as an urban model of procedures, rather than as a formal model. Academics and critics alike described it as an empirical model which was not based on grand technocratic planning, but rather on fragmentary interventions, in small and middle-sized operations that recomposed the city in a strategic manner (Montaner i Martorell 1990) in order to place Barcelona among the top European capital cities. This urban administration of such a model and its results was one of the main reasons for the city positive outcome as touristic destination and which now being called into question by the USM.

If tourism is generating different types of discontent in the city, these disgruntlements are also causing a new discourse concerning the model of city. A debate not only based on economic growth in terms of GDP, but also based on de-growth processes (Hall 2009) that offer an alternative and more sustainable discourse.

Among researchers there is a general consent that from when Barcelona hosted the Universal Forum of Cultures in 2004, an international event, the "Barcelona model" began to be questioned from different perspectives. There were some business sectors and the USM which considered that Barcelona dedicated excessive emphasis to tourism, promotion of large cultural events, services and real estate. Moreover, intellectuals from the left and the anarchist sector (Borja 2004, 2007; Capel 2005; Delgado 2005; Bohigas 2004) as well as local and international professionals (Monnet 2002; Marshall 2004), were questioning what appeared to be the conversion of the city into a theme park or the treatment of its residents as, above all, city consumers. Specifically the analysis of the USM focuses basically on the lack of attention to civic welfare, fundamentally in terms of housing policy, citizen integration and urban heritage. The general feeling that seems to have emerged from such criticism is that the city is not for its citizens any longer, but rather serves its promoters, tourists, tourist agencies, hotels, companies and the rest of the tourism sector. Concern about a tourism economy was not new in Barcelona. Furthermore during Barcelona's urban transformation to host the Olympic game, some criticism arose about the risk of foreign capital entering the city. From 2004 to 2011, the USM in Barcelona initiated a phase mostly focused against urban planning policies designed to construct and solidify the "Barcelona brand", rather than being concerned with the needs of its citizens. During this stage, tourism was one of the "enemies" to fight because it was strictly related the economy of scale and its externalities.

Despite the bankruptcy of the Lehman Brothers in 2008 and the subsequent worldwide economic crisis which followed, Barcelona experienced substantial growth in its tourism clearly marking it as one of the most remarkable economic and social phenomena of the twenty-first century (Garcia and Fava 2015). However, despite tourism being a resilient sector in Spain, large national and post-industrial economies suffered in this critical period of recession, and the general demise of cultural and natural resources provoked a new phase of discontent for the USMs. Only during 2008 and 2009 did Barcelona tourism have a period of stasis, but from 2010 onwards tourist numbers have been steadily increasing (Ajuntament de Barcelona 2015).

In 2012, the increasing number of tourists yet again began to alarm citizens living in close proximity to Barcelona's internationally recognised attractions.

A group of neighbours asked for a referendum on the condition of one Barcelona's main attractions, the famous *Rambla*. The questions raised concerned security, control, noise, and public order.[2] In 2013, the residents from the *Barceloneta* district, the port and beach district, fought against the construction of the new "One Ocean Port Vell" for mega-yachts which they feared would gentrify the area. In 2014 the so-called "Barceloneta Crisis" brought new issues to the forefront such as the protests against the increasing number of tourist flats and the changes in local shops which were now focused on providing what these new inhabitants and customers required, rather than what the local residents needed.[3]

Complaints about tourism and its social and economic effects are now diffused throughout the city, albeit more intense in areas more seriously affected or in districts where citizens are worried about losing their quality of social life or their properties' values being lowered. In November 2015 a new USM platform was launched.

The *Assemblea de Barris per un Turisme Sostenible* (ABTS) (Neighbourhood Assembly for a Sustainable Tourism)[4] gathers most of the USM[5] that are involved in and concerned about the difficulties in finding a peaceful coexistence between

---

[2]El sueño de pasear por la Rambla, *El País*, 6 June, 2012, p. 4. During the summer of 2012 increasing prostitution and numbers of bachelor parties on the Ramblas motivated citizens to protest and call for a more controlled tourist.

[3]Impromptu protests, involving 200 residents, against the British (many of whom had behaved badly) began and have continued daily. Barcelona fights back against the Britons behaving badly, The Times, 22, August, 2014.

[4]https://assembleabarris.wordpress.com/ Accessed 11 Feb 2016.

[5]USM inscribed in the Assemblea de Barris per un Turisme Sostenible: Assemblea de Joves de Ciutat Vella, Assemblea Gòtic, Associació de Veïnes i Veïns de l'Òstia, Associació de Veïns i Veïnes del Barri Gòtic, Ciutat Vella No Està En Venda, Fem Plaça, CUP Casc Antic/Barceloneta, CUP Horta-Guinardó, El Raval no està en venda, Veïns de La Rambla, Associació de Veïns i Veïnes Sagrada Família, SOS carrer Enric Granados, La Barceloneta Diu Prou, Recuperem el Niza, Plataforma Gràcia On Vas, Assemblea Social Guinardó-Can Baró, Defensem els Tres Turons, Plataforma Defensem el Park Güell, Plataforma de Guies de Turisme, Salvem pensions—Gràcia, Ecologistes en Acció Catalunya, Poble Nou per un Turisme Sostenible, Fem Sant Antoni, Parlament Ciutadà, Som Paral·lel, Plataforma No Hotel al Rec Comtal, FAVB.

mass tourism and the city's residents. The main objectives of the ABTS are for de-growth in tourism, to redistribute the profits generated by the tourism sector, which represents 14 % of Barcelona's GDP, and to promote economic alternatives.

Citizens' needs and their voices are represented by ABTS in the City Council's current participatory processes for regulating the tourism sector, which includes multiple measures concerning different aspects such as regulating tourist flats, the construction of new hotels, and retail sectors in specific areas.

While the USMs are asking for a new city model, they are also putting in evidence two essential questions: how to manage citizen and tourist density and how to conciliate the city's welfare with a productive activity such as tourism. Problems, which had already manifested themselves in the city of the middle nineteenth century, now need a real change of paradigm by the city's administration.

6 Conclusion: The New Agenda

The Barcelona City Council elected in 2015 is made up of an alternative-left and green coalition known as *Barcelona en Comú*. The party is driving forward a set of severe measures designed to continue correcting the previous excesses and impacts of tourism, the most important of which are: suspending application procedures and licenses for tourist accommodation establishments, student residences and youth hostels, studying measures to deal with illegal tourist accommodation, and creating a Special Plan for Tourist Accommodation Regulation and a Tourism and City Council. This plan was conceived to be an instrument of multisectoral participation in the area of tourism policies and strategies; now is, along with the City of Barcelona Strategic Tourism Plan, being updated for 2016–2020. One of the lines of action that is being put into effect, which is predicted to contribute to tourist decongestion in Barcelona in the medium term, is a policy of tourist promotion and management together with the public administrations and sectors within the Barcelona area. The creation of new tourist products outside the city of Barcelona aims to contribute to territorial balance.

The Strategic Tourist Plan is an unprecedented and unique commitment to urban destinations that marks Barcelona as a paradigmatic city leading the way in strategic planning precisely by virtue of the social and political nature of the aims of the project: to develop and promote a new tourism management model that relies on the participation of different sectors of the population and areas of municipal organisation; to relieve the most central and iconic parts of the city from the pressure of tourism; and to foster conciliation with citizens. These aims make the Strategic Plan a unique and daring proposal which could become a model and a field of research for other tourist destinations with similar problems. The participative methodology based on action and reflection is also a singular and paradigmatic element of the Strategic Plan that marks it as distinctive and original. The active and representative participation of social agents in the process of analysis, diagnosis and formulation of proposals at all stages of the plan played a key and decisive role.

The construction and promotion of new spots for the city's visitors, apart from the most iconic ones, is redrawing the map of Barcelona and consequently changing the appraisal and social perceptions of tourism, as well as the role of the public administration. New lines of research and reflection are opening: the evaluation of the true effectiveness of the measures and strategies of the Plan; the potential for decongestion and the effect of the new tourist attractions; and the role of private agents and citizens in the management of tourism.

Finally, it is undeniable that while the debate continues openly the results are uncertain. The public administration is driving forward a set of measures designed to reduce the negative impact of tourism, to minimise the supply and demand in the city and to foment a better territorial distribution of that supply and demand, but Barcelona as a destination continues to have an extremely powerful magnetic attraction for tourists, in particular through its most well-known icons and symbols like Gaudí's work, the *Rambla* and the *Barri Vell*. The traditional elements that were recognised and promoted by the first tourism promoters of the Mediterranean continue to be amongst the foremost attractions for tourists in Barcelona a century later: the sea, *Park Güell*, the wide avenues, the modernist architecture and the city's sociocultural dynamism.

References

Ajuntament de Barcelona (2015), Informe d'activitat turística. 17 November

Anton Clavé S, González F (2007) Introducción. La naturaleza del turista. De la turismofobia a la construcción social del espacio turístico. In: Anton Clavé S, González F (eds) A propósito del turismo. La construcción social del espacio turístico. UOC, Barcelona, pp 11–33

Ashworth G, Page S (2010) Urban tourism research: recent progress and current paradoxes. Tour Manage 32(1):1–15

Bohigas O (2004) Contra la incontinencia urbana: reconsideración moral de la arquitectura y la ciudad. Electa [Diputació de Barcelona, Xarxa de Municipis], Barcelona

Borja J (2004), Barcelona y su Urbanismo. Éxitos pasados, desafíos presentes, oportunidades futuras. In: Borja J, Muxí Z (eds) Urbanismo en el siglo XXI, Ediciones UPC Bilbao, Madrid, Valencia, Barcelona

Borja J (2007). El modelo global y el proyecto local. El país, 32. January 31. http://elpais.com/diario/2007/01/31/catalunya/1170209246_850215.html. Accessed 11 Feb 2016

Budowski G (1976) Tourism and environmental conversation: conflict, coexistence or symbiosis? Environ Conv 3(1):27–31

Capel H (2005) El modelo Barcelona: un examen critico. Serbal, Barcelona

Delgado M (2005) Elogi al vianant. Del model Barcelona a la Barcelona real. 1984 Edition, Barcelona

Garcia M, Fava N (2015) International seminar touristic territories: touristic imagery and the construction of contemporary landscape, Girona, 2014. Town Plan Rev 86(3):351–356

Hall CM (2009) Degrowing tourism: Décroissance, sustainable consumption and steady-state tourism. Int J Tour Hosp Res 20(1):46–61. doi:10.1080/13032917.2009.10518894

Lahuerta JJ (2004) Destrucción de Barcelona. Mudito & Co., Barcelona

Marshall T (ed) (2004) Transforming Barcelona. Routledge, New York, NY

Monnet N (2002) La formación del espacio público. Una mirada etnológica sobre el cas antic de Barcelona. Catarata, Barcelona

Montaner i Martorell JM (1990) El Modelo Barcelona. Geometría 10(2):2–19

Muñoz F (2005) Paisajes banales: bienvenidos a la sociedad del espectáculo. In: de Solà-Morales I, Costa X (eds) Metrópolis, ciudades, redes y paisajes. Gustavo Gili, Barcelona, pp 78–93

Nash D (1989) El turismo considerado como una forma de imperialismo. In: Smith V, Anfitriones e invitados. Antropología del turismo. Ediciones Endymion, Madrid, pp 69–91

Rämet J, Tolvanen A, Kinnunen I, Törn A et al (2005) Sustainable tourism. In: Jalkanen A, Nygren P (eds) Sustainable use of renewable natural resources–from principles to practices. University of Helsinki, Department of Forest Ecology, Publications 34. http://www.helsinki.fi/mmtdk/mmeko/sunare. Accessed 11 Feb 2016

Green Tourism: Attractions and Initiatives of Polish *Cittaslow* Cities

Barbara Maćkiewicz and Barbara Konecka-Szydłowska

Abstract Green tourism is a dynamically growing world trend. Also cities see a possible path of development in building a tourist offer based on sustainable, environmentally friendly and responsible tourism. They are increasingly aware of the great potential lying in the relationship between tourism and the natural environment in cities. Urban green tourism is also a response to the need, emphasised by the participants of the *3rd Global Summit on City Tourism*, to make a city enjoyable to all citizens, tourists and investors and to spread the benefits of urban tourism to its surroundings, thus reinforcing its impact and managing congestion. Applied to a city, the general principles of ecotourism, i.e. nature conservation, education, economic benefits for local communities, relevance of cultural resources, minimum environmental impact and maximum environmental sustainability, host community participation, natural areas, culture, and small-scale tourism, go well with the ideas of the Cittaslow movement. Thus, Cittaslow cities are units especially well prepared to develop urban green tourism. The ecological and landscape values that are a significant part of their endogenous capital could stimulate their socio-economic development in which urban green tourism would play a vital role. This chapter seeks to determine to what extent Polish Cittaslow cities see the possibility of development based on this form of tourism. A detailed examination is made of 23 cities belonging to the dynamically developing Polish National Cittaslow Network.

Keywords Polish National Cittaslow Network • Warmia-Mazuria voivodeship • Green tourism

B. Maćkiewicz (✉) • B. Konecka-Szydłowska
Institute of Socio-Economic Geography and Spatial Management, Adam Mickiewicz University, Poznań, Poland
e-mail: basic@amu.edu.pl; bako@amu.edu.pl

1 Introduction

Green tourism is a dynamically growing world trend. Also cities see a possible path of development in building a tourist offer based on sustainable, environmentally friendly and responsible tourism. They are increasingly aware of the great potential lying in the relationship between tourism and the natural environment in cities. Urban green tourism is also a response to the need, emphasised by the participants of the *3rd Global Summit on City Tourism* (held in Barcelona in December 2014 and promoted by UNWTO), to make a city enjoyable to all, i.e. residents, tourists and investors, and to spread the benefits of urban tourism to its surroundings, thus reinforcing its impact and managing congestion. Applied to a city, the general principles of ecotourism, i.e. nature conservation, education, economic benefits for local communities, relevance of cultural resources, minimum environmental impact and maximum environmental sustainability, host community participation, natural areas, culture, and small-scale tourism, go well with the ideas of the Cittaslow movement. Thus, Cittaslow cities are units especially well prepared to develop urban green tourism. The ecological and landscape values that are a significant part of their endogenous capital could stimulate their socio-economic development in which urban green tourism would play a vital role.

This chapter seeks to determine to what extent Polish Cittaslow cities see the possibility of development based on this form of tourism. A detailed examination is made of 23 towns belonging to the dynamically developing Polish National Cittaslow Network. To establish how far the attractions and initiatives of urban green tourism stimulate their socio-economic development, use is made of expert interviews with their mayors, people responsible for their promotion and members of local associations, and their official strategic documents are analysed, i.e. development strategies, local and supra-local revitalisation programmes, development plans, and their tourist offer. The study also meets the need for the promotion of small towns as local growth and sustainable development centres using their endogenous potential, emphasised by ESPON in one of its three scenarios of Europe's development until 2050 (ESPON Vision-Scenarios 2050 2014).

2 Polish National Cittaslow Network

The idea of the Cittaslow movement was born in 1999 in Italy. Its initiator was Paolo Saturnini, the mayor of the small Tuscan town of Greve in Chanti. As of December 2015, the network includes 209 towns in 30 countries, not only European ones, but also in Australia, Canada, China, Colombia, South Korea, Japan, New Zealand, Taiwan, and the South African Republic. However, for obvious reasons, Italian towns predominate: they make up nearly 35 % of the network. Still, it is worth emphasising that also in Poland the national network has been developing very dynamically since the time when the north-lying town of Reszel

Fig. 1 Polish National Cittaslow Network. *Source*: authors' own elaboration on the basis of http://www.cittaslow.org

applied to be admitted to the group of Cittaslow towns in 2004. As a result, the Polish network established in 2007 (then with Reszel, Lidzbark Warmiński, Biskupiec and Bisztynek) accounts today for 11 % of all Cittaslow towns, coming second as a national network of those towns in terms of size. As of December 2015, it embraces 23 units (Fig. 1). A decided majority concentrates in the north-eastern part of Poland and lies in Warmia-Mazuria voivodeship (18 units). Lublin, Silesia, Opole, Pomerania and Wielkopolska have one Cittaslow town each (Polish National Cittaslow Network 2015). This is no accidental distribution. It reflects the history of the Polish network, established in the north-eastern part of the country in Warmia-Mazuria in 2007. The neighbouring towns quickly found it useful to follow the idea. By 2015, 18 out of the 38 small towns of the region have been registered in the Cittaslow movement (Kwiatek-Sołtys and Mainet 2015). It is worth noting that, compared with other Polish regions, Warmia-Mazuria has special growth determinants, the most important of which include: a very high quality of its natural environment, a high tourist potential, a well-developed production of regional high-quality food, and a high percentage of crops grown under a controlled ecological farming system. In the strategic documents of Warmia-Mazuria voivodeship, development priorities focus on the natural environment. The Warmia-Mazuria Regional Operational Programme for the years 2014–2020 emphasises the key importance of cooperation in the fields of ecology and tourism. This region occupies the first place in the country in terms of non-governmental measures taken for environmental protection (Kołodziejczyk 2015). Apart from the International Association of Cittaslow Cities, Warmia-Mazuria is also a member of the European Network of Regional Culinary Heritage. In 2014 the Council of Ministers confirmed a territorial contract for Warmia and Mazuria, the priority list of which includes a special integrated revitalisation programme embracing towns from the Cittaslow network (Warmia-Mazuria Regional Development Agency 2015; Warszawa Council of Ministers 2014).

2.1 Socio-Economic Differences Among Towns of the Cittaslow Network

With one exception, the towns of the Polish Cittaslow network belong to the class of small units. In population terms, there is a predominance of towns with up to 10,000 residents (13 units), while 7 units have a population of 10,000 to 20,000. Only three, Bartoszyce, Działdowo and Prudnik, with more than 20,000, belong formally to the set of medium-sized towns.

To analyse differences in the socio-economic development of the Cittaslow towns in two aspects (demographic-economic and tourist-recreational), we used indicators and mathematical-statistical methods.

Indices of socio-economic phenomena are necessary to make a correct assessment of processes taking place in the social and economic spheres. In the methodological sense, an index is a feature, occurrence or phenomenon on the basis of which we conclude with certainty, or with a specified degree of probability, that the phenomenon of interest to us is actually present (Nowak 2007). All the indices used in the paper are growth stimulants, i.e. they are positive indices. They describe phenomena that are desirable when seen in terms of the aspects of socio-economic development under study (Table 1).

To obtain a linear arrangement, use was made of Perkal's synthetic index (z-score index, Perkal 1953; Smith 1972) in the following form (Runge 2007):

$$W_s = \frac{\sum_{j=1}^{p} z_{ij}}{p}$$

where:

W_s synthetic index
j number of a variable, 1, 2,...p
p total number of variables considered
z_{ij} standardised value of the j-th variable for the i-th object.

Table 1 Indices of socio-economic development

Population and economy (WPE)
1. Population dynamic in 2002–2012 (%)
2. Natural increase (‰)
3. Migration ratio (‰)
4. Number of enterprises per 1000 population
5. Population of working age (%)
6. People employed per 1000 population
7. Commuting to work (in-commuting /out-commuting)

Tourism and recreation (WTR)
1. Shopping facilities per 1000 residents
2. Entities providing accommodation per 1000 residents
3. Entities providing food per 1000 residents
4. Entities providing culture, recreation and amusement per 1000 residents
5. Share of woodland in town area (%)
6. Number of foreign tourists per 1000 residents
7. Foreign tourists' bednights per 1000 residents

Source: authors' own elaboration on the basis of data from the Central Statistical Office in Poland (GUS)

To use the synthetic index, it was necessary to start with standardising the values of indices describing the intensities of individual variables in the towns. For variables of a stimulant nature, standardisation was performed on the basis of the formula:

$$z_{ij} = \frac{x_{ij} - \overline{x}}{S_j}$$

where:

z_{ij} standardised value of the j-th variable for the i-th object
x_{ij} value of the j-th variable for the i-th object
$\overline{x}$ arithmetic mean of the values of the j-th variable
S_j standard deviation of the values of the j-th variable.

In the next, final stage of analysis, a two-dimensional classification was made of all towns belonging to the Cittaslow network (23 units) on the basis of their level of socio-economic development in terms of the combined population/economy (WPE) and tourism/recreation dimensions (WTR) (Figs. 2 and 3). This made it possible to distinguish the following four classes of towns (Table 2):

Class 1. The class of towns with a good fit of a high development level of the population and the economy and a high development level of tourism and recreation. It includes four towns: Murowana Goślina, Gołdap, Olsztynek, and Nowy Dwór Gdański.

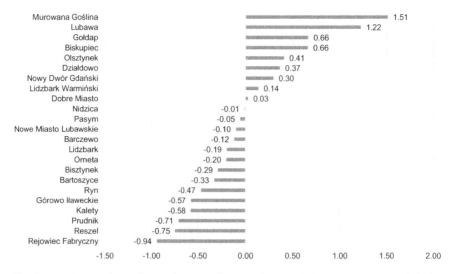

Fig. 2 Development level of towns in terms of the population and the economy—synthetic index WPE. *Source*: authors' own elaboration on the basis of data from the Central Statistical Office in Poland (GUS)

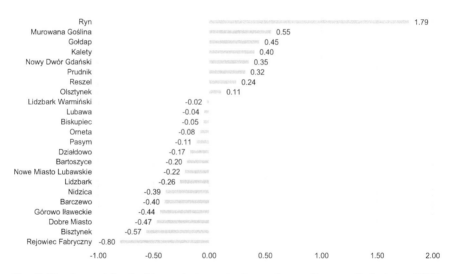

Fig. 3 Development level of towns in terms tourism and recreation—synthetic index WTR. *Source*: authors' own elaboration on the basis of data from the Central Statistical Office in Poland (GUS)

Class 2. The class of towns with a good fit of a low development level of the population and the economy and a low development level of tourism and recreation. It embraces three towns: Rejowiec Fabryczny, Bisztynek, and Górowo Iławeckie.

Table 2 A two-dimensional classification of towns of the Cittaslow network in population-economic and tourist-recreational terms

Population and economy	Tourism and recreation				
	Level of development	Very high WTR ≥ 0.5	High 0.5 > WTR ≥ 0	Average 0 > WTR > −0.5	Low WTR ≤ −0.5
	Very high WPE ≥ 0.5	Murowana Goślina	Gołdap,	Lubawa, Biskupiec	
	High 0.5 > WPE ≥ 0		Olsztynek, Nowy Dwór Gdański	Działdowo, Lidzbark Warmiński, Dobre Miasto	
	Average 0 > WPE > −0.5	Ryn		Nidzica, Pasym, Nowe Miasto Lubawskie, Barczewo, Lidzbark, Orneta, Bartoszyce	Bisztynek
	Low WPE ≤ −0.5		Kalety, Prudnik, Reszel	Górowo Iławeckie	Rejowiec Fabryczny

Source: authors' own elaboration

Class 3. The class with a moderately good fit of the development level of the population and the economy and that of tourism and recreation. This is the largest class, embracing as many as 12 towns, usually at an average level of development in both aspects.

Class 4. The class of towns with wide differences in the two aspects. There are four towns here: Ryn, Kalety, Prudnik and Reszel. Worth noting is Ryn, a town with a very high development level of tourism and recreation and a relatively low development level of the population and the economy.

The conducted analysis of the socio-economic development of the Polish Cittaslow towns allows stating that the network members are mostly those at an average and a low level of demographic-economic development (Table 2). In the case of those towns, the implementation of the Cittaslow idea may, in a longer time perspective, stimulate their local socio-economic development and improve the quality of life of the local communities. This process can already be observed in many Italian towns where the accession to the Cittaslow agreement has allowed them to reduce unemployment and breathe new life into the limping economy (Honoré 2005). A different case is presented by Murowana Goślina, a small towns at a high level of socio-economic development situated in the metropolitan area of the city of Poznań (Kaczmarek and Konecka-Szydłowska 2013; Konecka-Szydłowska and Maćkiewicz 2015). What seems to have been the chief reason motivating Murowana Goślina to join the Cittaslow network was its wish to stand out against the other small towns of the metropolitan area at an equally high development level as a place where people live well and in harmony with the environment, and which does not compete with the big city of Poznań, but which lives in a symbiosis with it (Kulupa 2010). For small towns located in metropolitan areas (such as Murowana Goślina close to Poznań or Créon and Blanquefort close to Bordeaux) the motives for joining the Cittaslow movement are closely related with attractiveness and the quality of life, issues that can encourage new potential inhabitants to settle down in a town. In view of urban shrinkage and population ageing, processes attracting new inhabitants should become an important element of such towns' development strategies and policies (Kwiatek-Sołtys and Mainet 2015).

The implementation of the Cittaslow idea in Warmia-Mazuria shows features of the process of spatial diffusion of an innovation (Hägerstrand 1967), which is understood in the geographical sense as a specific location of an idea bringing about spatial qualitative and quantitative changes in non-homogeneous socio-cultural elements in an area (Łoboda 1983). In this case innovation diffusion is understood as a growing number of Warmia-Mazuria towns entering the Cittaslow network. In terms of the conception of innovation diffusion, it can be said to be a contact type of diffusion, i.e. it manifests itself in the progress of the Cittaslow idea, readily recognisable in the geographical space of Poland. As in the conception of innovation diffusion, it is possible to distinguish several stages in the dissemination of the Cittaslow idea. The first is the penetration stage initiated in 2004 by the town of Reszel, the first to access the International Association of Cittaslow Cities. The next stage, currently occurring in Warmia-Mazuria, is one of expansion and consolidation. Over a relatively short time—the last 10 years—the Cittaslow network has been joined by a total of 18 towns from this voivodeship that additionally take part in the Supra-Local Revitalisation Programme for the Cittaslow Network. It is only in the future that one can expect a stage of saturation appearing in this part of Poland (at present further towns of this region are awaiting registration), and in the country's other regions, the stage of diffusion and consolidation of the Cittaslow idea. In the Polish conditions the chief role of 'emitters' and 'adaptors' of the Cittaslow idea goes to a town's local administrative authorities and political-social leaders. They are the source of initial impulses and it depends on them whether further steps will be taken towards registration in the Cittaslow network. The authorities and leaders also perform the role of generators of the opinion of local communities about benefits deriving from membership of the Association. The involvement of inhabitants in the implementation of the Cittaslow idea is not significant. In the Warmia-Mazuria towns only an average of 40 % of residents know it and identify with it, while in Murowana Goślina, situated in an agglomeration area in Wielkopolska voivodeship, this figure is less than 25 %. This follows from insufficient knowledge about the membership of their towns in the network and from a poor understanding of the idea itself. In the case of Poland, the Cittaslow movement, with its characteristic symbol of a snail, does not always evoke positive associations and may tend to be identified with backwardness, laziness and slowness, in contrast to Italy, where the idea of a slower pace of life goes well with the *'vita lenta'* type of lifestyle (Kulupa 2010; Grzelak-Kostulska and Hołowiecka 2011; Gruszecka-Tieśluk 2013).

3 Green Tourism Attractions and Initiatives

An inventory was made of the tourist offers of the towns belonging to the Polish National Cittaslow Network on the basis of their websites and strategic documents, i.e. primarily development strategies and local revitalisation programmes, and in the case of Cittaslow towns located in Warmia-Mazuria, also the strategy of the socio-economic development of Warmia-Mazuria voivodeship until 2025 entitled "The economic, social and spatial cohesion of Warmia and Mazuria with the regions of Europe", and the Supra-Local Revitalisation Programme for the Cittaslow Network (Sejmik Województwa Warmińsko-Mazurskiego 2013). The inventory showed all of them to ensure forms of recreation in accordance with the principles of urban green tourism defined by the Green Tourism Association as "... travel and exploration within and around an urban area that offers visitors enjoyment and appreciation of the city's natural areas and cultural resources, while inspiring physically active, intellectually stimulating and socially interactive experiences; promotes the city's long-term ecological health by promoting walking, cycling, public transportation; promotes sustainable local economic and community development and vitality; celebrates local heritage and the arts; is accessible and equitable to all" (Blackstone Corporation 1996, after Gibson et al. 2003). In all the towns belonging to the Polish National Cittaslow Network, specially designed hiking, hiking-cycling or cycling trails have been prepared for tourists and residents (some towns are planning to introduce an urban bike rental system). Some towns offer the possibility of water-based tourism, for example Ryn with its eco-marina, an ecological yachting mini-port on Lake Ryn in the town's centre. It was built in 2013 under the programme of constructing such ports in Warmia and Mazuria in order to create conditions for the development of ecological yachting tourism in this region. Also scheduled for the years to come is the modernisation of the yachting port at Pasym. In turn, Lidzbark Warmiński, Olsztynek and Nowe Miasto Lubawskie have canoe ports. In the nearest future the construction of canoe ports and pedal boat rentals is planned at Biskupiec, Dobre Miasto and Górowo Iławeckie. At Prudnik, in turn, the town and its vicinity have been adapted for horse-riding. It is worth emphasising that one of the towns, Gołdapia, develops a spa function based on its newly constructed graduation towers. Many towns also have educational paths relating to the natural environment, e.g. the *Prudnik Forest* didactic path at Prudnik, the *Green Loop* didactic-natural path at Kalety, the *Forest Secrets* nature-forest path at Reszel, or the *Plant Communities Around Lake Zielonka* nature path at Murowana Goślina, or connected with their cultural heritage, e.g. the *Historical Forest Trail of the Royal Town of Prudnik*, a path along the defence wall of the Chełmno Bishops Castle at Lubawa, or the city game *Quest— discoverers' expedition* at Lidzbark. In all the towns the priority task is the revitalisation of public space. This concerns entire town-planning patterns as well as selected facilities, e.g. castles, towers, water towers, or defence walls. Revitalisation is also applied to urban greenery, i.e. parks, cemeteries, or shore areas.

As a result, there is a clear improvement in the quality of those spaces and the creation of new functions. Sometimes the proposed development forms are highly original, e.g. a planned recreational-sensory park with an aromatic garden at Górowo Iławeckie. Also planned here is an ethnographic park, and at Ryn, the construction of a historical village of the *Teutonic Knights*. An important element of the tourist offer is the existing and planned cyclic cultural events, e.g. the *Ekołomyja' Ukrainian Culture Festival* at Górowo Iławeckie or the *Lidzbark organ concerts* at Lidzbark Warmiński.

All the towns have a variety of hotel and catering facilities, like inns, taverns, restaurants, or agritourist farms offering traditional dishes of regional cuisine prepared from local products. It is worth emphasising that in 14 out of the 23 Polish Cittaslow towns there are entities—restaurants, farms, food processing firms, schools, and associations—members of the European Network of Regional Culinary Heritage, the aim of which is to supply tourists and consumers with regional food. At Murowana Goślina the *Gostel's Castle* tavern offers discounts for hotel and catering services to tourists from other towns of the Cittaslow network. The towns also organise regular eco-picnics intended to promote local ecological products and ecological education. One organised a competition for a Tourist Eco-Route that would best present the natural assets of the region.

Apart from the green-tourist offer, the Cittaslow towns have also taken many other initiatives intended to arouse and sharpen the local, ecological and cultural awareness of their inhabitants. The most interesting ones include: an introduction to school menus of traditional regional dishes prepared from natural, regional products, practical classes in bee-keeping, an educational path in a waste disposal plant, the organisation of fairs and events promoting pro-ecological types of behaviour as well as the participation of local governments in the Warmia and Mazuria ECO-LIDER competition. It may well be expected that all those measures intended to build up the ecological responsibility and cultural sensitivity of residents of the Polish Cittaslow towns will contribute to an even better development of the local economies and businesses based on green tourism, thus enhancing local economic vitality.

4   Conclusion

The research has shown that most of the towns belonging to the Polish National Cittaslow Network, while highly diversified in terms of development, have offers for urban green tourism. All Polish Cittaslow towns offer basic green tourist attractions, steadily expanding their range. Not infrequently, the existing or planned attractions are original ideas arousing great interest. Especially readily visible are measures taken within the framework of the Polish Cittaslow Cities Network to which all Warmia-Mazuria Cittaslow towns belong. The chief goals listed in its supra-local revitalisation programme include building the image of Cittaslow towns as units attractive in economic and tourist terms and the development of their tourist offer. While it is still hard to assess the importance of green tourism for their economic development, it seems that it will grow in the future. Especially in the case of towns lagging behind in their economic situation, the promotion of this form of tourism can be an important element of their further development. This thesis is corroborated by Reszel, the town that initiated the establishment of the Polish National Cittaslow Network in 2004 and was the first to join the International Association in 2007, its inhabitants displaying the deepest knowledge concerning the Cittaslow project and most frequently convinced that the chance to improve their economic situation is via the development of tourism. It seems, therefore, that the implementation of a strategy based on the Cittaslow conception is a starting point for boosting the attractiveness and competitiveness of the small towns, thus making solid the foundations of their economic, increasingly tourism-based existence. However, one can expect visible results of those measures only in the future. It seems that the success of the development strategies of the Polish Cittaslow towns largely depends on how far they can popularise this idea among their local communities. There is much to show that the revitalisation of architectural objects alone or other forms of improvement in the quality of space may turn out to be insufficient. What raises some doubts, however, is the relatively low effectiveness of both the propagation and the implementation of the adopted conception. An especially weak point seems to be the low level of involvement of the local community, which follows, as the research shows, from the poor awareness of the residents, that of tourists being not much higher, as well as from a poor understanding of the idea itself.

References

Blackstone Corporation (1996) Developing an urban ecotourism strategy for metro Toronto: a feasibility assessment for the green tourism partnership. Blackstone Corporation, Toronto, ON
ESPON Vision-Scenarios 2050 (2014) http://www.espon.eu/export/sites/default/Documents/Publications/Territorial Vision/ESPON. Accessed 15 Apr 2015
Gibson A, Dodds R, Joppe M, Jamieson B (2003) Ecotourism in the city? Toronto's Green Tourism Association. Int J Contemp Hosp Manag 15(6):324–327. doi:10.1108/09596110310488168
Gruszecka-Tieśluk A (2013) Sieć Cittaslow-strategią rozwoju małych miast w Polsce? Studia Ekonomiczne, Wydawnictwo Uniwersytetu Ekonomicznego w Katowicach 144:383–393
Grzelak-Kostulska E, Hołowiecka B (2011) Kreowanie wizerunku miasta a rozwój funkcji turystycznej na przykładzie wybranych miast Polskiej Sieci Cittaslow. In: Rapacz A (ed) Gospodarka turystyczna w regionie. Przedsiębiorstwo. Samorząd. Współpraca. Prace Naukowe Uniwersytetu Ekonomicznego we Wrocławiu, 157, pp 652–666
Hägerstrand T (1967) Innovation diffusion as a spatial process. University of Chicago Press, Chicago, IL
Honoré C (2005) In praise of slowless: challenging the cult of speed. Harpe One, New York, NY
Kaczmarek U, Konecka-Szydłowska B (2013) Perspectives for development of small towns in Wielkopolska voivodeship. In: Burdack J, Kirszan A (eds) Kleinstädte in Mittel- und Osteuropa: Perspektiven und Strategien lokaler Entwicklung, 19. Forum ifl, Leipzig, pp 66–88
Kołodziejczyk D (2015) Ocena koordynacji i współpracy między instytucjami lokalnymi działającymi na rzecz rozwoju obszarów wiejskich (przypadek województwa warmińsko-mazurskiego). XXXI Seminarium Geografii Wsi, Opole, 27–28 kwietnia 2015
Konecka-Szydłowska B, Maćkiewicz B (2015) Endogenous capital of small towns in the Poznań agglomeration. Wydawnictwo Annales Universitatis Paedagogicae Cracoviensis, Studia Geographica Small Towns's Development Problems, Uniwersytet Pedagogiczny w Krakowie VIII, 178, pp 80–95
Kulupa R (2010) Możliwości funkcjonowania miasta Murowana Goślina w Międzynarodowym Stowarzyszeniu Miast Cittaslow. Praca magisterska napisana w Instytucie Geografii Społeczno-Ekonomicznej i Gospodarki Przestrzennej, UAM Poznań
Kwiatek-Sołtys A, Mainet H (2015) Cittaslow, a qualitative approach to small towns' local development. Miasto w badaniach geografów. Instytut Geografii i Gospodarki Przestrzennej, Kraków 2, pp 123–135
Łoboda J (1983) Rozwój koncepcji i modeli dyfuzji przestrzennej innowacji. Acta Universitatis Wratislaviensis, Studia Geograficzne Wrocław 585(37):216
Nowak S (2007) Metodologia badań socjologicznych. Państwowe Wydawnictwo Naukowe, Warszawa
Perkal J (1953) O wskaźnikach antropologicznych. Przegląd Antropologiczny, Polskie Towarzystwo Antropologiczne i Polskie Zakłady Antropologii Poznań 19:209–219
Polish National Cittaslow Network (2015) http://www.cittaslow.org. Accessed 10 Dec 2015

Runge J (2007) Metody badań w geografii społeczno-ekonomicznej. Wydawnictwo Uniwersytetu Śląskiego, Katowice

Sejmik Województwa Warmińsko-Mazurskiego (2013) The economic, social and spatial cohesion of Warmia and Mazuria with the regions of Europe (Strategy of the socio-economic development of Warmia-Mazuria voivodeship until 2025), Sejmik Województwa Warmińsko-Mazurskiego (Local Diet of Warmia-Mazuria Voivodeship), Olsztyn

Smith DM (1972) Geography and social indicators. S Afr Geogr J 54:43–57. doi:10.1080/03736245

Warmia-Mazuria Regional Development Agency (2015) Supra-Local Revitalisation Programme for the Cittaslow Network, Warmińsko-Mazurska Agencja Rozwoju Regionalnego S.A. w Olsztynie (Warmia-Mazuria Regional Development Agency), Olsztyn

Warszawa Council of Ministers (2014) Territorial contract for Warmia and Mazuria 2014-2020. Council of Ministers, Warszawa

Sports Tourism, Regeneration and Social Impacts: New Opportunities and Directions for Research, the Case of Medulin, Croatia

Nicholas Wise and Marko Perić

Abstract Regeneration is often regarded as the process of renewal, or the redevelopment of existing facilities and infrastructures. Scholars who study regeneration and tourism developments often focus on new infrastructures and economic impacts. However, there is a need for more case-specific focused research addressing social impacts of regeneration to better determine how developments create opportunities for residents and local communities. This chapter focuses specifically on sports tourism-led regeneration in Medulin, Croatia (on the Istrian Peninsula). The purpose of this research is to contribute insight and perspective on sport tourism by conceptually outlining an approach to measure and examine social impacts in future research. In Medulin, sports tourism training facilities have existed since the 1970s, but recent developments completed in 2014 aim to attract more tourists and amateur/professional level sports clubs to further sustain tourism during the winter months. To identify directions for future research, we discuss a number of conditions specific to sports tourism, social impacts and regeneration.

Keywords Regeneration • Sport tourism • Social impacts • Medulin • Croatia

1 Introduction

Tourism researches are becoming increasingly concerned with how local residents and communities are impacted by regeneration (Wise 2016), focusing on social legacies or 'softer' impacts (Clark and Kearns 2015; Wise and Whittam 2015). There exists a foundation of research focusing on economic impacts of new or upgraded infrastructures and improving the visitor profile (image) of a place. Forms of niche tourism such as sports tourism are becoming increasingly important to help a destination distinguish itself. As this chapter will discuss, investments in sports

N. Wise (✉)
Independent Researcher, Kinzers, PA, USA
e-mail: nwise5@kent.edu

M. Perić
Faculty of Tourism and Hospitality Management, University of Rijeka, Rijeka, Croatia
e-mail: markop@fthm.hr

© Springer International Publishing Switzerland 2017
N. Bellini, C. Pasquinelli (eds.), *Tourism in the City*,
DOI 10.1007/978-3-319-26877-4_22

tourism across the Croatia's Istria Region is an attempt to sustain opportunities during the months lacking traditional sea and sun tourists (Government of the Republic of Croatia 2013). Seasonal employment in Croatia is a concern; therefore, niche forms of tourism aim to combat this. Research into niche forms of tourism aim to address social and economic regeneration linked to associated tourism developments. Future research aims to contribute new insight and perspective on sports tourism by conceptually outlining an approach to measure and examine social impacts based on perceptions of local residents. This chapter addresses Medulin in the Istrian Peninsula of Croatia. The intension of this chapter, and future research, is to develop a framework to measure social conditions and associated impacts in other regions where investments in sports tourism drive ongoing regeneration. From a business and management perspective, while it is important to assess experiences and value delivery to tourists, this chapter is concerned with how the local community can benefit.

Regeneration is often regarded as the process of renewal, or the redevelopment of existing facilities and infrastructures. Investments in the sport, tourism and the leisure industries in post-industrial cities and wider regions link to nascent regeneration strategies adopted by many places. There is much work focusing on economic regeneration and associated benefits, but more work focusing on social regeneration and impacts on urban/regional communities is needed. This chapter offers preliminary conceptualisations for understanding the role of sport tourism and regional regeneration initiatives and seasonal declines in Medulin, Istria County, Croatia. Many cities in Croatia see financial declines during the winter months—which have significant consequences on residents who financially depend on tourism—especially those on the Istrian Peninsula where this work is being planned. Sport-led regeneration is an attempt to manage tourism during the off-season so these regions do not have to solely depend on traditional sea/sun tourists during summer months. Mild winter coastal climates in Istria are ideal for sport training and recreational activities and several cities have developed sport-led tourism programs to further attract visitors during off-season months. Future intensions of this research is to spatially identify physical infrastructural regeneration and how this links to wider planning agendas aimed at further developing off-season tourism. This research plan offers a discussion of sport management planning and sport tourism agendas in Medulin. This research has several objectives, from a sport and tourism management perspective this work is concerned with strategic regeneration and management plans linked to the use of upgraded facilities and recreational opportunities when discussing the case of Medulin. From a social sciences perspective, this work is concerned with social conditions and impacts on communities addressed in the discussion below. The ultimate goal of this research is to focus on impacts that gain new understanding on how regeneration influences residents, communities and social policy.

2 Sports Tourism Regeneration and Social Impacts

The concept of regeneration is complex and continually debated across a range of interdisciplinary perspectives (see Chalkley and Essex 1999; Edgell and Swanson 2013; Evans 2001; Gratton and Henry 2001; Matheson 2010; Smith 2012; Spirou 2010; Wise and Whittam 2015). For instance, in the United Kingdom and the United States, urban and regional regeneration represents attempts to redevelop and create new service sector opportunities following post-industrial decline (García 2005; Mooney 2004; Richards and Palmer 2010; Tallon 2010; Waitt and Gibson 2009). Many regeneration initiatives have attempted to utilise events based on sport and the promotion of tourism to achieve this goal (Getz 2003; Raj and Musgrave 2009; Smith 2012; Weed 2007), resulting in a range of new enterprise and entrepreneurial opportunities (Hall 2006; Preuss 2007). Enterprise opportunities are especially important as this links to a perceived social benefit—employment. When there are public-led initiatives, they often require private investment. Therefore, the promotion of urban regeneration initiatives has been accompanied by public-private partnerships. In cities such as Glasgow, sport and tourism are central to contemporary regeneration efforts due to shifts in demand and consumption patterns (García 2005; Mooney 2004). Cities globally are investing in large scale sporting events with the intention that there will bring lasting impact to the economy and the community. Critical scholars have noted that regeneration takes place in underdeveloped and underrepresented areas which often imped legacy initiatives (García 2005; Raj and Musgrave 2009). Investments in new infrastructure can result in economic benefits, but social impacts are sometimes limited (Wise 2016).

Sports tourism is a niche form of tourism and is seeing increased interest among academics (e.g. De Knop and Van Hoecke 2003; Downward 2005; Gibson 1998; Hinch and Higham 2001; Radicchi 2013; Weed and Bull 2009; Perić and Wise 2015). This field is gaining popularity because people seek new experiences and can actively or passively engage in sport as they desire (Radicchi 2013; Roche et al. 2013). Weed and Bull (2009) define sports tourism as the interaction of activities, people and places, and while travel away from an individual's familiar environment they are attracted to destinations to participate or spectate in sports or recreation that meet their own demands. For instance, people travel to Croatia to play tennis by participating in training sessions, or to spectate at tournaments (see Perić and Wise 2015). Given there exists socio-spatial dimensions in sports tourism, Bouchet et al. (2004) integrated notions of activities, people and place to propose a framework for analysing sport tourism consumption. They found consumer choice not only depends upon the actual destinations, but the sport services offered in relation to the experiences they seek in a particular place.

Harrison-Hill and Chalip (2005) found that sport and the host destination have to be cross-leveraged, meaning vertical and horizontal alliances need to exist such as providers, management, facilities and physical infrastructures to optimise the quality of experiences and attractiveness of a sports tourist destination. Moreover, the quality of new facilities, infrastructures and services at the destination provides essential support for the overall sport tourism experience and opportunities (Harrison-Hill and Chalip 2005). What is missing is a focus on how local residents gain; for instance, how infrastructures can support local well-being and engagement and new employment opportunities and involvement for local residents, because much of the focus has been on the activities themselves and more work is needed that considers the people who live in the actual place, as argued by Wise (2016). Sport creates opportunities, not only for tourists but for locals who reside in close proximity of new facilities and infrastructures. It is a challenge to manage social impacts. By suggesting a number of social conditions below, we see this as a framework to begin outlining a research approach that addresses social components that are often overlooked because of the emphasis on economic impacts.

Sport and tourism development/regeneration in the 1970s and into the 1980s was primarily public sector-led using taxpayer money to fund infrastructure projects. By the late-1980s, and even more so into the 1990s, public-private partnerships rapidly emerged—thus changing how urban infrastructure projects were funded and financed—resulting in increased profits among private investors (Lew 2007; Perić and Wise 2015; Smith 2012). Joint stock companies helped facilitate partnerships between the public and private sectors resulted in investment clustering. Intentions were to build on the strengths of shared resources and knowledge transfer to contribute added value to tourism products being offered and delivered for the purpose of economic regeneration (Deakin and Edwards 1993). In terms of product offering and the emergence of new leisure based activities (Rosentraub 2003), sport has been used as a driver to add further value to destinations and diversify opportunities for consumers (Smith 2012). Investing in sport and recreation opportunities helps establish, or enhance, a destination's reputation. Scott (1999) notes, for valuable products to be offered, new or upgraded infrastructures need to be made available not only for tourists but also to locals, who can benefit from employment, enterprise and new leisure opportunities locally. Given the extent of private sector financing and (expected) profit margins, there was little focus on social impacts. Chalip's (2006) work attempted to shift practical and conceptual perspectives by identifying how social outcomes were leveraged.

Because regeneration is a holistic concept in the social science and management studies, business and enterprise initiatives can tell us much about changing approaches (Deakin and Edwards 1993; Rosentraub 2003; Walters 2004). One of the main impacts of regeneration is to create new opportunities. According to Richards and Palmer (2010), destinations need to keep up with the pace of change or they risk stagnation and decline. Moreover, as we see increased competition among destination this has resulted in a range of new products and opportunities for consumers (Hong 2014; Richards and Palmer 2010; Smith 2012). These new opportunities are profit oriented, and local residents may be excluded through not having access or struggle to afford high prices to use facilities. Considering social impacts and issues requires more academic critique and insight. The regeneration literature offers much insight into how new infrastructures and tourism opportunities change places and local perceptions (Richards et al. 2013; Smith 2012).

Governments and organisations among the public sector have begun implementing new initiatives to measure social impact in recent years by developing social policies that include and promote local well-being (Deery et al. 2012; Wise and Whittam 2015). Alongside such policy implications, more research has been dedicated to critically assessing communities based on local perceptions of tourism, social tourism and community development (Deery et al. 2012; Dwyer 2005; Gunce 2003; Higgins-Desbiolles 2011; Richards et al. 2013; Smith 2012; Wise and Whittam 2015). In terms of impacts on people and communities, positive socio-cultural benefits are based on education, local experiences, improvements to residential facilities, maintaining cultural traditions and civic pride/sense of place (see Harrill 2004; Smith 2012; Wise 2015; Yen and Kerstetter 2009); each point aims to better support and engage local residents (Higgins-Desbiolles 2011). Sport tourism, specifically, is a form of tourism where local can engage and get involved in recreational activity, spectate and seek enterprise opportunities (Wise and Whittam 2015). However, it is still important to be critical of social impacts based on what sort of social conditions exist alongside physical regeneration. The chapter will now turn to the case of Medulin before offering further discussion of social conditions.

3 Medulin, Istria County, Croatia

Istria County, positioned in the north and westernmost of Croatia along the northern Adriatic coast, attracts visitors from countries in central-Europe. Although tourism infrastructures are already developed in Istria, it is still important to consider regenerative strategies linked to the recent upgrading of sporting facilities. Istria continually seeks to create opportunities to maintain its competitive advantage in Croatia and the Balkans. The Mediterranean climate makes the region attractive to tourists during the warm dry summer months. The moderate climate and range of sporting amenities enables year-round sports activity. Regenerating towns and cities to update sport tourism products, facilities and infrastructures represents an approach to capture and maintain your-round tourism. According to the Croatian Ministry of Tourism, in 2015 Istria County accounted for 23.5 % of the total tourist arrivals and 29.3 % of the total tourist overnight stays in Croatia (Ministry of Tourism 2016). These are observed as slight decreases from previous years (Ministry of Tourism 2015), which were just over 24 % and 30 % respectively. Investing in new sport tourism opportunities and new facilities is an attempt to increase tourism and create new enterprise opportunities for locals and businesses.

In Medulin, the regeneration of sports tourism infrastructure was recently completed in 2014 and the initiative is to generate tourism opportunities between the low seasons from November to April. During these months, due to the winter temperatures, this is not ideal for sea/sun tourists, but the cooler temperatures are ideal for sports tourism and winter training in coastal areas. Football training is ideal for clubs based in central and northern Europe. Another example of existing sports tourism in Istria is tennis camps and events in destinations such as Pula and

Umag (see Perić and Wise 2015). Moreover, planners are also further developing biking and running trails for additions leisure and recreational opportunities, which are expected to benefit locals as well.

Training facilities have been in operation in Medulin since the 1970s, but recent regeneration aims to attract more clubs to further develop the local sports tourism industry. Six FIFA sized football pitches have been upgraded, and these are managed by the hotels. To accommodate sports clubs, changing facilities, storage space for equipment and fitness/weightlifting facilities, in addition to conference/meeting rooms have been invested in. There are also nutritionists who work with sports clubs to ensure dietary requirements are met. Sports development is controlled by Arenaturist and the Park Plaza Belvedere, who maintain facilities and rents spaces. As noted sport-led investments create opportunities to sustain tourism in the off-season and assist with off-season unemployment or underemployment. Additionally, beyond economic benefits, locals can benefit from new facilities as sport and recreation encourage active-healthy lifestyles. Numerous debates will address how investments impact locals, but the public initiatives and private investments are a step towards year-round tourism in this region.

4 Discussion of Social Conditions

Softer impacts of tourism planning and development need to focus more on local residents and the community (Dwyer 2005; Deery et al. 2012; Wise 2016). Given the extensive physical sports tourism-led regeneration in Medulin, it is important to conceptualise an approach that seeks to outline and consider social impacts and directions as this research expands. Many scholars have discussed impacts gained by investing in sport infrastructure and tourism, what also needs to be further assessed is the impact and experience of *locals*. Pine and Gilmore (1998) stated we now live in experience-oriented economies, and providing and delivering experiences has become the focus in tourism developments (Prahalad and Ramaswamy 2004; Selstad 2007). Weed and Bull (2009) note sports tourism is the interaction in activities people have in particular places. Most sports tourism research focuses on the actual travellers; however, it is local people who continually engage with activities in their place, and thus sporting infrastructures can result in well-being and new enterprise initiatives for local residents (Smith 2012). This will add value to everyday life and activities for locals, offering more opportunities to experience sport through available leisure spaces, training or spectating.

Given the need to focus on local experiences and how locals gain and benefit from sports tourism activities and infrastructures, the first point that will be explored is how do public sector tourism planners and private sector tourism managers address the host of benefits available to all stakeholders, including the local community? This component of the research is currently being conducted. To inform this work, social conditions are being identified based on the work of Getz (2013) and Smith (2012) to develop a conceptual research framework. Research will be expanded through consideration of the following 14 points: (1) Destination development and regeneration has clear policies on social benefits for both tourists and locals; (2) Mutual understanding and tolerance between locals and tourists; (3) Local population is involved and supports event tourism organisation; (4) Local population is also benefitting from new sporting opportunities, and gain new experiences; (5) Mentorship, apprenticeship programs exist to train and involve locals; (6) There is a focus on local business strengths and the encouragement of local enterprise opportunities; (7) Plans to assist people from underprivileged communities; (8) Initiatives in place to assist persons with disability; (9) Local and national pride is increased; (10) Venues and facilities are co-managed to support local resident use; (11) Establishment of volunteer programmes; (12) Legacy training and participation incentives for locals; (13) Local population is aware of legacy agendas and benefits; and (14) Overall local interest in sports, events and tourism. The above 14 points represent our conceptual framework to evaluate and measuring social impacts. These points will be used in extensive surveys and discussed in interviews with various stakeholders.

Social change is about altering peoples' outlooks/attitudes, gaining support and encouraging cohesive involvement among members of a community. Geographical and sociological perspectives guide discussions of individual and social capital. Entrepreneurial and management perspectives focus on encouraging people to create new enterprises. Social capital also involves the formation of networks, norms and trusts that enable people to work together to peruse and achieve shared objectives (Smith 2012). This is essential in Medulin between the different organisations and the local residents. Urban development and planning for tourism can potentially have long-term impacts on societal relationships in cities and communities. Some may view investments in tourism as investments in someone else's interests and not necessarily the needs of the local residents (Spirou 2010). Therefore, new approaches to tourism planning and associated developments will be assessed to identify how changes impact a city and community.

5   Concluding Remarks

Tourism impacts are often assessed based on economic returns and income generation figures in a destination. There has been a shift from short-term financially driven projects to longer-term initiatives that promote social (and financial) wellbeing for communities and residents. Increasingly stakeholders, tourism officials and planners are concerned with measuring and managing impacts in an attempt to get local residents involved in tourism products and activities. Measuring and managing social impacts involve outlining and assessing what opportunities exist and how locals can or will benefit.

Tourism is an industry that depends on its resources, and a focus on sport-led regeneration seeks to create new opportunities for tourists and locals alike. No other industry's long-term economic success is so closely aligned with the success of local communities, specifically their well-being and involvement. Debates concerning change, renewal and revitalisation are linked to this notion of regeneration, with academics interested in impacts. Debates concerning regeneration impacts represent on-going debates as budgets are tightened, especially among the public sector. As noted above, since the 1980s private sector-led development has driven regeneration, resulting in capital gains for investors, but there is a need to identify wider societal impacts linked to understanding how local people and communities benefit, or do not benefit, from regeneration. More work is needed to analyse previous, current and planned regeneration initiatives in Croatia and elsewhere. Through research, scholars need to see if social conditions and social impacts have proved 'successful', and to distil what lessons can be learnt from differing experiences based on a range of perspectives and cases.

References

Bouchet P, Lebrun AM, Auvergne S (2004) Sport tourism consumer experiences: a comprehensive model. J Sport Tour 9(2):127–140

Chalip L (2006) Towards social leverage of sport events. J Sport Tour 11(2):109–127

Chalkley B, Essex S (1999) Urban development through hosting international events: a history of the Olympic Games. Plan Perspect 14(4):369–394

Clark J, Kearns A (2015) Pathways to a physical activity legacy: assessing the regeneration potential of multi-sport events using a prospective approach. Local Econ 30(8):888–909

De Knop P, Van Hoecke J (2003) The place of sport in the battle for the tourist: a figurational perspective of the development of sport tourism. Kinesiology 35(1):59–69

Deakin N, Edwards J (1993) The enterprise culture and the inner city. Routledge, London

Deery M, Jago L, Fredline L (2012) Rethinking social impacts of tourism research: a new research agenda. Tour Manage 33(1):64–73

Downward P (2005) Critical (realist) reflection on policy and management research in sport, tourism and sports tourism. Eur Sports Manage Q 5(3):302–322

Dwyer L (2005) Relevance of triple bottom line reporting to achievement of sustainable tourism: a scoping study. Tour Rev Int 9(1):79–93

Edgell DL, Swanson JR (2013) Tourism policy and planning: yesterday, today and tomorrow. Routledge, London

Evans G (2001) Cultural planning: an urban renaissance. Routledge, London

García B (2005) Deconstructing the city of culture: the long-term cultural legacies of Glasgow 1990. Urban Stud 42(5/6):841–868

Getz D (2003) Sport event tourism: planning, development and marketing. In: Hudson S (ed) Sport and adventure tourism. Haworth Hospitality Press, New York, NY, pp 49–85

Getz D (2013) Event tourism. Cognizant Communication Corporation, Putnam Valley, NY

Gibson HJ (1998) Sport tourism: a critical analysis of research. Sport Manage Rev 1(1):45–76

Government of the Republic of Croatia (2013) Strategija razvoja turizma Republike Hrvatske do 2020. Narodne novine 55:1119

Gratton C, Henry I (2001) Sport in the city: the role of sport in economic and social regeneration. Routledge, London

Gunce E (2003) Tourism and local attitudes in Girne, Northern Cyprus. Cities 20(3):181–195

Hall CM (2006) Urban entrepreneurship, corporate interests and sports mega-events: the thin policies of competitiveness within the hard outcomes of neoliberalism. Sociol Rev 54 (s2):59–70

Sports Tourism, Regeneration and Social Impacts 319

Harrill R (2004) Residents' attitudes toward tourism development: a literature review with implications for tourism planning. J Plan Lit 18(3):251–266

Harrison-Hill T, Chalip L (2005) Marketing sport tourism: creating synergy between sport and destination. Sport Soc 8(2):302–320

Higgins-Desbiolles F (2011) Resisting the hegemony of the market: reclaiming the social capacities of tourism. In: McCabe S, Minnaert L, Diekmann A (eds) Social tourism in Europe: theory and practice. Channel View Publications, Bristol, pp 53–68

Hinch TD, Higham JES (2001) Sport tourism: a framework for research. Int J Tour Res 3(1):45–58

Hong J (2014) Study on urban tourism development based on experience economy in Shanghai. Int J Bus Soc Sci 5(4):59–63

Lew AA (2007) Invited commentary: tourism planning and traditional urban planning theory—the planner as an agent of social change. Leisure/Loisir 31(2):383–391

Matheson CM (2010) Legacy planning, regeneration and events: the Glasgow Commonwealth Games. Local Econ 25(1):10–23

Ministry of Tourism (2015) Tourism in figures 2014. http://www.mint.hr/UserDocsImages/150701_Tourism014.pdf

Ministry of Tourism (2016) Turistički promet od siječnja do prosinca 2015. godine. http://www.mint.hr/UserDocsImages/160219_tpromet015.pdf

Mooney G (2004) Cultural policy as urban transformation? Critical reflections on Glasgow, European city of culture 1990. Local Econ 19(4):327–340

Perić M, Wise N (2015) Understanding the delivery of experience: conceptualising business models and sports tourism, assessing two case Studies in Istria, Croatia. Local Econ 30 (8):1000–1016

Pine BJ, Gilmore JH (1998) Welcome to the experience economy. Harv Bus Rev 76(4):97–105

Prahalad CK, Ramaswamy V (2004) Co-creation experiences: the next practice in value creation. J Interact Mark 18(3):5–14

Preuss H (2007) The impact and evaluation of major sporting events. Routledge, London

Radicchi E (2013) Tourism and sport: strategic synergies to enhance the sustainable development of a local context. Phys Cult Sport Stud Res 57(1):44–57

Raj R, Musgrave J (eds) (2009) Event management and sustainable regeneration. CABI, London

Richards G, Palmer R (2010) Eventful cities: cultural management and urban revitalisation. Elsevier, London

Richards G, de Brito MP, Wilks L (eds) (2013) Exploring the social impacts of events. Routledge, London

Roche S, Spake DF, Joseph M (2013) A model of sporting event tourism as economic development. Sport Bus Manage Int J 3(2):147–157

Rosentraub M (2003) Indianapolis: a sports strategy and the redefinition of downtown redevelopment. In: Judd D (ed) The Infrastructure of play. M.E. Sharp, New York, NY, pp 104–124

Scott A (1999) The cultural economy: geography and the creative field. Media Cult Soc 21 (6):807–817

Selstad L (2007) The social anthropology of the tourist experience. Exploring the "middle role". Scand J Hosp Tour 7(1):19–33

Smith A (2012) Events and urban regeneration. Routledge, London

Spirou C (2010) Urban tourism and urban change. Routledge, London

Tallon A (2010) Urban regeneration in the UK. Routledge, London

Waitt G, Gibson C (2009) Creative small cities: rethinking the creative economy in place. Urban Stud 46(5/6):1223–1246

Walters D (2004) A business model for the new economy. Int J Phys Distrib Logist Manage 34 (3/4):346–357

Weed M (2007) Editorial: event sports tourism. J Sport Tour 12(1):1–4

Weed M, Bull C (2009) Sport tourism: participants, policy and providers. Elsevier/Butterworth Heinemann, Oxford

Wise N (2015) Placing sense of community. J Community Psychol 43(7):920–929

Wise N (2016) Outlining triple bottom line contexts in urban tourism regeneration. Cities 53:30–34

Wise N, Whittam G (2015) Editorial: regeneration, enterprise, sport and tourism. Local Econ 30 (8):867–870

Yen I, Kerstetter D (2009) Tourism impacts, attitudes and behavioral intentions. Tour Anal 13 (5/6):545–564

A "New Normality" for Residents and Tourists: How Can a Disaster Become a Tourist Resource?

Silvia Mugnano and Fabio Carnelli

Abstract Although Italy is ranked as one of the five European Countries with a high probability of being exposed to a natural hazard, 75 % of Italian housing stock does not meet any anti-seismic criteria. In addition to this already fragile scenario, the fact that Italy is one of the countries characterised by a rich cultural heritage opens new issues regarding the impact of a disaster on this territory. The current social science debate is already pointing out that the disaster's recovery phase needs to move on from a physical and economic dimension towards a social and cultural one. However, much needs to be explored—especially in Europe—about how to deal with a tourist destination during and after a disaster. A "new normality" has to be found for the residents as well as for tourists and visitors. Beyond dark tourism, the recovery phase for a destination can work on finding new meanings and policies aimed at reshaping a new imagery which could encapsulate the tragic memory. The aim of this chapter is to present two Italian cases that in different ways have worked on the recovery/reconstruction phase within a touristic frame: the town of Longarone (1963 Vajont disaster) became a destination of a collective memory and the town of Comeglians (1976 Friuli earthquake) turned into an innovative tourist destination. Were these examples successful and can a lesson be learned from them?

Keywords Disaster tourism • Dark tourism • Tourist destination • Vajont • *Albergo diffuso* • Comeglians

1 Introduction

In the last decades the impact of natural hazards has increased due to the growth of population density in hazardous zones along with the increase of the frequency and intensity of extreme events as a consequence of climate changes (Intergovernmental Panel on Climate Change 2013). According to the statistics produced by UNEP (United Nations Environment Program 2010) regarding the occurrence of

S. Mugnano (✉) • F. Carnelli
University of Milan-Bicocca, Milan, Italy
e-mail: silvia.mugnano@unimib.it; f.carnelli5@campus.unimib.it

© Springer International Publishing Switzerland 2017   321
N. Bellini, C. Pasquinelli (eds.), *Tourism in the City*,
DOI 10.1007/978-3-319-26877-4_23

catastrophes worldwide from 1950 to 2008, this figure has increased threefold in the last 30 years. Or more precisely, as Wisner et al. (2003) stressed, what has increased is the number of disasters in terms of declaration of disaster areas, economic losses and the number of victims. Alexander (2005) reminds that "on average about 220 natural catastrophes, 70 technological disasters and three new armed conflicts occur each year" (Alexander 2005, p. 25).

However, not all places are affected by disasters in the same way; the disaster entity varies drastically depending on the local context. There is an important relationship between natural elements and the cultural, social and economic organisations of the affected society (Oliver-Smith and Hoffman 2002). As recent literature points out, the probability of a disaster having more devastating effects in one place than another depends on the local vulnerability of the place (Cutter et al. 2000). In other words, there is a correlation between the potential risk and the social resistance and reliance of a specific place (Kasperson et al. 1995; Cutter 1996).

This approach has been commonly used to argue that socially excluded communities or deprived areas are more in danger than others—implying geographical, social and economic disparities.

This theoretical approach can also give us the chance to provide an interesting contribution to the tourism debate. The tourist industry and tourist destinations are not immune to disasters. In general terms, in tourist destinations tourist and local communities are seen as two separate and sometimes conflicting populations; the question is to understand whether this might change if a disaster occurs.

The chapter aims to explore the social impact of a disaster and the innovative role that tourism can play. Although some tourist places do not have a low social vulnerable index in the pre-event phase, they might result as being more vulnerable and with a lower social reliance in responding and recovering from the event.

A tourist destination can become vulnerable to disasters from different perspectives:

- From the economic point of view, a tourist destination in a pre-disaster phase can have a very flourishing local economy which can be badly affected by the disaster. The economic organisation of the tourist industry is often characterised by a local or small and medium size local business (Cioccio and Michael 2007) which, in itself, is not an indicator of vulnerability but it can be seen as a risk factor. Moreover, if the tourist economy is based on international investors, these investors might no longer find economic benefits in investing in a devastated area.
- From a physical perspective, a disaster can have a strong impact on a tourist destination: besides damaging private houses with the high risk of people becoming homeless, a disaster in a tourist destination can also destroy parts of cultural/natural heritage that are core icon attractions of the area or core symbols for local identities. The tsunami that hit the Maldives in 2004 irreparably destroyed the coral reef; the 2005 Nepal earthquake caused thousands of victims, destroyed entire villages, left millions of homeless and also annihilated an inestimable cultural heritage.

- A sociological dimension should also be taken into account. A tourist destination is populated by various social groups such as local communities, temporary workers, temporary residents, tourists, etc. The impact and the consequences of a disaster on each of these populations might vary. A tourist destination has a high presence of temporary populations represented by both tourists (Burby and Wagner 1996) and seasonal or temporary workers who are less able to prepare or respond to a disaster. With respect to tourists that "are more vulnerable than locals because here they are less familiar to local hazards and the resources that can be relied on to avoid risk, and they are less independent". With respect to the seasonal workers again Faulkner stresses that "the level of staff turnover has not been taken sufficiently into account in the consideration [...]" (Faulkner 2001, p. 20). Several studies argued that in the rescue phase temporary populations are more difficult to help; i.e. it is more difficult to have access to information, the degree of local knowledge regarding safer places and so on.
- Last but not least, a tourist destination can result as being more vulnerable also from a symbolic viewpoint. The change in the image that a tourist destination might have after a natural disaster is a big price to pay (Cassedy 1991). A place that was a symbol of entertainment and holidays might suddenly become a place of death and destruction and this vision of mass devastation might be quite difficult to wash away (Chew and Jahari 2014).

In these terms, the idea of a *disaster tourism* is a pretty new concept in social sciences. As Nagai clearly reports quoting Hiji (2012), we find disaster tourists when "tourists can (1) see disaster heritages from which they can witness the gross intensity of the disasters, (2) experience the local treasure which existed before the disaster, (3) appreciate the reconstruction process through observing the state of the residents and the industries, (4) listen to the stories of the survivors, (5) learn something" (Nagai 2012, p. 10). In other words, this concept can highlight different aspects and combinations that affect tourism, places and the impact of the event. Tourism, therefore, might be seen, according to Nagai (2012), Korstanje and Ivanov (2012), as a cultural means to react and face the disaster in an innovative way. The multidimensional impact that disaster has on a tourist destination is incredibly complex to detect due to features already mentioned. The chapter argues that post-disaster phases might be seen as "a new normality", where the disaster might become a "new companion to live with", more than an enemy to avoid. Places and communities that have to deal with the memory of the disaster have even used it as a resource for new local development. In light of these preliminary considerations, it is necessary to define better what makes a tourist destination vulnerable and how tourism "interacts" with the different phases of a disaster in different ways, bridging the gap that is still wide between tourism and disaster literature.

2   Tourism Industry Within a Disaster

The relationship between the tourist industry and disasters is a rather unexplored topic (Cohen and Cohen 2012). The little systemic research that has been carried is mainly related to how a tourist destination can respond to a disaster. First of all, a disaster configures itself as a *continuum* that is longer than the actual event and its post-period (Oliver-Smith and Hoffman 2002). A commonly used model of emergency management is characterised by four temporal stages: mitigation, preparedness, response and recovery (National Governors' Association 1979).

In accordance with this heuristic model, the tourist industry also has to deal with the fact that "disasters [...] are frequent occurrences and require management, preparedness and response" (Hystad and Keller 2008, p. 152).

However, some research has been carried out and minimal proactive planning for the tourist industry was made (Drabek 1995; Faulkner 2001; Glaesser 2003; Hystad and Keller 2008; Kash and Darling 1998; Ritchie 2004). In this debate, the creation of a model on disaster management strategy to respond to disasters (Faulkner 2001) seems to be a central issue along with the need to create a governance system that allows the tourist sector to collaborate with the emergency unit. Nonetheless, some authors, as we will see in the next paragraph, have underlined unprecedented interrelations between tourism and emergency and shelter stage, as well as the recovery one.

We will take four dimensions into account: tourism, the place, the event and the temporal distance from the event. Looking at the interactions between those dimensions might shed new light on the debate. There are indeed some tourist places that have been hit by a disaster, other places that were not tourist destinations and that have turned into a dark tourism destination after a disaster or that are using the tourist economy as a regenerating tool for the area, even in cultural ways. Or, as Pezzullo (2010) has underlined in the case of the Katrina Hurricane, in New Orleans tourist facilities were useful during the emergency phase (i.e. tour buses were also used to evacuate survivors and tourist structures used as first aid bases); or touring was used as "field reports" for journalists and as a "lobbying tool" by politicians, becoming "a vital mode of interaction between political leaders making decisions about resources for disaster recovery" (Pezzullo 2010, p. 30). And, in the recovery phase, a new form of tourism—the *voluntourism*—was emerging and becoming very important. Volunteer tourists (students, religious associations, professional conferees) that travelled to and throughout New Orleans helped people to rebuild their houses and also "to re-image New Orleans" (Gotham 2006 in Pezzullo 2010, p. 32). As we noticed, tourism can be a resource even in unexpected ways and during the different phases of a disastrous event: a place might turn into a tourist destination in order to develop strategies of emergency management or as a part of the recovery process.

Furthermore, the desire of both local and national organisations and residents for a "new normality" could have different meanings and strategies, according to both previous characteristics and vulnerabilities of the place involved in the disaster and the management of the disaster itself. In the case of a tourist destination, a "new normality" turns into a "rehabilitation" of the physical, socio-economic and symbolic landscape, in order to restore the flow of tourists and the image of the place as "safe" and renewed. In other cases, the tourist dimension could upset the place: in the emergency phase, whether *voluntourism* does not really meet local needs or is perceived as inadequate; in this regard, dark tourism may just hinder the local desire for a "new normality", emphasising a not yet repaired trauma or an undesired present. On the contrary, it can contribute building a collective commemoration of the event or a celebration of the recovery phase. In this respect, the case of "dark tourism" related to Wenchuan earthquake (2008) is rather well known. The Chinese Government opened seismic memorial sites in 2010 in order to celebrate the recovery process driven by the Communist Party. In their visits, tourists experience feelings of "obligation and commemoration mixed with curiosity" (Tang 2014, p. 1338) at the same time, and *"gratification, appreciation and satisfaction* for economic and social recovery from the earthquake" (Tang 2014, p. 1338).

The role of tourism might be polyvalent in a place that might turn into a destination because of a disaster: the tourism industry can help and can even be used for the production of a collective (or partial) memory of the event, at both a government and resident level (as in the Wenchuan or Vajont cases—see next paragraph); from a different perspective, tourists can improve local economies and produce a "new normality" not even imagined or desired by survivors before they were hit by the "tragedy". In extreme cases, a locality can paradoxically disregard prevention or safety, in order to exploit tourism or the beauty of a hazardous place (i.e. tourism related to volcanos areas): in these cases, a "new normality" is presented within the conflicting values at stake.

3 Disaster Tourism Beyond Dark Tourism

The case of Hurricane Katrina, cited in the previous paragraph, is also relevant because it is one of the first cases in which the disaster has become a pivot for a peculiar form of tourism: *dark tourism*. Indeed, in the recovery phase, many tours were organised in the hardest hit zones of New Orleans, performing "public histories of the present" (Pezzullo 2010, p. 34). Indeed, according to Pezzullo (2010) tourists visiting the disaster areas were paying a *moral* tribute to the local community and to one of the most important cities in America by listening survivors' storytelling.

Dark tourism has recently been seen also as a recovery strategy for post-events. This term was first used by Foley and Lennon (1996) to define "the presentation and consumption (by visitors) of real and commodified death and disaster sites" (Foley and Lennon 1996, p. 198), connecting this phenomenon to Western modernity and mass media exposure of tragic events, too (Korstanje 2015). According to Stone and Sharpley (2008), they seem to follow the concept of *black spots*, the first notion of dark attractions connected to the mass *spectacularisation* of death, first introduced by Rojek (1993) and defined as "commercial [tourist] developments of grave sites and sites in which celebrities or large numbers of people have met with sudden and violent death" (Rojek in Stone and Sharpley 2008, p. 577): it can be a pilgrimage to Jean Dean's fatal car accident or Lockerbie, in Scotland, where a Pan Am plane crashed in 1988. In this regard, various authors distinguish different shades of "dark", according to various types of location, performance and empathy involved in the journey: for Miles (2002), for example, there is a difference "between 'dark' and 'darker' tourism based upon the location (...) between sites *associated with* and sites *of death*" (Stone and Sharpley 2008, p. 578), and this means that it is darker visiting Auschwitz than the US Holocaust Memorial in Washington DC.

More recently, dark tourism has become a more inclusive term. Dark tourism can include either visiting a spontaneous or official (Rittichainuwat 2008, Podoshen 2013) commemoration place or folk epigraphy practices (i.e. in the World Trade Center after 9/11, Sather-Wagstaff 2009) or museums dedicated to the death event (i.e. Holocaust museums in Cohen 2011), or even visiting a place specifically because it was hit by mass destruction (see for example Phuket 2 years after 2004 tsunami, Rittichainuwat 2008).

Therefore, what these cases have in common could not be only "death" (Seaton 1996) but the impact of an event on a place producing consequences that could represent a disaster; that is why we could go beyond dark tourism, trying to dissociate the implicit equivalence between "dark" and "death" and to better define specific cases in which disaster and tourism interact.

Considering disaster tourism as tourism in a place affected by a disaster (Kelman and Dodds 2009), we can interpret tourism within a disaster management framework, looking deeper into which strategies are elaborated by residents and tourists to reconfigure a new sense of *hereness*, useful in transforming a location into a destination (Chew and Jahari 2014, Kirshenblatt-Gimblett 1998); furthermore, precisely because of the need to rebuild a horizon of meanings after a disaster, death may paradoxically better hide or encapsulate "a second life as heritage" (Kirshenblatt-Gimblett 1998) to places that were hit by a disaster in different ways.

A "new normality" or "a second life" can, therefore, take different shapes. We will now present two Italian case studies that in different ways have worked on recovery and reconstruction phases using tourism as a pivot: the town of Longarone (1963 Vajont disaster) has become a destination of an alleged collective memory; the town of Comeglians (1976 Friuli earthquake) has turned into an innovative tourist destination. Therefore, we will focus on the relationship between tourism and the different phases of an event, beyond the concept of dark tourism.

3.1 The Vajont Case: Tourism as a Narration of Contested Memory

On October 9th, 1963, a massive landslide on Mount Toc (Veneto Region, North-East of Italy) provoked a *megatsunami* on an artificial lake (250 m high waves) that overtopped the Vajont Dam, swept away the town of Longarone and damaged (on the other side of the Mount) the town of Erto, causing around 1917 deaths. The reasons of this disaster, thanks to a long trial and different investigations, were finally attributable to negligence by the scientists that projected (at that time) the biggest Dam in the world: they were mainly interested in economic gains of the SADE company (that right in those years became ENEL, a State-owned firm) thanks to political complicity at all levels (Merlin 2001). Local communities were not involved in the project and all the clues (landslides, earthquakes, local knowledge) and scientific research suggesting that the Mount could have collapsed were systematically ignored—starting from the meaning of the Mount's name, that in the local language means "ill" (Merlin 2001). Even though there were some dark tourists immediately after the tragedy, some years later, during the trial and the reconstruction process, the Vajont valley was already "assuming another dimension for public consciousness: it became a tourist place to visit. With curiosity, perhaps with pity, never with rebellion"[1] (Merlin 2001, p. 166).

The process of defining responsibilities and producing a memory of the event was extremely conflictual (Ventura 2015): immediately after the disaster a "Committee of *survivors* for the defence of Vajont's rights" was formed in order to claim justice during the criminal trial against ENEL. The criminal trial established in 1971 that an ENEL and a State manager were accused of multiple manslaughter and unintentional disaster.

It was only the final sentence of the civil trial that set a compensation for damages for the survivors in 1997. And it was after this event and after the reconstruction process (Erto was divided in 1966 between the new Vajont Municipality and a 1971 New Erto. Longarone was rebuilt between 1967 and 1975) that an institutionalised memory was created in the Vajont valley. A new "Committee of *survived* people" (not "survivors") was created, in order to "pursue the aim of solidarity and moral and psychological support to the survived people to the tragedy of Vajont, as well as the right to disseminate the knowledge and preserve the memory of occurred events"[2] (Ventura 2015, p. 5); in 2003, the Vajont Foundation was created and in 2009 it contributed to the opening of the *Longarone Vajont Museum—Flashes of history*; in 2003, the Vajont victims' cemetery of Fortogna was rebuilt and "became a national monument" (http://www.prolocolongarone.it/) and in 2007, the top of the Dam was opened for guided tours carried out by

---

[1]The authors' translation of the original text.

[2]The authors' translation of the original text.

Informatori della Memoria (Memory informants), volunteers properly trained and educated in order to transmit the collective memory of the tragedy.

A tourist experience was built upon a combination of the local *"survived"* Committee's stories and the impressions given by the visitors about "places of memory" like the Dam, the Museum, the Cemetery, the new Longarone Church and the old Town bell of Longarone (the only building survived to the wave). Those two elements work together to build a dialectic circle of representations that configures a "new normality" for tourists. Since the 2000s, Longarone has been identified more and more by tourists with the Dam and the Dam has become the symbol of a history that is narrated through the Museum and by the *Memory informants*: in the tourists' experience, it is a heritage that exists if narrated through an institutionalised memory created at a local level that transmits the cultural efforts of survivors/ survived in facing the disaster in order to reconstruct their own *history*. A part of this memory could now exist only with the distance encapsulated in the heritage; tourists can contribute to cultivate this distance and this memory. The museum is defined by the local association that manages it as "a tool of knowledge of local history, indelibly marked by the worst tragedy of Post-war Italy. It intends to convey to the visitor a strong emotion and a real awareness that the value of life and the lessons of the past are essential foundations for building our future" (http://www.prolocolongarone.it, last accessed on 18 December 2015).

If the aftermath of the Vajont disaster is a hard and controversial history, nowadays tourism could be both a sector of its economy and a cultural way of transmitting the narration of part of the Longarone inhabitants' memory. At the same time, for tourists "Vajont" became the place of a public lesson on national history, an educational place where you must go in order to 'not forget the mistakes', and to experience a terrible truth and a compassionate feeling for the victims, that is their relationship with 'the limits of human trust in science' and with their national sense of belonging to a communal history (Fig. 1).

3.2 Comeglians: From a Disaster to an Innovative Policy for Tourist Industry

In 1976, the Friuli region (North-East of Italy) was affected by an earthquake. The epicentre was Gemona, there 993 people died and 80,000 lost their homes. The Gemona earthquake is very famous in Italian history because it was rather massive and it affected a very poor and deprived area. The process of reconstruction started quite soon. In some remote mountain areas near Gemona the re-construction phase was embedded into a more complex process of local development. Friuli was one of the regions that during the nineteenth century lost the highest number of people due to the migration phenomena and the process of urbanisation towards the industrial areas. The Friuli disaster has become famous due to the active and proactive behaviour of the victims. Immediately after the earthquake the local community

Fig. 1 A tour to Vajont Dam, Erto e Casso, Pordenone, Italy. *Source*: Davide Gangale

organised themselves: tent camp committees and a Committee of the committees were organised to coordinate the first housing aid. The government and voluntary aids came onto the scene later. According to Strassoldo and Cattarinussi (1978), the proactive collective and organised action fainted away in the recovery phase. There was a massive exodus of the local population from the affected areas (especially in the mountains) to the seaside areas. Within this scenario, innovation especially in the recovery phase came from the external agents. Among all, attention should be given to the case of an innovative project of recovery strongly connected with the tourist industry.

The mountain areas were the most deprived areas and, therefore, the process of reconstruction was seen also as a good opportunity to re-launch those areas. In 1978 a project, based on an academic work under the supervision of the University of Zurich, was proposed to convert an area into a tourist destination. Since 1982, the north area of Gemona—the towns of Maranzanis, Povolaro e Tualis—has become an interesting laboratory of innovation for tourism. Thanks to several EU Funds (Lander II) three towns have been rebuilt and turned into new forms of tourism facilities. Instead of building hotels, old houses have been renovated to host the tourists. The project was mainly based to promote a kind of tourism that included a strong involvement of the community. This new model of tourism facilities was named *Albergo diffuso*. Albergo diffuso of Comeglians is composed of several houses that have been turned into tourist accommodations. Actually it has a maximum capacity of 105 tourists distributed in 14 houses (which very soon will

Fig. 2 A view of Albergo Diffuso Comeglians, Udine, Italy. *Source*: Lucia Miotti

be more than 22 houses). Annually Comeglians has around 5500 arrivals including tourists and day visitors and its turnover is around 10,000 euros for bednights. Comeglians has been included in several trekking circuits and therefore the village does not only provide accommodations but it is also becoming a valid knot of day excursions. Data show that Comeglians is a tourist project that has tried to offer multifunctional services aiming to attract tourists and day hikers (2010, source: Albergo diffuso Comeglians).

Since then, *Albergo diffuso* has become a well-recognised innovative model of hospitality and has spread worldwide. It is presented as a model of sustainable development, which aims at the exploitation of local resources both tangible (cultural heritage, agriculture and handicrafts, small businesses) and intangible (traditions, knowledge, social ties). This model is an attractive form of sustainable tourism for both present and future generations because it promotes heritage and is oriented to the recovery of a locality's cultural identity and to the revival of traditional aspects (Fig. 2).

4   Conclusion

These original ways in which tourism and disaster *interact* can reveal how different tactics and strategies (De Certeau 2010) can play with different kinds of vulnerabilities and actors in disaster contexts and at different levels, in the re-configuration of a "new normality" for residents and tourists. Looking at a post-disaster phase as an attempt to reduce a place vulnerability in order to avoid a hypothetical future hazardous event, we can conclude that disaster tourism may also provide some tools for building or carrying out a sense of *hereness* that could offer cultural, social and economic means to face the disaster and the aftermath. Our attempt wants to go beyond a reductionist concept of dark tourism and how to manage a tourist destination hit by a disaster by focusing on some dimensions (place, temporal dimension, event and tourism), which, if analysed and correlated, let us understand in better ways how disaster tourism can be explained and how residents and tourists can "deal" with it. The need to study disasters in tourist areas is not only relevant because the tourist industry is expanding and tourist developments are frequently located in areas at risk, but because tourists, seasonal workers and temporary population might be more vulnerable when a disaster occurs. The intersection between tourism and disaster is not limited to disaster risk reduction or dark tourism and has to be more explored: as we have shown, tourism can be seen and might be analysed in different ways as a propulsive means in every phase of the disaster cycle.

References

Alexander D (2005) An interpretation of disaster in terms of changes in culture, society and international relations. In: Quarantelli E, Perry RW (eds) What is a disaster? New answers to old questions. IRCD, Boulder, CO, pp 25–39

Burby RJ, Wagner F (1996) Protecting tourists from death and injury in coastal storms. Disasters 20(1):49–60

Cassedy K (1991) Crisis management planning in the travel and tourism industry: a study of three destinations and a crisis management planning manual. PATA, San Francisco, CA

Chew EYT, Jahari SA (2014) Destination image as a mediator between perceived risks and revisit intention: a case of post-disaster Japan. Tour Manage 40(1):382–393

Cioccio L, Michael EJ (2007) Hazard or disaster: tourism management for the inevitable in Northeast Victoria. Tour Manage 28(1):1–11

Cohen EH (2011) Educational dark tourism at an *in populo* site: the Holocaust museum in Jerusalem. Ann Tour Res 38(1):193–209

Cohen E, Cohen SA (2012) Current sociological theories and issues in tourism. Ann Tour Res 39 (4):2177–2202

Cutter SL (1996) Vulnerability to environmental hazards. Prog Hum Geogr 20(4):529–539

Cutter SL, Mitchell JT, Scott MS (2000) Revealing the vulnerability of people and places: a case study of Georgetown County, SouthCarolina. Ann Assoc Am Geogr 90(4):713–737

De Certeau M (2010) L'invention du quotidien. 1 Arts de faire. Gallimard, Paris

Drabek TE (1995) Disaster responses within the tourist industry. Int J Mass Emerg Disasters 13 (1):7–23

Faulkner B (2001) Towards a framework for tourism disaster management. Tour Manage 22 (2):135–147

Foley M, Lennon JJ (1996) JFK and dark tourism: heart of darkness. J Int Herit Stud 2(4):198–211

Glaesser D (2003) Crisis management in the tourism industry. Butterworth Heinemann, Amsterdam

Hiji T (2012) Iwate Ken Otsuchicho Ni Okeru Fukko Tourim no Kanousei (the possibility of disaster tourism in Otsuchi Town in Iwate prefecture). Square 165(1):28–31

Hystad P, Keller PC (2008) Towards a destination tourism disaster management framework: Long-term lessons from a forest fire disaster. Tour Manage 29(1):151–162

IPCC (2013) IPCC WG I. Climate change 2013: the physical science basis. Summary for policymakers. https://www.ipcc.ch/pdf/assessmentreport/ar5/wg1/WGIAR5_SPM_brochure_en.pdf. Accessed 17 Dec 2015

Kash TJ, Darling JR (1998) Crisis management: prevention, diagnosis and intervention. Leadersh Org Dev J 19(4):179–186

Kasperson JX, Kasperson RE, Turner BL (1995) Regions at risk. Comparisons of threatened environments. United Nations University Press, Tokyo

Kelman I, Dodds R (2009) Developing a code of ethics for disaster tourism. Int J Mass Emerg Disasters 27(3):227–296

Kirshenblatt-Gimblett B (1998) Destination culture: tourism, museums, and heritage. University of California Press, Berkeley, CA

Korstanje M (2015) The anthropology of dark tourism. Exploring the contradictions of capitalism. CERS, Leeds

Korstanje M, Ivanov S (2012) Tourism as a form of new psychological resilience: the inception of dark tourism. CULTUR-Revista de Cultura e Turismo 6(4):56–71

Merlin T (2001) Sulla pelle viva. Come si costruisce una catastrofe. Il caso del Vajont, Cierre Edizioni, Verona

Miles W (2002) Auschwitz: museum interpretation and darker tourism. Ann Tour Res 29(4):1175–1178

National Governors' Association (1979) Comprehensive emergency management. A Governor's Guide, Washington, DC. https://training.fema.gov/hiedu/docs/comprehensive%20em%20-%20nga.doc. Accessed 10 Dec 2015

Nagai N (2012) Disaster tourism. The role of tourism in Post-Disaster period of Great East Japan Earthquake. Research paper. In: Erasmus University thesis repository. http://hdl.handle.net/2105/13252. Accessed 28 Dec 2015

Oliver-Smith A, Hoffman S (2002) Introduction: why anthropologists should study disaster. In: Hoffman S, Oliver-Smith A (eds) Catastrophe & culture: the anthropology of disaster. James Currey, Oxford, pp 3–22

Pezzullo PR (2010) Tourists and/as disasters: rebuilding, remembering, and responsibility in New Orleans. Tour Stud 9(1):23–41

Podoshen JS (2013) Dark tourism motivation: simulation, emotional contagion and topographic comparison. Tour Manage 35(1):263–271

Ritchie BW (2004) Chaos, crisis, and disaster: a strategic approach to crisis management in the tourism industry. Tour Manage 25(6):669–683

Rittichainuwat N (2008) Responding to disaster: Thai and Scandinavian Tourists'motivation to visit Phuket, Thailand. J Travel Res 46(4):422–432

Rojek C (1993) Ways of escape. Macmillan, Basingstoke

Sather-Wagstaff J (2009) Folk epigraphy at the World Trade Center, Oklahoma City, and beyond. In: Ruggles DF et al (eds) Intangible heritage embodied. Springer, New York, NY, pp 169–184

Seaton AV (1996) Guided by the dark: from thanatopsis to thanatourism. Int J Herit Stud 2(4):234–244

Stone P, Sharpley R (2008) Consuming dark-tourism a thanatological perspective. Ann Tour Res 35(2):574–595

Tang Y (2014) Dark touristic perception: motivation, experience and benefits interpreted from the visit to seismic memorial sites in Sichuan Province. J Mt Sci 11(5):1326–1341

UNEP (2010) 2009 annual report. Seizing the green opportunity. http://www.unep.org/PDF/UNEP_AR_2009_FINAL.pdf. Accessed 17 Dec 2015

Ventura S (2015) Il processo del Vajont e le memorie diverse di sopravvissuti e superstiti. Paper presented at the 3rd Italian Society for Applied Anthropology (SIAA) Conference, University of Florence, Prato, 17–19 December 2015

Wisner B et al (2003) At risk. Natural hazards, people's vulnerability and disasters. Routledge, London

Urban Tourism and City Development: Notes for an Integrated Policy Agenda

Nicola Bellini, Frank M. Go, and Cecilia Pasquinelli

Abstract This chapter draws conclusions by stressing that, through the wide coverage of different perspectives, this book describes the 'burst' of the city tourism concept, showing the several and relatively uncontrollable—and thus difficult to manage—nuances of tourism(s) in the urban context. In particular, the chapter discusses what tourism research is supposed to suggest to policymakers. It distinguishes three plausible scenarios in which the weight of urban tourism in development strategies may vary, i.e. marginal tourism, dominant tourism and surrogate tourism, and articulates them by emphasising different features and variations in how synergies between city tourism and urban development take place.

Keywords Urban development • Policy • Tourism development • Tourism planning

The frontiers of the city tourism debate depict a travel domain that is qualitatively—as well as quantitatively—widening and intersecting with the urban fabric, i.e. with the physical, cultural, social, political, productive and symbolic infrastructure characterising urban agglomerations. Through wide coverage of different perspectives—theoretical, empirical and methodological—this book describes the 'burst' of the city tourism concept, showing the several and relatively uncontrollable—and thus hardly manageable—nuances of tourism(s) in the urban context. From a research—and, even more, policy-making—perspective, this corresponds to an intricate weave where it is not only hard to orient actions but also sharply to distinguish the intertwined organisational, geographical, ethical and regulatory

N. Bellini (✉)
La Rochelle Tourism Management Institute, Groupe Sup de Co La Rochelle, La Rochelle, France
e-mail: bellinin@esc-larochelle.fr

F.M. Go
Erasmus University, Rotterdam, The Netherlands
e-mail: fgo@rsm.nl

C. Pasquinelli
GSSI Social Sciences, Gran Sasso Science Institute, L'Aquila, Italy
e-mail: cecilia.pasquinelli@gssi.infn.it

© Springer International Publishing Switzerland 2017
N. Bellini, C. Pasquinelli (eds.), *Tourism in the City*,
DOI 10.1007/978-3-319-26877-4_24

borders so as to understand the tensions and establish the critical mass necessary for pursuit of the goals which are "representative of all interests concerned" (Orbasli 2000, p. 99). Sustainability, inclusion, accessibility through transports and information technologies, participation in urban decision-making and city representation, as well as participation in the local labour market are all important for both tourism and city development. The chapters in this book show and discuss an array of issues that make integrating tourism into the urban agenda a complex undertaking. In particular, established top-down legislative frameworks with their formal rules and regulations, in which the urban authorities function, stand in stark contrast with the more informal kinds of decision-making that drive the conduct of entrepreneurs. This context complicates the significant linkage of public sector initiatives with private sector resources. In the meantime, scholars have shied away from fitting their own research into broader intellectual patterns evolving in transdisciplinary networks to co-create unexpected pathways and analytical and normative perspectives beyond tourism and urban studies attached to theories of modernity. Hence controversies in the three arenas of urban policy-making, urban tourism development, and social science research lack agreed-upon rules for debate. The discontinuity of values, norms and practices may explain why a consistent approach to integrating tourism development into the urban agenda has not yet become a political priority. However, mechanisms of hybridisation, integration, cross-fertilisation of local and tourism 'cultures' are evident in the practices of urban consumption, as well as in the processes of urban space production, as various chapters highlight in arguing for a necessary integration of tourism development and urban planning.

This book also stresses the relation between tourism performance and urban liveability, which has to be established as a frame wherein tensions and potential trade-offs, on the one hand, and potential synergies on the other, may converge on an emergent strategy.

In sum, this book raises a number of issues that urban policy makers can no longer neglect. Here, however, a deep contradiction emerges. Tourism has become an integral part of any strategy concerning local economic development in a variety of situations, most frequently in rural areas but also, of course, in urban settings. Yet, in parallel with the implicit consensus within scholarly networks on the negligibility of tourism in the process of urban and economic development, tourism research has to date had only a limited impact on actual strategies for urban development.

As said, this book intends to contribute not just to the scholarly debate, but also to policy practice. It therefore also provides interpretative frameworks that may work as an analytical ground for policy-making. This orientation was explicit in the call for papers launched at the Gran Sasso Science Institute for the L'Aquila workshop in 2015, as mentioned in the introduction to this book, and in the selection of the contributions both to the workshop itself and to this publication. This orientation is also in tune with the distinctive character of tourism research and the important role played in it by the production of "mode 2 knowledge", leading to contextualised, problem-solving results (Tribe 1997). Consequently, in this short concluding chapter the intention is to present and systematise (and partially add to) some of the items for the integrated policy agenda suggested by the authors who have contributed to this book.

So what is tourism research supposed to suggest to policymakers? Following the main hypothesis underlying this book (tourism can be integrated into the urban agenda), all its chapters converge in suggesting that important opportunities also lie on the prescriptive side of this hypothesis, i.e. integrating tourism policies into the wider framework of urban development policies and, at least in some respects, of urban planning as a whole. This does not imply reducing sensitivity to the negative impacts of tourism that generate anti-tourism feelings and movements and that can only be mitigated by corrective public policies (as in the case of Barcelona discussed by *Fava* and *Palau Rubio*) and residents' resilient practices (like those in Prague analysed by *Dumbrovskà*).

The rationale for integration can be understood in very pragmatic terms as the result of the many synergies that co-exist between tourism policies and urban development policies, as summarised in Table 1. In each case, achievement of the tourism policy objective is made possible by achievement of the more general urban policy objective. At the same time, the former contributes to the latter.

The weight of urban tourism in urban development strategies may of course vary, depending on the importance of tourism for a city's economy.

Here we distinguish three plausible scenarios:

(A) *Marginal tourism*: tourism may play only a marginal role in the economy of a city. This scenario is most likely to occur in large metropolitan areas, where tourism may be important in absolute terms but, both physically and economically, represents a relatively minor activity compared, e.g., to the financial or manufacturing sector: "their main economic rationale is not tourism" (Ashworth and Page 2011, p. 4). Yet in these cases, as discussed by *Čamprag* with reference to Frankfurt, tourism-led images may be aimed to soften the

Table 1 Synergies between urban development policies

Urban development policies	Urban tourism policies
Local competiveness, employment, entrepreneurship	Tourism industry: entrepreneurship, human capital, subsidies, support services
Infrastructure/Traffic management	Accessibility for tourists
Quality of the environment	Sustainable tourism initiatives
Cultural economy	Tourism attractors
Urban regeneration	New design/preservation/renovation of tourist spaces
City reputation/positioning/relational assets	Branding, marketing, visibility in global networks, e-reputation
Technology/Smart City	Smart tourism/management of the flows of city users
Soft infrastructure	Values linked to tourism (hospitality, openness to different cultures etc.)
Crisis management	Post-disaster tourism

established negative image of a cold financial metropolis, enriching the diversity of attractive public spaces and creating new identification points.

(B) *Dominant tourism*: tourism may be the main economic activity in the city (or at least one of the most important ones). This opposite scenario is typically applied by resort cities, historic cities and art cities, where—following *Rabbiosi* and *Giovanardi*—recombining old and emerging elements may set the path towards diversification and/or rejuvenation of the local tourism scene.

(C) *Surrogate tourism*: tourism may be proposed and emerge as a sustainable option, i.e. a substitute for declining economic activities, which draws importantly on urban development policies, particularly urban regeneration. This alternative scenario leverages place-specific models based on cultural legacy (as discussed by *Della Lucia, Trunfio* and *Go* and by *Borseková, Vaňová* and *Vitálišová*) or on some significant niches (like sport tourism-led regeneration, discussed by *Wise* and *Perić*).

Table 2 articulates these three scenarios by emphasising different characters and variations on the way synergies between urban tourism and urban development take place.

Table 2 Variations in the role of tourism policies

Role of tourism in city development	(A) *marginal*	(B) *dominant*	(C) *surrogate*
City attractions	Mostly used by non-tourists	Mostly used by tourists	New attractions created for use by both tourists and non-tourists
Main attitude towards heritage and tourism assets	Possibly re-defining tourist usage and value	Preserving	Re-inventing
Brand identity and Projected image; Authenticity	The metropolitan life—possibly more 'human' and welcoming—authentic experience	The attractive, unique, extraordinary place—original authenticity	The changing, sustainable city—re-authentication; staged authenticity
Features of urban tourism	Urban travellers/repeated visits	Urban tourists/once-in-a-lifetime visit	Urban tourists
City's relational assets	Widened	Confirmed	Substituted
City's soft infrastructure	Confirmed; improved, made more sustainable (?)	Confirmed; sustainable? (anti-tourism)	Re-designed configurations; networks of interrelationships
Contribution to local economy, employment and entrepreneurship	Adding, diversifying	Tourist mono-culture?	Conversion of traditional local crafts and skills

The chapters in this book signal a number of perspectives that, in combination with issues and urban models, would enable tourism policy to contribute to a more dynamic and effective urban development policy.

First, the emergence of new consumption patterns in tourism has the potential to reduce conflicts and increase efficiency in the use of urban resources. This is linked, above all, to the growing role of 'responsible' attitudes in tourism, as in the case of the 'enjoyable-to-all' urban green discussed by *Maćkiewicz* and *Konecka-Szydłowska*). In some respects, however, basic trends in the tourist market are also helping, e.g. consumption patterns based on the greater availability of time and money, such as senior travels (more evenly distributed throughout the year because seniors are not restricted by official calendar holidays) or luxury tourism (whenever this has an 'experiential' character).

Second, the emergence of the 'urban traveller' profile, as described by *Pasquinelli*, marks the evolution of tourists' role:

- from mere consumers to co-producers of experiences, therefore potentially feeding educated; international-minded, ethically-oriented contributions back into the city;
- from enclave visitors to actors who infiltrate the urban 'ordinary' reality in order to package tourist experiences including also non-tourist spaces and activities.

In very practical terms (as suggested by *Gronau* with reference to public transportation) this means that the demand generated by tourists may (usefully) complement existing local demand instead of competing with it. Even disaster tourism (following the arguments by *Mugnano* and *Carnelli*) may exhibit complementarity in the joint and innovative redesign of a 'new normality'.

Third, urban tourism may nourish a new breed of entrepreneurship often characterised by an original and/or advanced use of new technologies and which adopts innovative (if not alternative) business models, potentially rejuvenating the city's entrepreneurial clusters. In fact, the well-known toolbox of policies supporting new high-tech entrepreneurship (including incubators, accelerators, venture capital, business angels, etc.) is also applicable to the tourism sector. The case of the *Welcome City Lab* in Paris, an incubator set up specifically as an innovation platform for start-up companies in urban tourism, could be the benchmark for a whole generation of such initiatives. But also (as suggested by *Khiat* and *Montargot*) the new complexity of the relations with the customer positively challenges the local labour market and education system to provide human resources of sufficient quantity and quality to companies.

Fourth, urban tourism may foster a culture of innovation:

- By experimenting and developing 'smart city' technologies in several situations and with remarkable impacts (as discussed by *Garau*) in the field of the cultural economy/cultural tourism;
- By making human progress in technology become itself an attraction, either organised in a museum (like the increasingly popular science and technology museums) or as a living laboratory—as in the connection among art, creativity

and manufacturing that *Lazzeretti, Capone* and *Casadei* discussed in the case of Florence in this book.

Full exploitation of the synergies between tourism policies and urban development requires not only recognition of the benefits (static and dynamic) of urban tourism but also consensus in decision-making in order to overcome the gaps and pitfalls that have hitherto impeded the effective implementation of urban tourism policies embedded within an urban agenda. Some appear more serious than others, although not necessarily more evident.

First, especially (but not only) political leaders may perceive tourism as an easy option and a quick fix, underestimating the financial investments, human capital availability, knowledge and relational assets necessary to make tourism strategies viable and durable. Both the advocates and opponents of tourism development may refer to visions that are outdated, lacking serious investigation into the linkages with other sectors and industries (possibly under the resilient influence of industrialist paradigms) and into the actual impact of tourist activities (as suggested by the reading of the role of events in the chapters by *Caroli* and *Valentino* and by *Ferrucci, Sarti, Splendiani* and *Cordente Rodrìguez*). Overall, as emphasised by both *Lanquar* and *Andersson*, urban tourism requires a renewed effort to measure phenomena and monitor the impact of policies, thereby escaping from the trap of the simplified (either positive or negative) representations that so easily acquire visibility and crystallise in the political discourse.

Second, mandates may be unclear, and stakeholders may therefore be unable to identify potential and actual conflicts in the use of urban resources so as to define ways to deal with them. As *Uğur* explains: tourism policies must be inclusive and participatory, and they must collaboratively involve local communities in the tourism development process as well as in place branding. They can thus, as argued by *Kavaratzis,* reduce conflicts between internal perspectives and outward-looking ones by enriching the process with a plurality of inputs.

But is the political process really involving tourists or does it simply rely on the stereotypical attractiveness criteria suggested by territorial marketing (i.e. what the insiders think that the outsiders want)? Beyond the rhetoric of tourists as 'temporary residents', is there room for something more, for instance some kind of 'citizenship' giving voice to tourists directly and creating enabling conditions for them as co-producers (and not just consumers!) to help in shaping and legitimising local narratives. Already in the case of Venice (discussed by *Minoia*) the stabilisation of a cosmopolitan presence has given rise to a powerful constituency, whose role, however, is not balanced by a weakened and a local population that has often been displaced. Are there alternative and more balanced forms of raising awareness among tourists about the potentially positive role that they may play in urban governance? One possibility might consist in the 'new communicative space' created by social media and outlined by *Sevin* with reference to place branding. In other words, the new urban tourism seems to require not just updated and integrated *policies*, but a more radical re-thinking of urban *polities*. This is, in our opinion, the challenge that lies ahead for both research and policy practice:

disassembling the experiential ghettoes of traditional city tourism, perhaps relinquishing some of our sense of protective ownership of the urban fabric and identity, and accepting tourism as a constituent element of tomorrow's cities.

References

Ashworth G, Page SJ (2011) Urban tourism research: recent progress and current paradoxes. Tour Manage 32(1):1–15. doi:10.1016/j.tourman.2010.02.002
Orbasli A (2000) Tourists in historic towns urban conservation and heritage management. E & FN Spon, London
Tribe J (1997) The indiscipline of tourism. Ann Tour Res 24(3):638–657

Lightning Source UK Ltd.
Milton Keynes UK
UKOW06n1926140916

283011UK00016B/204/P